Christian Sisterhood, Race Relations,
and the YWCA, 1906–46

WOMEN IN AMERICAN HISTORY

Series Editors
Anne Firor Scott
Susan Armitage
Susan K. Cahn
Deborah Gray White

A list of books in the series appears at the end of this book.

Y.W.C.A
Call on us if
You
Want
Comfortable
Accommodations
Apply to Room Registry

Christian Sisterhood, Race Relations, and the YWCA, 1906–46

Nancy Marie Robertson

UNIVERSITY OF ILLINOIS PRESS
URBANA, CHICAGO, AND SPRINGFIELD

First Illinois paperback, 2010

Manufactured in the United States of America
2 3 4 5 6 C P 5 4 3 2 1

∞ This book is printed on acid-free paper.

The Library of Congress cataloged the cloth edition as follows:

Robertson, Nancy Marie, 1956–
Christian sisterhood, race relations, and the YWCA, 1906–46 /
Nancy Marie Robertson.
p. cm. — (Women in American history)
Includes bibliographical references and index.
ISBN 978-0-252-03193-9 (cloth : alk. paper)
1. Young Women's Christian Association. 2. Race relations—
Religious aspects—Christianity. 3. Race relations—United States.
4. Female friendship—Religious aspects—Christianity.
5. Christian women—Religious life.
I. Title.
BV1340.R58 2007
267'.597309041—dc22 2007005154

PAPERBACK ISBN 978-0-252-07710-4

Frontispiece: YWCA Room Registry Poster for Colored Work, 1919
(YWCA of the U.S.A. Records, Sophia Smith Collection, Smith College)

FOR

BRYCE ROBERTSON FRANKLIN

GINA LORRAINE KUNA ROBERTSON

IAN SCOTT KUNA ROBERTSON

LIANA MARIE KUNA ROBERTSON

MEAD FRANKLIN ROBERTSON

CONTENTS

ABBREVIATIONS

AME	African Methodist Episcopal Church
ASWPL	Association of Southern Women for the Prevention of Lynching
CIC	Commission on Interracial Cooperation
CME	Colored Methodist Episcopal Church
CTCA	Commission on Training Camp Activities
DAR	Daughters of the American Revolution
FCC	Federal Council of Churches
FEPC	Fair Employment Practices Committee
ICW	International Council of Women
LCA	Ladies' Christian Association
LCU	Ladies' Christian Union
NAACP	National Association for the Advancement of Colored People
NACW	National Association of Colored Women
NCCCW	National Committee on the Cause and Cure of War
NCNW	National Council of Negro Women
NCW	National Council of Women
NLC	Negro Leadership Conference
NTS	National Training School
NUL	National Urban League
SNCC	Student Nonviolent Coordinating Committee
WJCC	Women's Joint Congressional Committee
YLCA	Young Ladies' Christian Association
YM or YMCA	Young Men's Christian Association
YW or YWCA	Young Women's Christian Association

ACKNOWLEDGMENTS

I OWE A PROFOUND DEBT to many people—from many different communities—who helped me see this project through. Although it may not be obvious, *Christian Sisterhood, Race Relations, and the YWCA, 1906–46* grew out of the "sex wars" of the 1980s, when feminists fiercely debated how to understand the power dynamics embedded in personal relationships. Involvement in the feminist movement taught me a lot about power and justice, the personal and the political, and the need to be aware of how and when women are divided as well as united.

In a more conventional vein, I am grateful to the members of the New York University History Department who worked with me on a very early phase of this project. David M. Reimers read multiple drafts quickly. I greatly appreciate his thoughtfulness as a mentor. Daniel J. Walkowitz directed the seminar that sparked my interest in this project and he continued to advise me as my work progressed. I learned a lot from him about assisting others in developing projects that continues to inform both my writing and my teaching. Martha Hodes modeled how to constructively challenge a student to think big about a case study. While Sarah Deutsch was visiting NYU, she generously offered encouragement and comments that were invaluable. And, finally, Paul H. Mattingly saved me from embarrassing errors and assisted me in securing financial assistance at a critical juncture. Early on, both Mary Nolan and Susan Ware commented on this project and raised useful questions. In addition, Susan gave me the opportunity to begin a separate project on Anna Arnold Hedgeman as I was wrapping up this one.

I was fortunate to have arrived at NYU along with others who were committed to building a collegial home base. Many contributed to that environment, including Elaine Abelson, Adina Back, Barbara Balliet, Jon Bloom, Peter Eisenstadt, Melanie Gustafson, Margaret Hunt, Marilynn Johnson, Mollie Keller, Annelise Orleck, Claire Bond Potter, Robert W. Snyder, Pauline Toole, Suzanne Wasserman, Susan M. Yohn, and Renqiu Yu. The members of the Women's Interdisciplinary Methodology Seminar from around New York City were also an important part of my time there.

My writing group read innumerable versions of my work, in a setting of camaraderie and good food. Ilana Abramovitch, Ellen Gruber Garvey, Jane Holzka, Harriet Jackson, Ellen Kellman, Nina Warnke, and Vera Whisman were encouraging but tough as we worked together on our respective solitary projects. Several people researching projects related to the YWCA shared their findings with me and commented on my ideas. I am pleased to recognize the contributions of Regina Bannan, Elizabeth Brinson, Dorothea Browder, Michelle Busby, Carole Bucy, Nancy F. Cott, Janine Denomme, Celeste DeRoche, Paula Giddings, Amanda Izzo, Adrienne Lash Jones, Esther Katz, Susan Lynn, Karen Mittelman, Francesca Morgan, Nina Mjagkij, Clifford Putney, Nancy Boyd Sokoloff, Margaret Spratt, Frances Sanders Taylor, Judith Weisenfeld, and the late Thomas Winter. As I ventured into the larger academic community, a number of people commented on pieces that were precursors to the book. They include Elisabeth S. Clemens, Ruth Crocker, Mary Frederickson, Evelyn Brooks Higginbotham, John T. Kneebone, Debra C. Minkoff, Robyn Muncy, Priscilla Murolo, Heather Munro Prescott, Marion Roydhouse, David H. Smith, and Patricia Turner. I presented at various venues, but the discussion that ensued at Columbia University's Women and Society Seminar with longtime YWCA women and second-wave feminists was particularly meaningful. Thomas Dublin's welcome interest in the project was well timed.

Susan Yohn and Jane Holzka each read more versions of my manuscript than any friend could expect, while Sylvia D. Hoffert and Melissa Bingmann helped me think about the opening. Sherry Miller caught more typos than I care to remember. Philip Goff, the late Tony Sherrill, and Paul Harvey helped with matters of religion. Monroe H. Little and Justin H. Libby provided information that would have taken me ages to find out. David E. Spiech edited a late draft, and Amy N. Powell helped at the end.

I was fortunate to have landed in the collegial environs of Indiana University's School of Liberal Arts at Indiana University-Purdue University, Indianapolis (IUPUI), especially the History Department, the Women's Studies Program, and the Philanthropic Studies Program. On and off campus, Annie Gilbert Coleman, Kevin Cramer, Linda Santoro, Jill Carr, Cynthia B. Roy, Susan Brin Hyatt, Margaret Robertson Ferguson, Marianne S. Wokeck, Amy Jones Richardson, Cheryl Stonestreet, Tammara Tracy, Richard E Ward, Karen Ramsay Johnson, Erik Lindseth, Barbara Shaw, Carmen Aguilar, and the Friday-night pitch-ins helped me to put down roots in a new place. Friends back east who "won't let me come home a stranger" include Susan Yohn, Valerie Barr, Camilla Yohn Barr, Jane Holzka, Mark Winther, Chloe Holzka Winther, Rob Snyder, Clara Hemphill, Ellen Mutari, Deb Figart, Deb Edel, Penny Johnson, and Amy Hague. Three longtime compatriots provided comfort and cheer when it mattered the most; Jim Oleson has been a constant for more than half my life; John D'Emilio is always a voice of reality; and Mary Renda inspires me every time. The late Deb Trent held my feet to the fire; I regret not being able to tell her thanks.

For years the commitment of the YWCA women to social justice has been matched by their belief in the value of documents, without which, as Mary Beard once observed, there would be no history. Any recent historian of the YWCA owes an immense debt to the late Elizabeth Norris, who fought to protect the records of the YWCA during countless office moves and staff reductions. I commend the National Coordinating Board, the current executive body of the YWCA USA, for placing the records of the national YWCA at the Sophia Smith Collection at Smith College. That decision made last-minute fact-checking easier for me, but it also ensures access to this rich collection for future researchers. Over the years, the staff of the SSC, notably Amy Hague, Maida Goodwin, Susan Boone, and Sherrill Redmon, have assisted me during visits and with requests from afar. Kara McClurken meticulously provided research assistance when I could not easily get to Massachusetts.

Archivists and librarians at a number of other repositories assisted my research. I thank those at the Atlanta History Center; Brooklyn Public Library; Moorland-Spingarn Research Center, Howard University; National Archives and Records Administration (Washington, D.C.); New York Public Library; Rockefeller Archives Center; Schlesinger Library on the History of Women in America; Schomburg Center for Research in Black Culture; Southern Historical Collection at the Wilson Library, University of North Carolina at Chapel Hill; Robert W. Woodruff Library of the Atlanta University Center, Archives and Special Collections Department; Kautz Family YMCA Archives, University of Minnesota Libraries; and YWCA of the City of New York. Those who hosted me and made research trips possible include Julie Abraham, Mark Huey, Peter Brehm, Susan Yohn, Valerie Barr, Janice and Robert Robertson, Doug Robertson, Marie Kuna Robertson, and Helen Freniere Long. Staff members of several institutions graciously responded to e-mail requests for biographical information, including those at Clark Atlanta University, Cornell University, Hamline University, Houston Metropolitan Research Center, Indiana University, Lake Erie College, the Library of Virginia, Macalester College, Rhode Island State Archives, Union Theological Seminary and Presbyterian School of Christian Education, Urban Archives at Temple University, Vassar College, and Wellesley College.

Librarians at New York University's Bobst Library and the Tamiment Library as well as those at the Brooklyn Public Library were an incredible help early on. The passing of Debra Bernhardt is a loss to everyone interested in the history of social justice; I am grateful for her commitment to the Tamiment and also that she arranged for me to have continued access to Bobst. More recently, the staff of IUPUI's University Library has been a blessing. I taxed the personnel of the Interlibrary Loan Department, especially Karen Janke and Sharon Fish, as I requested one obscure item after another, but they were always efficient and gracious in their responses. Frances A. Huehls of the Joseph and Matthew Payton Philanthropic Studies Library has both obtained items for my use and been a sounding board for discussions about teaching and researching women and philanthropy. Kristi Palmer consistently provides her excellent reference skills to my students and me.

Money alone won't produce a book, but without financial assistance at key moments, I could not have undertaken nor completed this project. I benefitted from a Charlotte W. Newcombe Fellowship from the Woodrow Wilson Foundation; a Penfield Fellowship and a Helbein Scholarship from New York University; a Doctoral Fellowship in Nonprofit Governance from the Center on Philanthropy at Indiana University; and a Joseph A. Skinner Fellowship for Research in History and a Mary E. Woolley Fellowship, both from Mount Holyoke College. The latter award meant a lot to me because Woolley was on the YWCA's National Board during much of the period which this study covers. A grant from the Indiana University President's Arts and Humanities Initiative gave me a semester of release time to revise the manuscript, while a summer stipend from the Indiana Research Fund of IU's Center on Philanthropy provided additional support. As chair of IUPUI's History Department, Philip V. Scarpino wrote letters of support that helped me secure financial assistance. The University Seminars at Columbia University provided help in publication; a version of chapter 5 was presented to the University Seminar on Women and Society.

Joan Catapano, my acquisitions editor and the editor-in-chief of the University of Illinois Press, consistently supported this project and offered encouragement at a critical stage. The sharp editing pencil of Carol Bolton Betts made for a better-written book. I owe a special debt to the readers for the Press, Anne Firor Scott and Margaret Lamberts Bendroth. Each demanded that I clarify my points and expand my analysis (particularly on the role of religion) and helped me produce a better-argued book. Margaret Bendroth went above and beyond the call of duty with her subsequent responses to my revisions. The members of the acquisitions and marketing staffs at the Press helpfully moved the book along.

My maternal grandparents, Catherine Marie Chapman Huey and Ray Huey, were northerners. Robert Laird Robertson Sr. and Mary Frances Hackley Robertson, my paternal grandparents, were southerners. Their stories informed my attempts to understand the efforts of earlier generations of white Americans to make sense of race, religion, and culture. My parents, Janice Marie Huey Robertson and Robert Laird Robertson Jr., provided support of all kinds for my work. My siblings, Douglas L. Robertson, Kathryn A. Robertson, and Laura J. Robertson, consistently remind me that they are proud of their big sister. I have dedicated this book to the next generation, Bryce, Gina, Ian, Liana, and Mead, and their own struggles for justice.

Christian Sisterhood, Race Relations, and the YWCA, 1906–46

INTRODUCTION

IN THE EARLY TWENTIETH CENTURY, two Protestant women analyzed the importance of women in efforts to effect a Christian solution to racial problems. In 1907, Addie Waites Hunton declared, "Home is one of the three immutable things of life, and the glory of Christendom. Hence, it is true that to woman is allotted the highest and most blessed part of the work of racial uplift. Universally it is conceded that in this development of our home life, the salvation of the race is in the hands of its womanhood."[1] Shortly after World War I, Lily Hardy Hammond would echo Hunton's beliefs in the duty of women and the power of the home, writing, "[E]ssential to the advance of any race is the status of its women and their homes. Until Christian white women stand by negro women, giving them that human protection and respect which is the right of womanhood the world over, there will be little progress in racial solutions. Womanhood and motherhood are among the few things deeper than race."[2]

The two women had much in common. Both had southern parents; both attended school in the North but later returned to the South. Each was an early supporter of the National Association for the Advancement of Colored People. Each married a man who shared her concern for improving American race relations. In the early twentieth century, each wrote extensively about race. When the Young Women's Christian Association (YWCA, or YW) chose to educate its leaders and general membership about race, it published pieces by both women.

Yet, a critical difference overshadows these similarities. Addie Waites Hunton was the black descendant of slaves, and Lily Hardy Hammond was the white daughter of former slaveowners. Hunton's and Hammond's apparently similar assumptions about the power of Christian womanhood to correct racial wrongs are the starting place for this book. White women in the YWCA, especially class-privileged women, spoke of womanhood as universal; they argued that, as Hammond put it, there was a "bond of common womanhood deeper than all racial separateness."[3] In so doing, they suggested that *all* women had traits that bound them with other women. They referred to women as "sisters" and consistently invoked what they called "Christian sisterhood" as an important means to build a better world. The term both conveyed their motivation and legitimized their social activism at a time when women were supposedly relegated to the home.

This ideology resonated with many black women, who also spoke of the duty of women to promote social righteousness. White and black women believed women had a special mission to promote harmony in a divided world by bringing the familial values of the private realm into the public. Then, people working together—black and white, worker and industrialist, woman and man—would build the "Kingdom of God on Earth." Linking religion to politics, they argued that social problems would best be solved through democratic means.

Despite the shared rhetoric, however, there were always profound disagreements between black and white women in the YWCA, especially over efforts of white women, even white allies, to determine proper race relations. Black women in the YWCA used the language of Christianity in their efforts to persuade, cajole, and even shame their white sisters into extending the full blessings of fellowship and citizenship to all. In the 1920s, for instance, a white YWCA leader in New Jersey refused to admit black girls to a conference on "Weaving the Pattern of Christian Citizenship into Our Lives." In response, her black counterpart reminded her that the "ideal" of the YWCA was "to break down all barriers of race or creed so that each girl may develop to her best self." Only as they approached that ideal would it be possible to have any "sincerity of purpose" when discussing "Christian citizenship."[4] Throughout the first half of the twentieth century, black women struggled to force white women to recognize where their vision of common womanhood or Christian values fell short.

I began this project interested in analyzing how white women have understood the relationship between their gender and their race. Hammond envisioned a common womanhood, but how was her conception of womanhood shaped by her race (and class)? How well did she, and other white middle-class women, understand those influences? Examining race relations in the early twentieth-century YWCA permits exploring such questions. At the time, the YWCA was the only large national women's organization that had significant participation of both white and black women. At the same time, local associations in the South *and* the North were segregated.

While some have characterized the Y as no more than "a gym and swim club for the middle class,"[5] the YWCA provided social services, education, and leadership training for women, and it facilitated networks of female reformers. By 1920, the YWCA was the third-largest autonomous American women's organization and provided an arena where women struggled over definitions of "the race problem" and its solution. In these contests, white and black women articulated differing assumptions about gender, race, and Christianity.

Because the YWCA included both white and black women, white members—northern as well as southern—ended up in situations where they had to talk about, even with, black women and consider race relations at a time when many white Americans ignored the topic. The period from the founding of the national YWCA in 1906 to the 1946 national convention, when YW members called for desegregation, saw several changes in the YWCA's racial policies. In particular, white women went from justifying racial segregation as compatible with sisterhood, democracy, and Christianity to a policy, if not a practice, of desegregation. In some cases the YWCA took relatively progressive stands, but its members were rooted in their time. The debates in the YWCA among white women over the place of black women permit insights into a larger white Protestant mind-set.[6] Prior to the 1930s, for instance, both racially conservative and racially liberal whites believed in the desirability of harmony, the efficacy of education, and the necessity for racial segregation.

White and black women were able to work together, in large part, because of a shared religious commitment. YWCA women's vision of Christian sisterhood drew upon nineteenth-century ideals of womanhood as well as the values of evangelical Protestantism; the importance of those values lasted well into the twentieth century. Although studies of earlier American women have explicitly engaged religion, historians of twentieth-century women and social change have focused primarily on secular institutions, especially when their subjects are Protestants. This study reveals ways in which such a focus limits our understanding of both the history of American race relations and the continuing importance of religion.

To understand the role of religion in women's activism and racial reform in American history, one needs to look back to earlier understandings of evangelicalism.[7] Nineteenth-century evangelical churches included those in what would subsequently be referred to as "mainline" American denominations, particularly Baptist, Congregationalist, Episcopalian, Methodist, and Presbyterian. In the 1800s, evangelicals embraced a vision of creating a "Christian [i.e., Protestant] America" and of bringing in "the Kingdom of God on Earth." At a time when theology and church polity divided Christians, evangelicals argued that Protestants from different denominations should join voluntary associations to promote pragmatic programs; they intended such reforms to reshape both the individual and society as well as to provide unity across denominational lines. Prior to the Civil War, they created what many have called a "benevolent empire" of interlocking reform organizations that was national and highly organized to address the social issues of their day including slavery, women's rights, immigration, poverty, temperance, and morality. The pivotal role that evangelicals granted lay-run voluntary associations, legitimized by religion, as well as the faith they had in the redemptive power of domesticity allowed women to cast taking on public roles as a sanctified act.

Beginning in the second half of the nineteenth century, white and black Protestant women established YWCAs as one way to address the needs of women, although white YW women would not consider those of black women as of paramount importance until the 1920s. Over the course of the first half of the twentieth century, white women in the YWCA slowly shifted from racial policies rooted in segregation to those that favored desegregation, if not integration, a trajectory followed by other white Americans in the second half of the century. As such, the YWCA is of interest as a case study for racial change and because of its relation to the subsequent civil rights movement. As Americans reflected upon both the fiftieth anniversary of the 1954 Supreme Court decision in *Brown v. Board of Education* and the fortieth anniversary of the 1963 March on Washington, a number of memoirs surfaced that presented alternative accounts of the civil rights movement and the origins of white support for it. In story after story, black and white women spoke of the importance of college YWCAs for introducing them to a community of women committed to supporting women's empowerment and social justice. Aided by black mentors like Ella Baker as well as recently graduated white women like Constance Curry, white and black members of Christian student groups, particularly the YWCA, moved into the civil rights movement in the 1950s and 1960s.[8]

Addie Hunton and Lily Hammond expressed the visions of womanhood and racial reform that black and white women brought to bear as this story opens. Another pairing from the 1960s—Renetia Martin and Lilace Reid Barnes—presents us with one legacy of that history. A student at Berkeley in the late 1960s, Martin was active with both the Black Student Union and the campus YWCA. Gradually she was pulled into national YWCA leadership. There she met Barnes, former president of the association. According to Martin, Barnes was

> the epitome of the wealthy white lady. She always wore a hat and gloves and carried a handbag and was as cute as could be, with a little something off: a slightly skewed hat or a little bit of slip showing. Before every large student gathering, Lilace would send me a corsage that I was to wear as the students' leader. Prior to the 1970 convention, we had a string of meetings: the black women's conference, three days of student meetings, and a morning with the national student committee. By the time the conference arrived, I was wiped out. I couldn't imagine continuing on for another week. Lilace sent me an orchid to wear to the conference opening, and when I walked into the auditorium, there was a standing ovation, a truly uplifting moment. Lilace gave me the inspiration to persist and a symbol to remind me to stick to the task.[9]

At that meeting, Martin and other black women, along with white allies like Barnes, successfully pressured the larger membership to pass the "One Imperative" committing the YW to "the elimination of racism wherever it exists and by any means necessary."[10] Less than a quarter century earlier, Barnes had been present at the 1946 YWCA national convention where she had praised the "sisterhood of Christian women" found in the YWCA, and members had endorsed the YWCA's Interracial Charter, which called for the inclusion of black women into "the main stream of Association life."[11] Through the YWCA, individual black and white women forged a bridge between the women's organizations of the first part of the century and the civil rights, New Left, and feminist movements of the second half. These connections call into question those histories that see the 1930s to 1950s as a time when women's organizations became insignificant, scholars who locate the origins of the civil rights movement in the post–World War II era, and those who argue that growing secularism is the best way to understand the twentieth century.[12]

Focusing upon individual and institutional continuities, however, can lead one to overlook the contested nature of this history. White YW women often spoke of the changes in the YWCA's practices as natural—even inevitable—consequences of its Christian purpose; one longtime white YW staffer, Mary Sims, wrote house histories detailing "An Unfolding Purpose" and "The Purpose Widens."[13] African American women were less sanguine. They shared with their white sisters the belief that racial change was the Christian thing to do, but they did not fail to point out the struggle necessary to accomplish it. In 1947, Dorothy Height, a black staff member, visited Fort Worth, Texas, as part of an interracial team to study the "terrific progress" the city had made in implementing the Interracial Charter. Despite the fact that Height represented the national association on official business, she encountered white women who begrudged her even a cup of coffee and accused the team of coming "to cause trouble." People needed a lot of help to change, Height observed, and she concluded that "if we waited for attitudes to be changed just through hopeful encouragement, we'd be waiting forever."[14] Conflict as well as cooperation arose in the intersection of gender, race, and religion in the YWCA.

❖ ❖ ❖

In order to present this story, I have utilized a largely chronological approach, although, as the following chapter outline suggests, specific subthemes are the focus of individual chapters. Issues such as internationalism, the role of working women in the YWCA, the relations between men and women, divisions within the African American community, the goals of student YWCAs, or the backlash against social activism could have been explored in depth in virtually every chapter; I have addressed each as it was especially relevant to changing race relations.

The first chapter covers the history of the YWCA through the establishment of the Young Women's Christian Associations of the United States of America in 1906, which resulted from the merger of two competing women's organizations: one based mostly in northeastern cities and the other found largely on midwestern campuses.[15] Although both groups identified as evangelical Protestants, they differed in their visions of social change. The women used "Christian sisterhood," a grassroots female-oriented version of the social gospel, to find common ground. Christian sisterhood allowed urban associations, which identified religious work with improving social conditions, and campus groups, which saw religious efforts as those that assisted spiritual growth and overseas missions, to link social redemption with individual salvation. Despite escalating racial problems, white women (along with most of white America) regarded assisting white women and girls as their primary goal. After the merger, YW leaders were particularly concerned with ensuring the YWCA's expansion into all regions of the country. The chapter concludes with a discussion of a 1907 all-white conference in Asheville, North Carolina, which set the terms for restricted African American participation in the new organization.

Chapter 2 analyzes the expansion of race work in the association, through the efforts of Addie Waites Hunton and others, including Elizabeth Ross Haynes and Eva Bowles. Examining two interracial conferences in the South, in 1914 and 1915, reveals the assumptions that white women brought to their interactions with black Americans, most notably a commitment to white domination and racial segregation and a belief in a racial etiquette whereby black women were to defer to white women. A 1915 conference in Louisville would consolidate what came to be known as the "branch policy," where local black associations were structured as branches of white-run central associations. Although African American women had some control over the day-to-day operations of their branches, black YWCAs were usually financially dependent upon and administratively subordinated to (white) central associations.

World War I, as well as African American migration to northern cities, helped to promote a noticeable increase in the attention that whites throughout the nation paid to race problems. Chapter 3 discusses the expansion of YWCA programs for African American women during the war under the slogan "Everything that is done by the Y.W.C.A. for white women is done also for colored women." In the light of postwar tensions and racial violence, white and black YW women joined others in promoting interracial cooperation and education as solutions to race problems. While black YWCA members agreed with the emphasis upon mutual understanding between the "better classes" of each race, they accepted neither the idea that white women should direct the programs, nor a goal of segregation.

As the 1920s opened, the YWCA made two institutional changes that indirectly related to black women: members loosened the religious requirement for student members and they ratified the "Social Ideals of the Churches," which endorsed rights for workers. YW women built on gains of the Nineteenth Amendment and aimed to educate women as "Christian citizens" who would use their new power to lobby for legislation for women, workers, and peace. Supporting these changes, black women also challenged white domination of the racial agenda, and chapter 4 looks at the ensuing controversies. In the aftermath of meetings intended to ease tensions, black women made modest gains at the national and local levels; in 1922, for instance, the YWCA determined that national conventions would have integrated seating. The YWCA's actions in these years largely represented incremental change.

Nonetheless, liberalization of the religious requirement, support for workers' rights, and the YWCA's promotion of legislation prompted some conservative women's and patriotic organizations to attack the association (along with other women's organizations).

In the mid- to late 1920s, the Young *Men's* Christian Association (YMCA or YM) began to pressure the YWCA to merge in a campaign that reflected an increasing emphasis on heterosexual socializing. The YM also had a branch structure for African Americans; merger proposals were for a coeducational, but racially segregated, institution. Chapter 5 delineates the consequences of the interactions with the YM for the YW's racial policies. White *and* black women resisted merging because they feared both that women would lose leadership positions in a coeducational group and that men in the more conservative YM would modify the YW's progressive social agenda, including turning away from interracial endeavors toward less controversial and more financially rewarding recreational programming. Black women used white women's desire to remain in a single-sex organization to lobby successfully for a greater institutional commitment to interracial efforts.

The YWCA worked with other women's organizations to support the legislative programs of the New Deal in the 1930s, but its engagement with race issues differentiated it from most other white-dominated groups. Chapter 6 explores how some white women in the association came to recognize that simply educating individuals was insufficient to deal with the structural problems of segregation. Under pressure from black women, the white women of the YWCA shifted to political efforts, such as supporting antilynching laws, to complement their earlier reliance on education and cooperation to improve race problems. As some groups within the YWCA, especially industrial workers and students, moved ahead of the larger constituency, leaders faced the challenge of bringing the rest of the association along, particularly in light of the conservative backlash that local associations experienced as the YWCA added racial reform to an already controversial political agenda.

Chapter 7 looks at the YWCA general membership's decision to desegregate the association, notably through the unanimous adoption of the Interracial Charter in 1946, which called for the association to "pioneer in an interracial experience that shall be increasingly democratic and Christian" and urged local associations to examine all forms of segregation with an eye to eliminating them.[16] Institutionally, white YW women no longer viewed segregation as compatible with Christian sisterhood and now saw the purpose of democracy as protecting the rights of minorities as well as fostering self-governance and majority rule. The changes in the YWCA did not happen in a social vacuum. Women of both races recognized a new world order and spoke of the "opportunity to help build world security by furthering mutual respect and understanding among *all* peoples—the nucleus of a world-wide community dedicated to true Christian ideals of fellowship."[17] While the YWCA's early efforts on behalf of interracial cooperation and African Americans had placed it ahead of much of middle-class white America, by the late 1940s the rest of the United States had also begun to change. In their own words, women of the YWCA had moved from being a "spearhead" to a "cross section" of the community.[18] Members continued to define their role in the world in religious terms although they offered new understandings of what it meant to be in a Christian organization.

The epilogue examines the legacy of the YWCA's racial policies and practices as members struggled over the implications of the Interracial Charter and the meaning of integration. YWCAs had provided physical sites, while Christian sisterhood had allowed a rhetorical space for white and black women to meet, argue, and change. However slow and faltering the changes, they were significant both in their own right and for their impact on the larger society, but white and black YWCA women did not—could not—fully resolve the challenge of race relations for their association or America. The struggles in which they engaged remain with us, and we can learn much from their stories.

1 Building a National Organization

As the person credited with the creation of the Young Women's Christian Associations of the United States of America in 1906, Grace Hoadley Dodge holds a unique position in the YWCA's history. Born into the Phelps-Dodge wealth in 1856, committed to her family's philanthropic tradition, and proficient in organizational skills, she represented a transitional generation of white, class-privileged, female reformers.[1] An earlier group of women, represented by Louisa Lee Schuyler (a mentor to Dodge), had promoted efficiency and organization to address social problems. Relying on noblesse oblige, they had believed that they should direct the programs for others.[2] Like Schuyler, Dodge had little formal education; both were active as volunteers in a range of philanthropic and social reform efforts. But Dodge also embraced an approach that (at least rhetorically) repudiated the maternalism of the earlier generation. Privileged women, Dodge repeatedly said, "owe it to their laboring sisters" to strive toward "not working *for*, but *with*" them.[3] Active with clubs for white "working girls" prior to her involvement with the YWCA, she stated, "As long as we look upon them as a class whom we are to benefit and uplift, there can be no cooperation." She continued, "We must learn to know their grand-sacrificing lives, must make them friends from whom we are to receive more than we can ever give."[4] The headline of her obituary in the *New York Tribune* simply read, "Miss Grace Dodge, Girls' Friend, Dead."[5]

As the first president of the YWCA of the USA, Grace Dodge set the tone for its early years. "Working with, not for" their constituencies became a shibboleth for YW women as they sought to redeem both individuals and society. Christian sisterhood provided a powerful metaphor for evangelical Protestant women to work together. At the same time, familial language could cast some out, while masking profound tensions among those who remained. Until well after World War I, the YWCA focused on the needs of white women and girls. White members *were* interested in the situation of "colored" women, but the latter were only one of many groups whom members discussed—including "Indian girls," "heathen" women in other countries, "oriental women students who are studying in this country," foreign-born women and families, and even "fallen" women.[6] Other institutional priorities, most notably the commitment that white women had to building a national organization that included (white) southern associations, trumped the demands of black Protestant women who sought to bring the benefits of the association to their communities.

As black women and girls joined the association, they struggled to get their white sisters to work "with," not simply "for," them. African American members were not the only ones who resisted the efforts of white, class-privileged women to determine the YWCA's policies and practices. College students and industrial workers of both races would also spend the first half of the twentieth century working to force the YWCA to live up to the rhetoric of equality and reciprocity. To explain how and why white women initially responded to the situation of African Americans, we must examine their discussions of cross-class sisterhood, as well as their racism.

"A Sister's Kindness"

The Young Women's Christian Association began as part of the evangelical Protestant religious revivals in the United States and England in the late 1850s.[7] Moved by the enthusiasm of what one scholar has called the "layman's revival," a group of socially elite white women gathered in 1858 in the Chancellor's Room at New York University in New York City to form a weekly, nondenominational prayer circle.[8] Women, excluded from formal positions of power within organized churches, looked for ways to express their religious feelings in such all-female groups.[9] The group progressed from a prayer circle to a formal organization, the Ladies' Christian Union (LCU), which took as its purpose encouraging "the Christian women of all denominations in New-York to unite their efforts to do good among their own sex." The constitution restricted officers to "communicants in Evangelical Churches."[10]

whether residences should be self-sustaining, Mrs. Jacob Harley argued in favor, stating that the "independent principle God has implanted in the human heart is no light thing to be tampered with." She explained that when the young women themselves were asked whether rates should be lowered and the deficiency covered by a public appeal, they responded that they did "not wish to be dependent."[30] Throughout these years, working women resisted descriptions that cast them as charity cases.[31]

Couching sisterhood, home, and independence in religious terms, divinely sanctioned and identified with Protestantism, meant that YW women often expressed class issues in religious, cultural, or moral terms rather than economic ones. Acknowledging that "all are precious in our sight, as in the Master's," the officers of the New York YWCA rejoiced in 1875 about the increasing numbers of "women of culture and refinement" coming to a Bible class.[32] Some YWCAs explicitly limited their programs (especially residences) to white-collar workers (as opposed to factory or domestic workers), although a principle of self-selection also functioned. Historians have observed that it was women from lower-middle or middle-class backgrounds who were most likely to feel at ease in the residences with fairly strict rules to maintain respectability.[33]

Even when elite women addressed economic issues, their efforts to assert a commonality among women further muddied the waters. Grace Dodge often spoke of herself as a "working girl" whose "wages [had been] earned for her in advance." YW volunteers followed suit as they stressed the potential for mutuality among (some) women and the duty of elite women to avoid idleness.[34] Dodge's formulation simultaneously brought working women under the cloak of middle-class (even elite) respectability *and* granted privileged women the blessing that Protestantism bestowed on work. Debates among white women (and later white and black women) slipped among the discourses of economics, culture, morality, and Protestantism.

Shared language and values could not always mask the different interests of the various groups of women in the YWCA. A longtime YWCA staff member observed that many YWCA employment bureaus initially sought to place women in domestic positions at a time of high "demand for good household helpers."[35] In urging women to take these positions, YWCA leaders declared, "[no] young woman can be too well qualified, either by education or culture" to take a domestic position.[36] Such work did not, however, appeal to the working women who came to the YWCA. Many of them had held teaching jobs in their towns, but they were not always qualified for similar positions in cities. They began turning to the developing clerical occupations. Acknowledging the "popular prejudice against so-called 'service,'" in 1875, the YWCA in New York gave up trying to place women as "house servants," referring those seeking servants to "sister societies" established for that purpose.[37]

YWCAs began to offer some of the earliest courses that trained women in clerical skills such as typewriting and bookkeeping.[38] Working women's acceptance of some programs and rejection of others prompted associations to broaden their scope by eventually offering cafeterias, travelers' aid, health programs, educational courses, lectures, free libraries, concerts, gymnasiums, recreational activities, and vacation camps.[39] The evolution of programs suggests the ability, albeit limited, of white working women to influence what was offered them.[40]

Increasingly, many community associations also moderated religious requirements for participants (although certainly not expectations for high morals and respectability); many dropped the requirement of church membership for general members, even though most continued to restrict leadership positions to evangelical Protestants. Despite the revisions, associations remained culturally Protestant. By the turn of the century, then, the International Board of Women's and Young Women's Christian Associations was a network of women's groups based in urban areas, primarily in the Northeast, which addressed temporal, social, and mental needs as well as moral and religious ones.

"The Kingdom of God among Young Women"

In the 1870s, a related movement developed among college women seeking spiritual development. Influenced by the work of student Young *Men's* Christian Associations, a distinct organization for men, the student YWCAs focused more upon individual religious growth than did urban associations. The first student YWCA was organized in 1873 at Normal State University in Illinois. Several more sprang up in the ensuing years, fueled in part by the increasing numbers of female college students. In 1870, about one-fifth of all college students were female; ten years later, one-third were.[41] In addition to encouraging members to strive for individual salvation, the students supported foreign mission work. They used Bible study and religious meetings to persuade young women to commit to "a life of Christian service at home or in the mission field."[42] Strongest in the Midwest, the student organizations formed a national association in 1886 with headquarters in Chicago and eventually adopted the name American Committee of Young Women's

Christian Associations. Affiliation with the American Committee was possible only for associations that limited active membership to members of evangelical Protestant churches.

For some years, the American Committee and the International Board coexisted with each focusing on a different constituency—students in the case of the former and urban working women in the latter. But by the 1890s, the two began actively competing, particularly as the American Committee expanded into cities in response to college graduates who wished to continue their YWCA involvement. Religious differences between the two national bodies also led to tensions. Women in the International Board defended their "liberty of basis" as "nearer to Christ's teachings" than the restrictive membership rules for the American Committee.[43] For their part, women in the American Committee strongly opposed what they viewed as a lax membership requirement and argued that Young Women's *Christian* Associations should require evangelical church membership.[44] They were also wary of the liberal, if not secular, nature of the International Board's programs. International Board women defended their programs in *religious* terms, declaring that their seemingly secular efforts were "the means to a greater end; namely the 'moral and religious' improvement" of young women.[45]

In cities such as New York, there were associations affiliated with each national body, and women in both organizations increasingly recognized that competition posed problems.[46] Multiple small associations were weaker than a united effort. Funders and the larger community were confused by two different YWCAs. And public conflict between two "Christian" groups lessened the credibility of each.[47] The two organizations had discussed the idea of merging as early as 1891, and a legal dispute over jurisdiction in Washington, D.C., brought the existing tensions to a head in 1904.[48]

At that point, Grace Dodge offered to mediate between the two, a job she was uniquely suited for. The men in her family had had a long history of involvement with evangelical Protestantism and the YMCA. Dodge herself had expressed an interest in the YWCA in general but had not wanted to ally with either faction. Her religious conservatism interested her in the American Committee, while her involvement with groups that provided social services made her sympathetic to the International Board. The money she could bring to an organization no doubt also eased her entrée.

In much the way that the men in her family had sought to improve the efficiency of the industries they led, Grace Dodge promoted the consolidation, centralization, and professionalization of women's reform activities. Over the course of 1906, she presided over meetings of representatives from the International Board and the American Committee, who finally developed a compromise that permitted a merger. The final agreement allowed associations affiliated with either organization at the time of the merger to join the new national association. Thereafter, associations could belong only if active members belonged to an evangelical Protestant church.[49] The new organization was to be headquartered in New York City and staffed by secretaries, the YWCA's term for its trained professionals. Autonomous local associations would meet every two (later three) years at national conventions to set policy for the organization and elect the members of its National Board. Between conventions, the National Board was to function as the executive body.[50]

One hundred forty-seven city associations and four hundred sixty-nine student groups applied for membership, representing almost all of the associations affiliated with either organization. At the first convention of the newly constituted Young Women's Christian Associations of the United States of America, held in New York City in December 1906, delegates established that the purpose of the organization was "to advance the physical, social, intellectual, moral, and spiritual interests of young women."[51] YW women articulated a vision of Christian sisterhood that provided common ground for those women more oriented toward individual salvation with those committed to social salvation.

At the convention, Ida T. Thurston, a member of the new National Board, speaking on "Christian Cooperation among Women in Social and Business Life," called for "cooperation, not a reaching down, but a reaching out." Sounding like Grace Dodge, Thurston continued that such efforts would allow elite women, those who "suffer from idleness," to "learn the greater lesson, that it is the work not only for but with these other girls, that brings both the larger blessing. So both learn the beautiful meaning of sisterhood in Christ." But even as Thurston stressed the idea of mutuality—that both groups needed to learn about sisterhood—she spoke of privileged women assisting their "younger sisters." The benefits were not limited to women alone for, as Thurston noted, "every upward step of the working girl means an uplift for the whole community, for the whole country." Women had a mission, blessed by God, to improve the country, if not the world, by working with their sisters.[52]

At their next national convention, held two years later in St. Paul, delegates officially adopted a constitution for the national organization; members declared that the "ultimate purpose" would be to bring young women to "a knowledge of Jesus Christ as Saviour and Lord" and to "make the organization as a whole an effective agency in the bringing in of the Kingdom of God among young women." They clarified that the church requirement meant those churches "entitled to representation in the Federal Council of women in urban areas found the YWCA's provision of social services in a nondenominational setting appealing. At a time when whites denied African Americans access to "public" services, black women saw considerable value in the housing, training, recreational, and vocational offerings of YWCAs. They, like white women, also found value in an organization that transcended religious denominations. Black women had started an association in Philadelphia as early as 1870, but it and other early associations usually did not last long because of scarce resources in black communities and limited assistance, if not full-scale hostility, from the larger white community.[67]

More stability for black associations came at the turn of the century, but so did increasing segregation and violence in both the South and the North. New York, for instance, had a race riot in 1900.[68] Social service organizations, including most settlement houses and both YMs and YWs, increasingly provided facilities only on a segregated basis.[69] White women and girls increasingly sought to exclude African Americans from their associations. At the same time, African Americans sought to create institutions that they could control, utilizing the organizations both to meet immediate needs and to advance the race. Black women in Brooklyn had established a YWCA in 1903 and those in Manhattan followed in 1905.[70] African American YWCAs had little contact with local white associations and limited status with the International Board.

At the time of the 1906 merger, associations that served black women and girls existed in about ten cities, but the national organization regarded only four of those—Baltimore, Brooklyn, New York (i.e., Manhattan), and Washington, D.C.—as sufficiently well organized to affiliate.[71] There had been more activity for, if not with, black students, primarily at historically black schools such as Spelman Seminary and the Tuskegee Institute. At the time of the merger, there were associations in about a dozen such schools (out of the more than four hundred student associations that had applied for affiliation).[72]

While the new national body had recognized a limited number of black associations, the presence of others and the demands from African Americans for still more presented a potential challenge to white women. At the urging of Grace Dodge, some sixty white women, mostly from the South, met in Asheville, North Carolina, 7–17 June 1907, to discuss the "Colored Question" in the YWCA.[73] Even though the existing active African American community associations were in northern or border cities, accounts from the all-white Asheville conference focused on the implications of such programs in the South.

Southern white women were ambivalent about the work and their northern white sisters were not inclined to push them. A national staff member later wrote that the southern white women "stated that they were quite anxious and willing to help the colored girls in the southern states, [but] . . . on account of the prejudice they did not think it best to attempt it at that time."[74] Afterwards, the *Association Monthly* (the YWCA's journal) told its readers that the "southern ladies" had asked that work for "colored" women in southern cities be delayed for a year to allow "work among the white girls to be more fully organized." The "cordial recommendations" of the conference permitted affiliation of existing black student groups and urban associations. Any African American programs in southern cities, continued the article, were to be administered by the national headquarters in New York.[75] What the public account did not report was the final recommendation that "the National Board be asked to confine representation at the Southern Conference in the future always to white delegates" *and* that the National Board accepted the recommendation.[76]

Documentation for the 1907 Asheville conference is sketchy, but an analysis of the surviving records suggests four important and interlocking aspects of white women's understanding of the YWCA, the larger society, and their place in each. First, the white participants' priority was that the YWCA develop as a *national* organization. Next, they assumed that *white women,* both northern and southern, would control the organization *and* determine policies for black women. Third, they accepted *segregation* as necessary to programs for African Americans. Finally, they defined race primarily, or even solely, as a *southern* issue.

The YWCA's merger happened at a time of consolidation in many American arenas: business, the media, charities and foundations, voluntary associations, and religious bodies.[77] Efforts to unify the nation often revealed tensions between regionally based groups. In particular, many white southerners were wary of joining with northerners because of the legacy of the Civil War and Reconstruction. By the turn of the century, interlocking networks of men in business, education, politics, and philanthropic endeavors produced an ideology that emphasized a common interest in shared pursuits. Additionally, America's debut as an imperial power promoted an emphasis upon national unity and national identity.[78]

Creating national identity and building a national organization, however, were not simple acts. Mabel Cratty, the white northern general secretary, summarized the national organization's approach saying, "I came away with the feeling that we were under a certain amount of obligation not to make it too difficult for those who had conceded a great deal."[79] While her comments did not provide the details of the concessions, the context for her remarks made clear who she felt had conceded—white southern women. Although some white women's organizations, notably missionary groups, had a rich tradition in the South, the YWCA had taken a long time to develop there.[80]

Still negotiating longstanding tensions between the East and Midwest, YW women wanted to ensure it was truly national by promoting the association in the South. Helen A. Davis, a white northern staff member, later summed up the challenge facing the national body: "We had very little or no money or anything to begin with and the South had even less than certain parts of the North and West. We wanted to develop as evenly as we could all over the country."[81] At the time of the merger, while about 33 percent of all Americans lived in the South, the region had only about 14 percent of the city associations.[82] White YW women saw their priority as creating a national organization—of white women—and designed racial policies to promote that end.[83]

The Asheville conference was but one of many efforts by white people to address the race problems at the turn of the century—often in white-only meetings.[84] The white national YW leadership excluded black women from Asheville despite the fact that the latter had already organized their own associations. There was apparently no public comment or explanation for this exclusion at the time, which suggests that the YW leadership accepted white control of the organization as a basic assumption.

Segregation and white control were givens for most whites at the time. Cratty reported that the women in attendance understood that "any parallel work among white and colored people would mean attendance at conferences, etc. The real question was the question of the [national] convention."[85] The recommendations proposed by southern white women and approved by the National Board accepted segregation, permitted local white women to defer assisting black women, and gave local white women the right to determine who from a city could attend the national conventions.

White YW women repeatedly explained the YWCA's racial policies as an accommodation to southern white women's distaste for interracial socializing.[86] The idea that the race problem was a peculiarly southern problem was partially based on the reality that most African Americans lived in the South.[87] The approach also stemmed from the women's understanding of American history. Davis reviewed the goals of the National Board at Asheville: "They tried to gain the confidence of the South in carrying work on and not to go too rapidly. Many people felt that certain sections of the North and certain individuals have no right to go into other sections and impose themselves on those other sections."[88] Her final sentence hints at the lessons whites had drawn from history—the specter of freedmen and carpetbaggers run amok—resolved only by the end of Reconstruction and the subsequent implementation of Jim Crow segregation.[89]

The four issues fed into each other. Concern over black women's participation at the national conventions was not simply an issue of interracial socializing; it raised the possibility that black women at national conventions would have the power to affect policy for all members. The agreement between southern and northern whites that race was a particularly southern question aided national unity. By casting the issue as one of southern white women's concerns, the accounts both granted southern white women a greater say in policy and allowed northern white women to downplay growing racial tensions in the North.[90]

❖ ❖ ❖

In the early twentieth century, white YWCA members developed a female-oriented social gospel to unite competing associations into a new national body. Expanding on Grace Dodge's belief in women working *with* women, they linked individual and social salvation in order to promote the Kingdom of God among young women—or at least the white, native-born young women then entering the paid workforce or attending school. Some black Protestant women found Christian sisterhood's vision of saving souls *and* society appealing. When they approached the association, however, they encountered resistance if not outright exclusion, because of whites' belief that national integration necessitated racial segregation.

The 1907 Asheville conference captured white women's understanding of a Christian sisterhood that linked issues of national identity, power, and segregation. The meeting suggested critical ways in which white YWCA women both reflected and shaped larger trends in the United States. Most white people accepted the repudiation of Reconstruction and no longer regarded race relations as a critical national issue. A whites-only conference established that white people—especially southerners—were to control the race question. Northern whites deferred to white southerners ostensibly in the interests of national harmony, although the reality of African American life in northern cities belied the view that race relations were strictly a southern affair. Part of black women's attack on white domination and, eventually, segregation would be to offer alternative understandings of Christian sisterhood, but, first, they would have to convince their white sisters that the alleviation of racial problems should be a central part of the YWCA's mission.

2 Creating the Race Policy

CHARGED WITH IMPLEMENTING the "cordial recommendations" of the "southern ladies" at Asheville, the National Board faced the question of how to deal with African American associations—in particular, determining which ones the National Board would allow to affiliate with the YWCA. To determine the status of existing associations, the board hired Addie Waites Hunton as a "special worker" to evaluate them.[1] Hunton was a logical choice as she was active with the black clubwomen's movement and wrote frequently on African American women and their organizations.[2] In addition, she had assisted her husband, William Alphaeus Hunton, in his work as the first African American professional worker for the Young Men's Christian Association.[3] In the winter of 1907–8, Addie Hunton visited the associations, recommending affiliation for about half of the student and community groups out of those existing at fourteen schools and in about ten cities.[4]

White women were pleased with the YWCA's progress in the field. Accounting for the National Board's first year, Mabel Cratty, the YWCA's general secretary, reported that Hunton had "been brought into contact with 2,300 colored young women and is awake to the possibility of a larger and fuller womanhood for them through the Association movement, realizing in the Association the greatest possible factor in the work of uplifting her race."[5] Off and on over the next decade, Hunton advised the National Board, assisted local associations in organizing, mediated between white-dominated YWCAs and local black women, and recruited an impressive group of African American women into the YWCA to continue her efforts.

In a 1914 speech on the YWCA, Hunton heralded the achievements of black women in and out of the YWCA, announcing that "the wonderful progress of the Negro has had behind it the *propelling power* of its *women*."[6] Black YWCA women carved out a role for themselves as the "best element of our women" in their efforts to advance the race.[7] They used the language of collective self-help and uplift, but also of womanhood, respectability, and the social gospel, to develop strategies other than a full frontal assault on segregation. They ultimately favored what became known as the YWCA's "branch policy," which established racially segregated associations, yet allowed for black leadership.

At a time when many, if not most, whites were content to ignore the needs of African Americans, it was an accomplishment to get any assistance—financial, administrative, or moral—for black programs. Hunton and her colleagues sought to persuade white women that they (white women) had a Christian duty to improve race relations. While most white women in the organization overlooked black women, a few, including northerners like Grace Dodge and southerners like Maude Wilder Trawick, saw a place for black women and girls in the Kingdom of God. Debates over the role of black women in the organization, however, were never as simple as black versus white, or even blacks and a few white allies versus the majority of whites. In and out of the YWCA, African Americans also argued among themselves over the best way to advance the race.

"A Race Is as Good as Its Women"

It was the Student Committee of the National Board that requested Addie Hunton be hired to evaluate African American student associations.[8] The request may have come from the Student Committee, as opposed to the City Committee, because of the greater number of student associations. In addition, the southern white women at Asheville had been relatively comfortable with the expansion of black student associations because those YWCAs related directly to the national body, rather than to adjacent urban YWs. Community YWCAs in a given city, however, *were* expected to work together; the request from southern white women to delay work for black women in southern cities was, in part, a desire to avoid interactions with African Americans in their cities.

While Hunton concentrated on black schools, she also "unofficially" visited cities and reported back on which associations merited affiliation. The

National Board accepted her recommendations to include student associations at Agricultural and Mechanical College (Normal, Alabama), Langston University, the Normal and Industrial Institute (Ettricks, Virginia), Southern Christian Institute, Spelman Seminary, Talladega College, Tougaloo College, Tuskegee Institute, and Wilberforce University, as well as the community YWs in Baltimore, Brooklyn, New York, and Washington, D.C.[9]

Hunton, wishing to secure the existing work and promote additional efforts, defined her job as also "finding a suitable woman for the supervision of work in colored schools."[10] In the fall of 1908, the National Board called Elizabeth Ross (later Elizabeth Ross Haynes) to promote these efforts.[11] As a "special worker," Ross Haynes was given neither the job security nor the pay of a regular secretary. After two years, she resigned to get married and was replaced by Cecelia Holloway.[12] Holloway herself left when she married in 1912 and was succeeded by Josephine Pinyon.[13] Once married, Elizabeth Ross Haynes, along with Addie Hunton, returned to the YWCA for short-term assignments to promote work in cities while Holloway or Pinyon focused on students.

In accordance with the agreement worked out at Asheville, Hunton, Ross Haynes, Holloway, and Pinyon (in various combinations) promoted efforts from the New York headquarters, lending practical assistance to local black associations and reporting on their accomplishments. In their reports, the women provided more than a simple account of what had happened as they both promoted racial pride for African Americans and sought to win support from the larger white community. When Hunton described the activities of the YWCA to an audience already sympathetic to African Americans, as in a 1911 article for the *Crisis* (the publication of the National Association for the Advancement of Colored People), she focused on what black women were doing themselves to serve "their generation in a new and important movement for the salvation of womanhood." She wrote of the accomplishments of local black women in cities like Brooklyn and the leadership provided by black women on the national staff. The role of the white National Board was seemingly limited to its hiring those women.[14] When addressing those potentially less interested in race issues, such as the larger YWCA membership, Hunton did not fail to credit the efforts of "the colored race" in an "aggressive campaign for its own betterment."[15] But she also sought to convince that larger audience that work for African Americans was important to support. To do so, she utilized the discourses of womanhood, self-help, respectability, uplift, and the Kingdom of God, which resonated with her white audience.

Hunton focused on the importance of women. "A race is as good as its women—no better," she declared in an early YWCA publication.[16] Like white YW women, Hunton pointed to woman's efforts in building a good home as her special role. Home is "the glory of Christendom," she observed in 1907, and, she added, with the "development of our home life, the salvation of the race is in the hands of womanhood."[17] For all the similarities between white and black women's evocation of the home and woman's role, however, there was a social context that made the arguments different.

By the turn of the century, African Americans, individually and collectively, faced a sustained assault expressed through political, economic, social, and cultural means. The period, dubbed the "nadir" by one historian, saw the culmination of political disenfranchisement for black men, the economic dependency of sharecropping and severely constrained vocational choices, "separate and unequal" accommodations in everything from education to transportation through Jim Crow laws and customs, and an escalation of derogatory cultural images. When whites believed that laws or custom failed to keep African Americans in "their place," they turned to other means. The early twentieth century was a time of explosive racial violence, including an increase in both lynchings and race riots, as well as the continuing practice of white men sexually assaulting African American women and girls. As African Americans migrated to northern cities, they encountered de facto (if not de jure) segregation, discrimination, and racial violence.[18]

African American men and women (and, in some cases, white allies) founded a range of organizations in these years to respond to these difficulties, including the National Association of Colored Women (NACW), the National Association for the Advancement of Colored People (NAACP), and the National Urban League (NUL). Black women turned to the YWCA as part of this movement for collective self-help, in part, for the practical social services the YWCA offered. At a time when law or custom increasingly closed so-called public institutions such as schools or parks to African Americans, the educational or recreational facilities of black YWCAs (and YMCAs), as well as travelers' aid for newcomers, proved invaluable.

But the YWCA, with its emphasis on women, morality, and Christianity, also represented a means to counter the cultural assault (and, implicitly, economic, social, and political restrictions). A unifying aspect of white attacks on the black community was that they treated all African Americans as the same. Most whites saw blacks as immoral, uneducated, and potentially dangerous people who deserved neither civil rights, economic opportunities (beyond manual and servile labor), nor respect. In 1907, Addie Hunton publicly criticized the New South's efforts to make "absolutely one class of its [colored] citizens [as the] 'hewers of wood and drawers of water.'"[19] It was an approach that, among other things, did not accord black women the treatment afforded white women. Regardless of class or the ticket purchased, every black woman had to ride in a third-class Jim Crow car, rather than the "ladies'" compartment.

A consequence of growing segregation was that elite whites were less likely to come in contact with blacks and, especially, privileged blacks. Educated black women were concerned that whites were judging the race on the basis of poor blacks. Hunton observed that "there is a wide gulf—which seemingly grows wider—between the white people of the South and the better class of colored people. . . . [Those] who write about the moral degradation of the Negro woman know little or nothing of the best element of our women who are quietly and unobtrusively working out the salvation of the race. Because the Negro women with whom they come in contact exhibit none of those higher qualities that are based on virtue, it is assumed that these women are typical of all Negro women."[20] It was a vicious circle: segregation meant that privileged whites did not meet their black counterparts, and because they never met "the best element," whites saw no reason to question a political, economic, and social system that functioned to keep blacks away from them.

The confusion that existed when white women discussed class, morality, womanhood, or Protestantism was compounded when whites looked at African Americans.[21] Addie Waites Hunton and other African Americans who defended the black home and family and, particularly, the role of black women as good wives and mothers, were mounting a campaign to defend the black community and advance the race politically, economically, and socially through a moral discourse. They developed, as Evelyn Brooks Higginbotham has termed it, a "politics of respectability."[22] Black leaders, female and male, recognized that advancement for African Americans individually was limited in a white-dominated society that saw them as black only. Their solution was to educate whites on the existence of the "talented tenth" who expressed "white" values of morality, education, respectability, and culture, thereby challenging a racism that did not recognize educated and refined African Americans and, hopefully, winning white support. African American leaders also sought to lift up the "black masses," thereby working against racism that brutally kept their people down, but also eliminating a factor that might discredit the race in the eyes of white people. This class-based racial solidarity found black leaders seeking to work *with* whites as they worked *for* the larger black community.[23]

One of the most commonly used concepts in this campaign was that of "uplift." While the idea of uplift was common to general progressive-era reform rhetoric, here it became racially charged.[24] When whites did acknowledge racial problems, they usually emphasized the assistance that blacks needed. In 1906, the white YWCA of New York City, for instance, described the challenges facing it, including the "sisters of a darker hue coming into fellowship and asking for protection and care."[25] Uplift for black clubwomen like Addie Hunton, however, was rooted in racial self-help. They reported on needy African Americans but also stressed the role that more privileged black women could play to assist those in need. In a 1904 article, "Negro Womanhood Defended," Hunton praised "the Negro woman . . . [who] with the culture and character that education [gives] is constantly at work for the uplift of her race."[26]

Ultimately, though, Hunton recognized that African Americans needed assistance if local YWCAs were going to survive, and she relied on social gospel language to gain support. In 1913, the YWCA's National Board published her account, *Beginnings among Colored Women;* in it, Hunton praised both the National Board in "meeting a manifest need" *and* the efforts of "colored women themselves." She also hoped to "awaken to a larger co-operative sympathy all who believe in the democracy of Christianity."[27] She concluded the pamphlet with an appeal for "a greater financial investment" that would produce "not only the spiritual and moral regeneration of four and a half millions [*sic*] of women in the United States, but the advancement of the nation and the kingdom of God here on earth."[28] Like white social gospelers, Hunton conflated democracy and Christianity in defining a divine mission for Americans.[29]

Women's role, morality, uplift, and the Kingdom of God featured prominently in the discussions of the YWCA and African Americans in the early twentieth century. The issue, however, was not simply what the National Board—through white or black staff—would do to start work for African Americans, but how it would respond to efforts that local black women initiated. In her report for 1909, Elizabeth Ross Haynes described an "irrepressible popping up here and there throughout the South of some kind of organization called the Y.W.C.A."[30] Local black associations provided services similar to those offered for white women: housing, travelers' aid, employment bureaus, recreational opportunities, Bible classes, lectures or discussions on public affairs, and vocational education.

Both white and black national leaders were concerned, however, that some local efforts included other kinds of programs. In 1908, Ross Haynes advised the National Board that the work of African American YWCAs in Philadelphia, Baltimore, and Washington, D.C., was "not strictly confined to Association work but includes rescue work, Sunday school work, Epworth League work [the Methodist youth group], and kindergartens." In fact, in Philadelphia and Washington, the associations were working with children and older women, rather than young women, perhaps reflecting the fact that the black women migrating to cities to work included a larger number of *married* women than did comparable white women, who tended to be single.[31] In any event, such diversity of programming flew in the face of efforts to standardize YWCA work, and the national leadership encouraged Hunton and her compatriots to control the variations.

The African American national staffers walked a thin line between the demands of local black women and those of the white national body. Although national YW leaders explained that white associations also had to meet national standards for affiliation, local black leaders felt that they faced particular difficulties in obtaining recognition for their work.[32] Hunton and the others spent much of their time trying to explain or, in YW parlance, "interpret" each group to the other. Representing the national YW, Elizabeth Ross Haynes could sound like her white sisters, recommending in 1910 that, "in view of the fact that much Y.W.C.A. work in name only is being most unwisely started in cities, [it was] advisable to request forcibly such organizations to refrain from the use of the name Y.W.C.A. unless certain requirements are made."[33] Ross Haynes and the others cautioned that locals were trying to do too much, too fast, and were likely to fail.

On the other hand, Ross Haynes also warned the National Board that she was running into difficulty justifying its slow approach to African Americans: "although I did the best I could, my defense has not been sufficiently formidable to convince the inquirers of the truth of our sincere interest in them and their work."[34] The problem she and others realized was not simply the consequence of local black women's ambitions, but also the result of the Asheville accord, which had dictated that New York would oversee local black associations. The national YWCA did not make African American programs a financial priority and local white associations continued to ignore or discourage black efforts. The results were disheartening. "[We] were not able to carry on work from headquarters," a black member of the national staff later explained, "[and] because there was no touch with the [local] central Association, [colored work] died."[35]

To strengthen local programs, African Americans on the national staff favored a structure that increased the involvement of local white women with black associations. They succeeded in getting the (white) City Committee to recommend an interim policy, which the National Board approved in December 1910. The new guidelines suggested that "in cities where there is a central Association the [colored] work be organized as a branch of the central Association."[36] They built on the agreement that only one association in a city would be allowed to affiliate with the national association; the first association in a city was to be the "central association," while succeeding ones would be "branches."[37] While encouraging the branch structure for black YWCAs, Ross Haynes was not naive about continued white resistance. She obliquely referred to white racism as "existing conditions which have little tendency to yield" and asked that provisions be made that would allow black women to organize where white resistance remained.[38] In such cases (or where there was no white association), the National Board agreed that "if the colored population is sufficiently large and able to support its own work," a "Colored Young Women's Christian association" would be permitted to affiliate directly with the national body, although the goal would be a branch relationship as soon as possible.[39]

The branch relationship entailed at least three components: a member of the (white) central association was on the governing board of the black branch; the branch's activities were "subject to the Central's approval"; and the central was responsible for unmet debts.[40] While some local black associations remained autonomous, Pinyon and her fellow workers reported that increasing numbers were functioning as branches. By 1912, branch associations existed in New York, Brooklyn, St. Paul, Poughkeepsie, St. Louis, and Kansas City (Missouri), while independent associations still operated in Baltimore, Norfolk, Philadelphia, Washington, Dayton, and Charleston (South Carolina). Over time, most independent associations became branches.[41]

Different constituencies favored the branch relationship for different reasons. Some local white women continued to forestall any efforts to develop black associations, but others saw the relationship as a means to influence black associations. In 1911, two young white women in Richmond "felt the call to do some service for less favored women of their city" and sought to start a black YWCA.[42] That same year, white women in Poughkeepsie, New York, supported a branch because it offered courses in "domestic science" that promised to "help much in solving the question of domestic service in the city."[43] National white leaders favored the structure because it was in line with the goal that there be only one association in a given city. Local black women gained recognition for their efforts and, at times, some financial assistance, while African American national staff members observed that branches were more likely to survive than independent associations.

The apparent acceptance by Hunton and other black YWCA women of institutionalized segregation was complicated. Hunton personally opposed segregation; she became increasingly active with the NAACP after its establishment in 1909.[44] But Hunton and the others also had to be realistic in evaluating the needs of the black community and strategize how to access white resources. They focused their efforts not on fighting segregation, but on the issue of who would lead the efforts for African Americans. Here too they encountered obstacles. At times, it seemed as if white women regarded any black woman as less capable. In 1911, for instance, the white leadership of the New York City YWCA hired a white woman as the secretary for the black branch despite the opposition of black women.[45] Although Addie Hunton praised the white women of Richmond who wished to help "the less favored women of their city," she pointedly observed that the white women discovered that black women "had already accomplished the thing that the white women had in mind for them."[46] In consistently praising the efforts that African Americans exerted on their own behalf, Hunton and her compatriots attempted to demonstrate that even as African Americans needed assistance, they were not completely incapable. Hunton struggled to get whites to recognize that many African American women were already doing important work. In cases where they were not, the role of the YWCA was to find those with potential and train them.

While Hunton and the others appealed for financial assistance from whites for buildings and equipment, they placed particular emphasis upon developing black leadership through both paid staff and volunteers. Black women seeking to establish a new YWCA needed to ascertain that "a competent secretary can be employed" and that there existed a group of "representative women who have a fair understanding of needs, purposes, and plans of Association."[47] Reporting on the YWCA's efforts in 1911, Hunton wrote, "Our largest need at present is not more associations, although that need at several centers is alarmingly pressing. We must first find trained leaders."[48]

The YWCA had opened its National Training School (NTS) in 1908 in New York City to educate its professional workers. Not until 1911, however, did the school admit black women into its summer program.[49] Not all workers were able to get to New York; in addition, the volunteer members of local boards also needed training. In 1912, the employed and volunteer workers from local black associations began getting together in conferences.[50] Held once or twice a year for city workers, the meetings allowed women to build a network among themselves for information, training, and support.[51]

Stretched thin, Hunton and the others urged that the national staff concentrate on visiting the cities with the strongest chances of "developing model associations," while corresponding with others in order to restrain unwise expansion. In determining whether a locality was ready, Hunton recommended that organizing be limited to communities that could provide "permanent and adequate equipment" and see that "support for one year is assured."[52] The ability to raise money was an important aspect of a black branch's ability to determine its own fate; in 1913, white YW women living in the historically white neighborhood of Harlem sought to prevent the black YWCA from relocating there, as white Harlemites generally fought the racial transformation of the area. A substantial contribution from Grace Dodge, often supportive of African American groups, facilitated the black women's purchase of two houses on West 132nd Street despite the local white leadership's opposition.[53]

Despite limited support, if not full-scale resistance, from most white northerners and southerners, Addie Hunton and her associates had reason to take pride in their accomplishments. African American women at the national and local levels made the most of their opportunities. In 1913, Hunton reported that the YWCA had expanded from fourteen student associations of questionable merit in 1908 to more than ninety organizations. Community work had gone from four local associations to nineteen, with "small beginnings" in several others. They also pointed with pride to those associations, such as the one in St. Louis, where the branch had not had to rely on the central association to pay its debts.[54] Building on these efforts required persuading white women that the work was of value to them.

"Only through Mutual Sympathies and Understandings"

As early as 1909, black YWCA workers and white members of the City Committee pushed for a full-time staff member to oversee community associations. Citing a lack of funds, the National Board resisted. Its reluctance to commit funds to such a position contributed to an inherently unstable situation.[55] In 1912, the City Committee reported that while Hunton and Ross Haynes were conducting their work "admirably," it feared that their husbands might "at any time recall the loan."[56] Finally, in January 1913, the YWCA called

Eva Del Vakia Bowles as the first full-time professional to administer work for urban African Americans.[57] Educated at Ohio State University, with additional training at the New York School of Philanthropy, Bowles had prior experience with the black YWCA in New York City as well as in southern black schools and the Associated Charities of Columbus, Ohio. For almost two decades, she would direct the national efforts to promote work for and among African Americans in the YWCA.

At the end of the year, the National Board also established the Sub-Committee on Colored Work to oversee the work. The subcommittee included white board members as well as black and white staff members. Bowles welcomed the white-dominated committee's aid cautiously. She believed that it would assist in the development of the programs, but she recalled that "until recently," the situation of African Americans had been "approached with indifference." She continued, "There has been much discussion which has served often as an excuse for doing nothing."[58] She promoted the subcommittee at the national level and the branch relationship at the local as part of a specific strategy to improve African Americans' position. At a time of intense racial segregation, these structures brought white and black women together, even if in white-dominated settings. Like Hunton, Bowles regarded black women's efforts as indispensable to, but not sufficient to achieve, racial advancement.

Throughout her tenure at the YWCA, Bowles argued that contact between whites and blacks was necessary for racial improvement *and* that both groups benefitted from such contact. The branch relationship, she wrote at the end of her first year, was "valuable not only to the branch but to the Central Association as well. It is only through mutual sympathies and understandings that the development of all women is assured."[59] Promoting such relations would be no small task, as segregation continued to characterize work not only in the locals, but also at the national setting. At the 1913 national convention held in Richmond, the three black delegates representing Hampton Institute were forced to sit in the balcony.[60] Bowles's sister later reported that Bowles herself was unable to attend the convention even though she was the national staff member in charge of work for African Americans, "because no provisions were made for her attendance."[61] Nonetheless, Bowles viewed the branch relationship, limited as it was, as an opportunity to move white women by exposing them to educated African Americans such as herself.

She faced resistance not only from white southern women, but also from white northerners, who tended to downplay the issue of race relations. Bowles was fortunate to have assistance from a few white women who *were* interested in race matters, including Leila Frissell, a member of the National Board. From an abolitionist family and a member of the Sub-Committee on Colored Work, Frissell was exceptional among the board members in her commitment to the race question. Returning from a 1914 conference for black Christian students, Frissell rebuked her colleagues in New York in uncharacteristically blunt language: "If, as many people thought, the white people of the North were getting tired of the Southern race problem, thinking 'I have done enough there. There is no need for further work for me,' the time had surely come when we should be awakened to the knowledge that this is the time of all others when thoughtful help is more needed than ever."[62] She sought to explain the conference's importance in terms that would resonate with her white colleagues, concluding, "Anyone might wish to [have been] at the conference, because those present caught heavenly visions of the love of God, which makes the true brotherhood of man."[63]

The conference that Frissell attended, the Negro Christian Student Conference, was called by John R. Mott and brought more than six hundred people to Atlanta in May 1914 to discuss the situation of African American students.[64] Participants included almost five hundred black students from eighty-eight schools and colleges, as well as college presidents, newspaper editors, social workers, teachers, and religious leaders—including some fifty-three southern whites.[65] The presenters were a veritable who's who of people involved with the race question from a variety of viewpoints. Booker T. Washington was an invited speaker, but so were Lugenia Burns Hope and William Pickens (more closely identified with W. E. B. Du Bois). While the gathering was not strictly a YWCA conference, YW women were visible both as presenters and attendees. As Frissell's summary suggests, religious language dominated the conference and was the motivating factor for both white and black attendees.

The conference's purposes included encouraging African American students to engage in "Christian life callings" as well as urging that "Christian thought [be brought] to bear on present and future cooperation of the races."[66] The presence of both races at the conference was notable, and organizers designed the content to minimize conflict. One white observer praised the conference for excluding "all divisive questions, such as those of color, politics and social segregation." This exclusion, he went on, "[ensured] harmony and [begot] a sincere friendliness."[67] Representative of the emphasis on harmony was Maude Wilder Trawick's address entitled "The Social Message of the Church." The white president of the board of directors of the Nashville YWCA, she argued that the church would be "socially converted" when people remembered that "we should love our neighbor as ourselves." Invoking the progressive ideals of "efficiency" and "social justice," she concluded that "racial cooperation" was an integral part of any general effort to improve society.[68]

Speaking on the work of the National Board, Addie Hunton also emphasized that social service was a necessary component in the "extension of our Lord's Kingdom here on earth."[69] She reported in the "North as well as South, white and colored women are finding unity in service."[70] Echoing Hunton's stress on cooperation, Lily Hardy Hammond, a white Southern Methodist, told the predominantly black audience that the next few years "will see a great opening of the doors of opportunity for all your people . . . and it is we of the white race who must widen those doors and cooperate with you more privileged Negroes for the uplift of your race."[71] White and black women asserted a relation between divinely sanctioned service, women's role, self-help, and uplift that was by now familiar to anyone in the YWCA who had paid the slightest attention to racial efforts since Asheville.

What made this conference significant was its emphasis on the fate of Christianity around the world, especially in meeting "the claims and crisis of Africa." What, attendees asked, was to be the role of African American students in the missionary movement in Africa? Ronald White, a historian of the social gospel and race relations, has argued the focus on Africa dodged what was "uniquely American" and was part of an unwillingness of whites at the conference to address meaningful issues.[72] Josephine Pinyon, the YWCA secretary for black student work who attended the conference, evaluated the situation differently.

When John Mott identified "Negro students" with a "world issue rather than a race issue," he linked the race question at home with the evangelical Protestant mission to convert the world. Pinyon drove the point home in her report to her white colleagues: "Now there is something that will make people realize that the colored work is not a vague cause for sympathy and a casual interest, but a great big actual fact!—a force to be reckoned with, an integral and by no means negligible part of the responsibility assumed when the National Board was organized."[73] The connection between foreign mission work, an organizational priority of the YWCA and churches, and the situation of African Americans afforded Pinyon a chance to link race work to issues that her white colleagues *did* care about.

Sympathy and interest were not enough, she continued. Her colleagues needed to educate themselves so they could have informed discussions and develop useful plans. She softened her criticism a bit, admitting that she knew no more about immigrants or foreign missions than her white colleagues knew more about work for African Americans. But, she went on, it was time to repair the evident "lack of knowledge" and she proposed that "every secretary on the national staff be asked to include in her year's program the reading of certain books." She and Bowles could recommend a "fairly long list" of suitable titles. Only then, should the staff attempt to discuss "the whole question of the colored work."[74] Implicitly, Pinyon was challenging the notion that white women were inherently better equipped to lead than educated black women.

In the short run, white members at the national headquarters seemed to echo Pinyon's understanding that race work was an integral part of the YWCA. Louise Holmquist, the head of the Department of Method, spoke of Atlanta's representing "a new era in our colored work" and pointed out to the entire staff "the necessity of each one's work being part of everyone's work."[75] But matching actions to words was slow in coming. At the YWCA's national convention in California in May 1915, the National Board reported briefly that the Atlanta conference pointed "the way to a better cooperative effort between white and colored leaders."[76] At the same time, Pinyon was the only African American present. The proceedings, she later recounted, left her "resentful, bitter, disgusted" and she labeled the association a "spiritual farce, rather than a spiritual force."[77]

"There Can Be No Whole without Her"

By 1915, the YWCA had been promoting programs for African Americans for almost five years under the National Board's interim guidelines, which had revised the Asheville agreement. Because the National Board was in New York City, however, only women from the Northeast regularly attended its monthly meetings.[78] Grace Dodge urged that a more representative group meet to discuss the racial policy of the organization, and the Sub-Committee on Colored Work began planning a conference for spring 1915.[79] Surveying the field, YW leaders noticed an impressive growth in the programs, but also saw that the burden fell on the few national black staffers. In cities like Birmingham and Norfolk, local YWCAs were still failing.[80] National YW leaders argued that the difficulties were the result of both black and white women's "misunderstanding" the "true purpose" of the YWCA. They were encouraged that some southern white women were "awakening to [the] need of racial cooperation." But, they noted, the YW was facing increasing criticism (or competition) from groups like the NUL, the NACW, the NAACP, the Southern Methodist women's home mission movement, the Women's Christian Temperance Union, and the YMCA over the YW's failure to support efforts for black women and girls.[81]

Dodge's death in December 1914 delayed the meeting until October 1915, at which time twenty-eight people met in Louisville, Kentucky. Attendees included eight representatives (six white, two black) from the National Board and staff, seven white representatives of the South Atlantic and South Central Field Committees, six African American women "representing various movements in the South," and four white women and three white men active "in constructive work among Colored people in the South" other than the YWCA.[82] As at Asheville, YWCA leadership continued to see African Americans as a peculiarly southern question, pointing out earlier that year that blacks overwhelmingly—some 86 percent—lived in the South.[83] After meeting for two days, the interracial, white-dominated Louisville conference concluded that "the best method of cooperating in city Associations is through the branch relationship," a decision which built on the interim National Board policy.[84]

In its efforts to codify the "branch policy," YW women sought to clarify the administrative structures responsible for a branch. Branch members themselves were to select a Committee on Management, which would direct the day-to-day operations of the branch. For its part, the central association exercised control through an interracial, but usually white-dominated, body called the Affiliating Committee.[85] Eva Bowles and others at the national level urged that the latter committee be strictly advisory and function to promote mutual understanding, but in some cities, it actually administered the branch.[86]

Even in cases where the Affiliating Committee only gave advice, the central association wielded tremendous power over the branch. It was the (white) board of directors for the central association that had the right to refuse to open or even continue a black branch, just as it determined what would happen to programs and branches for white women and girls. The central association staff and board were also involved in hiring decisions, in some cases selecting white women to run the programs for African Americans. And, finally, central associations chose the women to represent their cities at the national conventions, which meant that southern white women could veto specific, or even all, black southern women from attending as delegates.[87]

In explaining the importance of the branch structure, the white-dominated Committee on Findings identified it as essential to building "mutual understanding and patience on the part of both our white and colored friends."[88] This language of mutuality was at the heart of the YWCA's approach to race in these years. The solution to problems would come when both groups understood each other and the YWCA's true purpose. Mutual understanding was a double-edged sword. On one hand, the idea recognized that both blacks and whites were involved and had a role to play in promoting social harmony. On the other hand, white women could use the rhetoric to mask differences especially over white dominance. In proposing the conference, the white-dominated Sub-Committee on Colored Work had reported that *both* whites and blacks had misunderstood the YWCA's purpose. It added that an additional source of black women's opposition to the YWCA stemmed from "[l]ack of faith and prejudice against the Association's apparent failure to live up to the breadth of its purpose."[89] As the subcommittee expressed it, then, the problem was not that the national group was slow in expanding its efforts; rather it was black women's perception that it was slow. White women failed to acknowledge that some local whites actively resisted the efforts of African Americans to develop YWCAs.

For her part, Eva Bowles heralded the Louisville conference for promoting interracial contact and acknowledging black women's abilities. She used the language of Christian sisterhood to explain the importance of such experiences for both groups: "The colored woman is beginning to find herself and realize . . . Christian sisterhood as one of the greatest factors towards ideal womanhood and also that they have a share in it and a contribution to make. . . . On the other hand, our more favored Christian sister is awaking to the realization of opportunity and responsibility towards this hindered group. The joy comes as they realize our women are a part and there can be no whole without her."[90] In an effort to challenge white domination (if not segregation), Bowles, like Hunton before her, continually tried to get white women to see their Christian duty to their black sisters but not lose sight of the latter's contributions. She did not advocate a full-scale attack on segregation but looked for ways to link white and black women.

In addition to promoting the branch relationship, the Committee on Findings called for a national committee of "white and colored women from or of the South" to advise the organization on racial issues and requested that the southern field committees develop "a working plan in accordance with the spirit of this conference."[91] Initially optimistic that Louisville demonstrated that a "small group of southern white women" had begun to see the need to work with African Americans, Josephine Pinyon used her follow-up reports to suggest concrete ways the YWCA could move beyond the racial divisions she had witnessed at the national convention earlier that year. She proposed that the southern fields each create an interracial committee that would function like the national Sub-Committee on Colored Work, thereby ensuring black voices in regional discussions.[92] The national subcommittee supported her recommendation and persuaded the South Atlantic Field Committee to establish a committee that included a white board member, a white staff member, and a black leader of community work. In December 1916, the biracial committee met for the first time with black and white members of the national staff to discuss plans for promoting programs in the South.[93] But change would be slow in coming.

"The Best Method"?

In determining the branch policy as "the best method of cooperating in city Associations," the Louisville conference established the structure of race relations in the YWCA for the coming years. Both whites and blacks would be in the association, although, for many of them, contact with the other race would be rare and carefully orchestrated. Contact was more likely to occur among select leaders—white women, for instance, who agreed to serve on interracial affiliating committees. Even those restricted activities required the constant vigilance of African American women. The biracial regional committee to facilitate programs for African Americans suggested by Pinyon and endorsed by the national Sub-Committee on Colored Work, for instance, did not meet a second time.[94]

Given the obvious limitations, what advantages did (some) black women find in participating in the YWCA? Many shared with their white sisters a commitment to a Protestantism that permitted a unity among different denominations that was often lacking in their church and mission groups.[95] Hunton praised the YWCA's having "broken down denomination barriers and exalted Christianity."[96] At a time when white social gospelers were usually silent about race, black women forged a space for discussions about race and the Kingdom of God, and some white women like Maude Trawick, Lily Hammond, Leila Frissell, and Grace Dodge joined them. Black women's opportunities to engage white women were limited in these years and they took advantage of the few that did exist.[97]

African American women identified other benefits as well. They were able to use branches to promote improvement in their communities through educational, recreational, and social programs. The significance of the associations went beyond the immediate needs of a given community. Addie Hunton observed that the African American facilities in Washington, D.C., and New York City permitted women from around the country to travel east for national meetings because the attendees "could stop in the Association homes" when hotels were closed to them.[98] The white central association was expected to be "responsible morally and sympathetically" for the branch, and it was also to pay the salary of the branch secretary.[99] Endorsement of the branch by a white organization could give the former legitimacy if it turned to the larger community for financial support.

An additional appeal of the YWCA for local African American leaders was the opportunity to attend YW conferences. Black employees and volunteers had met annually since 1912 and a comparable meeting for black students and their advisors began in the summer of 1916 in the wake of the Louisville gathering.[100] These meetings included formal training sessions, but they also provided advice from experienced professionals from the national office and other locals. The education offered in those meetings was useful to women who were barred from attending many schools or did not have the time or money to attend those schools open to them. Conferences also promoted connections to the national staff and among local leaders. These personal connections built on and supported the networks of African American women social reformers that existed in the early twentieth century.[101]

Finally the YWCA was appealing as a national women's organization that had at least some interest in participation by black women. Hunton, Ross Haynes, and the other black women were not denied opportunities for broader leadership only because of their race. The NAACP and the Urban League often denied black women top leadership positions. As Deborah Gray White has observed, at the turn of the twentieth century, black clubwomen used the NACW to create a power base for themselves in community welfare efforts, often in competition with black men.[102] Black YWCAs provided another venue for them. Black women often downplayed gender divisions in the black community. When they did publicly criticize black men, they presented their response as necessary to promote the race. In 1916, Addie Hunton addressed a Philadelphia audience calling for support of the black branch there. Her speech began with the now familiar tribute to the power of black women. But she continued with an explicit explanation of how black men had let the race down: "Many of the problems, both economic and political, can be better solved by the negro women than by the negro men who have, I regret to say, permitted themselves to become in too many instances pawns of some political party and have thus destroyed their usefulness and influence as a political factor."[103]

The leadership opportunities black women found in the YWCA point to an ironic result of racial segregation. Hollis Frissell, principal of Hampton Institute (and the brother of Leila Frissell of the National Board's Sub-Committee on Colored Work), popularized the concept of "the advantages of the disadvantages." Segregation meant that African Americans might serve as leaders of all-black groups. Branches afforded them experiences that they would not have had in white-dominated organizations. In 1910, Elizabeth Ross Haynes reported to the National Board that "the opening of city Associations will offer large opportunities for colored college girls to serve the less favored of their race, also furnishing them with professional opportunities."[104] While African Americans of the talented tenth were comfortable discussing their efforts to uplift others, they were more reticent about the material advantages that accrued to themselves: Ross Haynes's comment was not included in copies of the report that circulated outside the YWCA's headquarters.[105]

While some found in the YWCA's branches a way to advance the race, others in the African American community opposed either segregation or the proposed relationship to the white central association. In 1911, Cecelia Holloway reported that "the older colored people opposed a branch organized on racial lines" in Indianapolis. On the other hand, "newcomers" (presumably southern migrants) "indorsed [*sic*] the plan."[106] Established African American communities in other cities, notably Cleveland and Boston, also publicly opposed segregated Ys and especially their spread to the North—even when they provided important services. Mary White Ovington of the NAACP recalled that a black Bostonian, asked about the fate of young black migrants if a segregated YMCA was not built, replied, "Let them rot." And Boston, in fact, built neither a black YM nor YW.[107]

In the early twentieth century, however, many saw the choice not as between segregation and integration, but as between segregation and exclusion.[108] Resistance to segregation at the price of no facilities was not the norm. But even when a community accepted a separate association, people debated its relation to the white association. In Baltimore, there had been an independent black association prior to the establishment of the National Board. Local black leaders prided themselves that it had been "self sustaining" for "quite a number of years." When those in the central association and in New York encouraged it to become a branch, the *Afro-American Led-*

ger suggested that "those who have recently come into it and have given but little labor, money, and influence" needed to listen to those who had actually done the work before pushing them to consolidate.[109] While the Madison Avenue branch, as it became known, did subsequently affiliate with the central association, the variety of local experiences reveals competing ideas among black women themselves.

Not all black women were as optimistic as Bowles about the potential of the YWCA, but even many critics found aspects of it useful. Some women, Bowles observed, came to the YWCA and "get just some of the benefits from it" rather than throw themselves into the movement, as she favored.[110] These women participated in the YWCA, but also in a range of other groups, including the NAACP and the NACW, seeking to combine resources from and connections in each to advance the race.

❖ ❖ ❖

Debates over the YWCA's racial policies and practices in the years before the First World War saw points of commonality as well as disagreements between white and black women, northerners and southerners, national and local women, as well as divisions within each of those groups. The emphasis of women like Addie Hunton had been on drawing attention to the "propelling power" of African American women to refute images of them as immoral and as a way to justify leadership positions for themselves *and* lift up the race. While many of the implications of the branch policy codified at the 1915 Louisville conference—especially segregation and the domination by white central associations—were restrictive, promoting contact between white and black women represented a well-thought-out strategy for racial advancement. Eva Bowles relied on the ideas of mutual understanding and Christian sisterhood to create situations where white and black women had an opportunity to come together, even if initially only in the shared name of the YWCA, in the belief that whites would have to recognize "our women are a part and there can be no whole without her." As Americans contemplated entering the Great War, African Americans' place in the whole gained new importance.

3 Working for Democracy

IN 1917, LILY HARDY HAMMOND described the "Christian and patriotic" duty of white women to work for "racial adjustment."[1] The white daughter of former slaveowners, Hammond was a prolific writer on race relations of her day. In *Southern Women and Racial Adjustment,* she reported on white women's organized activities, especially those of the Women's Christian Temperance Union, church societies, and the YWCA.[2] Hammond praised the latter as laying the basis "for mutual understanding" between the races.[3] Observing that the war was "accelerating the trend toward coöperation," she argued that the migration of African Americans meant that race was also becoming an issue for northern white women, although southern white women had a critical role to play.[4]

At the forefront of southern white liberals in the early twentieth century, Lily Hammond had to negotiate the ideological terrain of the New South. She was married to John D. Hammond, who in 1911 became president of Paine Institute, a school for African Americans in Georgia run by white Southern Methodists. The Hammonds spoke at the 1914 Negro Christian Student Conference. In 1916, John Hammond was forced out of Paine, ostensibly for incompetence, but at a time when even discreet support for racial liberalism was controversial.[5]

Like Addie Hunton, Hammond looked to privileged black women to improve their race, writing that the "discovery of the educated colored woman is of deep significance. It is she who must lift her people."[6] Like YW women of all races, Hammond viewed the home as critical to social improvement, declaring that the "status of the Negro woman and the Negro home in the minds of the privileged white women will determine the status of the race."[7] Addie Hunton had hoped that white women would "awaken" to the demands of "the democracy of Christianity," and, in many ways, Lily Hammond was the answer to that appeal.[8] Black women in the YWCA saw enough in Hammond's writings to recommend them to their white counterparts, and Lily Hardy Hammond, as a southern white woman, provided a critical voice about race for white YWCA women in these years. She had, for instance, addressed the 1915 Louisville conference twice on the "problems facing both white and colored people in the South."[9]

Hammond's formulation of the "race question" and its solutions, however, differed in significant ways from Hunton's, and it was Hammond's view that more closely resonated with white YW women—northern or southern. Hammond portrayed "educated colored women" as almost completely dependent upon "privileged" white women, stating that the former "can do so little without our help." Given that most whites ignored racial problems, her belief that white women should turn things around was notable, but her assumption was that white women had to work *for,* not *with,* "these struggling, scattered, handicapped women." Coupled with the noblesse oblige was the belief that segregation was a necessary component for racial adjustment.[10]

Hammond was prescient in observing in 1917 that the World War was changing the scene. The consequences of war work, migration, industrialization, and postwar racial tensions irrevocably altered race relations in America. As the major women's organization involved in war relief, the YWCA expanded its programs dramatically in these years, including those for African Americans. Increasingly, white women in the YWCA came to see that, as Hammond put it, the "negro is no longer a sectional, but a national, concern," and they cooperated with her to educate the public to promote racial "reconciliation."[11] Most white women did not see race relations as a national *priority,* but, through the YWCA, they participated in an increasingly national discussion. Although white women defined the debate within the institution, African American women questioned those definitions and the ensuing policies and practices.

"To Make the World Safe for Democracy"

With the entry of the United States into World War I in April 1917, the YWCA joined most of the country in seeing the war as a crusade, one that had political and cultural, as well as religious, implications. An editorial in the YWCA's monthly magazine proclaimed, "The largest cause ever put up to mankind is the one now before us, 'to make the world safe for democracy.' In its highest sense this is the same thing as the Kingdom of God."[12] In their equation of democracy and Christianity, YW members saw the war as connected to their tradition of overseas missions.[13]

It was progressives who directed the American war effort, and they believed that it could redeem the United States as well as the world. Secretary of War Newton D. Baker came to his position as a midwestern reformer.[14] Not only did he face the challenge of creating a modern military machine from a small army, he, like other progressives, identified efficiency and purity as essential to such an effort. A new federal agency, the Commission on Training Camp Activities (CTCA), was established to coordinate voluntary organizations to provide wholesome support services at home and abroad, while avoiding duplication of programs and competition between groups. Ultimately, the federal government granted seven organizations affiliate status with the CTCA: the American Library Association, the Jewish Welfare Board, the Knights of Columbus, the Salvation Army, the War Camp Community Service, the Young Men's Christian Association, and the Young Women's Christian Association.[15] The groups conducted campaigns individually and collectively to raise money for their programs during the war and the subsequent demobilization. Although the federal government was able to utilize the newly established income tax, voluntary giving through bonds, loans, and donations covered two-thirds of war expenditures and was essential to the American war effort (as well as fitting in with the voluntarism associated with the war).

Although the YMCA received the lion's share of funds and provided the bulk of relief efforts to servicemen, the YWCA fared well. In 1916, the national YWCA's expenditures had been $663,690.[16] In November 1917, the YW's War Work Council, which had been organized in June of that year, campaigned for $5 million to cover expenses through 1918. In the summer of 1918, Secretary Baker and the secretary of the navy, Josephus Daniels, charged the seven relief agencies to conduct a United War Work Campaign for the week beginning, ironically as it turned out, on November 11 (the day the armistice went into effect). Of the $200 million budget, the YWCA was awarded roughly $15 million to cover its efforts from November 1918 to the end of 1919.[17]

The YWCA's experience providing facilities and social services imbued with morality throughout the country made the organization particularly appealing to wartime progressives, and its members prided themselves on its mobilization as the only women's group among the seven.[18] YWCA women worked with government agencies, not only in the CTCA, but also the Women in Industry section of the Labor Department.[19] The YWCA utilized its network of almost one thousand college and city associations to raise money and recruit workers to respond to the challenges that wartime participation brought women overseas and stateside.[20] The YWCA's War Work Council administered a range of programs and significantly extended the YWCA's operations.

In February 1917, the head of the Union Chrétienne des Jeunes Filles (the French equivalent of the YWCA) requested that the American YWCA provide assistance to French female factory workers, particularly for rest and relaxation. In June, the YM suggested that the YW also aid women with the American Expeditionary Forces. Although these women provided essential services, most were civilians and the military did not provide them even with housing. In the end, the YWCA sent more than three hundred white women to provide housing and recreation to some six thousand American women serving as nurses, telephone operators, stenographers, and workers with other American relief organizations. YW secretaries also worked with French munitions workers and clerks, as well as English WAACs.[21] Arguing that other welfare groups, whether male-run or coeducational, could not "prevent men's interests from taking precedence over those of women," the War Work Council heralded its efforts to "serve women as they need to be served."[22] As important as the YWCA's overseas efforts were, however, they paled in comparison to its homefront activities.

The groups responsible for servicemen were preoccupied with maintaining the men's morality and curtailing the dangers posed to the armed forces by prostitution and alcohol. Not surprisingly, groups varied as to their primary concern. The military emphasized the danger of venereal disease to the troops' fighting ability. Reformers were as concerned about the morality of the men as their efficiency and envisioned programs that made "men finer" and "strengthened the whole moral fiber of army life."[23] Members of the YWCA, however, were more concerned about the impact of servicemen on the female civilian population, arguing that it was necessary "to throw every safeguard around the communities that surround the camps."[24] Although these agencies worked together, their efforts were fraught with tension; each spoke of the need for regulation but did not always agree upon who needed protection. Was the teenage girl who succumbed to the "lure of the khaki" dangerous to the soldier or herself a victim?[25]

Beginning in June 1917, the YWCA opened hostess houses that served simultaneously to protect the female friends and relatives of servicemen and to provide a moralizing influence on the soldiers. The "houses," ranging from tents to a southern mansion, were located in or near training camps and cantonments, safely away from bars, red light districts, and other forms of commercialized leisure.[26] They offered a place for women and families to stay when visiting their family members in uniform.[27] Overseen by maternal figures, they also offered "homey" places where military men could read, play parlor games with other soldiers, or have a "bit of home cooking." Hostess houses varied as to how much socializing between men and women was permitted; not all camps, for instance, permitted dancing. In others, however, properly chaperoned dances, with young women and girls brought in from nearby areas, were a popular activity.[28]

The YWCA prized the attention it received for its hostess house efforts, "the most picturesque of war time activities," as one staff member dubbed them.[29] *The Independent,* noted for its social commentary, praised the hostess houses in a headline as "Oases in the Desert of Army Discipline," while *House Beautiful* described them as "Bringing Home to the Army Camps."[30] By the time the War Work Council disbanded in late 1919, the YWCA had administered more than one hundred twenty hostess house programs.[31] Supplementing these programs, the War Work Council promoted more than two hundred fifty recreation centers in communities adjacent to camps to provide additional supervised opportunities for servicemen to meet women and girls as part of the CTCA's efforts to enlist support of the civilian community for troops.[32] The national YWCA worked with local women to finance and staff the programs, utilizing existing YWCAs or establishing new institutions.[33]

Relief efforts fused practical services with morality; both, according to progressives, were needed to win the Great War. YW overseas centers and the hostess houses were wartime measures reflecting the YWCA's long-term commitment to assisting women and protecting their moral standards, but YW women knew the programs to be temporary. It was the "industrial army of women" mobilized during the war as the nation's "second line of defense" that YW women believed represented future opportunities.[34] Millions of men were necessary to fight a modern war, but so were millions of women; YW posters announced "For Every Fighter, a Woman Worker." The War Work Council provided cafeterias, housing, and recreation opportunities for women mobilized for wartime jobs, whether laundry workers outside a military base in New Mexico, federal clerical workers in Washington, D.C., or munitions workers in Bridgeport, Connecticut.[35] Many of the programs responded to immediate needs—places to eat, sleep, or rest. During postwar demobilization, as men returned and displaced women from jobs, the YWCA attempted to aid women who wished to continue employment. In October 1918, a journalist praised the YWCA's foresight in realizing that "readjustment will be necessary after the war, when women and girls accustomed to independence, will have to find different work to do."[36] YW members valued these services not only because increasing numbers of women held industrial jobs, but also because professional women gained opportunities to direct programs; both aspects, they argued, would affect women's employment after the war.[37] Like many, they assumed that the war would alter women's economic, political, and social position.

In retrospect, people's hopes (or fears) of a "new era" for women economically were not fulfilled.[38] Relatively quickly, women, white and black, left or were forced out of relatively advantageous jobs. Women's overall labor force participation in 1920 (20.4 percent) was roughly what it had been in 1910 (20.9 percent).[39] Whatever the impact of World War I work on women in the larger society, however, it had notable consequences for the YWCA itself. The YWCA estimated that it reached some three hundred thousand industrial women in these programs—roughly the same number as its *entire* membership in 1915.[40] While many of the industrial women and girls who were in contact with the YWCA during the war did not join it, others did.[41]

While the War Work Council featured the variety of offerings ranging from a club for young Hollywood actresses to clinics for the foreign war brides and children of American soldiers, it identified two groups who had "special needs to be met in special ways," namely the "foreign-born" and "colored."[42] The YWCA's Committee on Work for Foreign-born Women was responsible for the former. In 1910, the YWCA had begun to experiment with community centers called International Institutes to assist immigrants and their children. Offering programs similar to settlement houses, the institutes hired foreign-born and second-generation women as staff. Starting first in New York City, International Institutes developed across the country, primarily in industrial areas, and represented a shift from the YWCA's original focus on white, Protestant native-born women.[43] The YWCA tailored its war efforts for the immigrant community, at times translating government or Red Cross materials into other languages, while at other times hiring "nationality workers" to deliver relief efforts to non-English-speaking people.[44] Increasingly these programs reflected a commitment to cultural pluralism, even while other groups urged compulsory Americanization for ethnic Americans.[45]

Americans of both genders and many classes and nationalities united to support the war that was to end all wars and make the world safe for democracy, even as laws such as the Espionage and Sedition Acts combined with public opinion to promote conformity and punish those who protested the country's wartime policies. For their part, African Americans sought to use the war to question the meaning of American democracy and citizenship. The YWCA's programs for African American women and girls offered a chance to raise those questions *and* provided resources to push for change.

"Negro Women Have Heard the Reveille"

American leaders envisioned the Great War as a modern one that required the comprehensive mobilization of both the military and civilian forces; as part of that campaign, they brought (or even forced) groups into the war effort that they had previously overlooked, including African Americans. Given the essential role they played during the war, many African Americans expected the larger white society to recognize their contributions.[46] Toward the end of the war, Eva Bowles wrote, "Negro women have heard the reveille . . . and [contributed] their share to bring about world Christian democracy."[47] Throughout the war she worked to ensure that black women, men, and children would receive benefits as well.

On first glance, she succeeded. Bowles oversaw a dramatic expansion in services. Almost without fail, YWCA wartime publicity included statements like, "Everything that is done by the Y.W.C.A. for white women is done also for colored women."[48] When the War Work Council was organized, Eva Bowles was the only black member on the national staff; by 1920, there were twelve. At the start of the war, there had been sixteen local associations staffed by nine paid workers; by war's end, more than eighty paid workers ran forty-nine centers.[49] While the War Work Council funded the programs, the (now full) Committee on Colored Work directed them. The committee was interracial, but the responsibility for programs fell upon the African American secretaries, and Bowles went from being the Secretary for Colored Work in Cities to the "general leader" for all YWCA work for African Americans.[50]

Of particular importance to Bowles, and a point also made in the YWCA's publicity, was that all "activities are under the leadership of colored college women and social workers."[51] Hiring such women was made possible by the allocation from the War Work Council of $200,000 for work from late 1917 to the end of the war. In the years before the war, the YWCA had struggled to pay qualified African American women well enough to retain them.[52] During the war, Bowles recruited educated African American women and trained them; she brought women like Josephine Pinyon back to the YWCA, but also hired women who had previously not been involved with the association, like Catharine Lealtad and Crystal Bird.[53] "The war brought to us," she later reported, "many strong women whom we had not been able to reach before."[54] Building on existing networks, such as the NACW, Bowles helped forge connections among black women around the country.

As impressive as $200,000 was, the total War Work Council budget for the year was $5 million. At a time when African Americans represented roughly 10 percent of the overall population and the armed forces, they received only 4 percent of the YWCA's budget.[55] Despite the YWCA's claim of equality, the reality was discrimination, which was blindingly clear in the organization's overseas efforts. The YWCA's goal there was to assist female war relief workers and military auxiliaries. Since the vast majority of women in Europe (whether European or American) were white, the YWCA sent only white women to work with them. It was the YMCA that sent a small number of black women, including Addie Waites Hunton, to aid in its relief efforts for black servicemen.[56]

Although excluded from the YWCA's overseas efforts, African American women and girls joined in promoting morality and providing services at home. The issues of morality and work standards took on racial aspects as hostess houses, social centers, and services for female workers were adopted for African Americans. Some feared that reformers' preoccupation with protecting troops or the larger white community would have an adverse consequence for African Americans. As one journalist wrote, "The very fact that a safeguard is being thrown about white girls makes any menace to the colored girl more real. She is certainly subject to every strain and temptation in war times that is put upon her white sister."[57] Underlying this concern was the belief held by many whites that black women were inherently less moral. African American YW leaders embraced the programs to uphold black women's and girls' virtue with a vengeance.[58] Bowles praised the bravery of those women who maintained "the same ideal for the Negro girl as for the white," asserting that was necessary if black women were to be given the same opportunities.[59]

Like those for white Americans, social welfare efforts for African Americans included hostess houses, recreation centers, and programs for women workers.[60] A prolonged debate over whether, and eventually how, the government would mobilize black men for the military delayed the establishment of hostess houses for them. When the dust had settled, black men were indeed drafted (at a higher rate than whites) and recruited into segregated units, usually under the control of white officers. African Americans accounted for almost 10 percent of the four million men eventually placed in service and sent to training camps and cantonments around the country.[61] By November 1917, the YWCA's Committee on Colored Work proposed "since there would always be a certain number of colored troops at Camp Upton [on Long Island], that we erect a building to be used as a hostess house for colored girls and women, and this building be made a model for hostess houses at other camps."[62] Until that building officially opened the following April, programs for black troops and their visitors were conducted in an old barracks open to weather as well as people; the staff recounted walking through snow to get from one room to another.[63] The opening of these temporary quarters was greeted with much fanfare; among other guests at the celebration was Theodore Roosevelt. The YWCA gave extensive publicity to his $4,000 donation from his Nobel Peace Prize money, reporting that the former president directed that "Miss Eva Bowles be consulted in the disbursement of this item. My wife and I were very much struck by the work of Miss Bowles in connection with the colored hostess house."[64]

Eventually, the YWCA opened hostess houses for African Americans in seventeen camps from New York to Georgia and from Virginia to Kansas to serve the some 380,000 black men.[65] Like the hostess houses for white troops, these centers provided a place for black troops to socialize and for visiting female family members and friends to meet them away from the dangers of commercialized recreation and under the supervision of women deemed respectable. Comparisons with the facilities for white soldiers (designed by architects such as Julia Morgan) suggest that African Americans rarely received equal treatment. Nonetheless, at a time when surrounding white communities had little desire to make any provisions for black troops or female visitors and other welfare organizations offered limited or no facilities, the YWCA provided invaluable resources.[66]

The black women, who directed hostess houses, reported to the executive hostess for the camp, almost always a white woman, much in the way that the secretary for a black branch reported to the white leadership of the central association. African American women, however, received their placement and training from other black women.[67] To administer these programs, Bowles recruited broadly, drawing on existing black YWCAs and women's clubs.

One such woman was Lugenia Burns Hope of Atlanta, Georgia.[68] In 1908,

Hope had helped to found Neighborhood Union, which was responsible for promoting social programs for the urban poor and lobbying business and local government to provide adequate water, sanitation, health programs, and education. Hope headed the NACW's Department of Neighborhood Work. She had also long advised the YW, speaking, for instance, to a 1916 meeting of black professional and volunteer leaders on relations between black and white women in the association.[69] In early 1918, Bowles enlisted Hope to develop the training program for hostesses at Camp Upton. Training was necessary to teach the staff how to handle the hundreds, even thousands, of visitors to the camps; the African American hostess house at Camp Upton alone handled some five thousand visitors a week.[70] Hope's proficiency in local organizing, as well as her connections with other prominent black women, made her a logical selection to set up the initial training.

During World War I, the YWCA also tapped other local black clubwomen to assist with war relief efforts. Loosely federated through the NACW, these women and their groups already provided essential services, including health, education, travelers' aid, and daycare, to black communities. Black women's clubs in New Jersey, for instance, helped to raise money for the furnishings of the hostess house near Camp Dix and volunteered to staff it, while the South Carolina Federation of Colored Women's Clubs helped to raise money for the building near Camp Jackson.[71] Through this mobilization, the YWCA connected nationally prominent black women to an internationally known white-dominated organization and also brought locally based black women into contact with each.[72]

Like their white sisters, black women characterized the hostess houses as "homey" environments. Hope wrote that they provided places for soldiers "preparing for grim business" to feel "the delicate influence of home."[73] Given assumptions about the importance of a proper home in uplifting the race, the "hominess" of hostess houses took on additional weight. Black YW women suggested a critical aspect of the hostess houses was that women of the talented tenth could show poorer African Americans what a "proper home" should look like. Thus educated, the poor would build good homes when they returned from the war and, thereby, improve the race. As the author of a study of African American YWCA women's war efforts put it, the "house has seemed to give men an ideal of what their homes should be. One boy, reflecting on the beauties of the house and his joy in being back and his plans when he reached home, said, 'We have to hand this to the Kaiser. The World was asleep and he woke it up.'"[74] "Picturesque" though it was, hostess house work was temporary, and Bowles and her colleagues knew it.

They saw the programs in industrial and urban areas, however, as having the potential to transform the postwar position of African American women.

Of particular importance to Bowles and other black women was the economic position for women of their race. In addition to the difficulties faced by her white sister, the African American woman faced, Bowles noted, the "handicap which history, injustice, and prejudice had built around her race."[75] In describing black women's contribution to "the second line of defense," YW women emphasized their role as replacement workers releasing "White women for more skilled work" and replacing "Colored men who went into service" as well as white boys and, occasionally, white men. Even as black YW women emphasized the opportunities and challenges for black working women in new occupations, they cast that work as necessary to the war effort, seeking to downplay the image of African Americans as strikebreakers.[76] YW women and others faced a number of obstacles: the belief that black workers, especially women, were incompetent or lazy, the resistance of employers and unions to include them, and the violence directed against them in events like the East St. Louis race riots of 1917.

Northern industrialists heavily recruited southern African Americans into war industries because the war cut off the supply of immigrant labor. As African Americans compared the perceived opportunities of the urban North with the problems of daily life in the South, they found migration ever more appealing. The number of blacks leaving the rural South had already been increasing prior to World War I, but wartime conditions accelerated the moves. As they moved into cities, there was even more strain on communities to provide adequate housing, eating places, and services for new residents. Estimates suggest that upwards of 400,000 African Americans migrated from the South to the North during the war—a statistic every bit as significant as the 380,000 black men who served in the military.[77] At a time when African Americans represented perhaps 10 percent of the general population, they were more than 14 percent of workers. The latter statistic was not lost on the largely racist Wilson administration, which authorized the establishment of a division of the Labor Department to oversee "Negro Economics," headed by George E. Haynes (the husband of Elizabeth Ross Haynes).[78]

Haynes and his division concerned themselves with both mobilizing black workers and seeking to improve race relations. Ross Haynes volunteered as a "dollar-a-year" worker, but the needs of black women were often overlooked.[79] Concerned about the impact of migration on work conditions and housing for black women, in 1917 the YWCA hired a clubwoman and former state labor administrator, Mary E. Jackson, to undertake a survey of industrial conditions for black women.[80] Jackson traveled the country, particularly focusing on cities affected by migration such as Philadelphia, Baltimore, Louisville, St. Louis, and Chicago.[81] She found that black women were often in the least skilled positions, requiring dirty, heavy work for long hours; some were in traditional jobs such as laundresses and chopping cotton, but she also encountered them in railroad yards cleaning engines and in lumber yards carrying wood. Black women were overwhelmingly in unorganized occupations, although she also located a smaller number of women who were employed in jobs that African American women had not traditionally held, such as skilled trades in garment factories. Regardless of the occupation, black women almost inevitably were paid less than the white men or white women who had previously held the jobs.[82]

In good progressive fashion, Jackson investigated conditions and encouraged local women to continue studying the situation after she left.[83] She also organized working women she met into clubs. "[O]rganization is, after all," she told the readers of the *Crisis,* "the solution of industrial problems."[84] The Committee on Colored Work often sent additional secretaries to follow up on Jackson's work. These women, funded by the War Work Council, worked with African Americans and whites to provide recreation, housing, food services, and education.

When possible, they worked with existing black branches, but in most cases, it was a necessary to start a new group, often called "Blue Triangle" clubs or centers.[85] The involvement of national staff with national financial resources allowed local African American women to bypass indifferent or recalcitrant local white women. When the white women of Little Rock refused to support an association for African Americans, the national association sent an organizer and the financial support to cover the cost of a building.[86] National black secretaries consulted with local black community leaders in cities ranging from St. Louis to Philadelphia to determine what the priorities for the centers were; in some cases, they concentrated on providing supervised recreation for young women to supplement hostess houses, in other cases they focused on housing, while in still others, they promoted industrial clubs.[87] These centers, like branches, often came to serve as clearinghouses for civic or social agencies in the community.[88] What these programs would mean for the postwar era was not spelled out, but a report in early 1918 to the National Board's executive committee acknowledged that programs "once enlarged to this extent are more or less pledged for all time."[89]

Jackson, Bowles, and others publicized their findings to win long-term support for these efforts. Writing on the eve of the armistice, Jackson argued that it was necessary to educate "the public, the employers, and the girls themselves," and continued by explaining that the "work was both a war measure and a preparation for after the war."[90] The message was quite deliberate. To employers and the general public, YW women argued that, when properly trained, black women did the work as well (or better) than white workers. Race was not the factor limiting ability; Jackson explained that "errors were due to inexperience and human weakness rather than to some racial defect."[91] To "the girls" of both races, Jackson and her colleagues pointed out that it was necessary to educate and organize black workers so they would not undercut wages and depress working conditions. Bowles reported that the "Colored girl . . . has entered into a problem that not only affects her, but the white girl who has been fighting for standards; and together, they must understand their own interrelationships."[92] It was in white women's self-interest to do this, and Bowles was optimistic that, as Christians, black and white women could join forces: "Bearing the name of Christians our groups through Him can be friends and together walk the broad highway of Friendly Hearts."[93]

Jackson was less likely to appeal to Christian values, but no less likely to envision the races working together. While she acknowledged that white workers were often prejudiced against African American workers, she made a point of flagging places where they worked together "without antagonism" and offered examples of times when black women joined with white women in unions or other organized labor efforts.[94] Her examples (and the literature from the Committee on Colored Work was littered with similar ones) were a response to those who argued that prejudice was inevitable, if regrettable. No, the women of the YWCA maintained, it *was* possible for black and white women to work together; they had already done so in cities ranging from New York to St. Louis.

Among some white women, the argument about common interests got a hearing. While the white leadership of the War Work Council continued its often vague assertions of unity—the treasurer asserted, "All races of women, the Association feels, are inextricably bound in common sisterhood"[95]—the white national secretaries for industrial women, like Grace Coyle, addressed specific issues. In a 1918 internal memo on white industrial women from the East Central Field, Coyle admitted that at a recent YWCA conference "several delegates were utterly unwilling to work in the same room with them [i.e., black women]," although others argued that "Christianity demanded a sisterly attitude toward all girls, regardless of color." In her published account of the meeting, Coyle reported only that the topic was the "subject of much debate," and she focused on the passage of resolutions calling for white workers to take "an interest in the colored girls new in industry" and have "a democratic attitude" toward "the colored girls of our country."[96] That same year, Adela Ruffin, an African American woman who oversaw war work for African Americans in the South Atlantic Field, spoke at the conference for white southern city associations, which had a large industrial presence; attendees subsequently resoundingly endorsed a resolution condemning lynching.[97] While white working women did not determine policy in the association, they represented potential allies for African Americans.

"This Country Will Have a Sense of Duty to Them"

Wartime mobilization had a dramatic impact on the YWCA in general and African Americans in the association in particular. Prior to the war, the YWCA was but one of several national women's associations—the National American Woman Suffrage Association, the General Federation of Women's Clubs, the Women's Christian Temperance Union, the National Women's Trade Union League, and the Daughters of the American Revolution, among others—which at times worked together, while at other times competed. The particular fit between perceived wartime needs and the YWCA's expertise in housing, cafeterias, and recreation—all infused with Christian values—brought it resources and new recognition. "Nothing attracts attention more than getting money," wrote the treasurer of the War Work Council in 1918. She continued, "except dispensing money. The Association, so long a poor relation of the big philanthropies, is now spending with the best of them."[98] Individually, women gained administrative skills and leadership opportunities, while the association expanded. The number of permanent local associations increased by 15 percent. The membership grew by almost 40 percent to 500,000, making the organization one of the largest women's groups in the country. Wartime industrialization and urbanization had a noticeable impact on the YWCA in the South: from 1906 to 1920, the number of urban YWs in the region more than doubled, from twenty-one to fifty-two.[99] The war and initial demobilization efforts were very, very good for the YWCA.

As part of promoting an efficient national effort, wartime policies escalated a trend toward increasingly centralized bureaucracies and boosted the power of the National Board vis-à-vis local associations.[100] At its founding, the consolidated YWCA had established the National Board as its executive body, but locals were largely autonomous. The small national body had little identity separate from them. It could advise locals, but it could not dictate to them. During the war, it was the National Board that received and channeled money to the locals; in addition, it hired women to work at the local level. In the years from 1915 to 1920, the budget of the National Board increased tenfold. The number of paid staff went up by 70 percent, with a threefold increase at the national level.[101] The emphasis the national placed on its training staff as well as its power to transfer women from one association to another meant that the professional workers of the YWCA identified with other staff around the country and with the national body, while local volunteers and board members represented community interests. As the war ended, local and national leaders worked to regularize the relationship between central associations and wartime programs.

But, if the goal was to return to racial normalcy, the war had, in fact, forever altered the terrain of race relations in the United States. Wartime participation generated expectations for the postwar society. Elizabeth Ross Haynes urged support for black women workers who had "uncomplainingly met an emergency in the war." She continued, saying that "surely now this country will have a sense of duty to them."[102] At the heart of black optimism about the war was the argument that African American men and women had publicly participated as citizens, rather than as wards of the state. They had, as Theodore Roosevelt observed, discharged the "duties and responsibilities" of citizens, and citizens also had "rights and privileges."[103] Black men had served as soldiers, the quintessential responsibility of male citizens, but black women and girls, like their white sisters, had also mobilized, raising funds from their own communities and channeling them into well-publicized war relief efforts, as well as volunteering. Yes, the African American community had received benefits, but Bowles and others emphasized what blacks had accomplished themselves. Describing the African American YW program in St. Joseph, Missouri, one black woman wrote, "Here, as elsewhere, almost the entire amount was pledged by the colored people themselves."[104]

It was not simply that African Americans had helped their own; rather, they had helped the nation, even the world. Although the YWCA raised money from many communities, African Americans were particularly responsive to the campaigns; a report from the Student's Friendship War Fund indicated that African American students had done better than any other group of students in supporting the war at a "true sacrifice" to themselves.[105] At every opportunity, Bowles praised black women and the YWCA; in the fall of 1919, she reported at the white-dominated YWCA War Work Council's wrap-up meeting that "the war [gave] the opportunity to the colored woman to prove her ability for leadership. She had her chance and she made good."[106] Wartime accomplishments were proof not only that black women were *capable* of leading the work, but that they *deserved* to lead it.

Black women, making an argument that African Americans had earned new rights because of their wartime responsibilities, appealed explicitly to white America's belief in democracy and patriotism to strengthen that claim. In 1918, Mary Jackson warned that if black women were denied opportunities, "we cannot hope to rank as an ideal for world-wide democracy."[107] She advised that "it is now to the national advantage to give the Negro a square deal."[108] Bowles's final report on African Americans' contributions through the War Work Council declared that the "giant task that lies ahead now that the world has been saved for democracy is to make democracy safe."[109] The YWCA may not have lived up to its wartime slogan of "An Equal Chance for the Colored Girl," but African Americans built on the fact that some whites had felt it was important to cast wartime efforts in terms of equality.[110] Bowles showcased white women who acknowledged black Americans' contribution (and ensuing rights). As demobilization was winding down, she reported on a white college student who had stated, "Negro solders [*sic*] returned from France have fought our fight and borne some of the brunt of the struggle. . . . [They] will demand that their women as well as themselves get a square deal."[111] As African Americans saw it, America had made a promise to black America and it was time to honor it.[112] While that argument was not new, it was notable that some white Americans acknowledged the debt.

"Reconciliation between the Two Races"

In the initial period after the armistice, hostess houses and industrial centers remained important to deal with the difficulties of a prolonged demobilization and postwar industrial and social tensions. In 1919, the interracial Colored Work Committee reported to the National Board that its programs were "more important and perhaps more difficult than ever in the present situation, intensified as it is by labor conditions and the return of colored troops from abroad." African American YW workers hoped, the committee reported "by their practical Christian work to make some contribution toward the solving of the great race problem."[113] The staff, however, faced new challenges as wartime monies dried up and a developing economic recession placed severe financial pressures on the YWCA. In 1920, for the first time since the start of the war, the YWCA reduced its budget and began cutting back on programs. That year, the remaining funds from the United

War Work Campaign were divided among various programs; out of YWCA's share of $1,766,210, "colored work" programs were given $78,000 (or 4 percent)—$2,000 less than what the YWCA proposed to spend on social hygiene lectures.[114] The problem was not simply that funds were disappearing, but that the responsibility for programs for black women would have to revert to local communities.

At the same time, postwar "race friction" meant those programs were even more needed. Americans of all political persuasions—black and white, and, increasingly, northern as well as southern—saw a "great race problem" in postwar America. Beginning in 1917, cities from East St. Louis to Washington, D.C., and from Houston to Chicago witnessed brutal race riots, culminating in the "Red Summer" of 1919—a year that alone saw twenty-five riots.[115] Alongside industrial unrest and the nativist violence associated with the "100 per cent Americanism" of wartime propaganda, the race situation led many to agree with Lily Hardy Hammond in wondering, "[H]ave any of us seen a time of such confusion and strife?"[116] Gone was the wartime optimism that Americans would pull together.

In addition to race riots, racially motivated "strife" was evident in the dramatic increase in lynchings and the resurgence of the Ku Klux Klan.[117] For some conservative whites, riots and lynchings represented a response to a changing racial order. Will Alexander, a white southerner investigating racial tensions, recounted the response of an elderly white minister to the question of whether there had been trouble with African Americans in the community after the war. The minister replied, "No, we had to kill a few of them, but we didn't have any trouble with them."[118]

But other whites—southern and northern—saw racial violence as representing the rise of mob rule and a threat to democracy and order. White southern liberals, like Alexander, endorsed a strategy known as "interracial cooperation" to address problems. Associated primarily with the southern-based Commission on Interracial Cooperation (CIC), white northerners also promoted interracial cooperation through organizations like the FCC's Commission on Race Relations, the NUL, and the YMCA.[119] All these groups were male dominated, although men in the CIC eventually established an interracial women's division.[120] It was in the YWCA where women—black and white, northern and southern—struggled over the meaning and implementation of interracial cooperation and crafted a version that fit with Christian sisterhood.[121]

Interracialists (as its advocates were known) urged joint efforts by blacks and whites to ease racial tensions. They directed many of their efforts to whites and argued that it was in whites' self-interest to improve the situation facing blacks. Communities needed to better living conditions for blacks because disease and immorality in black areas could spill over to whites. They warned that, if not helped economically, blacks would bring down entire communities. Individuals and public officials ought to prevent lynchings so that order and the rule of law were maintained. Likewise, local and state governments should enforce equal citizenship rights to avoid making a mockery of democracy; admittedly, this often meant making "separate" truly equal. As good progressives, they emphasized the role of education to change society; newspaper editors, they urged, should avoid fanning the flames of racial hatred and should give favorable publicity to improvements in race relations. Interracial cooperation combined three premises. The first was that the "best elements of both races" needed to work together. Second, in doing so, they would promote mutual understanding and harmony and ease racial tensions. And, finally, these efforts could be carried on within the confines of a segregated society.[122]

In 1920, the YWCA's National Board published a small pamphlet, *Interracial Cooperation: Helpful Suggestions Concerning Relations of White and Colored Citizens,* that presented material from external and internal sources. The editors sought to respond to "the acute crisis in the relation between white and colored Americans."[123] The single longest article was Lily Hardy Hammond's essay entitled simply "Interracial Cooperation," which analyzed the place for *women* in the interracial movement. "Much depends upon men in fully Christianizing our race relations," she wrote. She continued, "[I]t cannot be done without them. But essential to the advance of any race is the status of its women and their homes. Until Christian white women stand by negro women, giving them that human protection and respect which is the right of womanhood the world over, there will be little progress in racial solutions. Womanhood and motherhood are among the few things deeper than race."[124] Building on what she had earlier referred to as the "bond of a common womanhood," she called upon "*women* to stand by *women* of every race, and in so doing to stand by Jesus Christ." Hammond was explicit that it was the job of "privileged white women" to work with the "better class of negroes," especially its women, to promote understanding. She hastened to reassure readers, however, that "God made us separate," and had given to "the negro [as well as whites] his race instinct and the desire to preserve his racial integrity."[125]

The shared identity of "common womanhood," especially the importance of home, seemingly united YW women—black and white—at a time when the world of politics and economics divided men. Interracialists placed particular importance on class-privileged white women's meeting their black counterparts through the YWCA. They observed that a problem with Jim Crow segregation was that the better classes of each race had increasingly less contact. Much as Addie Hunton had observed more than a decade previously, they pointed out that the result of educated whites' not knowing educated blacks was they based their beliefs about the race upon the "inefficients of the race, the handicapped, the unambitious, the physically and morally degenerate," from whom, as Lily Hammond put it, "we draw the bulk of our supply of unskilled laborers and servants."[126] The YWCA became an arena for white women to meet another class of black women through reports, talks, and conferences.

Meeting educated black women could be transformative for white women, since it called into question fundamental beliefs about African Americans. Eva Bowles reported that Elizabeth Preston Allen, the white board member on the South Atlantic Field's committee on race work, attributed the "beginnings of her change of thought from four years ago when she first met an educated colored woman. She [Allen] considered it the crowning work of her life to make women of her kind see. 'They cannot ostracize me for my views,' she says, 'perhaps it is because I am too old, and I tell them they have to listen to me because I surrendered at Appomattox.'"[127] Like their counterparts in the larger interracial movement, YW women believed that as the "better classes" of both races learned about each other, they, in turn, would educate members of their respective races about the true character of the other race.

Mutual understanding was to produce two desirable results: whites would turn away from racial demagogues, and blacks, who learned of the potential for revised race relations within the existing racial order, would find the demands of "radical" blacks (such as W. E. B. Du Bois) less appealing.[128] Like other interracialists, and social gospel advocates more generally, white YW women conceived of change as resulting from educating people to appreciate their common interests. The "great mistrust and lack of understanding of one race by the other menace all progress toward harmony," warned Helen P. Wallace, the white chairman of the Colored Work Committee. It was the YWCA that stood "as a harmonizer between races and bends its efforts toward a more constructive righteousness." People needed to learn from the YWCA's wartime programs "the place the Young Women's Christian Association can hold in the work of reconciliation between the two races destined to live side by side."[129]

The effort to make refined African American women visible—both to whites and to the larger black community—took on literal expression when, in 1919, the Committee on Colored Work proudly reported that an "attractive poster" had been completed in order to inform young black women about the YWCA's services. It was the first time a publicity poster had featured a "colored girl." Previously, the staff had been forced, in Eva Bowles's words, to "brown up posters" of white women or girls. The 1919 poster showcased a light-skinned African American young woman, neatly dressed with a stylish hat and carrying a suitcase, looking hopefully at the YWCA's blue triangle logo as the caption informed the viewer that she could "Call on Us if You Want Comfortable Accommodations." The figure was intended simultaneously as a presentation of the "better class" of black women to white viewers and as a symbol for a black audience of both race pride and the YWCA's potential.[130]

Harmony and mutual understanding were frequent tropes of progressives, social gospelers, and interracialists. In their analysis, misunderstandings, rather than irreconcilable differences, were at the heart of difficulties between whites and blacks (as well as capital and labor, and the native born and immigrant). All people—male and female, industrialist and worker, white and black—needed to work with each other to promote God's Kingdom on earth. Relying on a specifically Protestant view of individuals, society, and social change, they sought to reform society by educating individuals. The focus on individuals and mutual efforts made it difficult to accept that blacks and whites, individually or collectively, might have a different responsibility for social unrest.

Ostensibly, the black women who stayed with the YWCA embraced the language. Eva Bowles was every bit as likely to employ phrases like "mutual understanding" or "sisterhood" as her white counterparts. Yet black women's apparent agreement masked their efforts to change the institution and the white women they met. Black YW women resisted public criticism of white women in the association; when they did allude to problems, they usually did not identify the women or even the place. When they named individual white women, it was to praise them: Katharine Heath Hawes, for instance, "stood faithfully behind the work" during the war.[131] A year later, however, Eva Bowles reported that a "great step" had just occurred: the "illumination of Miss Katherine [*sic*] Hawes." Programs in her region, Bowles continued, would "now be assured . . . with the 'personality' hindrance removed."[132] Only after Hawes could be praised for seeing the light would Bowles suggest that Hawes had once been a hindrance.

In analyzing the interactions between southern black and white churchwomen, Mary Frederickson has argued that black women developed a strategy of praising white women and allowing them to appear to be the initiators of racial reform in order to gain necessary support.[133] Throughout the country, interracial cooperation was a carefully choreographed dance; despite the language of "mutual understanding," cooperation, and sisterhood, white women expected to be the lead partners and, in the YWCA, they were—publicly. Black women were, however, perfectly capable of engaging in what might be considered, to continue the metaphor, backleading. They concentrated their public comments on praising white women once the latter had made changes, as opposed to criticizing white women when there were problems.[134]

The last aspect of interracial cooperation that whites espoused was a commitment to segregation. The "recognition of womanhood as a thing deeper even than race," Lily Hammond told her readers, would contribute to settling the "race question" because "all other things needed will come out of it—full racial justice, true racial separateness, full human cooperation and respect."[135] The "need" for racial separateness combined three elements: a concern about interracial sex, an aversion to integration, and a commitment to white dominance. Hammond hastened to assure white women that support for interracial cooperation would not endanger the white race: "If we knew the negro better we should find that the preservation of racial purity is not entrusted to us alone." It was the "least-developed folk of both races" who bore the responsibility for "millions of mulattoes" because their "racial instinct" was dormant.[136] In defending their involvement in a struggle for justice, white women in the YWCA declared a clear boundary that they would not cross. "Certainly racial purity in our experience," wrote one white liberal northern YWCA leader, "seems to us to be the way in which the fullest development and happiness can come."[137]

Many whites linked sex and almost any form of social contact through the term "social equality," which could refer to anything from sharing a meal to intermarriage; in the minds of many whites, the former inevitably led to the latter.[138] Hammond and other white interracialists attempted to reassure white America that a properly developed racial instinct meant that African Americans were also not interested in crossing social-sexual lines; "the desire of the better classes of both races," she wrote in 1913, is "to keep white and blacks racially, and therefore socially, distinct."[139]

African Americans promoting interracial cooperation frequently included a disclaimer that they did not desire "social equality" either. Adela Ruffin advised her largely white audience, "Tradition and customs compelled us to explain that constructive work for young women had nothing in it which might be construed to be an attempt to establish social equality—whatever that term may mean."[140] Whatever their private views about segregation, black women active with the YWCA shied away from challenging that social norm. The reasons not to do so were plentiful: other concerns (such as economic equality) were more pressing, advocating full-scale social interaction would have doomed their efforts, and, finally, many of them were concerned about protecting the image of African American women as virtuous. White society simply did not discuss interracial sex without painting black men as rapists and black women as immoral temptresses.

Even when white YW women did not raise the specter of interracial sex, most seemed to have taken the "color line" for granted and viewed work for black women and girls as categorically different from other programs. Helen Wallace, the white chairman of the Colored Work Committee, was a vocal advocate for improving race relations as the "true working out of the ideal of democracy." She delineated the challenges that faced those developing work for African Americans by contrasting the programs with those for immigrants: "the problems of Association work with the different white races in America are more simple obviously because [they are] applied to the group in process of being absorbed into full membership in the parent Association. The International Institutes are way stations toward an American Association, while the Association among colored women does not thus [lead] into the parent work."[141] Commenting on Wallace's assessment, Bowles praised it, but expressed concern that southern white-dominated field committees were attempting to establish authority over programs for African Americans. She sought to reassure white southerners that "we from Headquarters must continue to understand that we can only go as far and fast as any particular section is ready," but went on to question their right to direct the programs.[142]

Bowles was responding, in part, to a criticism that wartime practices represented a deviation from the 1915 Louisville agreement. During the war, programs for African Americans had been established whether or not local whites approved. By the end of the war, the War Work Council was paying the salaries of almost one hundred black women in local programs.[143] Internal records of the Colored Work Committee reveal that southern white women had continually asserted their right to control the programs. Bowles had successfully resisted these efforts, explaining that the national body was experimenting and it was too early to allow the field committee authority. In the spring of 1919, for instance, she reported to the Colored Work Committee that a southern field committee had "felt this work should be under the field, rather than headquarters." Bowles argued that national staff should discuss the issue and the next month reported that discussion had determined "this was not the opportune time to give the fields complete supervision of the work."[144]

In accepting Helen Wallace's rationale for segregation, Bowles attempted to create a bulwark against white domination. If whites and blacks were so separate, if "Colored work can not 'lead' itself into white work," then the association needed to be wary about establishing (white) field control. Bowles explained that "our first attempt at field supervision with its immediate attempt to be entirely separate from Headquarters warns us of a many headed instrument that would finally wreck all the ideals of [united] strength and harmony which the Movement must ever hold." Generally Bowles spent less of her time arguing that whites were not capable and more on how well suited black women were to leading the programs "among colored women and girls."[145]

The efforts of white women to assert control over black programs were not limited to the South. In 1919 a white secretary "unofficially" warned Catharine Lealtad of plans to move her to another position and place a southern white woman in the position. Lealtad and Bowles met with a white executive to discuss the situation. Lealtad reported that the executive argued in favor of bringing in the southern white woman "because a southern white woman who was really sincere and just in her attitude toward colored people would be an asset." The white executive added "that there were certain circumstances in which such an individual could do even more for the work than a colored woman." Lealtad indicated that she would not stay with the YWCA under such conditions and Bowles was emphatic that "a white woman could not do for colored girls what one of their own could do." As rumors of the incident spread through the African American community, outsiders also protested the idea and, eventually, the national staff dropped the plan.[146] In writing to Lugenia Burns Hope, the white head of the Field Work Department contended that the proposed reorganization had been intended simply to make better use of Lealtad's strengths and that the white woman was not intended as a replacement. The white woman attributed the "misunderstanding" to the inadequacy of the "English language . . . these days to express one's thought."[147]

The inadequacy of the English language was not simply the function of personal limitations; rather the disagreements reflected differing assumptions about the implications of mutuality and the "better classes." In her final report to the War Work Council, Bowles declared, "The time is past for white leadership for colored people. As white and colored women, we must understand each other, we must think and plan together for upon all of us rests the responsibility of the girlhood of our nation."[148] Black YW women melded their community's activities, the leadership of black women, and wartime opportunities into an argument promoting "race pride" as a way to advance both African Americans and the nation. Dealing with tensions between white and black workers in St. Louis, Mary Jackson reported that they eased when "we talked efficiency, responsibility, leadership, and race pride."[149] Even as they utilized the common language of mutuality and togetherness, black women sought to advance the race, not simply adjust the races.

White women expressed an uneasy reaction to ideas of race pride and race consciousness. At times, they employed these ideas alongside "racial instinct" as the basis for interracial cooperation, while at other times, they feared that this sense of racial identity threatened society. One cause for "race friction," the YWCA advised in its 1920 pamphlet, was the "[growing] race consciousness on the part of the negro." While acknowledging that a cause for that consciousness was that African Americans were "not being accorded that for which they have fought and the continued effort to deprive them of the rights of citizenship," the focus was on African Americans' "disappointment" at the situation.[150] Even those whites who did not desire the return to racial "normalcy" cautioned patience. "Sometimes asking for *all* you want is the best way to get nothing," advised R. B. Eleazar of the CIC.[151]

Even as black and white interracialists shared a public commitment to the better people of each race working together to promote harmony within the parameters of a segregated society, every element was contested. An uneasy agreement between white and black women characterized the YWCA's approach to race relations and some black women began to draw the line at segregation. Addie Hunton shifted her energies to the NAACP, which was becoming more black and more viable, as well as the International Council of Women of the Darker Races.[152] In early 1920, Catharine Lealtad, who had survived the effort to replace her, left the YWCA, arguing that it had violated a commitment to equal accommodations for black women at a December 1919 student convention in Des Moines, Iowa. Lealtad publicly described how "the Christian spirit, for which they [the YWCA staff] stood, had been put to the acid test in Des Moines, and . . . they failed us [black people] utterly." She continued by noting the failure of the black national staff to protest the situation.[153] In a private letter to Lugenia Burns Hope, she opened by writing, "I could hardly retain my own self-respect or the respect of the people of my race and remain with the Association." She decried the lack of support from Eva Bowles, writing that she (Lealtad) had become "so disgusted with the whole crowd [of national black secretaries] and their 'milk and water' policies that I resigned."[154]

The black secretaries who stayed with the YWCA walked a tightrope between maintaining their own self-respect *and* a desire to work with white women as they attempted to advance their race; it was not an easy balance. Bowles chose her battles carefully. She joined Lealtad in a behind-the-scenes protest of the proposal for a white woman to run programs for African Americans, but she did not support Lealtad in her public criticism of segregation in the YWCA. Bowles placed emphasis not on eliminating segregation, but on ensuring that, *if* there was separate work, black women would control it. And, she stressed, the ultimate goal was that black and white women would work together.

Reporting on the accomplishments of African Americans from 1915 to 1920, Bowles wrote that "as Colored women we have shared in plans and promotion with equal justice and opportunity. We can never afford to lose this fundamental principle through compromise. When we cannot carry out a righteous principle, we will continue to exercise the virtue of patience to which we are heir and which God awards in due time."[155] Black women might choose to wait until white women were ready, but God was on the side of the righteous and patient. The question, as Bowles constructed it, was when white women would move, not if. The gains for Bowles were often incremental: an Elizabeth Preston Allen here, a Katharine Heath Hawes there. But each one was proof of God's power and the righteousness of black women's case.

Following the armistice, Eva Bowles had told her white colleagues, "Our problem is now a national problem. It is God's challenge to America."[156] By 1920, the National Board itself was reporting that the "assimilation of our foreign population, racial relationships, industrial problems, promotion of health and social morality, the woman movement, are phrases familiar to us all. They represent difficult national problems."[157] It was an assessment that acknowledged race as a national issue, albeit without necessarily making it the priority in bringing in the Kingdom of God.

❖ ❖ ❖

YWCA women heralded the association's accomplishments during the war and the praise they garnered from people like Theodore Roosevelt, notably for the work they did with African Americans. Perhaps the most important gain of the war years for African American women, small though it was,

was that some white women had begun to see race relations as a problem in both the South and the North. At a time when most white Americans ignored the plight of African Americans or blamed them for their status, white YW women believed that what *they* thought about African Americans would "determine the status of the [Negro] race."[158] In assuming the responsibility for determining the position of African Americans, however, white women often limited African American women's agency in improving their own situation.

For their part, through wartime activities, African American women developed social capital that they would rely on in years to come. Experience in the YWCA offered access to financial resources and national attention. Wartime programs helped to integrate them into a national effort that went beyond isolated local efforts. They found ways to explain their goals in terms they thought white women would understand. Reporting on the accomplishments of 1920, Eva Bowles explained that white women needed to understand that the black woman "will consent to work *with,* but resents anything that savors of being worked *for.*"[159] Women like Bowles who remained with the YWCA put on a public face of accepting white women's terms for debates over race relations, even as they negotiated those terms sub rosa. Others like Catharine Lealtad put their energies elsewhere. Competing approaches by different white women, divisions between white and black women, *and* conflicts among black women shaped the YWCA's debates on race.

Interracial cooperation was a strategy that sanctioned a role for educated women of both races in resolving together the problems of postwar America, but within the context of segregation. "Mutual understanding" did not mean complete agreement, and white women did not always see "sisterhood" as the basis for equality. Rather, they cast themselves as big sisters, ready to assist others as their Christian duty.[160] Their conceptions of mutual understanding and sisterhood prevented most white women from acknowledging important differences in how whites and African Americans regarded their shared world.

4 Developing Christian Citizenship

BY THE WINTER OF 1920, the YWCA faced an onslaught of negative publicity in the black press. "I suppose it is not too much to say that the National Y.W.C.A. is in sort of public disfavor with the race," Mabel Cratty, the general secretary, told an interracial meeting discussing the YW's racial practices.[1] Several events had led to the outbreak, but the treatment of Mary Talbert, president of the NACW, by the American YWCA in France in the summer of 1920 generated much of the attention.[2] Talbert, a member of the American delegation to the meeting of the International Council of Women (ICW), arrived in Paris after an all-night train ride.[3] With other delegates, she went to the American Women's Club, which the YWCA administered. Talbert began to enter the dining room when Harriet Dunn, the YW secretary in charge, turned her away. Dunn was vague about why, but claimed that arrangements had been made for Talbert elsewhere. To Dunn's chagrin, others pointed out that the club was already serving breakfast to Dr. Mary F. Waring, a light-skinned African American woman also in the delegation. Only after the intervention of Myra Kingman Merriman, the white chair of the American delegation, were Talbert and her daughter grudgingly permitted a cup of coffee before leaving to find other accommodations. Every other woman in the U.S. delegation, and even male guests, had been served in the YWCA's dining room, and it seemed obvious to Talbert that Dunn had excluded her because she was visibly black.[4]

Featured in black periodicals ranging from the *New York Age* to the *Savannah Tribune,* Talbert observed that she had been admitted to every other facility in Europe, often seated in places of honor, and it was only an *Ameri-*

can institution that excluded her.[5] Talbert and her advocates raised two related issues in their criticism of the YW: the expansion of segregation and the manner in which the association treated Talbert, not only in Paris, but also in its discussion of the affair. Mary White Ovington, the white chairman of the NAACP, wrote to the YW's National Board several times that winter, observing at one point that to "segregate in New Orleans is inevitable. To segregate in Cleveland, Ohio, is not necessary as we learned when we had our conference there, but it is explainable. But to segregate in Paris seems to say to the colored women of this country that the YWCA believes in the principle of segregation and would separate white and colored women anywhere on the globe."[6] That a YW secretary had "drawn the color line" in *France* was particularly inflammatory; throughout World War I, white Americans had sought to limit the contact between black Americans and the French.[7]

W. E. B. Du Bois, editor of the *Crisis,* focused his criticism on the treatment of Talbert, not only by the American Women's Club, but also by the National Board as it attempted to handle the fallout from the incident. Initially, the YWCA flatly denied Talbert's account. Relying on an interview with Harriet Dunn, the National Board emphasized that the problem had occurred because Talbert did not have reservations and noted that some white women in the delegation (including Merriman) also had to stay elsewhere. In their minds, the fact that not all white women could stay at the club was proof that racial prejudice was not the cause of Talbert's exclusion. Dunn also implied that the YWCA had not resisted serving Talbert and reported that "everyone" there "felt that Mrs. Talbert was in the wrong and that she was extremely rude in all she had to say."[8]

The account written by Dunn and circulated by the YWCA, Du Bois wrote, "practically branded Mrs. Talbert an ill-bred liar." He continued, noting that the YWCA followed a pattern whereby a "colored person is insulted and resents the insult. Immediately without any attempt to find the exact truth, white apologists hasten to say *first,* he was not insulted; *secondly,* he was impudent; *thirdly,* his attitude represents the impossible demand of colored people who do not realize the difficulties of the race problem." He went on, "[W]e do assume that the Y.W.C.A. does not stand for the deliberate and unnecessary insult of colored women of ability and breeding and we have the right to expect that when unfortunately such an occurrence does take place that the one responsible for it should be punished and the proper apology made to the victim." He concluded his response—sent to the YWCA's National Board, but also published in the *Crisis*—by "wondering whether your board has either the Christianity or womanhood to do these things."[9]

A longtime observer—and public supporter of the YWCA—Du Bois based his criticism of it on its identity as a Christian women's group.

Once it was clear that a prominent white woman, Myra Merriman, was prepared to publicly back Talbert's account, the National Board modified its response. In its final statement, issued in January 1921, the executive committee concluded that it was "impossible to get an entirely accurate and dispassionate account of the matter." It acknowledged an "obligation to work toward an equal opportunity for colored girls and women," but suggested that both sides were guilty of "misunderstanding" and "antagonisms." It was necessary for each to be committed to "'working together' toward a truly Christian society." The closest the national YWCA came to an apology was its concluding sentence that "[i]t regrets deeply that a colored woman found cause for resentment in the manner of her reception at the American Women's Club in Paris."[10] Even so, representatives of the National Board continued to fault Talbert for going to the press with her criticisms rather than coming to them directly.[11]

The "Paris Incident" or, more precisely, the competing interpretations of it, revealed fault lines in the strategy of interracial cooperation. White and black women had hoped that the best women of both races could promote harmony and build that truly Christian society. As the head of the National Association of Colored Women, Talbert was, in Du Bois's words, "the foremost woman in America of Negro descent." For years the YW had identified women of the NACW, in particular, as "the best type of colored women," but the "best" women were supposed to be the advocates for mutual understanding, not challengers.[12]

White women expressed dismay as much over *how* Talbert handled the event—that she had made her criticisms public—as they did over what Dunn had done. Even in internal discussions, they remained at a loss to explain how what they deemed "an unfortunate circumstance" could engender such "avidity and bitterness" in the black press. They were upset that Talbert's public criticism had exposed the YW to "scurrilous" attacks.[13] Interracial cooperation called for a specific racial etiquette.[14] The "best women" idea inextricably linked morality, Christianity, entitlement, refinement, respectability, and class position. A discussion about any one component easily shifted to another. Women of the best sorts—black or white—had proper manners. They were to be dispassionate, acting on principle rather than personal feelings. Disagreements were best handled privately. When African Americans no longer abided by these rules of social conduct, they could be deemed "ill-bred." Talbert's defenders—black and white—repeated Merriman's testimony that Talbert did not "at any time do or say anything rude or unladylike." Manners were a central signifier of her status as one of the "best" women, and they were particularly important for African American women who, as a group, lacked the economic resources of their white sisters.[15]

One longtime YW leader, Elizabeth Ross Haynes, attempted to explain to her white compatriots the nature of black dissatisfaction over what had happened in Paris and after. She did not mince words, labeling the behavior in Paris a "blunder" that needed to be corrected. "The heart of the people at the head of the Y.W.C.A. in Paris was not right and it hurt us and the negroes of this country are asking the question have we become part of an organization that is fostering race prejudice in our country."[16] For Ross Haynes, the problem was not so much how one black woman felt about her encounter with the YWCA, but the institutional nature of the incident.

For many white YW women, discussions over the "proper" way to handle disagreements often reduced debates over structural practices to personal feelings and failings, which were to be handled by calls for understanding among Christian sisters. For their part, black women articulated a more systemic understanding of race issues. As the decade unfolded, Christian sisterhood was no longer simply a moral or social vision. It became the basis for political efforts as women carved out their new identity as full-fledged citizens. What citizenship, and specifically female Christian citizenship, meant would have differing implications for women of different races.

"A Power Put into Our Hands"

It was with a triumphant tone that the YWCA held its first national convention after World War I in Cleveland in April 1920. In addition to the end of the war, women celebrated the recognition they had received for their patriotic contributions to the war effort. The war had seen white and black women alike living up to the responsibilities of citizenship, and the end of the war saw them laying claim to one of its most esteemed privileges: the vote. Even Woodrow Wilson, at best a questionable ally to the woman suffrage movement, had acknowledged that the nation had incurred a debt to women during the war; suffrage was not only payment of that obligation, but an important expression of democracy itself.[17]

The victory of the Allied Powers set the stage for the YWCA's ensuing activities. With 500,000 members, the YWCA was now the nation's third-largest independent women's organization, surpassed only by the General

Federation of Women's Clubs (1,000,000 members) and the Women's Christian Temperance Union (800,000). As many as 3,000,000 women and girls participated in programs and used the facilities of YWCAs, even if they did not have full membership.[18] But size alone did not determine the importance of the association to its members; being part of the "Christian woman movement" was essential to them. Increasingly, they discussed the YW's identity in democratic terms as well.[19] The National Board's *Report* to the convention addressed topics ranging from the "democratic support" of YWCAs in towns to the "democratic control" in self-governing clubs.[20] Group after group, including younger women, students, and working-class women, asserted the right to have their say—initially for themselves, but ultimately in the entire body. "Never again will college students be content to let people outside colleges direct their Association affairs," reported the National Board.[21]

What might simply have been a continuation of wartime language to make the world safe for democracy was put to the test at the 1920 convention as two groups, college students and industrial women, demanded changes in the association. Students wanted to amend the YWCA's constitution so that a young woman who declared her purpose "to live as a true follower of the Lord Jesus Christ" could be a full, voting member of her campus YWCA. The "personal membership basis" was a shift away from the existing requirement of formal membership in an evangelical Protestant church. At the same time, industrial women demanded that the YW endorse the "Social Ideals of the Churches," a program for workers' rights developed by the Federal Council of Churches that included a six-day work week, the abolition of child labor, and support for collective bargaining.

The two groups and their respective allies found power in new institutional structures. At the 1920 convention, students met separately for part of the time in the Student Assembly, but they also joined the general business of the convention. Since the 1910s, working women had organized in local clubs and had met in regional conferences; industrial secretaries at the national level, along with some at the local, accepted the demands for self-governing clubs for working women.[22] In the fall of 1919, the YW had sponsored a national conference for working women in Washington, D.C. where working women (and the middle-class secretaries who worked with them) laid the groundwork for their efforts at the convention.[23]

The similarity in the debates for change is striking as advocates for each change blended religious and political ideas in their arguments. Student after student, from Boston University to Randolph-Macon to Central Wesleyan College to Wilberforce University, argued that limiting YWCA membership to evangelical Protestants interfered with attracting new women; the YWCA, they reported, was seen as an exclusive group, not in keeping with the "democratic nature" of their schools. Students who were not members of Protestant churches could participate in activities, but they could not vote; "We preach Christian democracy," commented the student from Mount Holyoke, "and we do not have it in our association." How could they lead their fellow students to Christ, the students asked, if those students could not join the YW?[24]

It was for an older woman, Bertha Condé, the National Secretary for Students, to gently suggest to her colleagues what might happen if students' wishes were not heeded. The last speaker before the vote was taken, Condé declared, "If I know students, I know this one thing: That they do not want to part company with the Young Women's Christian Association but they do claim a right, which is the inalienable right of every student movement of every country in this world, namely the right to govern themselves in their policies, and to do that thing which will feed the springs of their spiritual lives and equip them for all kinds of Christian leadership in the world."[25] Like the students themselves, Condé spoke in terms of democracy and religion, but she also implicitly told delegates that students might leave the association if their wishes were not heeded.

A few current students were among the opponents; it was, overwhelmingly, older women who spoke against liberalizing the membership requirements. They raised both religious and political reasons for retaining the existing commitment to evangelical Protestant churches. Effie Price (Mrs. Thomas) Gladding of the National Board told delegates that the proposal was "disloyal to the great evangelical church." It raised the potential, warned a delegate from St. Louis, of opening the YW's gates to "Romanists, Unitarians, Jews, and [Christian] Scientists." And, finally, Helen Gould Shepard, also on the National Board, cautioned the membership that she had been studying "the great currents leading away from Christianity, and it seems . . . that the fundamental step of departure in those movements and in the political movements for subversion of our government . . . is the emphasizing of brotherhood instead of the atonement of Jesus Christ and his divinity."[26]

For the women upholding tradition, the question was not as simple as what should the students do, but rather what were the implications of the proposed change for the entire association. Students provided the future leadership for community YWCAs.[27] Conservative religious women recognized that there would be pressure from some to liberalize the membership requirements for city associations—a concern justified by the fact that the Boston association had already submitted a resolution proposing a personal membership basis for city YWCAs.[28] While the rules governing constitutional changes meant that the proposal for community membership would not go into effect for three conventions, the signs of a sea change in institutional identity were in the air. Despite warnings that the revision was an attack on the church and, therefore, was "not only taking a blow at Christianity, but also one at an American institution," members overwhelmingly approved the proposal for a personal membership for students.[29]

The following day, delegates took up a series of recommendations related to the "Social Ideals of the Churches."[30] Gertrude B. (Mrs. William D.) Mitchell of St. Paul presented the National Board's proposal, which began simply, "We believe that in Jesus Christ is to be found the solution of the world's need." The "great issue" of the day, declared the board, was "our economic life and social relationships." Women of the YWCA had the responsibility (in quintessential social gospel terms) "to associate young women in personal loyalty to Jesus Christ as Saviour and Lord, *and* to become a social force for the extension of the Kingdom of God."[31] Like the supporters of religious liberalization, advocates for the social ideals appealed to both democratic and religious values to win support. Frieda Keller, a working woman from Philadelphia, argued that the ideals were the principles of Jesus. "Christ was the greatest leader," she told her audience. "He was a carpenter, an industrial worker, and so we feel that because He viewed the situation from the inside out, that we can pretty well believe that his principles are sound." For her part, Helen Ramsey, a student from the University of Wisconsin, reported that the "students are behind it solid." She continued, "We women, with our new responsibility for citizenship, can do much to make our whole life and all its institutions truly Christian."[32] Despite hearing that a business journal was urging businessmen to withhold funds from the YWCA if the ideals were endorsed, members unanimously did so.[33]

Members then easily passed an accompanying recommendation calling for the YWCA to prepare "women for responsible citizenship and to direct their energies toward the achievement of social righteousness." They debated, however, the next recommendation, which specified *what* responsible citizenship meant: the National Board was to study social and economic conditions affecting women and was to "use its resources and influence to help secure such legislation as shall promote the welfare of young women."[34] At this point, delegates expressed more unease; Effie Gladding explained she planned to use her vote "as a church member and as a member of the Association, and as a Christian citizen." Yet, she cautioned against committing the organization as a whole to legislation; at a time when "great economists were anxious and unsettled over these great questions," it was "rash" for women to rush in. Helen Shepard was even more concerned: women could use their "influence for what we think is right," but entering into politics would only bring "dissension" into the body. Shepard warned that the push to go into politics was the result of "the trend of our time toward radical socialism."[35]

Supporters of the proposal, such as a delegate from Tacoma, responded that women had already been educating themselves on the legislative process. Acknowledging some women's resistance to entering the political realm, she argued, "It is a safe thing to study all you want, but we are having a force, a power put into our hands, that we must use." Members passed this recommendation as well, although not unanimously. The next day, Shepard, a founding member of the National Board, returned to the floor of the convention to publicly resign her membership and issued a press release explaining her alarm over the direction of the YWCA.[36] Born in 1868 and the daughter (and an heir) of Jay Gould, Helen Gould Shepard represented an older generation of wealthy supporters of the YWCA. Along with Grace Dodge, she had been a substantial funder of the National Board. Like Dodge, Shepard personally interested herself in the well-being of young women. She told the convention she had originally joined the YWCA because of her "warm and friendly feeling for the women in industry."[37] A journalist reporting on the convention to the readers of *Good Housekeeping* observed that the fight "was probably the most bitter that has ever been waged within any organization similar to the Y.W.C.A., [. . . but] for many obvious reasons it was almost entirely underground."[38] In her study of the industrial department, Mary Frederickson found that industrial women threatened to leave the YWCA if the social ideals were not passed, but the proceedings do not record such a threat.[39] Shepard's public display of her disapproval was exceptional for either side in the debate.

The YWCA of the early 1920s was no longer Shepard's organization and working women demanded more than friendly feelings. Industrial clubs had expanded dramatically from 375 to 823 during World War I. Industrial women spoke for themselves.[40] They were supported by professional workers like Florence Simms and Grace Coyle. Secretaries increasingly were college educated and promoted ideas of group development and self-governance associated with progressive educators like John Dewey. Coyle, in particular, expanded on the possibilities of "group work" for "schooling" members in "real democracy."[41]

Even other wealthy white women who supported the YWCA had a changing vision of the YW's role. Before the 1920 convention, Abby Aldrich Rockefeller, a member of the National Board, urged that members support legislation to solve social problems. Opposition to this activism, she argued, might stem from a concern of being "thought socialistic if we advocate the passing of a law that is in advance of commercial public opinion." And some believed that it "may antagonize our financial support." Despite this, Rockefeller argued that women had a "Christian duty" to support laws for the "young women to whom we have given our moral support."[42]

To implement the recommendation regarding legislation, the National Board established a Legislative Service Division as a clearinghouse to educate members on federal and state laws.[43] Local associations followed up by creating their own legislative committees. In June 1921, the YWCA joined a coalition of other white-dominated women's organizations, the Women's Joint Congressional Committee (WJCC), to push for legislation.[44] Other members included the League of Women Voters, the General Federation of Women's Clubs, the Daughters of the American Revolution, the Women's Trade Union League, and the National Consumers' League. Members of the "Women's Lobby on Capitol Hill" testified on behalf of a permanent women's bureau in the Labor Department and for laws like the Sheppard-Towner Act to promote maternal and infant health.[45]

YWCA women made explicit connections between their religion and politics in these activities. A series of leaflets from the early 1920s proclaimed, "Politics Needs Christian Citizenship" and informed readers about how to develop groups to learn about legislation, specifically for women and children.[46] The point of the YWCA's efforts, however, was not simply to educate women about issues so they could lobby others to act in accordance with "the spirit of Christianity" (although that was important), but to help women and girls develop as citizens capable of participating in democratic institutions ranging from YWCA clubs to national politics. The emphasis on females as self-governing countered societal definitions of women as dependent, rather than independent, beings and resonated with these women's understanding of what it was to be an American as well as a Christian (i.e., Protestant).[47] However *conservative* calls for "Christian citizenship" may sound today, white YWCA women's claim to it was troubling to many at the time because of its *radicalism*.

The criticism from women like Helen Gould Shepard during the 1920 convention foreshadowed post-convention attacks on the YWCA (and other women's groups). Rockefeller had been right to anticipate that there might be consequences for the financial well-being of the organization. In cities ranging from Los Angeles to Pittsburgh, businessmen threatened to cut off financial support if local associations did not repudiate the actions of the convention.[48] Endorsement of the social ideals of child labor legislation and old age pensions was "rank socialism," complained Harry M. Haldeman of the Better America Foundation, based in Los Angeles.[49] Not one to avoid hyperbole, he warned, "Business men will refuse to supply the ammunition with which they are to be shot" and urged businesses to refuse to support the Los Angeles YWCA.[50] The Employers Association of Pittsburgh advised its members that the YWCA had adopted a program "destructive of the very basis of America's progress and civilization."[51] In a campaign that won it national attention, it called for businesses to cut donations to the YWCA.[52]

Assessing the impact of the attacks is difficult. After Shepard resigned, she withdrew her contribution for the year of about $4,000. In the meantime, Abby Rockefeller's husband (John D. Rockefeller Jr.) announced a gift of $500,000 to the National Board.[53] But for local YWs, the situation was less sanguine. Critics and supporters of the YW alike noted that the Pittsburgh YW raised only $90,000 of its $200,000 goal for its campaign in early 1921. Likewise, initial reports from Los Angeles suggested a drop-off in funds received there.[54]

Several women's organizations active with the WJCC, including the YWCA, found themselves showcased on "spider web charts" circulated to demonstrate an international, Moscow-led conspiracy among progressive women.[55] For its part, the national YWCA downplayed the financial impact of its endorsement of the social ideals. In 1922, the National Board reported that "careful study has revealed that it did not bring us financial loss."[56] Even when the sums dropped off, supporters of the ideals stressed that the number of contributors had increased; "girls on small salaries" were stepping up to replace Helen Gould Shepard's largesse.[57] Although having hundreds of small contributors certainly fit with the YWCA's goals to democratize the organization, their monetary contributions usually did not equal those of a few wealthy donors. Perhaps attempting to minimize some local associations' dissatisfaction over the difficulties, the national YWCA attributed less-successful fundraising to general economic hardship—an explanation that was plausible during the recession of the early 1920s but grew less so as the decade progressed.

"How Difficult It Is for White Women to 'Think Black'"

The forty-four African American women at the 1920 convention faced both new opportunities and continuing restrictions. There was a sense of expansion and inclusion, that black women and girls were an intrinsic part of a bigger project. One report after another—war work, industrial, student, city—discussed African American women and girls as members of other groups. Token or not, African American women were visible in the debates on the floor of the convention. Clementine Hodges, the delegate from Wilberforce University, urged passage of the personal membership basis; she declared that "the appeal of eight hundred negro girls" was for the membership to be expanded. She told her audience that "it will be a benefit not only to our people and not only to the Anglo-Saxon races, but to the entire inhabitants of this universe," as a more inclusive association would help build "a new world."[58]

The accepted wisdom among whites was that the ideals were intended to support workers (whom most whites thought of as white). African Americans, however, often read a racial message into the first ideal: that the YWCA, like the churches, should stand for "[e]qual rights and justice for all men in all stations of life."[59] At the convention itself, Mary J. McCrorey, from the black branch in Charlotte, spoke on an accompanying recommendation that the YWCA "enlist in the fellowship of our Association larger and larger numbers of young women."[60] A seemingly innocuous idea (who could oppose bringing more women into the association?), the proposal in McCrorey's hands became a chance to describe "that class of women who have been more handicapped than any other women in the world." Commitment to a larger fellowship was, she concluded, an opportunity "to spread this work over the Southland, and give to the women of our race the great privileges of this Association."[61] Delegates endorsed the idea that "common fellowship" was a key aspect of the YWCA's goal to establish "right human relationships" in the face of "misunderstanding." They went on to affirm that "education, legislation, and cooperation, are but a means to [that] end," thereby linking their traditional strategies of education and cooperation with the new one of legislation.[62]

The YWCA noted more concrete gains for black women and girls. The National Board announced that the first YWCA building built expressly for African Americans had been finished in 1919 in New York City and hailed it to be "as adequate to their [i.e., African Americans'] needs as any that has ever been built for white girls."[63] At a meeting for city associations, members pointed out that black women were now on the local boards of directors for entire cities—not just black branches.[64] Even as the YW's national leadership credited the YWCA for being an important arena for the promotion of Christian understanding, however, it excluded African Americans from the convention banquet. Accounts differed over whether the resistance to an interracial meal came from the waiters at the hotel or white southern delegates, but African Americans criticized the YW for caving to racial prejudice. The *Cleveland Advocate* advised that "thinking Colored people" were asking, "How long will these institutions continue to prostitute the word 'Christian'?"[65]

Problems went beyond social segregation to issues of power and self-government. Delegates at the meeting of city associations heralded the presence of black women on the boards of directors for (three) cities, but they also acknowledged that "in other cities this is not possible because of local conditions over which the local Association has no control."[66] Black women, in and out of the YW, were concerned about efforts by white southern women to regain direction of local association work. By 1920, national war relief funds were disappearing and with them the ability of the national staff to develop work at the local level. As the country returned to normalcy, white southern YW women increased their demands for a return to the prewar policies established at the 1915 Louisville conference.

Even as Eva Bowles worked to ensure that black wartime centers would meet the standards for branches and, therefore, be entitled to some autonomy, YWCA women differed over what the branch policy meant in practice.[67] The findings from the Louisville meeting had concluded "that the best method of cooperating in city Associations is through the branch relationship."[68] But did "best" mean "only"? What about communities where white women were not ready to support a black branch? The white executive secretary for the South Atlantic Field Committee, Amy Smith, was reported to say that Louisville meant that things should be done "according to the ideas of the white women or no way."[69] Black women who had been at Louisville, like Lugenia Burns Hope, expressed outrage that it was even suggested that they would have ever agreed to a policy of white control. "We were misrepresented," she later wrote, and added, "Colored women who attended that Conference, who were not paid workers, protest against this interpretation."[70] Prior to the YW's national convention, leading southern black women, including Hope, McCrorey, Charlotte Hawkins Brown, and Mary McLeod Bethune, met in Atlanta to "discuss and seek remedy for the troubles existing in the work of the Y.W.C.A. among the colored women of the South."[71] Relying on personal, professional, and institutional connections, they challenged the local, regional, and national YWCAs.[72]

The women drafted recommendations to the National Board and delegated Hope and Lucy Laney to meet with Mabel Cratty and Eva Bowles to explain their concerns.[73] Their appeal was signed by sixteen women, "representing 300,000 negro women of the South." It challenged the "distinct misrepresentation of the colored women present at the Louisville conference as to their position regarding the development of the YWCA work among negroes in the South"; called for an investigation of the causes of African Americans' dissatisfaction with work in the South; urged that supervision of work be from the national headquarters in New York rather than the field office in Richmond; and demanded that "in all work affecting our people full recognition of leadership be given Negro women"—including representation on the National Board. Black women focused their criticisms on white southern women's efforts to control what was happening, but they also questioned the judgment of northern white women and the black members of the national staff.[74] Their particular target was the Colored City Secretary for the South Atlantic Field Committee, Adela F. Ruffin. White southern women had selected and felt comfortable with Ruffin, but the black women in Hope's group distrusted her and regarded her as having "too much 'Uncle Tom' in her attitude," in one of the more charitable descriptions.[75]

In the immediate aftermath of the meeting, Hope and her associates solicited advice, including from Eva Bowles. Bowles's response, significantly a handwritten letter from her home, rather than a typed letter from the office, advised, "Have definite recommendations. Ruffin is a politician and she will fight to the end."[76] Correspondence between Bowles and Hope points to the importance of the connections among black women in and out of the YWCA. Relations between Bowles and Hope were not always easy. Years later Bowles would obliquely refer to tensions when she wrote Hope that "even if we do have difficult times I enjoy being with you."[77] Yet, they forged an effective alliance that was largely invisible to white women. As Deborah Gray White has written of many black clubwomen: they were allies, not friends, but they united to advance the race.[78]

The YWCA's 1920 national convention began shortly after the appeal was sent and McCrorey, Hope, and Laney came to Cleveland. While members of the national staff listened to the complaints and seemed sympathetic, they suggested that the issues were more suitably handled by the regional body. The regional representatives, in turn, refused to meet with them, offering little explanation why.[79] But the matter had reached the point where the YWCA could not ignore it, and the staff arranged a meeting between the black women and women from the South Atlantic Field for early July.

In the meantime, Hope and her associates made their concerns public by sharing the appeal with African American leaders, including newspaper editors. In an editorial entitled "Too Much Paternalism in 'Ys,'" the *Cleve-*

land Advocate decried segregation in the YW and YM. If segregation was necessary, it continued, then full control over black branches ought to be wielded by black "men and women of superior attainments" whose abilities surpassed those of the "mediocre officials" from the white associations who functioned as "overseers."[80] In and out of the YWCA, African Americans discussed whether to continue working within the association.

Representatives of the National Board, the South Atlantic Field Committee, and the network of southern African American women finally met in Richmond, Virginia, on 3 July 1920 to discuss the administration of African American YW programs in the South. Representing the National Board were staff members Eva Bowles, Helen Davis, Mabel Head, and Katharine Scott. Representing the field committee were two of its board members (i.e., volunteer workers), Katharine Heath Hawes and Martha McNeill, as well as two paid staff members, Leona Macgeorge and Adela Ruffin. Lugenia Burns Hope, Lucy Laney, and Mary J. McCrorey rounded out the meeting as "invited guests."[81]

The Richmond meeting that Saturday in July existed on two levels. One was recorded in a forty-plus-page transcript that remained with the YWCA national headquarters. The second was reported in the seven-page "Circulated Minutes" that were shared with all the women. Katharine Heath Hawes, chairman of the South Atlantic Field Committee, distilled in those minutes what she saw as the essentials of the meeting; in so doing, she demonstrated an inability, shared by the white women present, to comprehend the African American women's points.[82] The black women, Hawes later reported, "talked, but they didnt [*sic*] say a thing the whole morning. . . . We talked around, and around and around."[83] McCrorey observed that Hawes's account made it appear "that there were no complaints, no issues—*nothing*, but just an outing to Richmond to see the S. Atlantic Field Office and its 'dignitaries.'"[84] Comparing the circulated minutes with the full transcript reveals important points that the white women missed.

The women in Richmond spent the better part of a day discussing the appeal that Hope had drafted. Black women gained grudging acknowledgment from the white women that there might have been a misstatement as to the conclusion of the Louisville meeting. "Any interpretation that the colored work could go no faster than the white women of the South would permit," summarized Hawes, "was an unfortunate expression of the historical fact that the Young Women's Christian Association never, in any place or any part of its work, can go faster than the people of that community will permit."[85] But even this formulation, observed one black woman subsequently, still begged the question of who were the "'people' of the 'community'" who would determine the pace.[86]

The white women seemed to take it for granted that reasonable black women were prepared to defer to white women who knew better. Hawes recorded that "Miss Laney brought up the point that in her judgment the colored women would prefer to wait until they could become a branch of the central white association than to endeavor to organize independent work against the judgment of the white women of the community."[87] Lucy Laney actually made quite a different point. She saw waiting for white women as a necessary step because of the white women's unwillingness to work with African Americans unless they (white women) were in control. Her emphasis, politely stated, was on the intransigence of southern white women rather than their judgment. To the women assembled in Richmond, she had said, "You can never adjust things with the white people unless the white Association were the central Association. The colored people would prefer to wait until the white people wanted them so that they could become a branch."[88] Where Laney was critical, Hawes assumed deference.

The white women, from both the field committee and the National Board, generally reacted to the black women's critique in one of two ways, each of which functioned to deny a *racial* basis to problems. The first was to argue that a difficulty was the result of an institutional situation that applied to many groups, not just black women, while the second was to suggest that the policy was sound, but individuals had erred in their implementation of it.

In response to observations about the high turnover among African American staff (thirty resignations out of forty-nine positions), the white representatives of the South Atlantic Field Committee explained there was high turnover among all paid workers. "They do not stay anywhere," commented Martha McNeill, chairman of the field's Committee on Colored Work.[89] Black women, in contrast, attributed the resignations to a situation in which, as one African American woman later wrote, "it is at times impossible to remain in the work and keep one's self-respect."[90]

White women dismissed black women's criticisms of the branch policy by likening the branches for African Americans with other specialized work. Leona Macgeorge, a white southern staff member, observed, "We must keep in mind that the branch relationship is the plan that is used in all our branches—Japanese, student, industrial, foreign-born, nurses. The same organic relationship exists with all the branches regardless of racial adjustment." Furthermore, Mabel Head noted, women from branches for foreign-born or industrial women were also often not members of the central board.

Bowles and Laney pointedly observed that many more boards of central associations included representatives of these other groups; African American women were on only three boards out of those in the more than sixty cities that had programming for African Americans.[91]

The tendency to see the problems as shared by other groups and, therefore, not racial was complemented by the fact that white women frequently attributed problems to individuals' misunderstandings or shortcomings, rather than any structural aspect of the YWCA. "The human element always enters everything," said Katharine Hawes. She advised, "If we do not learn to cut out talking about personal things and if the work is not big enough to keep our minds to it, if we cannot stop discussing our little personal things, trivial things, both white and colored people, then we are in a bad way." Her subsequent characterization of black women's concerns at Richmond was that only "personalities, really, [were] at the bottom of it."[92] If the problems were personal, rather than institutional, the association could not do much about them.

For her part, Hawes was particularly rankled by one recommendation that Hope and her group had presented. The request began with the observation that "the Southern white woman does not understand us." Continuing, the women asked that they "be permitted to form independent organizations wherever the branch relationship is not desirable or where there is no central association."[93] Hawes exploded: "It has no basis whatever, to say of the Southern woman that she does not care. A whole lot of us have gone out of our way to do all that we can."[94] What for black women was primarily an issue of their ability to control their own work, questioning how well white women understood it, became in Hawes's mind an accusation that she did not care. She also disagreed with *how* the black women had conducted their challenge. Hope and southern black women had publicly aired their disagreements with the regional YWCA, and Hawes was "hurt" that the complaints had been sent to her colleagues at national headquarters.

In person, Hope was conciliatory. "You are a broadminded woman," she told Hawes. But, she emphasized, black women needed to represent themselves on boards. "[If] the southern [white] woman is not interested enough to get our point of view, how can she suddenly decide that she can handle the whole question?" Hope observed. The only black women that white women knew were their servants, she added. White women did not know the three hundred thousand "representative women" in clubs that she and her group spoke for.[95]

Toward the end of the meeting, Helen Davis, a white woman and the highest-ranking staff member representing the National Board, tried to ease things by calling for women to work together and suggested somewhat vaguely they would have "more equal representation on the boards." Hope followed up by requesting that "there be a negro representative on the field committee, a person who would interpret not as a paid worker, but as a representative of the race and educate the field committee so far as we are concerned and help us to know them better and interpret them to us." Once Davis admitted the plan seemed "logical" and the National Board would discuss it, Hope pressed the point, asking why not a representative, then, on the National Board itself. This would mean that black women's "suggestions and criticisms would not have to come from outside." Hope attempted to use white women's concerns about bad public relations as leverage to establish procedures that would give black women some control.

Still committed to the idea that many of the problems were personal rather than structural, Davis attempted to forge an agreement about what had happened that day, half asking, half saying, "Could we report that we went into the field and had certain questions answered and found that certain other questions could not be answered since they were human questions." It would be "advisable" to have a larger conference for representatives from the YWCAs in all three southern regions "to face the problem, as a great national problem." And, while she acknowledged that the issue of representation on boards had arisen, she described it only as "the opinion of the colored women."[96]

After the meeting, McCrorey, Laney, and Hope shared their frustrations with other African Americans. White women had conceded little of lasting consequence. As one of Hope's correspondents observed, "It appears to me that it is their purpose at times to wear us out and finally to ride over us."[97] The matter was not settled, however, and later that month, at the biennial meeting of the NACW, Hope introduced a motion to its executive committee arguing in the interests of "direct representation," that black women be given representation at all levels of the YWCA. The committee endorsed the recommendation in the hopes of "making the work more effective."[98]

Back at the YW, black women used these criticisms as they attempted to negotiate change. Returning from the NACW biennial convention, one national staff member, Mary Jackson, reported that "the program of the Young Women's Christian Association did not meet with [its] approval . . . and for that reason was not endorsed by that federation." Jackson reminded her white counterparts that the NACW was very powerful and that the success of the YWCA depended on "the cooperation of such sister organizations." For her part, Bowles urged that the YWCA sponsor a conference in New York of "Outstanding Colored Women" to explain the YW's policies.[99] Bowles felt that it was essential that national white YW women meet black women leaders who were independent of local associations. She explained to white women that they (white women) would be able to explain the organization and win the black women over. She spoke of interracial contacts as useful for educating black women, suggesting "that the unrest among the colored people would be lessened somewhat if the colored women had a better understanding of the Association policy and purpose."[100]

In her personal correspondence with black women, however, Bowles argued that introducing white women to black women would change the *white women*. She wrote Hope that "our white women do not properly appreciate the strength of our colored women throughout the country. . . . We want our own colored women to be able to help make policies. . . . Am hoping to arrange a conference soon in order to set forth the association principles as they are. Hope the strongest women will attend."[101] Bowles characterized the meeting as a chance for black women to tell the YWCA "how difficult it is for white women to 'think black.'"[102] Black women essentially used "good cop/bad cop" tactics whereby Hope and others outside the YWCA demanded change (perhaps unreasonably), while Bowles and Jackson offered concessions from within to push the association along.

Nineteen of the most prominent black women met with the YWCA's executive committee to discuss the problems at the "Outstanding Colored Women Meeting" in December 1920. By then, the YWCA was also embroiled in the fallout from the exclusion of Mary Talbert in Paris. At the end of the day, Mary McLeod Bethune presented a statement from the women declaring that as "a factor and a force for the uplift of the womanhood of the world," they needed to be in positions of authority, including on the National Board. For its part, the white executive committee issued a statement flagging the "mutual friendliness" and the new understanding gained by both sides.[103]

In February 1921, the YWCA hosted another interracial meeting of about sixty women, fairly evenly divided between the two races, in Louisville, to address the policies and practices of the association at all levels. Like the 1915 conference before it, the 1921 meeting in Louisville would become the benchmark for racial practices in the association in the ensuing years. Although top national leadership (staff and board) were in attendance, the majority of attendees were southern black and white women active at the local and field levels. In addition, a few women from outside the YWCA who knew about work in the South were invited; Eva Bowles saw to it that Charlotte Hawkins Brown was there to represent the voice of the "outstanding colored women" who had been at the December meeting.[104]

The two-day conference included "frank" discussions initiated by Mabel Cratty's opening comments. Cratty praised the importance of the work while reporting the criticism the YW had been receiving; but she then warned the audience that "our organization cannot continue putting as much of its time on this one phase as it is now putting—so much more than on any other single piece of work. . . . We cannot just fiddle on this while Rome burns on other parts of our work."[105] The YWCA was facing financial crisis and the national organization was spending a lot of money to make the conference happen.

White and black women discussed the problems in the YWCA, including the criticisms coming from Hope's group and the meeting in Richmond, although evidently many local white women had heard little of what was going on. White and black women reported on the accomplishments at the local and regional levels. They also heard from the white and black women who had been in attendance at a meeting in Memphis in October 1920, which had initiated a women's division within the CIC.

Black women put white women on notice that African Americans were by no means committed to segregation. In the short run, black YW women focused on preventing the expansion of segregation. When Leslie Blanchard, the white executive secretary for students, suggested that separate groups for black students might be started in northern colleges, Elizabeth Ross Haynes made quick end of the idea, saying that "the northern student is not going to organize [separately]. We don't need to say they are, they won't."[106]

As at many interracial meetings of the decade, emotions at Louisville were simultaneously intensified and channeled by religious customs. Meetings opened with, and occasionally were interrupted by, prayers and devotions. Southern white women, such as Katharine Hawes, repented of their errors before a forgiving audience. Hawes admitted that at Richmond she had been "sore as a boil," angry that the black women "had nailed all of us down here at headquarters and hadnt [*sic*] given us a chance, as I saw it, to speak for ourselves. I was mad for fair. Now," she commented ruefully, "wasn't that a nice Christian lady to be Chairman of the Field Committee."[107]

Throughout the conference, black and white women joined in singing spirituals and hymns. It was rare that YWCA women held an event in these years without singing, and the Louisville conference was no exception. Lucy

Sheppard, a black delegate from Louisville, for instance, led the entire assembly in singing "Lord I Want to Be a Christian in My Heart."[108] In addition to singing themselves, the white women listened to the black women sing. As the meeting wrapped up, the "colored delegates" sang "I Ain't Going to Study War No More" and "Religion Is a Fortune."[109] For white YW women, as with many white Americans at the time, listening to spirituals combined religion and entertainment.[110] For their part, African Americans inflected social commentary into the songs. "Religion Is a Fortune" opened with the questions, "Oh when shall I see Jesus / And reign with Him above?" and concluded with, "When shall I be delivered / From this vain world of sin?" Black women reminded their white sisters that God was the ultimate judge of sinners in a wicked world.

In and out of the YWCA, interracial cooperation was presented through a religious medium. As the final member speaking from the floor, Charlotte Hawkins Brown concluded that the women had taken a "long step forward . . . in acknowledging the fundamentals of Christianity, the fatherhood of God and the brotherhood of men."[111] But the connection between race and Christianity raised different themes for white and black women. For white women, the motif was frequently that of sin, while for black women, it was suffering. As Mabel Cratty wrapped up the meeting, she recounted reading an unusual definition of patriotism as beginning with "recognizing the sins of one's country." She continued, "You know patriotism has something to do with the Fatherland, and we are all aiming to be citizens in the Fatherland of God. . . . Have we qualified on that first entrance into this Fatherland? Have we made the beginning which is the recognition of the failures and mistakes and sins of our own race?"[112]

Blacks and whites had historically linked the suffering of African Americans with the redemptive suffering of Christ. Reflecting years later on white women's reaction to meeting Adela Ruffin, a white YW woman described the encounter. Ruffin carried upon "her person marks of her rearing in a harsh white world. Why would we not call it Christ-like virtue, if she turned the other cheek to humiliations that our kind heaped on her, and showed kindly goodwill even to her white tormentors, whom she steadfastly looked upon as potential brothers?"[113] The point was not simply that suffering was expected of Christians in this world, but that it redeemed them. A 1923 statement on the educational work of the YW included as a goal "to strengthen the faith of the present colored generation and conserve the spiritual strength which comes through having suffered."[114] In these years, YW women referred frequently to sin and suffering as they explored Christianity and race relations.

In their "Findings" for the 1921 Louisville conference, the women held out that the "great responsibility" of local associations was to "interpret the Christian purpose of the Association to the community." Toward that end, they urged that "as soon as practicable," both the field committees and local associations should establish interracial committees on "colored work."[115] The 1921 Louisville conference, in sum, evidenced the central tropes of interracial cooperation, but also revealed how they were changing: the best women of each race would work toward mutual understanding to build a Christian society, but black women increasingly expressed public doubts about segregation. The conference did not repudiate the idea of the branch relationship, but it did place more emphasis upon structures at the regional and local level to enable black women to participate. White women finally conceded that black women should have some voice in the association, or at least that part of the association that directly touched their lives.

"Interpret to the Community"

By spring 1921, much of the public debate over the YW's racial policies was dying down. Lugenia Burns Hope and other black women in the NACW apparently reduced their public challenges of the YWCA. They continued to express criticism amongst themselves but increasingly sought involvement with other groups, especially the women's division of the CIC.[116] They maintained contact with those women still active with the YWCA, such as Eva Bowles or Elizabeth Ross Haynes, regarding the YW as but one among many options to advance the race.

In the following months and years, black YW members made gains at the local, regional, and national levels. Women at all levels sought to make the wartime expansion of programs permanent. The new building for African Americans in New York City on 137th Street was described as a model for other locals.[117] White women praised the quality of branches around the country, but African American women had a more jaundiced view.[118] A black staff member in the Springfield, Ohio, branch in the 1920s, Anna Arnold, recalled that her "branch did not have a gymnasium, swimming pool, or cafeteria, nor an adequate staff." She went on, "[I]t was in this community that I fully recognized that 'separate' meant inferior, despised and unequal. I knew nothing about civil rights organizations or the struggle even then going on over the question of 'separate but equal.'" When Arnold sought to gain access to the better facilities of the central association for her members, the board of directors responded that the community was not ready to integrate while the Community Chest would not grant the funds to improve the branch's facilities. "We are," continued the board, "making progress in understanding and ask for the patience of the branch leadership as they interpret this to the Negro community."[119] White women wielded significant power because the budgets of the branches were generally contingent upon support from the white-controlled central association.[120]

The administrative structure of local branches was modified somewhat to increase African American women's power. The 1921 Louisville conference consolidated the notion that two different committees should be developed for a black branch: a Committee on Management and a Committee on Colored Work. Members of the branch (i.e., African Americans) sat on the former and directed the operations of the branch. Members of the central association (i.e., white women) and an *equal* number of women from the branch were on the latter committee. Bowles failed in an effort to require that branch members would nominate the white women who served on any Committee on Colored Work, but she did get bylaws that established that the (white) president of the central association was to consult with the chairman of the committee of management (i.e., a black woman) when appointing the white members.[121]

While the Committee on Colored Work sounded similar to the old Affiliating Committee (discussed at the first Louisville conference), which had often administered the branch, national leaders made the differences explicit. The primary function of the Committee on Colored Work, Mary Sims of the national City Department told the 1924 convention, was to work toward "the better understanding of both races."[122] The frequency with which Bowles and the national staff reminded locals that the interracial Committees on Colored Work were not supposed to be running the branches suggests that adjusting the relationship remained an uphill struggle.[123]

In limited cases, black women's power was further increased. By 1923, eight cities had black women on local boards of directors for the entire city: New York, Brooklyn, Jersey City, Newark, Philadelphia, Cincinnati, Detroit, and Chicago. Although the number was small, out of the approximately sixty-five cities that had black branches, it represented an increase from three cities in 1920.[124] All in all, the national staff could identify changes at the local level, although there were regional variations.

Changes at the regional level were also ambiguous. First proposed at the 1915 Louisville conference, the regional Sub-Committee on Colored Work was supposed to ease relations at the field level. The South Central Field Committee already had an interracial one and, in the following months, the South Atlantic Field Committee followed suit and appointed Charlotte Hawkins Brown as the "colored member-at-large." However, like other nonresident members (i.e., those who did not live in Richmond, where meetings took place), she was not granted funds to travel to meetings. Brown wrote to Antoinette Lapham, secretary of the National Board, apparently commenting that it seemed to be merely a "figure head" position. In response Lapham described the job as one of explaining the association to her community, rather than attending meetings, writing that Brown's "chief service" would be "to interpret to the community and the groups with whom you come in contact our purpose and our hopes." Lapham went on to ask, "Is it not a valuable service to render to an organization when one can be an intelligent interpreter to and from a committee."[125] Lapham did not indicate any viable format by which Brown could interpret her community *to* the field committee, let alone have a say in policy.

Ironically, the two greatest achievements at the regional level, the replacement of field committee control by oversight from New York and the removal of Adela Ruffin, came as the result of increased financial cutbacks in the YW in the 1920s. Outside consultants found too much duplication between the local, regional, and national levels, and, at the beginning of 1922, the YWCA abolished the field structure in the interests of efficiency (not racial equity).[126] Additional retrenchment led to the elimination of one of the positions for African American women on the national staff by 1924, and Adela Ruffin left to work for a North Carolina branch, leaving Eva Bowles and Cordella Winn to handle city work.[127]

The YWCA also implemented changes at the national level. In December 1921, as part of the reorganization of the National Board, the YWCA created a Council on Colored Work. An equal number of black and white women, including both northerners and southerners, made up the council. The white women on the council, such as Abby Rockefeller, were members of the National Board. Most black members, such as Charlotte Hawkins Brown, came from outside the YW, although some, like Elizabeth Ross Haynes, had worked for the national organization, while others, like Fannie (Mrs. Frank) Williams of St. Louis, were active with local associations. The council was to advise the National Board on issues relating to better racial understanding and, thus, parallel what the local Committees on Colored Work did for city associations.[128] For the remainder of the decade, the council was a venue for staff and board members with differing views to discuss racial practices.

Although never publicly described as a response to the criticism of segregation at the Cleveland convention, the planning committee for the 1922 national convention, scheduled for Hot Springs, Arkansas, determined baseline standards for the convention, which included no segregated seating at the convention itself and no exclusion of African Americans from official social gatherings. These guidelines were used at subsequent national conventions (although not at all national meetings). The YWCA would not hold another national convention in the South for almost fifty years.[129]

And, in 1924, YWCA delegates at the national convention in New York City finally elected an African American to sit on the National Board, thus acceding to a major demand of black critics of the association. They chose Elizabeth Ross Haynes, who had been the first black full-time staff member at the national level and had continued to advise the association. During the 1921 Louisville conference, even as she criticized the YWCA for the treatment of Mary Talbert, Ross Haynes announced to the black and white women assembled that "I tell you that I as a negro woman stand for the Y.W.C.A."[130] White women saw her as reasonable; the southern white woman who seconded her nomination declared "that only by such working together of the best types of women could the race problem be solved."[131]

As a member of the National Board rather than on the staff, Ross Haynes may have felt more leeway than Bowles to comment on the YWCA, but she too worked through outside women. Upon hearing that Margaret Murray Washington would meet with Mary Westbrook (chairman of the Council on Colored Work), she privately wrote Washington in late 1924, "I am not asking that you do one thing special for her, except to give her a conference and tell her brutally frankly what you think of the Negro end of our Y.W.C.A. I wish you could see some of the confidential letters from Y.W.'s to me."[132]

Working within the parameters that white women established, the black women who remained active with the YWCA forged a third way between the alternatives of complete separation or white domination. They rejected both Lugenia Hope's vision for independent black associations *and* Amy Smith's idea that it was white women's way or no way. Certainly, they valued the organization as an important vehicle to get resources to rural African Americans migrating to both northern and southern cities at a time of limited public assistance.[133] But those services could be (and were) provided by more autonomous organizations. Black YWCA women also stressed the importance of the organization as (in their words) "biracial," if not integrated, without accepting white definitions and domination. Bowles called for "an interracial movement which acknowledges Colored women as women and accords to them the privileges and rights of Christian citizenship."[134] Bowles was laying claim to being the true Christian sister; to leave the YWCA was potentially to accept white class-privileged women's definition of *themselves* as Christian women, with other women being black Christian women. Bowles explained that the "first principle" of the work was that "we go as far as both the white and colored groups are agreed to go together."[135] The phrase sounded deceptively like the principle that many white women believed was established at the first Louisville conference. For Bowles, however, the emphasis was on "together" and, as the decade wore on, she employed notions of "togetherness" at every opportunity.

"To Create Right Public Opinion"

In the 1920 discussions on how to promote Christian citizenship, YW women had proposed a triumvirate of "education, legislation, and cooperation." While promoting education and cooperation as means to address a variety of topics, members of the YWCA were emphatic that the association should support legislative efforts only for a narrow range of issues tied to the social ideals; by the 1922 national convention, they included international relations, especially peace issues, in that agenda.[136]

Women in the YWCA saw their involvement in peace as a women's issue, but they also saw it in light of their "Christian internationalism," even as the larger society turned toward isolationism.[137] Women throughout the YW were interested in what was happening around the world, dating back to their support for the YWCA's overseas missionary efforts.[138] International issues ranging from "world fellowship" to peace garnered support even among the more conservative elements in the YW's sisterhood. In 1920, members at the national convention had voted to see that one-third of the national budget go for overseas work.[139] In the short run, the emphasis on the YW's overseas work appeared to work against efforts for African Americans at home, as the YWCA devoted financial and political efforts to support the former and not the latter. Black women responded by redefining international issues to link them with race issues: first, by establishing their contribution to peace and, second, by arguing that world peace began at home.

At the 1924 convention, De Orona McCrorey, from Talladega College (a historically black school in Alabama), reported that her group was learning that world peace was not "a matter of concern only to the white world; the colored student must realize that she must join hands with the rest of the world to bring peace about."[140] Like white women, black women laid claim to having a big vision. Eva Bowles suggested that the world could not do without the "contribution of the Negro race." Having cultivated "the spirit of patience and Christlike humility" for over three hundred years, she continued, it might be "the Negro's contribution which is needed to bring the Peace for which the world is seeking."[141]

Black women also argued that whites who were serious about peace needed to look at what was happening in America. McCrorey was hopeful that there was now a sense that "world fellowship, to the white students, can no longer mean friendship with the foreign student only, but must mean fellowship with the Negro student at their door."[142] Another YW writer pointed out that "the smallest racial factor" was significant because of "the predictions that the cause of coming wars is likely to be largely racial."[143]

As African Americans surveyed the American landscape in the early 1920s, one of the most alarming trends was the rise of lynchings, a threat to peace as well as justice. In October 1922, the executive committee of the National Board discussed Mary B. Talbert's request for endorsement of the Anti-Lynching Crusaders, a black women's group seeking federal antilynching legislation. The executive committee refused the request on the grounds "that they could not cooperate in creating another organization since they believe already existing organizations can be relied upon to back the Dyer Anti-Lynching Bill."[144] The following year, the Council on Colored Work reported that "several" members felt that the National Board should "publicly state its position on the question of lynching," but members could not come to agreement about supporting legislation and could only agree to "try for an expression of a Christian attitude toward lynching."[145] In 1924, the council declared that, although "the growing interpretation of brotherhood has reduced the toll of life through lynchings," an education campaign was still necessary. The council, in a statement that was ratified by the National Board and publicly reported, expressed what it saw as the duty for members: "As law enforcement depends upon right attitudes of mind, we . . . would urge upon our entire association body a new and earnest effort to create right public opinion toward the complete eradication of mob violence and lynching."[146] As white women expanded their legislative agenda to address international as well as industrial issues, interracial questions remained in the realm of education and voluntary efforts.

One possible reason why white YW women shunned political solutions to racial problems was the lesson they drew from the prevailing historical interpretation of Reconstruction. The Fourteenth and Fifteenth Amendments, wrote one such woman in 1921, "were the attempt of a dominant group to impose an idea upon the country" and had, therefore, never been enforced. It was, she continued, "unlikely to be questioned" that the amendments were adopted "seventy-five years too soon." Laws were effective only when the larger population agreed to them, a criterion that was not, however, consistently applied to other priorities.[147]

YWCA women developed a deliberate educational campaign to change the hearts and minds of American women and girls. Members of both races argued that students, girls, and younger women were more amenable to changing and could be educated into new racial understandings.[148] Making students the focus of interracial education also represented their potential role as future leaders of the association. And students, as "educated" women, were the quintessential "better" women.[149] During World War I, Adela Ruffin and other black leaders had visited white colleges and white student conferences. The events were often short and choreographed, but they could have a lasting effect. Katharine Lumpkin, a white Georgian, described the almost conversionary impact of simply considering sharing a meal with a black woman; she and her friends, "a little company of Eves . . . found ourselves called upon to pick from the Tree of Life the apple that would open our eyes to see what was good and evil."[150] Lumpkin continued her involvement with the YW as a national student secretary in the 1920s. She and her associates worked to expand the number of white students who met educated African Americans—"Negroes of culture"—although the process was a slow one: a lecture this time, perhaps participation in a discussion session another time, maybe leaving study guides for future meetings, always with an eye out to see if the students were ready and to ensure that there was no negative publicity.

It was the student governing body, the National Student Assembly, that in 1924 mandated *proportional* black representation on the regional governing bodies for the southern divisions and a black representative on the council overseeing Pennsylvania, Maryland, Delaware, and Washington, D.C. That year, students also selected Emma McAlister, an African American student from Spelman, as an officer of their assembly. In a piece for the *Crisis*, Josephine Pinyon Holmes attributed much of the change in goals and tone found at the 1924 convention to the strong, interracial delegation of students. In an article entitled "Youth Cannot Wait," she reported that the delegates of the Student Assembly had passed a resolution stating, "We . . . pledge ourselves to seek anew to know the mind of Jesus in regards to our race relationships and to know students of other races that we may rid ourselves of prejudice and may promote justice and understanding."[151] They then succeeded in getting the entire convention to ratify the resolution.

Although students were the focus of most systematic efforts, women in the YWCA concerned themselves with community women as well. At a minimum, college women would eventually graduate and the question became, What would happen when they left the campus? Leslie Blanchard, the senior secretary for student work, told the 1921 Louisville conference that their goal for college women was that "when they leave college they will stand in their communities for the right kind of Christian womanhood and for the right relationship between the races."[152] Community efforts were even slower than those of students. YW leaders attributed some difficulties to the presumed conservatism of older people as well as the fact that city associations were dependent on the larger community for financial support. But an added difficulty was the vagueness of white women's goals. Local Committees on Colored Work were supposed to look for opportunities to foster racial understanding in cities as well as promote work for African Americans. Reports from city associations in the North and South indicated that some set about to educate themselves and others on problems facing African Americans and to promote understanding between the races.

Some black women found these efforts problematic. Anna Arnold recounted her experience as the branch secretary in Springfield, Ohio, in the mid-1920s: "The adults to whom I spoke were usually good Christian white people, who thought of themselves as 'liberal' if they invited a Negro speaker to their meetings. . . . The first [question] was always 'What do Negroes want?' It did not occur to them that the question itself was an insult. I lashed out at them with the bitterness and venom born of Mississippi and, now, the midwest and they loved it in a way for it relieved them of their shame for a moment, even as it purged me."[153] Interracial contact welded race and Christianity in emotionally charged experiences.[154]

As incremental as these efforts were, some found them too controversial. In 1925, the *Manufacturers Record*, a southern business journal, printed a letter from a Lida B. Robertson under a headline reading, "Claims that at Y.W.C.A. Camp at Blue Ridge, N.C. Intermarriage of Whites and Negroes was Advocated." Professing that "we can scarcely believe" the claim, the editor reported that white YW students had discussions in which the "marriage of the whites to negroes was advocated as the Christian thing to do."[155] In response to queries from members, Emma Bailey Speer, president of the National Board, defended the YWCA, writing that no representative of the national body had "advocated racial intermarriage." While she conceded that someone in a discussion group might have made the claim, she went on to attribute the charge to white concerns about social equality. Speer observed that "there are many people to whom one cannot even suggest courtesy and respect between the races who do not in the next sentence bring up the question of intermarriage and say that being kind to a Negro ends logically in social relationships and in marriages."[156] Part of the national secretaries' efforts to promote interracial contact entailed smoothing the ruffled feathers of community leaders when they heard (distorted) reports of what was happening at the YWCA.[157]

The YWCA's approach invited challenges even from internal allies. Following a 1923 discussion on proposals for the Council on Colored Work to take a public stance against lynching, Sallie Hanna, a white member from Texas, conveyed her sense of feeling beleaguered. She was "aware of the difficulties of the Colored Woman, but she felt that there should be more of an effort to understand what the [southern] white woman is also experiencing at this time." Her anguish was clear as she continued, explaining that she "had a feeling of being on the defensive and belonging to a group that was unfair."[158] Constructing the solution to race relations as one that required mutuality could allow white women to see their difficulties as analogous to those of black women.

YW women moved slowly, hemmed in by concerns over public reaction, their larger constituency, and their own assumptions about effective social change and realistic goals. Interracial cooperation made race a priority for some Americans in these years, but it prescribed the actions that they would take to promote racial justice. The efficacy for developing mutual understanding among the better classes was seemingly confirmed by the actions of student members; at the same time, that class-based approach made less visible the efforts of another group that also supported concrete actions to assist African Americans, namely industrial women.

While the rhetoric about industrial women often assumed that they were white, the actual programs and clubs sometimes recognized the presence of black working women. During World War I, Eva Bowles and Mary Jackson strove to see that working women of all races might find common ground. By 1921, however, budget cuts reduced the size of the industrial staff at the national level and Jackson was reassigned as the secretary of the black branch in Nashville.[159] Bowles increasingly was forced to turn to white industrial secretaries and members at the national and local levels as allies and there was some success. At the 1924 convention (where the members of the Student Assembly pledged "to rid ourselves of prejudice"), the Industrial Assembly also declared interracial issues a key priority.[160] The following year, a pamphlet on programming for industrial clubs suggested that activities for members could include writing legislators urging support for the Dyer antilynching bill. Although industrial departments, conferences, and assemblies remained dominated by white women, they represented an important structural base for new notions about race relations that could be conveyed back to the membership at large.

❖ ❖ ❖

At the 1922 national convention, focused on "The Business of Peace," Mabel Cratty asked delegates to face the future. The YWCA had come a long way from the establishment of the National Board in 1906. It was now "a democracy, that is a fellowship of more or less like-minded women associating themselves together in order that they may help one another, in order that they may be a force for righteousness." They were not just any fellowship, but "a Christian fellowship of women and girls."[161] Although the YWCA never completely discarded the language of "uplift," the women increasingly spoke of democracy and self-governance. Throughout the 1920s, white and black women developed the YW as a "force for righteousness." However slow, condescending, or faltering white YWCA women's steps were, their words and actions meant that the association was ahead of comparable middle-class, white-dominated groups. Wielding power as *female* Christian citizens was unsettling to defenders of the status quo and they became the target of other whites who sought to solve race problems through intimidation, suppression, and violence as well as those who mounted attacks on women for their involvement in politics.

Interracial cooperation emphasized what white and black women shared as the best women and as Christian sisters. White women believed that there were appropriate ways to handle situations. When problems did arise, they advocated quiet education (often behind the scenes) rather than public agitation as the appropriate response for addressing the situation. When explaining problems, they relied on ideas like "misunderstanding," in part, because they usually viewed problems as individual and isolated, rather than as representative of larger organizational (or societal) patterns.

Black women's ability to force changes in the policies and practices of the YWCA cannot be attributed simply to their ability to adopt and adapt white women's rhetoric. Other institutional situations, ranging from budget cuts to the YWCA's commitment to internationalism, shaped race relations. Ironically, however, it was a challenge from another quarter, namely their brothers in the YMCA (white and black), that would push white women to redefine the "Christian fellowship" of women and girls and would provide black women with new leverage in their efforts to be heard.

5 Defending a Women's Organization

COMMENTING ON THE RELATIONS between the Young Women's Christian Association and the Young Men's Christian Association, a YWCA member declared in 1929, "We believe that it is important for women to work with men, but not until they have learned to work with women. In the churches," she continued, "women have usually held subsidiary positions. They have prepared the food and washed the dishes, while men have made the decisions."[1] This anonymous woman reveals how women, particularly leaders, in the YWCA reacted to postwar efforts by the YMCA to expand its work to include women and girls. What was at stake for these women was the continuing existence of the "woman movement."

Publicly and privately, the women cast doubt upon men's intentions. To the 1928 national convention, Mary Shipman (Mrs. S. B. L.) Penrose of Walla Walla, Washington, explained, "I feel perfectly convinced that our dear brethren are not trying to do any evil to us. They are just trying to do us good, and we have the very best of friends [in the YMCA]; but there are some individuals, and they are forceful ones, who do not grasp the situation."[2] Penrose, a white woman, did not speak for only the white membership. Black women in the association were every bit as concerned. The following year, Lucy Slowe, a member of the YWCA's Council on Colored Work and the dean of women at Howard University, told the council that "there is nothing to be gained by the women working in cooperation with the men and it seems regrettable that the women do not seem to object to the subjugation of their thinking to the men's."[3] White and black, national and local, volunteer and staff, throughout the 1920s, women rallied to defend their organization.

They used the language of war to describe the crisis they faced. The YMCA's efforts to expand services to women were an "invasion of the women's field." A 1926 study of the two organizations spoke of "open warfare" in Mississippi. The general secretary for the Cincinnati YWCA summed up the state of affairs there in 1928: "while I believe in the outlawry of war, I am afraid that local combats will be necessary for a few years yet."[4] Perhaps the most common term used by both associations for the challenge facing them was the "occupation of the field," referring to attempts by both Ys to expand the number of their locals, especially in rural areas and towns and small cities historically overlooked by both. Men were also likely to use psychological or sociological language to describe their goals. YM men criticized the "artificiality" of single-sex spaces and highlighted the "wholesomeness" and popularity of coeducational programs. They argued for recreational activities that would replicate the "family unit" and promote a partnership between men and women.[5] Men, and the women joining the YMCA in these years, supported the YM's extending programs to women and girls and urged joint activities. Some, particularly Walter Wood of Philadelphia, urged that the two associations formally merge.[6]

As women of their times, many in the YW did not reject the psychosexual language of normality and family; in 1924, Henrietta Roelofs, of the national staff, told the convention that the YWCA had an important contribution to the "acute" national problem of "family life and marriage."[7] These individuals argued, however, that women would be ready for true partnership with men only when women developed themselves and that could be done best in single-sex groups like their own.[8] Their constant invocation of domestic imagery (preparing food or washing dishes, for example) suggests that they had no illusions about the equality to be found in the family unit. But, the issue was never simply what individual women would face in a coeducational setting. Merging threatened their institutional identity, especially their commitment to being a "social force for the extension of the Kingdom of God."

Like the YWCA, the YMCA had racially segregated branches at the local level in the South and in the North. The men's proposals for cooperating urged that local associations should become *coeducational* but remain *racially segregated.* Thus, a discussion about gender related to debates about race. An argument about "women" and "men" looked different for "white women" and "colored women," as well as for "white men" and "colored men."

In seeking to distinguish themselves from the YM, and thereby provide a rationale for their continuing separate existence, women in the YW, white and black, emphasized the role their organization was playing in promoting interracial fellowship. Differing institutional histories and experiences in the YM and YW encouraged white men and white women to see their roles in American society differently even though, as individuals, they may have begun with similar social and racial attitudes.[9] These differences crystallized during the 1920s debate over coeducation. As Lucy Slowe's remark suggests, black women shared ideas about the gender aspects of the situation with white women, but they also saw the debate in racial terms and would succeed in persuading some white women to see it that way as well. Despite explanations of an essentialist or social basis for the differences between men and women, institutional causes were also important. Herbert Shenton, a sociologist who studied the Ys in 1930, explained that differences were "largely [due to] differences in organization and point of view of the two associations, not simply the general differences between men and women."[10] What, then, were the sources of differences between the two organizations?

"The Business Side of Religion"

The YMCA's founding in the United States in 1851 predated the first official YWCA by fifteen years. The YM initially undertook to bring young Protestant men, then moving to cities from the countryside, into the churches.[11] As with the YW, the YM subsequently expanded that mission to offer residences, cafeterias, and classes, with an evangelical tone. Some YMs did have "ladies' auxiliaries," but they usually functioned to promote programs for boys and young men. The women's groups were welcomed for the resources they provided—raising money, serving meals, caring for "curtains and furnishings"—and, in the words of one YMCA historian, "to adorn social events." Even in cases where local associations allowed women or girls use of facilities, in 1869 the YM's governing body required male-only membership for local associations.[12]

In the late nineteenth and early twentieth centuries, an internal struggle in the YMCA resulted in a change in priorities. The YMCA, for the most part, discarded its evangelical mission and stressed providing services, especially in physical fitness, to young men and boys in order to focus on the "whole man." YMCAs adopted the "four-fold program," which linked physical, intellectual, social, and spiritual development. From a twenty-first-century perspective, the YMCA's shift away from evangelism to services seems to have been a liberal move. Yet with it, the YMCA shifted away from addressing the needs of men and boys of all classes. It narrowed its constituency, focusing on middle- and lower-middle-class men and boys whose aspirations were compatible with those of the businessmen who supported the YMCA.[13] The YMCA became one of the primary vehicles that late nineteenth-century reformers favored to promote "muscular Christianity."[14] By 1899, the majority of men in the association stressed activities that were tied to buildings, as opposed to community-based work or reform efforts.[15] From 1900 to 1930, YMCAs engaged in a campaign to build more and bigger facilities and a YMCA building became an expected feature of the American urban landscape.[16] The YMCA no longer sought to expand its membership in poorer areas but provided services to those who could afford to pay for them.[17]

In the late nineteenth century, men in the YMCA committed themselves to a set of principles intended to avoid political or religious controversy. The association had been torn apart over the political divisions that culminated in the Civil War; the lesson they derived was to deliberately avoid divisive issues. They established a key principle: "when questions of moral reform become political party questions, our association, *as such,* can have no relation with them." In 1887, the Chicago YMCA board of directors, for instance, shut down a debate club that was merely discussing politics.[18]

Institutionally, the YMCA stressed the autonomy of local associations, and members structured the organization so that the locals had more power than national divisions. The national YMCA provided no real financial assistance to locals and could do little besides recommend changes. The policies of YMCAs remained heavily aligned to the interests of the local businesses that supported them and, in some cases, owned their buildings. Not only did businessmen dominate associations, but the YMCA utilized business methods in its structure and operations. The strength of identification between industry and the YMCA led the *Atlanta Constitution* to editorialize in 1885 that the "Y.M.C.A. is the business side of religion."[19]

The case of one local YMCA reveals the underlying political implications of the YM's orientation. In 1907, working-class members and a sympathetic staff in the Philadelphia YMCA brought in pro-union speakers and used the industrial YMCAs to aid a union drive. In response, the business-dominated board cut funding for working-class YMCAs. To the extent that they continued to offer programs for working men, they provided training in an atmosphere deliberately freed of union influence.[20] By the 1910s, the national YM described its position as functioning in "the zone of agreement between the employer and the employee," meaning that YMCAs would seek to mediate between industrialists and workers, and to promote only those activities on which both sides could agree. In practice, since local businessmen often financially supported industrial YMs, workers wielded little clout.[21]

Like the YW, the YMCA permitted only one YM per city to affiliate with the national body; all others were branches of the local central association. In 1891, however, it exempted African American branches from the rule.[22] These associations became linked through the national staff, segregated conventions, and training programs, and they had little contact with or influence on local white YMCAs. By 1925, W. E. B. Du Bois warned of "an independent autonomous colored Y.M.C.A.—national, even international in scope—whose connection with the white Y.M.C.A. is daily growing less and less and confined more and more to general policies and the rare personal contacts of a few officials."[23]

Black men active with the YMCA, like William Alphaeus Hunton and Channing Tobias, saw promoting black-controlled and autonomous branches as an important strategy for racial advancement, including, ultimately, challenging segregation. Like their white brothers, the black men of the YMCA emphasized buildings as key to the programs they wished to offer. From 1912 to 1933, aided by challenge grants from Julius Rosenwald, they succeeded in building some twenty facilities for black men and boys, in cities ranging from Indianapolis to Dallas, that matched those of white branches, if not central associations. Like black YWs, the buildings were important community centers for African Americans. And like black women, black men saw the Y as a strategy to advance the race, not simply to provide social services, however needed. The difference between black men and black women was their gendered strategies of race work. For black men, the key was to build manhood, which required independence from white domination and control over property.[24]

The differences between men and women in the Ys were not simply rooted in gender, but had structural origins. Individually, black and white men in the YMCA, especially those in the New York headquarters or those involved with African American associations, were often liberal—perhaps as liberal as their female counterparts in the YWCA. Institutionally, they operated under different conditions. The relative importance of local associations vis-à-vis the national organization and the separation of black work from the rest of the association gave progressive men little opportunity to influence others at either the national or local levels.[25] Individual men or associations suggesting political action were sure to hear references to the "zone of agreement." If they succeeded in passing a resolution at a national convention, they had no means to enforce it.[26]

In contrast, the national YW had a greater ability to influence locals. It often provided needed administrative and, occasionally, financial assistance, and locals were more amenable to its pressure. Local secretaries in the YWCA had a greater sense of connection to the national association and with each other, since many were trained at the NTS in New York, controlled by National Board staff. Men in the YMCA, in contrast, received their training at several different schools.[27]

A comparison of the Philadelphia YM and YW is instructive. Shortly after the local YM board had succeeded in limiting the power of working-class men and progressive secretaries, wealthy women in the YWCA tried to exclude working women and fire a secretary sympathetic to workers.[28] The industrial women appealed to the YWCA's National Board, which sued the local and gained control over it. The national group handed the YW over to local progressive women. While the YM in Philadelphia helped companies hostile to unions in the following years by training workers for them, the YW supported the Bryn Mawr Summer School for Women Workers. Nationally, the 1920s saw the expansion of YW programs and self-governing clubs for workers, while the percentage of industrial members in the YM dropped from 23 percent to 13 percent.[29]

Although avoiding—or attempting to avoid—controversy over religion and stepping away from the kind of religious activity that one might now associate with the Salvation Army, YM men continued to describe their programs as religiously based, often contrasting their activities with the social gospel orientation of the YWCA (to the latter's detriment). Particularly at the local level, many saw their programs (and staff) as more Christian than those of the YWCA because they retained a commitment to traditional morality. As one local YM secretary summed it up in 1926: the "Y W program as I have observed it [is] a social service one [without] the so called Christian features which we promote."[30] Religious values then, as well as economics, psychology, gender, and politics, informed discussions between the two organizations.

By the mid-1920s, the YWCA's 600,000 plus members made it the second-largest independent women's organization in the United States, but the YM, with nearly 1,000,000 members, was even bigger.[31] In 1925, Mildred Corbett, the YW secretary who was perhaps most familiar with the YM, estimated that the national YM spent almost four times what the YW did, and that the difference was even more pronounced at the local level.[32] Age, size, and budget, as well as the fact that the YM was a male organization, gave it a greater share of the public's attention. Much to the dismay of YW women, the general public and funders often assumed the YW was an auxiliary of the YM.[33] YM men did not help matters when they suggested that *they* had been instrumental in helping to start the YW; the YM had, in the words of one of its leaders, attempted to fulfill "the obligations of an older brother to a younger sister."[34] It was the YM's definition of what a Y was that most people were familiar with: a building-centered organization that focused on providing the services that communities sought in a moral setting—nothing controversial.

The national leaders of the YWCA, in contrast, stressed their connection to "a world-wide fellowship of Christian women."[35] By the 1920s, the YWCA featured programs such as Girl Reserve clubs, which did not require elaborate facilities.[36] It was a pragmatic choice for a poorer organization. YWCAs were not as well funded; it was strategic to value other kinds of activities besides the recreation and physical fitness programs of the YM.[37] With limited resources, a smaller number of members, occupation of fewer towns and cities, and a potentially controversial social agenda, the YWCA was vulnerable when the YMCA began to redefine its constituency to include women.

"The Trend of the Day"

The YMCA had begun to provide services and open facilities to women in increasing numbers during World War I.[38] The decision reflected the loss of a male clientele, rather than a new appreciation for women. After the war, many YM workers realized that women could be tapped to fill associations at times of day when men did not use them (because they were at work). Anecdotal evidence as well as more formal studies revealed to the YMCA that women and girls were a growing source of income within the organization. Requiring little financial outlay on the YM's part and seemingly no changes in its programming, opening YMCAs to women represented a financial boon. With its greater financial resources, the YMCA was able to reach women and girls whom the YWCA could not afford to serve, especially in the smaller cities and towns to which the YW had not yet expanded.

Increasingly some YM men suggested that the YW and the YM should cooperate, if not actually merge. Important funders of both organizations, such as the Rockefellers, urged merger because they felt it created a more centralized and efficient organization.[39] Using business language of the day, one YMCA editorialist observed in 1929 that the "most significant trend of the day perhaps is that which centers around the idea of the merger. Chain stores, railway consolidations, steel combinations, radio monopoly, church union, denominations coming together, community churches, and—shall we put it in print—the merging of the two Christian Associations." In his mind, factors encouraging this trend for the Y included the possibility for the "reduction of overhead expense" and "dealing with the family as a unit."[40]

As the second factor suggests, the bitter debate between the YM and the YW throughout the 1920s was also part of a general trend toward coeducational ventures.[41] The aftermath of woman suffrage and the rise of a consumer-driven economy fused to promote a new heterosocial culture everywhere from college campuses to reform organizations. Yet, women who chose—or were forced—to work in coeducational groups frequently found themselves without real power. Research on settlement houses in smaller cities suggests that women were often forced out of positions of power as the settlements became organizationally secure and financially stable.[42] In 1923, the Presbyterian Woman's Board of Home Missions was merged with the (male) Presbyterian Board of National Missions. While the women were guaranteed representation on the new board, they were given only minority representation.[43]

Presbyterian women were not alone. The 1920s witnessed the merger or elimination of other women's church groups.[44] Women expressed such discontent over the situation that in the late 1920s the FCC, along with the Council of Women for Home Missions and the Federation of Woman's Boards of Foreign Missions, commissioned a study on the "relative place of women in the church in the United States." Conducted by YWCA workers, the commission's report listed the number of mergers of benevolent boards as well as churches. The report included the complaints of women such as the one who observed that with the new boards, "women make the money [but] the men spend it."[45] Did this woman deliberately challenge gender expectations of men as producers and women as consumers? We cannot know. But what is obvious is that women harbored no illusions about working with men. By the time the YMCA proposed joint activities, if not merger, women in the YWCA had a wealth of information about what happened to women in coeducational settings.

In 1924, the YW was sufficiently alarmed about the YM's escalating work for women and girls that the national convention authorized the National Board to study the situation.[46] In 1925 and 1926, the YMCA and YWCA established a joint commission to discuss relationships. Discovering that the policies and practices of local associations were widely disparate, they gathered case studies of what was happening. In 1929, the two obtained $16,500 from John D. Rockefeller Jr. to commission an investigation, conducted by a sociologist, to research the question more formally.[47]

Examining the records from both associations makes it clear that multiple debates were going on simultaneously, with men and women talking past each other. A reason repeatedly given by YW women as to why they opposed merging was that women would lose power in a male-dominated organization. Even if there were programs for women and girls, led by women, the overall policy would be set by men. Presumably individual women feared for their own positions as well as those of women more generally. Although men attempted to reassure the women that men would not run the show, men primarily countered this argument with one that pointed to the wholesomeness and popularity of coeducation for both sexes.

Women's concern over their potential loss of power went beyond the position of women. YW members were also concerned that in a coeducational institution, the more conservative agenda of the men would trump that of the women. While some men attempted to respond to this issue, others offered an alternate vision of the Ys. They did not so much argue against social activism, as they assumed that the programs of the YMCA set the model for what all Ys did.

What for men then were debates about wholesomeness, efficiency, and giving communities what they wanted were, for women, questions about women's power both in the organization and to change society. Men frequently commented that they did not know what the YWCA meant by terms like "fellowship of women" or "woman movement," but they did acknowledge that there was something there that they did not understand. What men—or at least white men—were silent about was the third reason that YW women gave for remaining sex segregated. White and black women argued that the coeducational, but racially segregated, associations would damage the YWCA's efforts toward promoting racial fellowship. As women and men sought to understand the changes in their society and organizations in the 1920s, conversations shifted in and out of competing debates: women's power versus wholesomeness, social change versus community services, and Christian fellowship versus racial solidarity.

"Cooperation Does Not Mean Waiting on Tables"

One of the first arguments women raised in defense of the YW was the issue of power for women. The YMCA might provide services for women,

women argued, but women gained neither leadership skills nor executive jobs. Usually, male secretaries or boards of directors chose the women who would administer the YM's programs. A male-dominated Y stood in sharp contrast to a female-run YWCA. YW women were presumably not surprised when one YM leader observed that a survey of YM secretaries reported that many did not understand "the difference between doing work 'for' and work 'with' women and girls. . . . Some see no difference at all."[48]

Over and over, women raised questions about the issue of power and control, utilizing gender-linked metaphors and familial-based language to make their points. "The Y.W.C.A. is not a glorified auxiliary," responded one local YWCA worker. "Cooperation does not mean waiting on tables."[49] A YM secretary summed up the view of women about their experiences in the church: "The women bear their full share, and more, of the work; but they have been assigned the position rather of auxiliaries than of principals. It is the men who do all the crowing."[50] Some YM men were more forthcoming than others about the power differential between men and women. Henry Israel of the national YMCA bluntly wrote that YMCA secretaries were "not deeply concerned [about merger talk] because they are fairly certain who will run the thing in the end."[51]

Other men from the YMCA attempted to allay women's concerns about losing power in a new organization. To do so, they used women's newly won suffrage as an argument that women were now equal and no longer needed to be separate in order to exercise power. Walter Wood, the general secretary of the Philadelphia YM, had dramatically expanded programs for women and girls there. As the leading proponent of merging, he frequently participated in intra- and inter-organizational discussions. Men and women, he announced to one joint meeting in 1925, now "stand on equal footing and are so recognized." Later, he questioned the need for "an independent woman's movement." Emma Bailey Speer, the white president of the YWCA's National Board, responded somewhat tartly that men and women were supposedly equal in the church, but it did not work out that way. Wood challenged the YWCA's idea that women could get ahead only in their own group. As proof, he offered a somewhat muddled example of an African American bishop who dedicated an African American church saying that no white men would be denied privileges in the building. While admitting that the example was not quite parallel, Wood seemed to think this example spoke to the issue. Significantly, Wood overlooked the fact that the issue was not whether the YWCA permitted individual men to participate in its programs, or even whether men and women should work together. Rather, the question posed by Speer regarded the relative power of men and women in coeducational organizations.[52]

Many in the YMCA made the positive case for joint activities, if not merging. They argued that single-sex spaces were, at best, old-fashioned, and they emphasized the "natural desire of young people to be together," pointing to a "fundamental need" for "wholesome relationships" between the opposite sexes and dangers in work with only one sex.[53] As one local leader wrote, it was time to take social activities "out of the hands of both the prude and the pervert."[54] Ultimately, they pointed to the popularity of the YMCA's programs.

Wood and men in the YMCA proposed that the approach for Christian associations should be to focus on the family and not segregated individuals, for "in serving the community there is need for unity of administration because the family is the unit."[55] Their fusion of economic ideas with psychological ones was powerful in the 1920s. Women in the YWCA drew their own conclusions about the gender basis for both discourses. Speaking before the 1928 national convention, Martha B. Finley, first vice president of the National Board, opposed a male world of business to a female sphere of democracy. She attributed the pressure to merge with the YMCA to the "'Big Business' psychology which rates efficiency and economy so highly that the more subtle values created by truly democratic processes are in danger of being lost." Because of the "relative position of men and women in society," she went on to say, efficiency and economy were more likely to be identified "with systems devised and controlled by men."[56] By implication, she was also casting democracy as female.

The men's arguments for mergers founded on the family unit were in accord with discussions of the day in favor of companionate marriages. Covered in both the contemporary scholarly and popular literature, the companionate marriage was intended to counter the image of the patriarchal Victorian family. The modern marriage, advocates said, was a partnership that should rely on equality, mutual affection, and sexual interest for both women and men.[57] Those who applied the ideas to Ys called for cooperation if not full-scale integration, whereby the Ys would look to the family unit as a model.[58] Essentially, the YM made an argument for what might be called a companionate merger.

References to "wholesome heterosexuality" or the "pervert" are clues to an important characteristic of the 1920s—an attack on the homosociality of nineteenth-century life and institutions like the Ys. In the case of the YMCA, it is hard to overstate the level of the attack. As George Chauncey Jr.

and John Donald Gustav-Wrathall have pointed out, it had been forced to rethink what fellowship—even Christian fellowship—meant for men in the first three decades of the twentieth century. There had been national coverage of at least two major sex scandals involving YMCAs—in Portland, Oregon, in 1912 and the Newport Naval Training Station, Rhode Island, in 1919–20—that featured prominent men, including ministers, charged with soliciting other men for sex. The institutional response was striking. For much of the nineteenth century, secretaries for YMs had disproportionately married later or not at all; by 1930 male secretaries were married at even higher rates than the general population.[59] It was increasingly less viable to defend the YMCA as a "men's movement." YM leaders' promotion of the family unit was a defense of their legitimacy in a changing society.[60]

Defending that organization in the 1920s included attacks on women and the YWCA. The YWCA's National Board reported in 1928 that some men in the YM saw the YW as "objectionably feminist, subversive of the best interest of women and the family," and others saw it as "dominated by underdeveloped women whose experience is one-sided, and attracts to itself the less normal types of women."[61] YW women were not inured to the discourse and they too employed words like wholesome and natural when describing their goals. In the 1920s, along with charges to study relations with the YM, peace initiatives, and workers' rights, the YW developed a Commission on the Family in the Life of Today. Although commission members defined "the emotional adjustment of unmarried women" as an important topic, their expression of concern for family and marriage turned to studying issues like the Maternity and Infancy Act (the Sheppard-Towner Act) and urging passage of the Child Labor Amendment and stricter enforcement of Prohibition.[62]

Even at the grassroots, YW members held onto many of the values associated with an earlier homosocial world. A 1926 study of more than five hundred girls and women who attended YWCA conferences found that while 52 percent of them thought of "old maid" as a displeasing term, even greater percentages reacted negatively to "flapper" (64 percent), "petting" (75 percent), and smoking (67 percent)—key elements of 1920s heterosociability.[63] Married board members, lifelong unmarried secretaries, and (not yet married) business, industrial, and college girls in the YWCA continued to embrace the value of sisterhood. At least in the 1920s, YW women rarely publicly responded to charges of abnormality. Despite the seeming "twinness" of the two organizations, single-sexed fellowship played out differently for the members of each.[64]

Whatever their reaction to the charges, the women were vociferous in their criticism of the "family unit" concept, arguing that it was a naive, if not disingenuous, idea. As the national YW secretary for the development of rural communities asked a local YMCA official, "The family is the unit—for what? It is an intriguing idea—'To do the Housework? To play the small boy's baseball? To carry on the father's business?'"[65] In an article entitled "What Does the Woman Want: Men Wonder, But Women Know," written for the YM, Emma Bailey Speer set about telling men, "We object to being consulted only about the church carpet or the church kitchen when morals are under consideration or the spiritual training of our sons and daughters. . . . We want to do our own thinking, and that process leads to amusement when some worthy brother thinks he is 'saving the family' by getting Mr. Jones and Mrs. Robinson into the same swimming pool."[66] Speer attempted to return the debate from a discussion of heterosexuality to one of power. Or, perhaps for some women, the two were the flip sides of the same issue.

The debate about power for women in a coeducational organization paralleled the discussion about black women in the YWCA. The criticism of work being done "for, not with" a group and the frequency with which the dominant group just "did not get" the demands of the subordinated group are two of the more striking similarities. At a 1925 interracial meeting on race work in the YMCA, Mildred Corbett explained women's concerns. The issue, she told the assembly, was "the inherent value of women's leadership." The white male discussion leader, a self-described student of psychology and father of four daughters, clearly felt attacked for not "understanding women." Although the discussion leader seemed unable to follow Corbett's points, she was struck by the insightfulness of a black male secretary who observed, "It seems to me that these women are evidently up against something which the colored race well understands."[67] The issue for women, however, was not simply their leadership, but also their progressive social agenda.

"Even If We Have to Walk a Little More Slowly"

Women endorsing cooperation with men acknowledged that the latter's conservatism would have an effect on the efforts to promote social righteousness. Speaking at the 1926 convention on the influence of women's organizations on legislation, Anna Garlin Spencer, a minister and reformer, admonished the delegates to "let every woman's organization remember this: . . . we do want to walk with men even if we have to walk a little more slowly."[68] Many women in the YWCA were not willing to pay that price, however, and fought to maintain the independence of the YW.

The relationship between the YM and the YW was not made any easier by the fact that, in some cities, the YM used the public's perception of the differences to benefit itself at the expense of the YW. The national YM, for instance, had endorsed a watered-down version of the "Social Ideals of the Churches" in 1919.[69] When the Employers Association of Pittsburgh had attacked the local YW for its stand, the general secretary of the Pittsburgh YMCA had sought to reassure the business community that the YM had not passed the ideals and that his association was "totally free of outside influences."[70] The editor of *Industry,* a vocal critic of the YW, praised the YMCA for operating within the "zone of agreement," in contrast to the "realm of controversy" inhabited by the YWCA.[71]

The YWCA's commitment to the social gospel led some YM men to question its religious commitment. "Why is it that the YWCA's are so liberal that they are even letting in absolutely unchristian leadership on their directing boards and placing some secretaries on their staffs who are not Christian?" was a question proposed by one man for a joint meeting of YM and YW secretaries. The YW's impact on its members was disturbing to men. "Why do Y.W.C.A. or Girl Reserve girls [the YWCA youth program] so seldom take standards on dress, mode of dancing, petting, and delight?" asked another one.[72] What was being challenged, however, was not simply the YWCA's support of social Christianity, nor its ongoing loosening of religious requirements for membership, but *who* was in that fellowship. One YMCA secretary explained it was hard to work with the YWCA because, "In the city the Y.W.C.A. girl is from the uneducated group, the Y.M.C.A. is not."[73] The debate over coeducation happened while the industrial membership of the YW was expanding and that of the YM was contracting. Working women and girls diversified the YWCA religiously and culturally, as well as economically.

In the face of attacks by business interests and some YMCAs' capitalization on them, women must have found particularly galling the assertions of one male advocate of the merger. In 1930, J. Quincy Ames of Chicago argued that it was only a fluke that the YM had failed to pass the tougher version of the social ideals.[74] Men in the YM, he admitted, had avoided politics partially out of a concern of the abuse that would be brought on them. The YW, he said, was freer to act because it need not fear such attacks: the "feeling of chivalry" extended to women would soften any criticism.[75]

Yet, women in the YWCA *had* been attacked for their stands on workers' rights, women's issues, internationalism, and peace. By the time Ames was writing, the attacks were orchestrated and affected YWCAs around the country.[76] In 1928, the Massachusetts chapter of the Daughters of the American Revolution (DAR) circulated a blacklist of speakers that included YW staff and board members, while the YWCA itself appeared on the list of organizations suspect because of their ties to others.[77] Conservative women's groups, businessmen, military leaders, and "professional patriots" shared information and published each other's findings in an effort to discredit the social agenda of progressive women's organizations and the attacks escalated throughout the 1920s.[78]

While the FCC and some church groups were also targets, many observed that women's groups were particularly likely to be criticized. Henrietta Roelofs, a national staff member, advised YWCA members that when "women's organizations contented themselves with work that contemplated merely palliative measures of a philanthropic sort, no criticism was encountered, but when they sought to discover the causes of and means of preventing poverty, sickness, unequal opportunity and war, the opponents shouted: 'radicalism,' 'Socialism,' 'communism,' 'Bolshevism,' 'pacifism.'" Members needed to be prepared to respond to these attacks and she offered tips on what women could say to win over detractors.[79]

Measured responses were not always successful. In 1926 and 1927 in Fort Wayne, Indiana, a "gentleman 'with military interests'" accused staff members of the YW of being linked to the "spider web chart" of "conspicuous radicals." After the staff members explained their actions, their board backed them. Subsequent threats by the local Community Chest to deny the YWCA funding, however, led to the resignation of the two staff members.[80] The Community Chest then demanded, and won, veto power over hiring at local social welfare organizations. More than twenty years later, the policy was still in effect and YW women remained edgy about the "troubles of 1926."[81] Increasingly in the 1920s, Community Chests sought to promote conservative programming in their recipient agencies.[82]

The Community Chest and funders in communities were often more oriented to the men of YMCA than they were to the YWCA. The YMCA was more established. Leaders of the Community Chest were more likely to be men; women, if on Community Chest boards at all, were limited to token positions.[83] Supporting the YM over the YW was a way that funders could curtail the YWCA's activism. Given the past activism of the Philadelphia YWCA (especially compared to that of its male counterpart), it seems striking that it was the Philadelphia YMCA and its leader, Walter Wood, that were at the forefront of merging the associations.[84] Wood's vision was that the Ys, as Christian community service groups, were to provide programs demanded by the constituency, not to involve themselves in changing laws or public opinion. Wood argued that granting both sexes "identical status" in such groups would produce "economic efficiency, social normalcy and Christian emphasis."[85] Women in the YW countered with their commitment to the woman movement and educating public opinion.[86]

"A Christian Fellowship of Women"

Coeducational but racially segregated Ys raised another set of issues for the women. In its 1926 report, the National Board argued that these Ys would face all the problems of any joint work between men and women, but they also might tend to "substitute a race solidarity for the working together of colored and white women which has been a much desired goal for the Young Women's Christian Association in the last few years." Or, as Mildred Corbett put it, such structures would foster "race solidarity" rather than "Christian fellowship of women."[87] The report suggests that Eva Bowles had made some headway in getting the YWCA to accept "togetherness," at least rhetorically, as the basis for work. Both white and black women feared that coeducational but segregated Ys could interfere with the YWCA's interracial efforts. When the women's home mission bodies had been merged into men's boards, for instance, their interracial efforts had gone into decline.[88] While the YM responded in some way to women's concerns about power and the YW's progressive policies, they quite literally read women's concerns about race out of the record (as will be seen below).

Bowles's defense of interracial cooperation brought to the surface tensions between black men and black women over the best strategy to advance the race. Bowles argued that the interconnections, however limited, found in the YWCA permitted local black branches to influence local white associations and possibly the national body and greater society as well. She and her colleagues took some satisfaction in reporting to the Council on Colored Work that some African American YM men thought "the progress of the colored women" in the YW was because the women were "organizationally a part of the governing group."[89] Most YM leaders, such as Channing Tobias, were convinced of the effectiveness of *their* strategy of promoting a parallel structure of autonomous YMCAs. In 1928, Tobias told the YW's council, "All along we have felt that there was advantage in group solidarity although we realize the many disadvantages and appreciate some of the interracial advantage that you enjoyed as a result of your kind of an organization."[90] Black women in the YWCA were adamant about not giving up their fellowship, and they fought to prevent the expansion of separate facilities to new places.

Implementing these commitments was not always easy. In 1929, the secretary of the black YWCA in Orange, New Jersey, led a campaign, backed by the black YW national staff, against the efforts of a local white funder and the black YMCA to build a pool for the use of the black community. The local black YW secretary resisted the idea because she "felt that such a segregated pool would retard the day when the white and Negro groups would use the same facilities." A black member of the national staff told an observer that hard choices were necessary to advance the race; when African Americans, she said, "come to the point where they are willing to sacrifice personal comfort and privilege for the good of the group, they will be able to achieve those things for which they struggle."[91] Under intense pressure from funders, the YM, and white women on the local board of directors, the black YW staff finally acquiesced to the pool.

Surveying the national scene, Bowles commented that the pressure for coeducational work for African Americans came from white funders, the larger white community, and, occasionally, black men. She declared that "men fall more easily for the bait of buildings than do the women, for they see their own work in terms of equipment." In 1930, she reported to local associations, "Thus far we have had no instance where our colored women have asked to be part of a men's movement, but in several instances the men have attempted to absorb the work of the women."[92] Bowles and other African American women believed that black men expected to control such coeducational black facilities. Carolyn (Mrs. J. B.) Blanton, a black volunteer on the Council on Colored Work, told her compatriots that it "is instinctive in men to want to domineer women."[93] Black women had to negotiate with white women for power in a women's organization, but they were also well aware of the potential for conflict with black men in a race-based group.

Some black men, like their white brothers, pointed to the popularity of coeducational efforts as "proof" that Ys should offer them; this popularity, however, made them all the more suspect to black women. African American women in Lynchburg, Virginia, turned down an offer to join African American men on a campaign for a joint building, complaining that those girls and boys "tempted to come to the building for a social good time more than anything else" would require greater "chaperonage."[94] Because assaults on the African American community often took the form of questioning the virtue of African Americans, black women saw the debate over coeducation not only in moral terms, but also in political ones, and argued that it posed not only gender problems, but racial ones.

Ultimately, however, Eva Bowles downplayed disagreements between black men and black women in her presentations. In her 1929 report, she wrote, "The situation which faces both organizations is acute between Negro men and Negro women. They are more the victims than the aggressors. The pressure placed upon them is from the white group that had no contributions as yet to make for joint work."[95] There certainly were cases of black YMs attempting to start programs for women and girls; overall, however, the official study of YM and YW relations noted that black men had a much higher rate of cooperation with black women than the white men had with white women.[96] Recognizing that African American men and women shared common concerns, Bowles tended to blame white men for the whole idea, declaring that "there is no initiative or especial desire from the colored people themselves to actually do work together. The idea has been promoted principally upon the suggestion and urgency of the white group, especially white men, to house all colored work under one roof."[97] Cordella Winn reported on pressures to merge the black Ys in one city and noted that "it is thought that the big business concerns of the city are behind this movement for cooperation, and the women may lose out if they do not comply."[98]

Both African American men and women believed that local white communities wanted to reduce financial support for African Americans and fund only one center for both black men and women. Eva Bowles and Channing Tobias lobbied to see that discussions of joint activities and cooperation would include an examination of the "racial situation." While they disagreed about strategies to advance the race, they did agree that proposals for joint work represented an attack on their communities. They observed that funders were urging that "colored work" be "under one roof" even before coeducational associations had been successfully designed and implemented for white people. The fact that white men in the YMCA and some white women in the YWCA were willing to have African American males and females try something not yet implemented satisfactorily for whites raised their suspicions. In a joint statement to a YM/YW group exploring cooperation in the mid-1920s, Bowles and Tobias conveyed their sense of outrage that these proposals disregarded the "Christian organization consciousness of the colored group."[99] In other words, they saw the proposals as a challenge to the morality of African Americans and, therefore, a political attack on the race.

While the white men in the YMCA had acknowledged and sometimes responded to the other questions raised by the YWCA (Would women have power? What about the differing social agendas?), they were almost completely silent on the question of race. White men rarely talked about the African American constituency as an important part of the YMCA, nor did they respond to the question of dangers of race solidarity. An early agenda for the joint commission included a vague reference to the special issues for African Americans. As the commission drew to a close, Mildred Corbett was responsible for circulating a draft of its findings for review to Mabel Cratty, of the YWCA, and Wirt Wiley of the national YM. The *only* part that was crossed off in the YM's copy, presumably by Wiley, was a reference to the concerns about the disregard for the Christian consciousness of African Americans. And therefore, the published "Tentative Conclusions" circulated for the next couple of years were silent on the issue of race.[100]

"If They Would Stop Trying to Dam the Y.M.C.A."

Two events marked the end of the debate over the relationship between men and women and/or the YM and the YW. The first was the publication of the "Reconnaissance Study: YMCA-YWCA Relations in the Field in the U.S.A." in 1930. The report, more than four hundred pages in length, included a survey of more than 90 percent of local YMCAs and YWCAs, complete with scores of charts, as well as surveys of individual people, additional interviews, a compilation of relevant policy statements, and a chronology of the efforts of the national bodies to cooperate. The report was made irrelevant almost as soon as it was published by the second event, the decision in 1933 by the YMCA, at the instigation of Walter Wood, to permit associations to determine membership requirements. The step effectively sanctioned the locals' practice of opening their facilities to women and girls. Both these events confirmed the YW's concerns about what men were doing.

The reconnaissance study revealed that the men's efforts for women tended to be segregated programs for girls and women; about two-thirds of YMCAs were offering something for women. On the other hand, despite the stereotype of women's refusal to cooperate, YWs were more likely to carry out (or try to carry out) joint programs with YMs.[101] For all of men's talk about promoting wholesome relations between the sexes, what they offered were sex-segregated services for women under the control of men and for which YMCAs received fees. YW women were understandably suspicious that the men of the YM were really looking for money. The suspicion seemed confirmed by a 1931 YM-commissioned study that concluded that the "facts gathered" indicated that the YM was interested in "the whole family" more because of "over-building" (i.e., needing to fill their facilities) and the potential to gain more donations, rather than "any genuine appreciation" for assisting the family.[102]

Increasingly, men treated the YM's expansion as inevitable. In 1928, J. W. Ogg, a YM leader, wrote to a colleague criticizing the YW. Nobody, he wrote, really knew what the YWCA wanted or what its ideas were. Women needed to recognize that "there is a great force at work in the field (meaning the tendency toward combined service for men and women)." They needed to stop "trying to combat this force" but, rather, see if they could harness it. As he continued his letter, he adopted the metaphor of a "great flood" facing the YWCA. The flood, however, became the YMCA itself. Perhaps, he wondered rhetorically, "if they [the women of the YWCA] wouldn't get farther if they would stop trying to dam the Y.M.C.A." and try to work with it.[103] What working *with* the YMCA meant when men were not prepared to work *with* women was not explained.

By 1933, men of the YMCA were no longer bothering to ask the YW to work with them and one YM report estimated that 90 percent of YMCAs were doing work for women and girls.[104] At their national convention that year, members voted to permit locals to establish their own policies for female membership. Locals could count women members to determine the number of representatives at national conventions, but they did not have to let them vote. A subsequent YMCA study found that only about half of the local associations that allowed women to join permitted them to vote. As the YMCA increased its work for women and girls, it became even less likely to cooperate with the YW. Most female secretaries in the YMCA worked only with women and girls, shutting those staff members out of power in the association as a whole.[105] The association did not permit women on national governing bodies until the 1950s. Women of the YW had been correct to worry about women's power in a coeducational organization.

The debate between the two organizations had a lasting impact on women in the YWCA. In particular, they were forced to articulate the relationship between being single-sex and being diverse in other ways. White women were clear that they opposed merging with the YMCA because of the threat to their own power in an organization as well as their ability to choose the organization's priorities. The YW's leadership continually referred to the importance of Christian fellowship. We know less about the "average" member. But in the 1920s, the YWCA's membership went up by 20 percent, suggesting that many women and girls found its combination of programs, female power, and social activism appealing.[106] The YW lost some of its constituency to the YM, but it had managed to withstand the pressure from both men and funders to give up its independence as a women's group. Black women challenged their white sisters to preserve the Christian values of black Americans and built on the YW's being a Christian fellowship of women in their efforts to advance the race.

"Working Together as Women"

African American women had struggled to gain control over the programs for black members. Yet black-directed programs for a black constituency had a downside: they suggested that only African Americans were interested in race issues *and* that race issues were their only interest. Eva Bowles argued that the YWCA needed to do more. For years, Bowles had been using the language of "working together," but now white women had a reason to listen to her. As white women sought to forge an institutional identity for the YW as distinct from the YM, they placed increasing value on their involvement with race issues and interracial activities. Building on this interest, Bowles tried to do two things simultaneously. First, she tried to persuade white women to expand support for African American and interracial projects; second, she held out that black women were not interested only in race but, like all women, had broader interests.

In 1928, the City Department indicated to the national convention that its first challenge was expanding to new areas and "next in importance" was increasing work among African Americans.[107] Facing competition from the YM for "occupation of the field," the national convention encouraged local YW associations to expand their offerings to black women and girls, including clubs for black women and girls within existing white associations if financial resources did not permit separate facilities. The YWCA in Elizabeth, an industrial city in northeastern New Jersey, started three clubs in the 1920s for African American women and girls that sometimes met in the central association building. With a black population of less than 5 percent out of something over 100,000, the black community was not seen as large enough to sustain a segregated branch.[108] In 1928, the YWCA of Boston opened its swimming pool to African American girls' clubs.[109] The following year, Boston, as well as Toledo, elected a black woman to its board of directors, although neither city had a black branch.[110]

In the late 1920s and early 1930s, some whites and African Americans favored replacing the old Committees on Colored Work with Committees on Race Relations or Interracial Committees.[111] The charge of these local committees was no longer to advise the branch, but to assist the association in developing good race relations.[112] Two black national staff members later described these committees, "The great asset of such a committee is the recognition, by the white people in the Association, of their responsibility not for colored people but for white and colored people in respect to their attitudes toward one another, and to the kinds of institutions which grow up in their city which vitally affect the peace and understanding between these two groups."[113]

Some white women, especially in the student and industrial programs, had experiences working with African American women as peers and on issues other than race. White student secretaries, such as Katharine Du Pre Lumpkin or Elizabeth Webb, visited college campuses and student conferences with African American secretaries, such as Frances Williams and Juliette Derricotte.[114] Derricotte later reported that upon arrival at one Midwest school, things were so tense that "the colored girls wouldn't talk to me when Miss —— [the white secretary] was around. And the white girls wouldn't talk to her when I was around." Derricotte and her white coworker challenged the women as Christians and left them with a study plan for the year. When Derricotte returned, she found that the women were now educating their campus: "Programs of Negro music or Negro poetry were put on. Bars were taken down." But for Derricotte, the real success was the following year, when "the whole Y.W.C.A. dropped the interracial issues and together, white and colored, went out to clean up on the campus the things that were not Christian. So I learned," she concluded, "that the most worth while thing to do is to be yourself and do your own work, not just to attack the interracial question."[115]

Difficulties, both personal and programmatic, did arise. In 1936, when Frances Williams reflected back on the 1920s, she told the National Student Council that Katharine Lumpkin was "the first southern girl whom I liked." Yet, she continued, "Katharine did not like me." Williams attributed Lumpkin's attitude to a time that Williams had sat in the "white waiting room" for the Atlanta train station. Both women were committed to advancing racial justice and Williams reported that they did not let their "personal differences interfere with the work." She credited Lumpkin for moving white students "to the place where they were the most dominating factor in the national student movement."[116] But black women had to struggle to make the relationships function in practice as principle dictated. In the mid-1920s, Williams wrote two black colleagues in the student department that she had a "long talk" with Lumpkin and that Lumpkin "got everything she wanted to get out of her system." Williams criticized Lumpkin for allowing YW staffers to go over her (Williams's) head when complaining to Lumpkin. Each woman was a national secretary for student work (responsible for her own constituency as well as to work together), but clearly many treated Lumpkin as senior. That, Williams wrote, needed to change.[117]

For her part, Lumpkin also acknowledged that relationships between black and white women were changing. *Her* first experience with a black staffer had been her contact with Adela Ruffin, who had accommodated to white southern racial mores. But with the World War I expansion, a new generation of black women, including Derricotte and Williams, had joined the YWCA. At the end of 1923, Lumpkin wrote the executive in charge of the student division that "at any time the colored staff will feel that on principle [accommodating segregation] cannot be done" and would upset the longstanding institutional (and social) acceptance of it. Lumpkin wrote that she was sympathetic to the stand that women like Derricotte were taking, but she wondered what the impact on their programs would be. She worried that the YWCA might be pushing faster than the constituency would allow. In insisting on integrated meals, for instance, would they lose their audience (and chance to change whites)?[118]

Even if students could accept the changes, there was another problem. YW leaders never intended student work as an end in itself. The YWCA saw it as a chance to train the leaders of the future, but, as the Council on Colored Work noted, there were few provisions to assist those students in continuing their efforts once they graduated and returned to communities that had not moved along.[119] As important as student work was, it alone would not be enough to change the association or society.

Like Derricotte in her analysis of the importance of working on other issues, Bowles looked for chances to bring white and black women together in new ways. Reporting in 1926 on black women's involvement in peace efforts, Bowles observed, "*Our real inter-racial progress is the by-product of working together as women on something other than race.* Not until then can we arrive into a natural state of living together."[120] Bowles looked for opportunities to create bridges between black and white women. Writing on racial understanding in 1929, Bowles held out her vision: "We should comprehend clearly that the Negro group itself must have a chance to develop its program and its leadership to the point where the relationships can be based upon more fundamental elements than race."[121] More than a decade earlier, Lily Hardy Hammond had called upon white women to recognize "womanhood as a thing deeper even than race," so they would take up their duty to help black women.[122] Bowles now called upon black and white women to find issues to work on other than race relations in order to build a Christian fellowship.

For Bowles, one of the most promising groups to take on this challenge was industrial women. Ever since the World War, she had tried to persuade white working women that their position was affected by that of black women. Promoting industrial work was a way to remind whites that black women had identities and issues beyond those of race. Advising northern associations who were developing programs "among colored women and girls" for the first time, Bowles wrote in 1925 that the "responsibility of the Industrial Department is to develop a consciousness in both white and colored groups that their interests are dependent upon each other."[123] Bowles was hampered in her efforts by the absence of a black industrial secretary at the national level. She worked with white Industrial Department members like Lucy Carner and Eleanor Copenhaver, but, since the end of World War I, there had been no national staff member whose priority was black working women or race relations among working women.[124]

The problem was further compounded because local black associations rarely had more than one secretary and those that did focused on other groups, especially the Girl Reserves. On one hand, the commitment to that program represented a chance to train the YW leaders of the future; on the other hand, it was the result of the emphasis upon the talented tenth as a strategy and a tendency of local secretaries to work with women and girls with whom they shared class and cultural values. Focusing limited resources on more privileged black women and girls meant that there was not always support for programs for working women. Economic fault lines between black women were there, whether or not they were acknowledged.[125]

Despite these limits, there were some gains among working women. The theme of the 1926 Industrial Assembly was "Unity in Industry Regardless of Race and Nationality." Alice Craney, a white working-class woman, reported on an interracial industrial group in Indianapolis consisting of four white and four African American women who met to talk and study. Craney spelled out the lessons to her fellow delegates: "The group hopes to make every girl conscious of the fact that every girl is her neighbor and no girl can be overworked, underpaid, segregated and unemployed without affecting every other industrial woman."[126] The goal of strengthening labor's position provided white working women with an incentive to work with black women. Change in both the South and the North was, not surprisingly, incremental.

Both students and industrial women used their separate structures to push the larger organization, sometimes by just modeling that it was possible for black and white women to meet together—even in the South. In 1927, largely due to demands of the student associations, the first interracial southern city conference was held in Richmond. A new Jim Crow law limited how much could be done, but it was a change from previous meetings.[127] Building on the policy of interracial accommodations at the 1922 convention, staff and volunteers of the national Council on Colored Work saw to it that each convention moved forward. In 1926, the council called upon the National Board to commit itself to holding conventions only in cities "where the principles of Christian sisterhood can be looked up to."[128] It took months of correspondence to see to it that black delegates would be served coffee in a hotel café, that delegations who traveled together could sit together, and that black members would not be housed in private homes. Sometimes hotels would accommodate (just for the conference, and only if delegates displayed a convention tag), sometimes they refused, sometimes they reneged on their promises.[129] Once the YW had established the precedent, other groups found it easier to hold interracial meetings in a city; in 1928, Bowles reported that the FCC had referred to the YWCA "as a pioneer in arranging national meetings so that such meetings could be truly interracial."[130]

But perhaps the most important activity that brought black and white women together in the decade was resisting the YMCA.[131] As the problems with the YMCA began to escalate in the mid-1920s, Eva Bowles and Mildred Corbett were in contact to discover what were the experiences of black, as well as white, associations approaching joint work. "We have the same problem with a great big plus," Bowles wrote Corbett. She continued, "I am sure that the only way we can be helpful is to be pioneers together."[132] For white women, the situation had started as a gender question only. For black women, it had always been about both race and gender. Through conflict with the YM, some white YW women came to see the struggle over gender integration in racial terms. As they justified their existence as a Christian sisterhood, they had, to some extent, to live up to that. Further, the attention they began to draw from other groups, who noticed that the YWCA was pioneering on the racial front, was a source of institutional pride.

❖ ❖ ❖

Long past 1930, white and black YW women maintained a belief in the distinct role a women's organization could play. Their faith challenges those who have argued that this decade represented the death knell for what was known as the "woman movement" and the total ascendancy of coeducation.[133] The YWCA did increasingly offer coeducational activities, but power remained in the hands of women; the association continued to restrict active (i.e., voting) membership and leadership to women and girls. Christian fellowship and citizenship legitimized both the YWCA's existence and its activism.

By the time of the 1930 reconnaissance study, Eva Bowles could look back on more than two decades of developing work among African Americans; from four recognized associations in 1907, there were now sixty-five. Twenty-five cities had black women on the general boards of directors, including places without a black branch. Some 150 communities without branches had programs for African American girls and women, including some that were interracial.[134] Each year she delivered an annual report noting accomplishments, praising colleagues, and suggesting next steps. On occasion, however, her weariness seeped out. In the fall of 1926, a meeting called the Interracial Conference of Church Women was held in Eaglesmere, Pennsylvania. Mary (Mrs. Richard) Westbrook, a longtime member of the YW's Council on Colored Work, had been instrumental in organizing it. Many of the attendees were affiliated with the YW; some reported to the council about the meeting. White YW women prided themselves on the relative accomplishments of the YWCA, explaining that churchwomen, in general, lagged behind the women of the YW. Sallie Hanna, a board member from Texas, "felt the best things that were said were said by our folks." Eva Bowles, in her comments, confirmed that the YW had a lot to offer the churchwomen, but she also expressed reservations. "Our movement has gone far in advance of the methods used at this conference," she told the Council on Colored Work, but "to a large extent our constituency is still in this stage."[135]

Other black women were even more critical of where interracial efforts were. Alice Dunbar-Nelson, poet, novelist, and columnist, was an advisor to the Girl Reserves in Washington, D.C. She attended the next Eaglesmere conference, in 1928, and reported to the readership of the black press that it "was the colored women, by the way, who kept the discussion on a frank and open plane; who struggled hardest to prevent the conference from degenerating into a sentimental mutual admiration society." Interracial meetings had to do more, she argued. "Mountain-peaks of religious experience are wonderful in personal retrospect, but far better [is] a searching after actual facts and conditions in various communities, and definite ways and means to better those conditions." In her diary, she was even more critical of the "churchly ladies," such as Mary Westbrook, who were "all smug and satisfied and too smiling."[136]

White middle- and upper-class women had defined a role for their organization as a place where the best white women and black women could come to a mutual understanding and ease racial tensions. They defended that space against a male assault by emphasizing being a Christian fellowship of women. It is possible to see that goal as an opportunistic effort of white women to maintain a place for themselves. Knowing they would lose power to white men in a coeducational group, they cast about for any possible justification for a sex-segregated organization that they, as white women, controlled. Opportunistic or not, this institutional purpose gave African American women an opening wedge when analyzing the institution's priorities and programs. Dunbar-Nelson herself was a contemporary of Bowles (both were born in 1875), but younger black women, including Juliette Derricotte and Frances Williams, were coming to maturity in the YWCA. They, and the white women like Katharine Lumpkin and Elizabeth Webb, with whom they most closely worked, were coming to expect more of interracial cooperation and fellowship than a cathartic experience for the white women present.

6 Changing Strategies

ON THE AFTERNOON OF NOVEMBER 6, 1931, a Ford Model A roadster traveled down a small road in rural Georgia. The occupants of the car, Juliette Derricotte, a former YWCA secretary and a dean at Fisk University, and Edward Davis, Nina Johnson, and Miriam Price, three Fisk students, were en route to Athens, Georgia, for supper with Derricotte's mother. The four African Americans were driving in order to avoid the humiliation and inconvenience of segregated public transportation. Outside of Dalton, Georgia, their car met a Model T sedan occupied by Roy Henton, a white farmer, and his wife. The two cars sideswiped each other and were forced off the road. Henton's car turned over, but it was slowed down by hitting a mailbox and the Hentons emerged relatively unscathed. Derricotte's car flipped over, landing upright in a ditch with its occupants thrown out.[1]

The four were taken to white physicians in town, as there were no African American doctors in the county. After lengthy examinations, Derricotte and Johnson, more seriously injured than Davis or Price, were moved to the house of Alice Wilson, an African American woman described as a "practical," but untrained, nurse. Hamilton Memorial Hospital, the only hospital in town and supported by public funds, was known not to admit African Americans. The white physicians normally placed their black patients who needed medical treatment in Wilson's home; in the absence of an emergency, African Americans usually went to the "colored" hospitals in Chattanooga or Atlanta. Asking to be called if Johnson's or Derricotte's condition changed, the white doctors left, planning to return in the morning.

Later that evening, officials from Fisk arrived with their own doctor and took Derricotte and Johnson by ambulance to Walden Hospital, the "colored" hospital in Chattanooga some thirty-five miles away. Johnson died en route. Derricotte, slipping in and out of consciousness and suffering from internal hemorrhaging, died the following evening. Thirty-four at the time, she spent her final hours in a hospital that lacked basic equipment such as an X-ray machine or a full nursing staff, and in surroundings that white Americans would have regarded as substandard in the two white hospitals in the city.

Reaction was immediate. Derricotte's many activities and acquaintances meant that her death touched people across the country. E. Franklin Frazier, on the faculty at Fisk, mobilized protests both on the campus and in the community, and Langston Hughes was involved in similar efforts at Hampton. A freshman at Fisk in 1931, John Hope Franklin later recounted how Derricotte's death fit in with subsequent stories of the deaths of Charles Drew and Bessie Smith and the knowledge among African Americans that segregation led to the deaths of black Americans. Outrage went beyond the campus as African Americans followed the event in the black press; "Hospital Bars Dying Women," announced the *Norfolk Journal and Guide* the next week.[2]

Other responses were more muted. The *New York Times* made no mention of the medical treatment—or lack thereof—that Derricotte received. The white president of Fisk counseled waiting for a complete investigation to determine the full story. His initial efforts to uncover the events were continued by a white representative of the Commission on Interracial Cooperation (CIC), Arthur Raper, aided by the victim's brother, J. Flipper Derricotte. The YWCA cooperated with the CIC's efforts. Concerned that this report would be incomplete, Walter White undertook an inquiry for the NAACP and Du Bois published the results of both in the *Crisis*.[3]

Articles appeared not only in the publications of the CIC, NAACP, and YWCA, but also in the progressive and religious press, for example, the *Nation* and *Women and Missions*, as well as in black papers, such as the *New York Age* and the *Afro-American*.[4] Accounts of the tragedy varied dramatically. Stories, particularly those from African Americans, reported that doctors and the hospital had denied aid to Derricotte and Johnson. According to one account, the accident had been a hit-and-run and the white driver never stopped. In another, he demanded money for the damage to his car. Versions differed over how long it had taken for help to arrive and whether the young women would have survived had they been immediately taken to a hospital. The townspeople of Dalton disagreed amongst themselves as to whether their hospital would have refused the women medical treatment.

In the end, Ethel Gilbert, a white publicity officer for Fisk and a friend of Derricotte's, cut to the heart of the matter. Arriving in Chattanooga to be with Derricotte in her final hours, she reflected on what she saw. In a letter to a YWCA secretary, she noted bitterly, "If anybody makes a report that says in effect 'everything that could be done was done,' it means that everything that could be done for Negroes was done."[5] Derricotte's and Johnson's treatment starkly revealed the consequences of the "separate and unequal" system and pointed to the limitations of a strategy for racial adjustment that relied on educating individual whites, while accepting segregation.

"Clearing the Way for the Multitudes"

If late 1931 was the nadir in YW women's hopes for the effectiveness of interracial cooperation, their national convention the previous year had marked a high point. Both white and black women heralded the YWCA's 1930 national convention, held in Detroit, as representing a significant moment in race relations in the association and a model for the larger society. Years of hard work had allowed the "fellowship to pioneer in the establishment of more Christian relationships between the races." The some one hundred black women in attendance were "a natural part of the whole."[6] Helen A. Davis, now associate general secretary, reported to the Council on Colored Work that it was the first convention that "did not have some difficulty in some realm of understanding in regard to the interracial interpretation of our program." Mary Sims, white, and Cordella Winn, black, each noted that in all but two of the twenty-eight local delegations that had women of both races, "the women came as one delegation—living, working, and playing together."[7] Black women were leaders, as were white women, in discussion sessions. The Industrial Assembly selected Floria Pinkney, an African American garment worker from Brooklyn, to represent the assembly at the World YWCA's meeting to be held in Geneva, Switzerland, that summer. A white secretary praised the vote, describing the women as paying more attention to "the qualifications and experience" of the nominees than to "their color."[8] For her part, Winnifred Wygal, one of the white student secretaries, noted that the entire assembly sang "Negro Spirituals and the Negro National Anthem" ("Lift Every Voice and Sing") during an evening songfest.[9]

The significance extended beyond a week in Michigan. Elizabeth Ross

Haynes and Cordella Winn spoke of the vision provided to local associations of what was possible.[10] Eva Bowles (featured in the *New York World*) and Mary Sims (writing for the *Crisis*) educated a wider audience about the "naturalness" of interactions among women. Each stressed that she saw little "race consciousness" at the meeting. Sims observed that the "Negro delegates were seldom, if ever, seen in groups—at times two or three together, not more." On the one or two occasions that black women did meet by themselves, "to discuss such problems as the developing of leadership among Negro women," Sims was pleased to note that the women felt "as free to meet without fearing it to be called a segregated meeting as they felt in the many more instances free to be a part of a mixed gathering."[11] She continued that the "business of the convention and the more informal discussions were not concerned with the relations between the races at this particular convention." The concerns of black women and girls as well as race relations did arise, but largely as they affected (or were affected by) the key topics for the convention: the economy, the YMCA, peace, and religion. Black women were becoming a "natural" part of the organization.[12]

Eva Bowles reminded her colleagues and informed the public that the accomplishments at Detroit did not "just happen." They reflected "years of education and development of race relations in local Associations [and] the difficult and perplexing discussions within the National Council on Colored Work over a period of years." The progress, she said "gives one the buoyancy to travel with confidence and expectancy toward goals that are ever receding but clearing the way for the multitudes to follow."[13]

Both black and white women saw the process as necessarily slow. Perhaps implicitly criticizing those in the student division who were pushing for faster change, Sims told the readership of the *Crisis* that "Negro and white women alike seem to be learning the difficult lesson of building from experience to higher levels rather than the constant judging of immediate situations in the light of wished for ideal conditions."[14] While the student and industrial departments remained the "chronic irritant" for change on racial issues, the association faced the challenge of bringing the rest of the YWCA along, especially as students' and industrial women's participation in the YWCA declined relative to community YWs and more middle-class members.[15] Pioneers were a good educational device, but YW women needed to think about the larger membership, which saw race, at best, as one of only several issues facing the association.

Women at the 1930 convention focused on four challenges: the economy, relations with the YMCA, peace efforts, and the YWCA's identity as a religious organization. Economic difficulties came up in a variety of ways: individual women were having problems, communities were suffering, and the association faced financial cutbacks at the local and national levels. Members voted to support federal legislation to help the economy as they struggled with their own funding needs. Community difficulties produced escalating demands on associations, precisely as their own funds were decreasing. YWCAs found themselves developing relief efforts, not the preventive programs the association historically favored.[16] Ongoing competition with the YMCA did not make things better as the men continued to expand into areas and secure higher allocations from funders.[17] On the peace front—connected to their Christian internationalism and membership in a world fellowship of women—members were more sanguine. They had actively supported the successful campaign for the Kellogg-Briand peace pact, joining with others to submit some twelve thousand petitions to U.S. senators.[18] Despite continuing international tensions, American ratification of the treaty in 1928 encouraged the women about their ability to contribute to the resolution of international problems.

Religion was one of the most perplexing issues for members as they faced questions over the place of religion in their organization. Beginning in 1920, when the association had loosened the religious requirement for students, YWCAs increasingly favored a personal affirmation of faith, rather than formal church membership, as the basis for YW membership. Every national convention in the 1920s featured discussions about the topic; community YWCAs relaxed their requirement at the 1926 convention, the students followed with an even looser requirement in 1928, and now the cities were considering the same. Members who had supported moving from church membership to personal declarations defended the changes as promoting the religiosity of the organization. Women and girls needed to have an active, meaningful faith, not merely have joined a church, they explained. But even as they defined themselves as religious, the language and meaning of religion had changed dramatically. By 1928, student YWCAs no longer spoke of Jesus Christ as "our Lord and Saviour"; rather they sought "to understand Jesus and to follow Him." Community YWCAs were making a similar shift; their revised purpose would call for members to "understand Jesus, to share his love for all people, and to grow in the knowledge and love of God."[19]

YW women continued to evoke God and Jesus, but not in the way that evangelical Protestants of the nineteenth or early twentieth centuries had.[20] The emphasis upon personal faith and Jesus as a friend or leader, as well as the decline in the traditional religious activities (such as vespers and Bible classes) and the growing participation of non-Protestant women and girls in the organization, posed problems for the YWCA by the late 1920s. What exactly was Christian or even religious about it anymore? The YWCA faced challenges from conservative critics (including some YM men), but questions also came from those who were struggling with the meaning of religion in modern America more generally.[21] A committee established to evaluate the program of the National Board reported in 1930 that "over and over again there appeared in reports the emphasis on the need for help in religious thinking. Requests for help in religion [from local associations] would seem to constitute the greatest unmet need."[22]

One response some YW women gave was to say something to the effect that "why, everything that we do is religious."[23] But most acknowledged that this was not particularly satisfying; if everything they did was religious, religion had been watered down to nothing. Women throughout the organization were struggling for some sense of meaning in "this machine age," when old ways no longer satisfied. As the National Board put it, "[T]here is keen realization that progress has been greater in the interpretation of religion in terms of social action than the expression of it as a satisfying philosophy of life for the individual."[24] Religion permeated the 1930 convention in small discussion groups, debates on the floor of the convention, and in the addresses to delegates. In typical YW fashion, the 1930 convention addressed the question by passing a series of resolutions calling for "clarity of thought" about the matter. Delegates confirmed the importance of "a continuing search for a deeper understanding of Jesus," as well as the goals of "an ever more inclusive fellowship among women" and "establishing righteousness upon earth."[25] The combination reflected their longstanding link between personal faith and social activism. For much of the YWCA's history, women had legitimized their activities by describing them in religious terms. But the relation between individual faith and social salvation had quietly changed. Eva Bowles was not alone in her sentiments when she wrote in 1930 that "race relations is one powerful channel through which the values in Christianity are truly expressed."[26] In this formulation, social righteousness had shifted from being a consequence of women's religiosity to being proof of it.

YW leaders featured as one expression of Christianity and interracial cooperation the election of Juliette Derricotte to the National Board of the YWCA. She was chosen, Bowles explained, "solely upon her qualification and not because she was colored. This, to my way of thinking, clears away the sentimental approach on the part of whites toward Negro representation based upon color, and gives the Negro the courage to feel that one is chosen because of merit."[27] And Derricotte was certainly meritorious.

Juliette Aline Derricotte was the epitome of the "better class of negroes" to whom YWCA leaders sought to introduce white women in order to promote harmonious race relations. In the 1920s, Derricotte had served as a traveling secretary for college YWCAs. In that capacity she visited almost every African American college that had a YWCA and many white schools as well. Recognizing her abilities, the National Student Assembly had selected her as one of two African American delegates at the World's Student Christian Federation in England in 1924 and one of three delegates (of any race) to the 1928 conference in India. Following her time in India, Derricotte had conducted a lecture tour in several countries, including China and Japan. Derricotte had an international stature far above that of most YWCA women of any race. She left the YWCA in 1929 to be dean of women at Fisk University.

Derricotte had provided many white women with their first exposure to an educated black woman.[28] Her articles in the YWCA's *Womans Press* and women's missionary publications introduced her to an unknown number of YWCA members and churchwomen, while a smaller number knew her personally from conferences, interracial discussions on college campuses, or working with her. In a survey from the early 1930s on interracial issues, the anonymous white respondents reported that personal contact with notable African Americans, including Derricotte, had the "greatest power in changing attitudes [toward African Americans]."[29] At the same time, she was well liked and respected by the black women with whom she worked and served.

With Derricotte's election as the second black woman on the National Board, the Detroit convention saw the culmination of the strategy of interracial cooperation as modified throughout the 1920s. Exposed to refined, articulate black women, white women could be educated to recognize the former's abilities. Mutual understanding was possible as black and white women promoted racial adjustment and built the Kingdom of God. Women could work together on issues of mutual concern and lessen race consciousness. Insisting on interracial accommodations at its conventions, the YWCA went further than many groups, although it did not challenge segregation in local associations where law or custom made it necessary. All in all, YW women pointed to their organization as an important model for Americans about what was possible.

"To Substitute Justice for Kindness"

The Christian tropes of sin and suffering had provided ways for white and black women to make sense of race relations and their respective roles.

Throughout the 1930s, the idea of race prejudice as a sin continued, but some began to question the ease with which they were countenancing suffering. Following the 1930 convention, Lucy Slowe, dean of women at Howard University, told the Council on Colored Work, "Prejudice is harmful to both races. The white girls who are not taught to live with other races have their characters warped while the colored girls have their souls seared and their faith in Christianity as professed destroyed."[30] Permitting suffering to continue could destroy characters, if not souls, and was not always redemptive.

Focusing on sin and suffering kept interracial efforts tied to the feelings and actions of individual women, reflecting, in part, the individualistic orientation of Protestantism. Despite a language of social righteousness, people often treated race relations as simply personal matters. Lily Hammond had warned against white people's tendency to emphasize their "friendliness" to "the Negroes" rather than address their needs.[31] She criticized a belief that "individual kindness . . . to individual Negroes" fulfilled their Christian obligation.[32] In the 1930s, a white YW secretary reported on her work in a southern city that "one of the chief difficulties is getting white women to substitute justice for kindness."[33]

Derricotte's final hours foregrounded the issue of justice and the consequences of the social conditions for African Americans. Both the NAACP and the CIC reported on the kindness of the Dalton residents, particularly the attending physicians. But segregation was the result of the "social pattern of a community," not simply the attitudes of individual people.[34] The accident made it harder for white women to speak of segregation only in individual terms. It was not simply a humiliation that black women, as Christians, might be expected to endure and overcome.

In her diary the day of Derricotte's burial, Winnifred Wygal reflected on the loss of her friend and colleague. She commented that Derricotte had "told me a year ago that she had no business with that car. That it was her wicked pride which made her want to have a car so as to not have to sit 'Jim Crow' in Nashville streetcars." Wygal's description of the "racial torture" Derricotte endured after the accident suggests that she did not share Derricotte's self-assessment of being sinful.[35] Wygal's commitment to her friend prompted her to accept an assignment to go south to find out what had actually happened in Dalton. In writing to Leslie Blanchard, her supervisor, she suggested that "perhaps we use this terrible tragedy to open minds heretofore untouched on all racial relations."[36]

Within the YW, one group was prepared to take the next step. In December 1931, white members of the Headquarters Committee of the National Student Council not only issued a statement that decried Derricotte's death, but committed themselves "to an unremitting effort for a new and different civilization where segregation shall be abolished."[37] Although the women emphasized that they signed as individuals, not for the student council or the YWCA, it was the first public statement issued by a national YW body that explicitly named and criticized "segregation." Interracial cooperation—talks, study guides, meetings, meals—*had* changed these women.[38] But even they realized the difficulties of moving forward. In their discussions, some pointed out the danger that they might be "running too far ahead of our constituency."[39] In charging Wygal to investigate what had happened in Dalton, Blanchard had warned that despite efforts by herself and Anna Rice (now the general secretary of the YW), the National Board seemed unwilling to do much.[40] White women were by no means agreed that ending segregation was the YWCA's priority.

In the early 1930s, not surprisingly, economic problems resulting from the Great Depression were the focus of many of the YWCA's efforts. Financial constraints necessitated retrenchment at headquarters; from 1929 to 1932, the National Board saw budget cuts of 38 percent.[41] After outside evaluation, the YW abolished a departmental structure that was based on constituencies (industrial, colored, Girl Reserve, business and professional) in 1931. Replacing those structures were divisions that reflected the functions that national staff would carry out (research, advice to locals, leadership training) and the cut national staff positions.[42]

The reorganization had racial consequences. Due, in part, to the belief that race consciousness was preventing true racial progress, black staffers were distributed among the different divisions. Rather than head up the "colored secretaries" in the City Department, Eva Bowles was integrated into the research division, while Cordella Winn joined the division to assist local associations. A black woman, Marion Cuthbert, was subsequently hired by the leadership division. Grace Coyle, the executive of the research division, described the structure as fostering interracial efforts because "work among Negroes and whites is a common responsibility for both Negro and white staff and that responsibility should, therefore be carried on in interracial groups in which colored and white members are related to the total work." In addition, Coyle explained, integrating black women into these new divisions meant they could advise the general constituency on nonracial issues. Marion Cuthbert, for instance, was to be a "resource on educational method" for women of all races.[43] Bowles wrote key black YWCA leaders around the country to explain the arrangements, announcing that the decision was "a real achievement in an interracial set-up." Of particular value was that the change had come "naturally and without promotion." And, she added, there was a "release" now that the staff would be able to "face our problem as a whole instead of through departments."[44]

Very quickly problems arose. As part of restructuring, the Council on Colored Work was abolished; after all, if everyone was tackling race issues and race consciousness was a problem, then having a structure that focused on race was out of step. Yet, without the council, there appear to have been few channels for the black staff to raise racial or interracial problems.[45] When the National Committee on Public Affairs omitted any discussion of race issues from the agenda for the 1932 convention, Bowles did not find out until after the program was finalized.[46] For the first time in years, the YW did not allocate money to send Bowles to the CIC's annual meeting. By the time she discussed the issue with her supervisors, no conference money remained in the budget.[47] In addition, a study of the YWCA following the reorganization found that while white staff members did oversee programs for black women, the reverse was rarely the case.[48]

Perhaps the final straw for Bowles was that she apparently found herself reporting to people whom she had previously supervised, including her sister, Cordella Winn.[49] In April 1932, Bowles resigned her position. Fifty-seven at the time, and having worked for the YWCA for more than twenty years, Bowles left to work briefly for the National Colored Merchants Association; she then worked for the local black YWCA in Cincinnati until she turned sixty and retired. At the time, some in the black community perceived that the white leadership had forced Bowles out.[50] Fragmentary evidence reveals that some white women at the YW *had* found her difficult to work with. The National Board member who had chaired the Committee on Colored Work in the 1920s described Bowles as "a very militant type," while characterizing Winn as "more cooperative and pleasant."[51]

Fifty years later, Bowles's niece, Clarice Winn Davis, wrote that Bowles left when she realized that the reorganization "would diminish 'participation of Negroes in the policymaking' of the organization."[52] Since 1906, when she was the first paid secretary for a local association (New York), until 1932, Eva Bowles was the public face for the YWCA's national racial policies and practices. Her stated preference for a strategy to advance the race had black and white women working together, ideally on issues that did not always revolve around race. Her departure, coming shortly after Derricotte's death, marked the end of the era of interracial cooperation. Although members of the next generation of black women in the YWCA also aspired to a "nonracial" world and recognized the need to bring white women along, they would promote other strategies to clear the way for, as Bowles had once put it, "the multitudes to follow."

"Not Because It Is a Negro Question"

As the 1930s unfolded, the economic uncertainty facing Americans only became worse. Persuaded of the additional hardships that black Americans experienced, attendees at the 1932 convention in Minneapolis recommended that "the Association increase its efforts to secure for the Negro race enlarged economic opportunities" as part of the public affairs program.[53] But race issues were more explicitly addressed when delegates succeeded in bringing a resolution condemning lynching to the floor of the convention. With the "great economic pressure" of the Depression, racial violence was on the upswing. After almost a decade of declining figures, 1930 witnessed a tripling in the number of lynchings from the year before. In addition, lynchings in states like California and Maryland challenged the notion of it as a southern phenomenon.[54]

Small groups within the YWCA—a regional conference in 1918 and the Council on Colored Work in 1924—had previously spoken out about the problem, but the national body as a whole had never taken a stand. At the 1932 national convention, Sallie L. Hanna, a white Texan active with the Association of Southern Women for the Prevention of Lynching (ASWPL) and former president of the national YWCA, led the campaign for a resolution condemning lynching as "contrary to all ideals of government and religion." The resolution called for local associations "to foster right public opinion" to prevent "mob rule."[55]

YWCA women offered several reasons to condemn lynching. They argued that lynching had an effect upon the greater black community. As important to the white women was the impact that lynching had on their programs overseas and on white women (and children) at home. This combination of reasons meant that they talked about lynching not only as a "Negro" question or a southern problem, but as one that had an impact on all Americans. Frances Gunner of the Ashland Place branch in Brooklyn provided a context for the 1932 resolution. Condemning lynching, she explained, was as "fundamental" as "condemning war or unemployment." She urged passage "not because it is a Negro question, because it is not. It is a national question."[56] It was, however, an issue that affected African Americans and whites differently.

The members argued that the impact of lynchings on the African American community was twofold. The first, perhaps most obvious, was the danger and fear that all African Americans faced. "Negroes," wrote Frances Williams, a black member on the national staff, "live on in a world that does not insure physical safety."[57] Second, there was a spiritual danger, as Lucy Slowe had pointed out, because African Americans facing prejudice "have their souls seared and their faith in Christianity as professed destroyed."

Just as lynching, along with other forms of racial prejudice, threatened the Christian faith of African Americans at home, reports of lynching and racial violence in the United States were compromising the efforts of YWCA women overseas. Foreign work remained for YWCA women an important concern. Women worried about the impact of lynching on those programs. Lynching "brings contempt upon America as the only country where such crimes occur, discredits our civilization, and discounts the Christian religion around the globe," explained the sole representative for the state of Florida at the convention.[58] Their Christian internationalism meant that many of these white women were among the first Americans to see improving race relations as a national priority.

YW women also attempted to win support for their views and actions by explaining how racial practices affected white people. Those whites who condoned mob violence by their silence "must accept a share of its guilt," argued the white Floridian.[59] In a pamphlet for YWCA members on interracial matters, Gertrude Ware Bunce, a white member of the National Board, wrote, "When a man accused of a crime but not tried for it is burned at the stake, his few moments of suffering are as nothing compared to the moral degradation of the community."[60] Even more disturbing were the reports that women and children, "for whom we have a responsibility and a concern," attended lynchings.[61] As Lucy Slowe had put it, the flip side of blacks' doubting Christianity was that whites "have their characters warped."

With minimal discussion, members of the YWCA 1932 convention endorsed the resolution against lynching. In the ensuing years, the National Public Affairs Committee and local committees sought to educate members and the larger community about the issue and worked to prevent lynchings. The members of the YWCA were not alone in these activities. Members of the CIC, churchwomen (especially with the Southern Methodist mission movement), and the white women of the newly formed ASWPL joined forces to eradicate lynching. Overlapping membership tied these groups together.

Founded in 1930, the ASWPL, for instance, mobilized networks of women from both local YWCAs and church groups to publicize lynchings and urge local officials to act to prevent them. In turn, the YWCA publicly endorsed the ASWPL.[62]

Different groups opposed lynching for different reasons. In her study of interracial cooperation between white and black churchwomen, Mary Frederickson has pointed out that some white women who were opposed to social welfare programs or civil rights for African Americans came out against lynching.[63] Others have observed that a statement against lynching was relatively inexpensive compared to providing funds for ongoing programs.[64] Those interested in law and order, including ultraconservatives, argued that no matter how great "the crime which causes lynching, the crime of lynching was greater . . . for it lynches the law and the sovereignty of the state."[65] The range of support is strikingly demonstrated by the fact that, at the 1932 national convention, the proposal against lynching came from local women, many of whom were southerners. This was despite (or actually because) the New York-based national staff members had resisted placing the proposal before the convention, arguing that not enough education had been done and fearing that the proposal would fail. White and black leaders at the national level recognized that they and some local YW leaders were "ahead of the rank and file in the Association and the community" and frequently advised going slowly.[66] In this case, they apparently underestimated the will of the organization.

To Break Down "the Barriers of Race"

Preparing for the 1934 national convention in Philadelphia, black and white women in New York met to discuss whether "the time [has] come when the national Association and the National Board should have a stated policy on race."[67] Delegated to prepare a brief outline of the "objectives of the YWCA considered in relation to its Interracial Work," Henrietta Roelofs (white) and Marion Cuthbert (black) defined the YW as "idealistic," "practical," and "experimental." From these premises, they proposed that the YWCA seek the "inclusion of Negroes in the entire Association life and program in the same manner as other members."[68] Part of what made such inclusion possible, Cuthbert explained in the ensuing discussion, was the similarity between the races. She spelled it out for her colleagues: "Time and again, Negro and white people try to locate something that shall make Negroes stand out as distinctly different people—Negro art, Negro something. You do not have anything essentially different in American Negro culture."[69] The issue for black YW women was not assimilating into white culture, but getting white Americans to recognize that American culture, along with true Christianity, was not race-based.

Most northern white board and staff members in the meeting doubted that the organization was prepared to go as far as the "inclusion of Negroes . . . in the same manner as other members." Mary Billings French, chair of the executive committee, expressed concern that no white southern women were present to weigh in and worried that that group was feeling like a beleaguered minority. For her part, Emma Bailey Speer, president of the National Board, suggested it might be possible to win agreement, but the association would have to undertake a program of education. "If," she told her colleagues, "we could carry on intelligent, accurate, scientific education through articles and studies and eventfully bring out good books on the subject, we would then be fulfilling one of our functions as a Christian organization."[70]

Lillian Alexander, an African American on the National Board, politely but firmly challenged French and Speer. "We have been working on this problem more or less sincerely and directly for almost twenty-five years and I wonder if we intend to go any further along. Just writing more pamphlets, talking more—how long?" As for the "minority in the South," she went on, "there comes a time when one must use the force of majorities. With the 99.98 percent majority why should we fail to do what each one of you says is the right thing to do?" She then warned white women that change was in the air. A new generation of African Americans was not going to be as accommodating as hers; "I do not see how the Negroes have kept loyal to American white people for so long, but how much longer will we remain that? We older ones who have felt this loyalty are dying off."[71]

As the convention drew close, the committee ensured that a series of articles appear in the association's magazine to prepare the membership to take some action at the convention, including a "Symposium on Race" with four white southern women.[72] Louise Young, based in Nashville, but a member of the National Board, advised the readers that to come to a proper appreciation of the "brotherhood of man as it touches race . . . [m]ost of us . . . have to be born again if we are to enter the Kingdom. This rebirth of the spirit most often comes as a religious experience."[73] The Public Affairs Committee also polled white southern women for their reactions to the goal of "inclusion." Rose H. Quinn, a Georgia woman, declared her personal support for the statement, but emphasized that "not enough of the membership [was] committed to interracial cooperation in [Georgia] to justify even a statement." It would be better to move the membership along before taking such a position. A group of white southern leaders meeting in North Carolina was even more adamant, refusing to present the idea to their local boards, arguing that "we would kill off 95% of the Southern Associations." The only positive note that the white national staff member, herself "born and raised in the South," could find was that ten years earlier the women would not have even discussed the topic "and certainly not with such calmness."[74]

In the end, the women at headquarters managed to develop a "guiding principle" that was vague enough to speak to Roelofs' and Cuthbert's proposal, but not produce immediate opposition from more conservative women. The board introduced it to the convention more as an expression of the association's "religious commitment" than as statement on race. For the following biennium, locals "should continue to work for the building of a society nearer to the Kingdom of God." The first step was trying "to create within the Association a fellowship in which the barriers of race, nationality, class, education and social status are broken down in pursuit of the common objective of a better life for all." Recognizing both the constraints from the larger community as well as the potential for YWCAs to serve as a model for others, the board added that locals should also attempt "to create an understanding of this objective in the community."[75]

But even as they relied on time-honored ideas of education, understanding, and fellowship, YWCA members took an important step at the convention that distinguished them from many other whites: they endorsed *federal* antilynching legislation.[76] As a result, the National Public Affairs Committee would issue educational materials explaining how local associations could lobby their congressman, and various locals went on record as favoring the federal legislation.[77] Representatives of the National Board would also testify on behalf of the YWCA before Congress for the Costigan-Wagner Act.[78] In campaigning against lynching, white women continued to rely on a belief in the harmony of interests between whites and African Americans. Increasing racial violence forced some white women to consider whether the federal government was needed to solve some race problems.

In contrast, Jessie Daniel Ames and the ASWPL never supported federal antilynching laws, relying instead on education. Federal legislation, Ames believed, was at best ineffective; at worst, it alienated southerners. The divergent attitudes toward the federal government's role reflected differences in the racial and regional composition of their memberships. The YWCA included white and black women, northerners and southerners, in contrast to the ASWPL, which was limited to southern white women. The presence of northern white and black women, as well as southern black women, influenced the YWCA's choice of strategies and the willingness to adopt a strategy that many, though not all, southern white women opposed.[79]

Antilynching laws became the opening wedge for white women in the association to add legislation to the already tried and true tactics of cooperation and education to address race problems. At the 1934 convention, the membership also called for the support of federal policies to aid in interracial cooperation and to help African Americans gain economic and "basic civil rights."[80] YWCA public affairs committees at both the local and national levels worked to put such mandates into effect, conducting studies of local civil rights conditions and encouraging members to lobby for governmental action.[81]

Even these actions, however, did not represent a frontal assault on segregation. The resolution to "encourage and support the federal government in policies of interracial cooperation" referred to the problem of "separation," deliberately drawing back from using the word "segregation."[82] Alexander may have been right that the majority of national white leaders supported institutional change, but they still differed on how to move the larger organization—a reflection of deliberate choices in selecting national leaders.[83] Was the best policy to be out in front of locals? How far out could they afford to be? When did it make sense to stop and try to help those who were not as advanced to catch up? Every discussion that addressed racial issues—ranging from the public affairs agenda to the question of whether to hold the national convention in the South—bumped against these questions.

Black women in the organization were concerned not only by what appeared to be the delay tactics ("more pamphlets?"), but by the expansion of segregation to northern cities. While some southern YWCAs were making progress, associations in "New England" or the "North" were adopting more restrictive policies (sometimes worse than what was found in southern cities that had hashed an issue out); the "bi-racial pattern" was "no longer characteristic only of the South, but [had] invaded northern communities," observed Cordella Winn. In addition, the economic situation was increasing racial tensions everywhere.[84] Speaking before the 1934 convention, Mary McLeod Bethune observed that attitudes would need to change before any of the proposed measures would be effective. Pointing to discrimination right there in Philadelphia's hotels, she told the women, "The Y.W.C.A. needs to speed up its action and get some backbone. We are tired of you women putting the entire responsibility for existing conditions on the shoulders of Southern Women."[85]

Despite the number of cities where black women served on citywide boards of directors, segregated associations continued in most cities, North and South.[86] National conventions were supposed to have interracial accommodations, but such guarantees did not even exist for other meetings, such as conferences of city secretaries or business and professional women.[87] Some groups, particularly those meeting outside the South, experimented with fully integrated meetings—a group of industrial women in Indianapolis or a group of the YWCA's high school girls in Colorado—but these remained the activities of a few rather than the majority.[88] Black women in and out of the YWCA emphasized that it had far to go to break down the "barriers of race."

Ultimately, the YWCA's (and others') efforts on behalf of federal antilynching laws failed.[89] They were more effective at the local and state level. Frances Williams pointed to successes in localities from Maryland to California in educating communities about the harm caused by lynchings.[90] Lynching declined over the decade, particularly in those areas where local women's groups had been active.[91] While supporting legislation, YW women never abandoned educational efforts. After Pennsylvania passed a civil rights law in September 1935, Williams developed an analysis of the bill to be shared with locals to educate them on its implications. "It applied only to public places and therefore no man pushes on any one's private life those he does not wish to include," she reassured women. But women needed to do more than study the bill for themselves; they needed to talk to others in the state and "enlist the active interest in keeping Pennsylvania from giving way to hysteria."[92] Having lived through the failure of Prohibition, women in the YWCA were aware that it was necessary to build support for laws even after they passed.

"Not in the Midst of Things"

Throughout the 1930s, white and black members of the YWCA reported on their involvement with the political programs of the New Deal. They continued to work with the WJCC to lobby for legislation as well as the inclusion of women in government positions—for women to be active citizens.[93] They noted with pride those staff and board members holding elected or appointive office, both nationally and locally. In 1932, President Herbert Hoover had selected longtime National Board member Mary Woolley for the American delegation to an international conference on disarmament in Geneva.[94] In 1938, Crystal Bird Fauset, a former staff member for programs for young girls, was the first African American woman elected to a state legislature (Pennsylvania).[95] Numerically more significant were the large numbers of women moving back and forth between lower-level positions in agencies such as the Works Progress Administration and the National Youth Administration and the YWCA.[96] So many women had gone from the YW to the Women's Bureau that one YW staffer referred to the bureau as the "graduate school" of the association.[97]

As such, the YWCA sounds much like many of the other women's voluntary associations that were critical to the creation of the American welfare state.[98] The YWCA corporately, and members individually, joined with others, but by the 1930s the YWCA did not have the national stature that it had had during World War I. In 1933, Henrietta Roelofs, a white staff member active with the YWCA's social agenda, wrote to Mary Dreier, a National Board member, and Lucy Randolph Mason, a former YW staffer, expressing concern that Secretary of Labor Frances Perkins did not really know much about the YW. Asking their assistance in drawing Perkins's attention to the YWCA's ability to provide assistance for programs for unemployed women, Roelofs concluded her letter to Dreier, almost wistfully, "I feel that the Y.W.C.A. is not in the midst of things as perhaps we ought to be."[99]

Accounting for the diminishing importance of the YWCA is complicated. A general societal belief that women's organizations were passé did not help. The extent to which people thought it was an auxiliary of the relatively apolitical YMCA also hurt. Ongoing financial crises lessened its visibility and effectiveness. An era that associated reform with secularism also rendered it less important.[100] What also seems to have been a factor was its identity as an interracial organization that gave it some stature but may have affected its ability to be a political player in 1930s America.

The YWCA supported the legislative efforts for racial justice, including antilynching bills, favored by groups like the NAACP and the National Council of Negro Women (NCNW). Because of their institutional autonomy, white women in the YWCA had some leeway that many other white women active with the New Deal did not. The white women tied to the Roosevelt administration remained constrained by the political limits on FDR. Despite the influence of Eleanor Roosevelt, for instance, that network of white reformers never publicly backed the federal antilynching laws, although many, if not most, personally favored the laws.[101] Virginia Foster Durr, a white southern woman, wrote of the early support of the Women's Division of the Democratic National Committee (DNC) for legislation to outlaw the poll tax; she remembered that Jim Farley, the chairman of the DNC, went to Franklin Roosevelt, saying, "You've got to shut up these damn women in the Democratic Committee because it's making trouble on the Hill with the Southern senators and congressmen." And the women withdrew their public support. White women associated with the Democratic Party worked closely with the white men of the New Deal even as they criticized them; increasingly, their power came from a connection to prominent white men, rather than to women.[102]

Most of the issues that YWCA women supported in the 1930s and 1940s—passage of federal antilynching laws, establishment of a permanent fair employment practices commission, the extension of social security coverage to domestic workers, and an end to poll taxes—went down to defeat in those years. In establishing their significance, then, black and white women in the YWCA were limited if they relied on conventional political yardsticks. They focused instead on their identity as a cross section of the society that was pioneering on the racial front.

Part of the difference between how white and black women balanced being both a cross section and pioneers had to do with the importance of the association in their lives. National white YW women often spoke of the opportunities to express their religious commitment through corporate action, and social action through the YW was a way to do that.[103] Many on the national staff and National Board had been involved with the YWCA for decades. Yet, for the most part, white women associated with the YWCA, even the national leaders, were never as nationally known as women like Molly Dewson, Frances Perkins, and Florence Kelley. Although a few, such as Mary Woolley, achieved prominence outside the YWCA, more often YW leaders like Mabel Cratty or Emma Bailey Speer developed their standing as representatives of the YW. As the YWCA became identified as an interracial organization, and race became more important in American society, speaking on behalf of an interracial group gave them legitimacy in the larger political arena. They needed African American women's continuing presence in their association, however, in order to have this authority.

In comparison, African American women who were active with the YWCA appear to have been relatively more prominent than their white counterparts.[104] It truly was a place, Cordella Winn reported on the eve of her retirement, where white women had the "opportunity to know the best group of Negroes."[105] Black women who went on in politics, such as Crystal Bird Fauset, or were subsequently active with other organizations, including Dorothy Height, had spent substantial time in the YWCA.[106] Describing local women, Winn declared that "practically every Negro woman worker in Negro social institutions or agencies had at one time been a Y.W.C.A. worker."[107] For many of them, it was still one of the few opportunities to be in an interracial women's organization.

Others found hope in a group where white women were beginning to make connections between a personal approach to race relations and a more systemic one. Representing the generation following Winn, Juanita Saddler, an African American student staff member, pointed to the importance of a 1932 YWCA seminar of white women who understood the relation "between economics, religion, and race." No longer were YW meetings places where white women merely commented "plaintively about its being the first time they knew there were educated Negroes."[108] After years of resisting legislative efforts to advance racial issues, in the 1930s, the YWCA rapidly expanded the race-related legislation on its agenda. Alongside support for telling the government to take on these issues, however, was the slow pace at which white women in the YWCA were prepared to take on racial issues—and especially segregation—within the association itself.

"Preserving the Association's Cross-section Character"

Throughout the decade, women in the YWCA tried to balance being an inclusive fellowship with the fact that many popular programs were for more homogeneous subsets—students, industrial women, African Americans. Such groups were necessary, the National Board pointed out to the 1936 national convention, "in helping diverse elements to feel at home in the Association . . . while preserving the Association's cross-section character" and giving the association the "basis for dealing effectively with social conditions affecting its varied constituency." No one objected to the idea that "age and occupation should be recognized as the major bases for grouping the constituency." Questions did arise, however, about groups based on race and nationality. The National Board's report to the convention, held in Colorado Springs, recommended that the YWCA also recognize that nationality "should also be recognized as the basis for grouping in communities where conditions and numbers warrant it," while race "as a basis for grouping should be recognized as valuable under some circumstances, but should be scrutinized to discover if it tends to segregation."[109] Years of questioning from black women on the National Board and staff, as well as the activities of students and industrial women, had finally paid off in getting the board to present to the membership a formulation that explicitly identified *segregation* as something to be questioned. The committee charged with bringing the National Board's recommendations to the floor of the convention, however, reworded the proposal, combining the two to read "Nationality and race should also be recognized as a basis for grouping in those communities where conditions and numbers warrant it." Significantly, the committee on the report was made up of representatives of local associations drawn from all the regions of the country and included no one from the National Board.[110]

As debate emerged at the convention, a number of issues arose. Those particularly associated with "nationality groups" argued that "race" and "nationality" were not parallel categories and did not present the same challenge to the membership. But the bulk of the discussion was on whether omitting the criticism of segregation was appropriate. Representing the southern region, Elizabeth C. Scott (Mrs. Frederic R. Scott II), of Richmond, Virginia, urged leaving out the passage, arguing, "We all know that understanding and sympathy between the races have never been achieved by legislation. It has been tried and it has failed." It was important that the association allow for different viewpoints and "proceed by the best educational methods, not by too much pressure toward the eventual fulfillment of our purpose." Delegates seemed relatively united on a statement of general principle that "in all cases these groupings look toward the progressive inclusion of individuals and groups into full fellowship of the Association." It was the word "segregation" that seemed most problematic. Edith Sawyer of the national staff wondered if it was "a technical word which means one thing in the North and another in the South. . . . Perhaps we could use the idea if we changed the word." In the end, those who advocated for the word won; by a vote of 379 to 152, the section was amended to read "both nationality and race should also be recognized as the basis for groupings in those communities where conditions and numbers warrant it, but such groups should be scrutinized to discover if they tend toward segregation." Speaking on behalf of the change, noticeably, were white students and representatives of northern cities; it is less clear whether some southern women also accepted the provision with the idea that "where conditions and numbers warrant" groups gave them breathing room.[111]

The inclusion of the word "segregation" in a statement of "guiding principles" was significant. Two implications increasingly became issues for the organization in the decade to follow. Black women, speaking on behalf of scrutinizing separate groupings, observed that questioning the purpose of black branches could slow down the work in those communities. Celestine Smith, an African American on the national staff, noted that white women still conceived of the work as programs "for," not "with," black women. She went on, black women were beginning to say, "We aren't a service group over here on this side any more. We are a group of women who want to work side by side with a group that can work side by side with us."[112] Black women of Addie Hunton's day had accepted segregated YWs as the price of getting any facilities in their community; three decades later black YW women were questioning that bargain.

And that questioning pointed to the other critical implication of the resolution on segregation—that YW women began to look at the YWCA not simply as the solution to race problems, but as a location for problems. Without minimizing earlier decisions to foster right opinion, oppose lynching, or urge civil rights legislation, demanding that YWCA women change their own organization was potentially more controversial. Reviews of the YWCA's employment practices, for instance, revealed that black women were paid less for the same work. The suggestion that perhaps this was because black women were not as qualified was subsequently discredited in a Russell Sage–sponsored survey that determined that black women who worked for the association were more qualified *and* paid less than white women.[113] Black women rebuked their white colleagues by observing that the real cause for lower pay was "the feeling on the part of many [white] people that it does not cost the Negro so much to live."[114] It was not a feeling that stood up to the light of reasoned examination.

Throughout the 1930s, the national YW conducted several studies of the association, attempting to determine general practices at the local and national levels as well as the relation between the two parts. The studies were intended to standardize practices and policies, with a particular emphasis on promoting democracy at all levels. One part of *The Standards Study* was an investigation of the branch structure. National staffers were alarmed to discover that 40 percent of the branches studied barred black women from voting for association leadership. They reminded locals that the only nationally permissible requirement for voting members was the religious requirement; preventing black women from voting was "unconstitutional." The study also noted that any association limiting membership to white women and girls was "automatically disaffiliated from the national organization."[115] There appear to have been no efforts to carry through on the threat; presumably local associations modified the wording without necessarily the practice.

By the late 1930s, then, an uneasy balance existed in the YWCA. Women from a variety of perspectives continued to speak of Christian fellowship and the need for democracy in and out of the association. They remained committed to building the Kingdom of God. But agreements about segregation or going only "as far as both the white and colored groups are agreed to go together" were coming undone. The branch structure itself was being questioned: was it a way into the fellowship or a permanent barrier? On these matters, the majority of YW members could not agree on a policy. A new wave of criticism from outside the association only heightened the tensions.

In the 1920s, most attacks had focused upon the YWCA's support for workers' rights, peace, and internationalism. Increasingly, racial issues became a focus of the conservative critique of the YWCA. In 1930, a president general of the DAR had criticized a YW and YM conference where the "Communistic principles of atheism, sex freedom, and race equality were openly taught."[116] In the mid-1930s, the self-described "Super-Expert-Patriot," Elizabeth Kirkpatrick Dilling, published two books on the communist threat to America, *The Red Network* (1934) and *The Roosevelt Red Record* (1936), both of which included the YWCA's interracial projects on her lists of dangers facing the country. She asserted that any "intermingling" would lead to efforts for "social equality" and claimed that "Red propaganda" from the YWCA's National Board was "advocating mixture of colored and whites in social affairs and swimming pools."[117]

While the YWCA got off relatively lightly in the two volumes, Dilling consolidated her findings in a 1939 pamphlet entitled *Should Christians Support the Y's?* With only a few comments about the YM, she saved her energies for the YW. The YW's efforts to foster a religion that entailed "working toward a better social order" revealed the YWCA as one of "Moscow's henchmen." Attempting to educate "sincere" Christians about the "Anti-Christian Communist activities" of the YWCA so they would stop supporting it, she identified red flags ranging from the Industrial Department's inclusion of the "Internationale" on a songsheet and students' opposition to ROTC, to the endorsement of birth control and the YWCA's general "Inter-racial Propaganda." Summing up, she advised, "the word 'Christian' in Young Women's Christian Association should either be dropped or changed to 'Communist.'"[118]

Elizabeth Dilling was a woman with a cause, as well as the financial means to further it. She and her compatriots pointed with alarm to the growing popularity of the Communist Party throughout the decade, but their focus was alerting Americans to the dangers posed by groups that the general public did not realize were "red" and, therefore, supported. Dilling's charges had the most effect on the YW when released prior to fundraising campaigns, and local associations were wary about the attacks. One can sense the relief of the secretary from Waukegan, Illinois, in 1936, when she reported to the National Board that "as far as I know only one person accused us of being Communist" during their annual fundraising campaign.[119]

In the minds of its critics, the YWCA's combination of a female fellowship, political activism, and religious liberalism was proof positive that the association was red-dominated and areligious. YW women *and* their conservative opponents made connections between race, religion, and women's activism, although they drew very different conclusions about how to evaluate those links. The YWCA tried to stand its ground against the attacks, changing—or attempting to change—the terms of the debate. Theresa Wilber Paist, president of the YWCA, wrote local presidents in the mid-1930s that it was essential for them to be prepared to "interpret more adequately" the YWCA's purpose and program to their communities. It was, she wrote, "the Christian liberalism of the Association" that was under fire. Over and over, she laid claim to the YWCA as a Christian (not simply religious) organization.[120] And as such, members were obligated to address social and economic issues. Paist and other YW women used a Christian discourse to defend themselves against an anticommunist one. Even when they were successful, it required constant education of the larger community about what the YWCA was doing and why.

❖ ❖ ❖

Juliette Derricotte's death in 1931 became part of a larger story in the African American community about the hazards of racial segregation.[121] For many *white* YWCA women, Derricotte had represented their major, if not only, exposure to an educated black woman and they too were distressed by the events. But the 1920s' principle that the solution to race problems lay in the minds of *individuals* left them unprepared to handle the full implications of a racially segregated *social system.*

Until the 1930s, white interracialists did not question segregation as they promoted racial adjustment. Whatever the individual views of the black women who stayed with the YWCA, they too had not *publicly* challenged segregation. In the winter of 1919–20, when Catharine Lealtad had been refused accommodations at the YWCA in Des Moines, Eva Bowles had not backed her. Times had changed; as Lillian Alexander advised her colleagues, many no longer felt loyalty to the old ways. Juliette Derricotte might have worried that avoiding "Jim Crow" was a sign of "wicked pride." Other black women saw pride as a matter of human dignity rather than sin. As a national student secretary, Frances Williams insisted that black students not ride in Jim Crow cars; for one conference, she chartered an entire Pullman car so the students could travel "in keeping with their dignity and life." It was, she also reported, the only time she ever had trouble with white colleagues over money.[122]

By then, Williams was advising the National Board (not just the student division) on interracial issues. Assisting on the arrangements for the 1938 convention (to be held in Columbus, Ohio), she suggested to Lillian Alexander that rather than the YWCA's working out private arrangements with hotels to ensure equitable treatment for the black delegates, they might be better off testing Ohio's civil rights law. She urged that "we . . . be ready to regard any delegate so involved as a person who is helping the laws of our country to function rather than someone who is stirring up trouble."[123] Williams knew full well that engaging in court cases was even more alarming to association women than were legislative efforts, but she was no Eva Bowles, nor even Juliette Derricotte. Justice required more than whites to be kind or African Americans to turn the other cheek. At stake was not only the meaning of sisterhood, but competing conceptions of Christian citizenship and American democracy.

7 Struggling over Segregation

IN 1941, CHARLOTTE MACCRACKEN joined the staff of the YWCA in Elizabeth, New Jersey, as its Secretary for Business and Industrial Girls. Late that year, she reported to the board of directors on a meeting of the "Senior Business Girls" club. Members of the club were white working women, in their early to mid-twenties, who held jobs in nonindustrial occupations such as clerical work or retail sales. MacCracken exemplified the YW's professional staff who sought to work *with* members, not tell them what to do. She reported, "Much of the business session was centered around the discussion of the suggested minstrel show in October. Although the members had been told it was against Y.W.C.A. policy they still felt very keenly on the matter. After some discussion and some statements made by the Secretary as to this policy in other cities, the minstrel show was dropped."[1] Although MacCracken's report was short and written in an impersonal third-person voice, it reveals her discomfort in trying to get the "girls" to do the right thing without having to forbid the activity herself.

In her follow-up, MacCracken stated her satisfaction that things had worked out, reporting that the club had held "a Kitchen-Hat Party" instead. She described the event where "each member came wearing a hat created out of some kitchen implement. This party took the place of the suggested minstrel and the Secretary was pleased that the members seem to have as much fun as they had anticipated from the minstrel show."[2]

Located in northeastern New Jersey, Elizabeth was an industrial city with a population of about 110,000. With African Americans comprising 4 percent of that figure, the city was not large enough to support a separate branch for

African American women and girls. Instead, as in cities with similar demographics, the YWCA conducted activities on a segregated basis with separate clubs for black and white women and girls. In such cases, African Americans were found in some programs and clubs more than others. Nationally, for instance, 20 percent of participants in the YW's industrial departments were African American, while only 6 percent of business and professional members were.[3]

White women and girls had been performing minstrel shows in the Elizabeth YWCA almost since its inception in 1920.[4] By 1941, the context for them had changed. While minstrel shows remained a popular form of amateur entertainment across the country, the conflict over them in Elizabeth pointed to a growing debate within the YWCA over the definition of American democracy. At their national convention the previous year, YW women had reaffirmed their traditional idea of democracy as self-governance. With almost no discussion, members approved a recommendation from those responsible for *The Standards Study* that "program groups be recognized as self-governing responsible units."[5] But, at the same time, Mary Billings French, president of the YWCA, speaking of democracy as a guiding "emphasis" for the association, reminded the women that "concern for the rights of minority groups is [also] characteristic of democracy."[6]

Whatever their idea of democracy, YW women almost inevitably linked it to Christianity. It was not simply that democracy was a way to promote Christianity, although they made that connection. In describing the emphasis on democracy, the National Board explained that it was "the true method of achieving corporate Christian goals."[7] The issue for these women was the way in which the two were fused. In its "Emphases" for future work, the board argued that the "democratic process" was an expression "of one of the fundamental teachings of Christianity—the worth of the individual."[8] Discussions on any issue for the YW, then, easily shifted between the political and the theological. In particular, debates in the 1940s over racial policies that kept African Americans on the margins of association life were couched in both democratic and religious terms.

Throughout the decade, the debates focused upon segregation in the YWCA at both the national and local levels, in the South and in the North, and in areas with large minority populations and those with small ones; finally the culmination arrived in 1946 when the association passed its Interracial Charter. With that act, the YWCA broke the identification forged in the YWCA more than a quarter of century earlier: that segregation was compatible with Christian sisterhood, racial justice, and American democracy. The changes in the YWCA itself were significant, but so too were those in the larger society: the impact of World War II, the early years of the cold war, and decolonization prompted a societal appreciation for American internationalism. Changes in policy and practices within the YWCA resonated with shifts in the ways that many white Americans came to think about race relations.

"An Inclusive, Christian, Democratic Fellowship"

At the 1940 convention, the National Board proposed—and members accepted with almost no discussion—that the "major emphases" for the next time period should be: "the Christian Purpose," "Democracy," and "World Community." It is hard to imagine someone speaking against any of these, but disagreements did arise over the ensuing resolutions. By far, the greatest amount of time was given to the developing world war. Members engaged in a passionate debate between pacifists, who favored keeping the United States out of the conflict, and interventionists, who advocated lifting the arms embargo on Great Britain. The interventionists won, although the pacifists gained a victory by getting the convention to condemn compulsory military training.[9] Women on both sides saw themselves as part of a world community *and* as advocates for world peace. The pacifists, for instance, argued for peace on the grounds of internationalism rather than isolationism. Representing the pacifist view, Harriet White of Bates College argued, "I really and truly want peace for the United States, not only for the United States but because I feel that the United States at peace means a better world."[10] And likewise, the interventionists combined a commitment to peace with their internationalism. Mrs. Robert Miles, of Kentucky, speaking on behalf of keeping options open (including lifting the arms embargo on Great Britain), spoke of it as a necessary step in working toward "a just peace" after the war.[11]

Delegates faced other questions as well. Although they adopted the general recommendations of the standards study as a matter of course, the delegates discussed at greater length the implications for local associations. Arguing that "democratic management" called for "broadly representative" boards of directors, the committee presenting the study recommended that locals see to it that *their* boards were representative. Members reported on how they ensured the elections of industrial and business girls to boards, but quickly moved to the issue of race. Beulah (Mrs. A. E.) Bowie, a member of the black branch in Houston, pointedly asked, "[H]ow long are we going to have people do things for us. When shall we begin to do them for ourselves?" For her part, Elizabeth C. Scott (white) of Richmond observed that her association was one of two in the South with an African American on its board. But, she continued, this was an issue that southern associations were agonizing over. If southern associations did not live up to the ideal, but worked on interracial programs and common concerns, she wanted "the convention to realize that there is integrity in what we are trying to do."[12]

Scott's formulation captured well the position of many southern white women (and some northern ones). Many agreed with the large goals (e.g., to build an inclusive fellowship), but stressed limits to translating those goals into practice. They asked that the convention accept that they were acting in good faith, albeit slowly. This concern was not limited to southern women. Mary Clayton (Mrs. Ralph) Earle of Philadelphia advised the delegates, "We all like to be pioneers, but sometimes we pioneer so far ahead that we are not followed closely enough by our constituency. We are also responsible to our communities."[13] White women at the 1940 convention were prepared to grant white sisters the benefit of the doubt. Mary Noel Arrowsmith, national staff member and on the standards study commission, clarified for the convention that "nobody" thought that the recommendations would go into effect overnight.[14]

For their part, black YW women made public the difficult position they were facing: Myra Jones (Mrs. Henry C.) Bryant, the first black member of the National Board from a southern association (Birmingham), spoke to a resolution on the relation between branches and central associations. Bryant observed that there "was a great deal said about the difficulty which our white members face in the South working out their method of participation of all groups in the Association." She continued, "[I]t seems there has not been any thought about the difficulties which the Negro woman faces also in the South, in this method of participation. She has to work just as carefully and tread just as silently as her white sister in the South, because we have a constituency, too, which is talking and thinking about what we do." Black women valued the "inclusive, Christian, democratic fellowship" of the YWCA. If, Bryant concluded, white women needed to be shown how to get to that goal, black women were willing to lead the way.[15]

As was frequently the case, it was students who also raised the topic of race. Rachel Good, representing the Student Assembly of YWCAs, presented a resolution urging that the associations, both nationally and locally, recognize that the YWCA's "belief in co-operative relationships" required the "ultimate elimination of all segregation."[16] By the time Mrs. George H.

Wood, chairman of the Committee on Resolutions, presented the resolution to the entire membership for consideration, it had been changed. The revised resolution commended the students for their efforts and called for the National Board "to appoint a commission to gather up the experiences of local Associations on the effects of segregation and discrimination in the Association and in community life, and to report their findings to the next convention."[17] Delegates approved the resolution without debate. It was but a study; there had been several in the preceding years. They usually took longer than anyone planned; investigating bodies customarily couched the final reports in language that accommodated almost everyone; and the national body had virtually no means of enforcing anything.[18]

On the last day, a group of delegates jocularly summed up the actions taken at the 1940 convention in a poem that concluded with the lines:

> We want national help and also minority rights,
> And boy-friends to take us out on Saturday nights.
> But of all the things which we are now asking for,
> The main one is this: That we all don't want war.
> If what we have sketched for this on-coming triennium
> Is done, don't you think it will bring the millennium?[19]

Convention attendees laughed and applauded, but their worldwide Christian woman movement was facing internal and external strains. Even the assurance of a divine plan was not going to ease the upcoming challenges.

"Toward the Same Ultimate Christian Goal"

Whatever their hesitancies had been about the war, YWCA women, individually and as a group, supported the war once the United States entered it in December 1941. As with the First World War, the Second brought mixed blessings. After years of fiscal cutbacks, the national association was able to expand programs; its budget increased fivefold from 1940 to 1945 (the national group alone spent about $4,850,000 in that last year).[20] The expansion of jobs for white women and minorities in the labor force was of great satisfaction, as was the entrance of women into the armed forces.[21] As in World War I, the YWCA joined other voluntary associations to provide assistance to servicemen and women (through the United Service Organizations) and to communities (through the American War-Community Services)—the only agency in both.[22] Although the YWCA did not see the dramatic expansion of permanent programs in the short run that it had seen in World War I, it was able to sponsor programs (and gain attention) in smaller cities and towns where finances had prevented it from expanding. Relying on monies raised nationally, rather than only local support, it also experimented with community planning efforts and interracial programs.

While proud of their achievements, women mourned the direct casualties of war—the "deep wounds of civilization" that it inflicted.[23] Included in those was the increase in racial violence that accompanied the war: race riots, lynchings, and discrimination. Like others fighting for civil rights, women in the YWCA attempted to use the war to persuade other white Americans of the need for change. In early 1941, Eleanor Copenhaver Anderson, a white secretary long associated with industrial women, presented a statement to the Senate Committee on the Judiciary on behalf of the YWCA in favor of legislation to outlaw the poll tax. She argued in part that the tax, which kept poor whites and African Americans from being able to vote, leaves "us doubly vulnerable to external criticism, as well as to internal criticism."[24] The concern over America's reputation overseas escalated with the United States' entry into World War II. Americans feared that Germany and Japan would use the mistreatment of African Americans in propaganda efforts in both the United States and around the world. In a pamphlet distributed by YWCAs, Lillian Smith warned that the "Axis nations have agents in our country to promote conflict and violence." The enemy sought to find "sensitive areas" and "trouble spots" to manipulate, and one such spot, she pointed out, was clearly the treatment of African Americans. People needed, she continued, to serve as "troubleshooters for democracy" by doing what they could to improve racial tensions in the country as their part of the war effort.[25]

The war years were a time of increased racial demands in the United States. African Americans spoke of the Double V—the victory for democracy overseas *and* at home. Representatives of the NAACP told a 1942 meeting of African American YWCA workers, "We must contend on two fronts—one against the external enemy and one against the groups who have betrayed freedom and equality within our own borders."[26] Advocates of changes in racial practices and policies used the importance of winning the war to sanction many changes. In describing her association's interracial efforts, one local YWCA secretary recounted that they had "been capitalizing on the fact that wartime is a favorable one in which to achieve certain desired changes."[27]

National and local public affairs committee members used wartime necessity as well as Christianity and democracy in their legislative efforts. Emily Hickman, chairman of the National Public Affairs Committee, testified before both houses of Congress on behalf of legislation to prevent employment discrimination. The YWCA was interested in such laws because it is a Christian organization, she explained. As such, it was committed to the spiritual welfare of its members. Man may not "live by bread alone, neither can he live without it," she told the congressmen. Beyond that, the YWCA was concerned about "American democracy with equal opportunities for all." How can the YWCA teach that ideal, she asked, if there is "serious discrimination?"[28]

But women in the YWCA did more than lobby congressmen. In their efforts to promote a consistent policy against segregation, local African American leaders unanimously voted in 1942 to discontinue the Negro Leadership Conference (NLC), which was held, in part, because not all regional meetings accepted black women. They were prepared to give up the benefits of training and association that they received at the NLC without a commitment that all of them would be able to attend other leaders' meetings. Hereafter, they looked forward to "calling a national human relationships conference, interracial in character, with common programs to be emphasized rather than differences."[29]

Black women also moved forward in their campaign to get the YWCA to back legal challenges to discriminatory behavior. In the late 1930s, Frances Williams had worked with Walter White of the NAACP to educate the YW's National Board on the importance of such legal efforts. In 1944, a black national staff member, Yolanda Barnett, filed suit *with* the support of the National Board against the Texas and Pacific Railroad company because a conductor refused to seat her in the dining car. The settlement of a thousand dollars the following year established a precedent for suing southern railroad companies in the courts of northern states where they did business.[30]

Fern Babcock, a white secretary for student work, took the opportunity to educate southern students about both Barnett's "legal right and the religious validity of her position." Other white women were less convinced. Lillian Norwood, sponsor for the student Y at Texas Wesleyan, wrote the president of the National Board suggesting that Barnett would have been better to have turned the other cheek, writing, "I trust that Miss Barnett will recognize that she, as a Christian leader, has come face to face with a testing of her loyalty to Christ, and that she shares with HIM in being persecuted and mistreated.... May she bear this in mind, and keep this and probably other experiences in her heart as 'marks of Christ,' which Paul was proud to bear." Norwood went on to explain that "as Christians, we are doing real pioneer work, in breaking down racial barriers, and we might as well take with us the Mind of Christ, and accept injustices. The colored people, who are Christian will have something to rely on, when remembering He suffered for their sake, and they too will have to suffer."[31] Like other white women in these years, Norwood had a commitment to breaking racial barriers, rooted in her faith, but it had its limits. What is striking in her letter is not so much her resistance to Barnett's legal efforts, but the ways in which her notion of common Christianity kept her from seeing how black women "suffered" differently. If the YWCA was going to move its larger membership along, it was going to require a sustained educational effort.

In 1942, the YWCA finally created a commission to carry through the convention mandate to study local associations in regards to "the effects of segregation and discrimination." The Commission to Gather Interracial Experience included board and staff members, white and black, as well as a few women from outside the organization. Juliet O. Bell, a white researcher (and a southerner not from the association), and Helen J. Wilkins, a black woman who had been active with several local YWs, jointly conducted the study.[32] Bell and Wilkins sent an initial questionnaire to the 400-plus local associations and received back about 60 percent; this portion of the study allowed them to generate statistical accounts (especially regarding the participation of African Americans in aspects of association life ranging from voting to eating). They followed up with a second questionnaire asking specific locals more qualitative questions about how they had handled various interracial situations, and, finally, interracial teams visited nine cities to determine more information.

In their 1944 report, Bell and Wilkins found that African Americans accounted for 10 percent of participants in YWCA programs and a slightly higher percentage of voting members.[33] Breaking the figures down by region and program, they found a higher percentage of black women in the South (18 percent) and East (14.4 percent) than the Central (8.8 percent) and West (12.2 percent). Programs for industrial women and younger girls were more likely to have African American participation than were programs for business and professional women or "home women," the latter being a new constituency of married women, not working outside the home, who were usually older than women in the other groups. But the primary issue was not whether black women participated, but how many (or how few) activities were interracial. Here the numbers were more modest. On the high end were industrial programs in the East (12.5 percent were racially inclusive). In contrast, no programs in the South were inclusive.[34] Beyond surveying the general membership, Bell and Wilkins examined the patterns for voting members, volunteers and staff, and representation on boards of directors, as well as doing a qualitative assessment of impact on the larger community. All told, the commission's 116-page report confirmed the suspicions of those who questioned the inclusive nature of the association. In a less obvious manner, it also suggested the necessity of moving beyond the "prophetic minority" strategy adopted by the leadership of student associations. Substantial change would happen in the organization only as advocates figured out how to win over the large numbers of relatively class-privileged women of the community YWCAs. The traditional torchbearers for change, students and industrial women, increasingly represented a smaller proportion of the overall membership and, in the case of industrial women, saw an erosion of their institutional power base—self-governing clubs and the Industrial Assembly.[35]

If members at the convention had thought that authorizing a study would allow them to sidestep continuing challenges to the YW's racial policies, they were mistaken. Bell and Wilkins, and the commission as a whole, went beyond the original mandate to "gather interracial experiences" by developing a series of recommendations to both the National Board and local associations. The purpose of the YWCA should be the "measuring rod for all policies and practices." Only those that "contribute to the Christian and Democratic inclusiveness of the Associations" should continue. All associations should adopt as a "conscious goal" the "inclusion of Negro women and girls in the main stream of Association life."[36] To effect this goal, the commission developed specific recommendations for both the national and local associations, calling for measures ranging from black women's participating with full responsibility on boards and committees to associations' rethinking segregation in residences, camps, and cafeterias.

In early 1944, the National Board adopted the provisions that affected itself and then started the process of educating the locals. Gas rationing meant the YWCA did not hold a national convention during the war, but in spring 1944, members met in regional conferences and discussed the study and recommendations. The National Board reported that most of the criticisms came from women in the southern region. They ranged from those who read the report as insisting upon ending social segregation, which the board took to mean "personal acts" such as having tea, to those who felt that such a study should not have been carried out during wartime, to those who self-identified as working "toward the same ultimate Christian goal" but stressed the slow pace of the South and worried that the association would be divided regionally.[37] One white South Carolina woman read the report "as a Southerner and Sociologist" and praised the surveys "as statistically accurate and as objective as possible, considering the emotional nature of the material under analysis and the personal interests of the surveyors in the problem." On the other hand, the Mobile, Alabama, board reported that "because of the use of sociological terms the impression given was that the makers of the report wished to conceal in mysterious verbiage their real intentions (There are only six college graduates on our board and none with a major in sociology)."[38] Those supporting the recommendations had their work cut out for them.

"One World under God"

The YWCA met in Atlantic City in early March 1946 for its seventeenth national convention. Its theme of "one world under God" captured both its religious commitments and postwar optimism. Wartime needs had shaped many of the arguments during the war to support civil rights and other issues; women at the convention returned to the more traditional idea of women and peace. In her opening comments to the 1946 convention, Mary Shotwell Ingraham, president of the National Board, told the delegates that they were at a key moment in history: "Man broke the atom, woman must break the pattern—there must be no more war; there must be harmony among men."[39] She stood "wide-armed," as one black staff member later explained, for "this, my Father's world."[40] One of the early events was a report on women around the world, including their wartime experiences and the role the YWCA had played. Lilace Reid Barnes, active with the YWCA as both a staff member and a volunteer, invoked YWCA traditions to hail the "sisterhood of Christian women" and conclude the session with a prayer.[41]

The next day, the convention passed proposals revising logistical aspects of their constitution. Then the women met in smaller discussion groups before returning to address the theme of "one nation indivisible" and the Bell and Wilkins report. Ingraham herself met with members of southern associations who had come to the convention prepared to vote against the report. Board and staff members explained how the study had been structured and the various educational efforts that had been conducted to explain the study to local associations and gain input from them. In particular, in the fall of 1945, associations had been polled as to what they had accomplished since the study was first conducted; in 1942, some eighty-seven associations had interracial boards, while in 1945, one hundred twenty-three did. This was an effort to respond to those who said changes could not be made. Myra Smith, who had supervised the study, offered that for every association who said it "'cannot possibly move in this direction,' . . . I can give you the name of another Association in the same state that is doing so." Smith also made a point of saying that the North also had segregation and that the problem was not only a southern problem.[42]

Revised slightly in light of local feedback, the conclusions of the report were presented to the convention as "The Interracial Charter" and a series of recommendations. In its opening, the charter advised, "Today racial tensions threaten not only the well being of our communities but also the possibility of a peaceful world." It reminded women of their historical commitment to the "building of a society nearer to the Kingdom of God." And it concluded with a pledge "to pioneer in an interracial experience that shall be increasingly democratic and Christian."[43]

Presided over by Ingraham, members began by discussing and voting on the thirty-five recommendations, which ranged from suggesting that only those who favored full inclusion should be on local boards of directors to urging the elimination of wage differentials for white and African American workers. Debate began tentatively with associations talking about what they had accomplished, as well as concerns about going "too fast." Ingraham urged the delegates to lay out all the problems; after all, they would be going home and someone was bound to ask, "Was such-and-such a thing said?"[44] With this, delegates became explicit about the difficulties stemming from both social mores and legal restrictions.

In one of the most widely quoted comments, Sallie Summer, of Nashville, reported that her association agreed in principle with the policies, "but it is very difficult to put them in in Nashville at present. . . . We have made progress . . . [but we] do not know when we shall be able to do more than we have done. The present moment, the feeling of the [Nashville] Board is that the policy is most difficult to effect in Nashville; one reason is that the women have moved much farther forward in their thinking than the men of Nashville; the YWCA has been more progressive than the YMCA. We are having to slow our process until such time as the men are able to move along with us; we do not have the support of the [Community] Chest Board at the present time on interracial practices."[45] Summer captured the stated views of those critics who were in Atlantic City: they themselves believed in the goal for the long run, but they thought that community mores or men or the laws would make implementing the recommendations difficult. They found reassurance in the provisions that acknowledged that laws would limit some associations' ability to make change. Helen Wilkins (by that time Helen Wilkins Claytor) emphasized that "every Association is not expected to travel at the same rate of speed, or start at the same place. It is the direction in which the Associations are traveling that is important."[46] Supporters of the charter also felt required to state that while they supported integration in the YWCA, they also supported people's right to avoid social integration in their private lives.[47]

In the end, members passed the recommendations. When they turned to the Interracial Charter itself, they passed it unanimously, even though when Ingraham polled the audience, no one thought it would be easy to implement.[48] Not surprisingly, the black press featured the YWCA's action. "Women Way Ahead," read an editorial in the *New York Age,* while the *Chicago Defender* announced, "YWCA Lowers Curtain on Race Bias." But the *New York Times,* the *Christian Science Monitor,* and the *Los Angeles Times* also found the event of interest.[49] Given that only forty years earlier, white women in the association had accepted segregation as compatible with Christian sisterhood, the Interracial Charter was an accomplishment. It was perhaps not as absolute as the YW has sometimes presented it; some delegates left before the vote, and some associations, in fact, left the YWCA in the following years.[50] The YW's history reveals much about how and why middle-class, white-dominated, mainstream America began to recognize segregation as an American problem, as well as how others resisted that change.

The 1946 Interracial Charter's commitment to desegregation was a part of a growing national assault on segregation. A day after the YW's decision, the Federal Council of Churches called upon Protestant churches to work toward a "non-segregated church and a non-segregated society." Later that month, men of the YMCA at their national convention called for the elimination of segregation in their organization, although not with the degree of specificity of the YW.[51] In less than a decade, at least on paper, segregation was challenged in institutions ranging from real estate to baseball and from schools to the armed forces, although most other white-dominated women's groups took little or no action on race and some, such as the General Federation of Women's Clubs, remained completely segregated.[52]

As increasing numbers of American whites (especially in the North) came to endorse desegregation, the YWCA helped build support for the idea. Its members, along with other white Americans, were shaped by postwar events. In laying out its agenda for the next two years, the YWCA's National Public Affairs Committee argued that Americans' "contribution to a world order . . . depends upon what we accomplish in community relations at home.

The integrity of our democracy is tested by its treatment of minorities."[53] Writing on behalf of federal antilynching laws, the president of the National Board explained that as "an international organization, the Young Women's Christian Association continues to work to help build a world of peace and justice." She went on to discuss the country's role. "We know that the eyes of the world are upon us; our record of treatment of minorities falls far short of the standards of democracy."[54]

The YWCA was not alone in its concern over the United States' postwar international reputation. In late 1946, President Harry Truman had appointed a committee to study civil rights. The committee issued its report, *To Secure These Rights,* in 1947. In addition to moral and economic reasons for supporting civil rights, its members argued for an international one. At the conclusion of the report, they wrote that they were "concerned with the good opinion of the peoples of the world."[55] American leaders worried that the United States' position in the world was affected by the growing popularity of Communism and they recognized that a key area for US/USSR rivalry would be the Third World. According to one State Department estimate at the time, almost 50 percent of Soviet propaganda focused on U.S. race relations.[56] Women in the YWCA, among others, realized that the new countries emerging after the war included those with large populations of people of color who might readily identify with the plight of African Americans.[57] By 1952, in a statement entitled "International Implications of the Interracial Charter," the YWCA spoke of the relation between "our democracy" and the "treatment of minorities" and called for Americans to realize that they were "in a world scene in which colored peoples are in the majority."[58] The YW's traditional Christian internationalism fit with the liberal internationalism of cold war America.

"In the Main Stream: Do We Sink or Swim?"

Shortly after the 1946 convention's endorsement of the Interracial Charter, African American national staff members met with the division responsible for community YWCAs to clarify what would "result from the so-called inclusiveness of the YWCA Convention action." Women of both races discussed both what integration meant and how associations would implement the policy. One black staff member queried, "[N]ow that we are in the main stream, do we sink or swim?"[59] The discussion revealed deep divisions among the staff members. Not all splits were along race lines, but they did show differences in how white and black women looked at integration. Black women were particularly concerned that some women thought that the convention action meant that work "on the Negro question" was no longer needed, and it was time to "choose some other emphasis."[60] In response, they pointed to the need for continuing work.[61] The difficulties they faced anticipated the problems that even more Americans would confront during the 1950s and 1960s civil rights movement.

One of the challenges facing the women was how to continue in an integrated organization the advantages found in segregated institutions. Some 70 percent of African American members were in segregated associations in the 1940s. Those branches brought African American women and girls into the organization and provided them with a sense of race pride. They also offered needed services to their communities.[62] Branches, as African Americans pointed out, were places that afforded "the sense of being 'at home in our own building,' [and] the freedom from fear of incivility or discriminatory acts."[63] Both the members and the leaders benefitted from the branches' self-governance. The women—both volunteers and staff—who led those branches had gained important training and leadership opportunities.[64] Even though the vast majority of African American women in the YWCA favored integration, they questioned whether integration would be implemented in such a way as "to really result in the advancement of the Negro group."[65]

Most white and black women agreed that integrated YWCAs were not likely to hire African American women in positions of top leadership. As one local association reported about women from the branches, "They know very well that they would not carry these jobs if the total program were an integrated one at Central."[66] The authors of a 1949 YWCA study about policies and practices at the local level acknowledged that in associations without branches, no African Americans served as executive directors. In the case of one interracial branch, the study continued, there was a "coexecutive"; in three other areas there were "associate executive directors with city-wide responsibility." The authors summed up the sentiments about the future: "Many 'integrated' Associations are not large enough to justify an associate executive director, and where such a position is possible, it would not always be the branch executive who would be best qualified to hold it."[67] Whites were reluctant to hire African Americans in positions of leadership over whites.

Some African American women supporting integration felt that losing out on these jobs was a price that they would have to pay, much as the members of the Negro Leadership Conference had voted themselves out of existence. Fannie Pitt Byrd, a staff member of the Harlem YWCA, urged the readers of the *New York Age*, "[Principle] rather than expediency must be [the] golden rule. Our race must learn that to reach its long-range goal: full citizenship—we must increasingly face a sacrifice of short-term gains. We must give up what may be some 'advantages' of segregation for the slower process of integration."[68]

At the same time, advocates for African Americans challenged the grounds on which the women were seen as less qualified. The YWCA's own studies had shown that African American women leading in the YWCA were often better educated than their white counterparts, although they were paid less.[69] One study issued a rebuke to local associations that said they could not find "Negro women of leadership caliber" by suggesting that these women had not felt welcomed at the YWCA and had turned to other groups.[70] At the 1946 convention, a white woman from California complained that her association might be required to have African American women on their board, saying that "we have found great difficulty in recruiting Negro members with the ability, willingness or stick-to-it-iveness to serve on every committee where we should like to have had them." In moderated words, Constance Ridley (Mrs. Jesse) Heslip, an African American from Toledo on the National Board, responded that the issue was not "ability and stick-to-it-iveness on their part," but that black women were "sometimes doubtful of the attitude of the majority group."[71]

African American women continued to question the attitudes of the majority group not only toward providing leadership opportunities for them, but also about offering a place that afforded African Americans "the sense of being 'at home'" and freedom from discrimination. What would inclusion into an organization that remained white-dominated mean to these women and girls? They had reason to be alarmed when a 1949 evaluation of programs revealed that the percentage of black women and girls in the "educational and recreational" programs had declined from 9.8 percent in 1945 to 8.6 percent in 1947.[72]

To address these concerns, the YWCA mounted an impressive educational campaign. It publicized what women were doing to promote integration (to show that it could be done) and provided guides for how to make changes.[73] When necessary, it also worked to educate the YWCA membership and the larger public on other studies—preparing a guide, for instance, to the 1947 report from the President's Committee on Civil Rights. Entitled *The Christian Citizen and Civil Rights: A Guide to Study and Action,* it suggested ways in which YW women continued to link their religion and their social activism.[74] Most frequently addressed to white Americans, these studies established a role for the YWCA, as a voluntary association, in promoting political change. In *Step by Step with Interracial Groups,* Dorothy Height explained that "etiquette in race relations" was about politeness but included "respect for *the rights* and feelings of others."[75]

While the educational efforts were clearly necessary, the YWCA tended to focus on whites. Black critics observed that the discussions on integration focused only on its significance for whites. In this scenario, minorities were important "as merely a 'plus' to the white group." Stressing how segregation hurt whites was a way to win whites over to supporting desegregation, but it could function to overlook what was happening for black women. Most of the resources at the national level went to assist white associations, not the branches or programs for minorities.[76]

African American staff and volunteers were aware of what African American women and girls faced in the locals. They pointed out that the policy of integration would be effective only if it was explained to the African American community as well as to the white.[77] This need was made more urgent by cases where it appeared as if black branches were being closed for reasons other than ending segregation. In at least one case, a local YWCA shut down its branch "in favor of an integrated program with the most sincere desire to 'do the right thing'; but it took the step only when it was having financial difficulties." Local African Americans were suspicious about the timing and worried that integration was a ruse to discontinue programs for the black community.[78]

Ultimately, YW women disagreed over what inclusion in the mainstream meant: one or two people of color? Representation in the association comparable to representation in the larger population? Fifty-fifty? Frequently the white leadership of local associations described activities with "only one or two Negro girls" as interracial.[79] African Americans argued that small numbers signified token representation rather than integration: "in many cases we merely sit on boards with no chance for leadership in that mixed group."[80] Even when events concerned African Americans, white women often set up the program and *then* invited black women to participate. African American women on boards and committees frequently found that white women did not listen to their opinions.[81] In some cases, "inclusion" was implemented by the establishment of more branches for blacks, particularly in the South where black branches expanded from thirty-two in 1941 to fifty-two in 1948.[82] Clearly, local associations adopted different strategies in working "toward the same ultimate Christian goal."

If African American women expressed concern over token representation, white women frequently worried that with an "open door policy," "Negroes will flock in" and "Negroes will move in and white people lose out." In some cities, white women and girls stopped attending events they perceived as "Negro." While "white flight" might have been a problem, there was, in fact, little proof that African Americans were flocking to central associations in large numbers.[83] To white women's surprise, African American women and girls did not always join "integrated" YWCAs. African American women, aware of the past history of exclusion, the possibility of snubs in the present, and the advantages of black-controlled spaces, anticipated that members of their community might not join newly integrated efforts.[84] Black women knew that white-dominated associations did not always open all activities to all people at once. White women frequently failed to communicate when an event was open to "all" whether that meant everybody or just white people.[85] In one study, African American board and staff members indicated, "We attend board meetings but we never know when 'we' means the total Board and staff and when 'we' means only the white members. Sometimes luncheon meetings are planned for everyone; at other times branch people are excluded. Since all are planned by the Board it is difficult to know when to come and when to stay away." As other African American leaders simply put it, "Why should I get myself into that kind of situation?"[86] The Interracial Charter raised as many questions about race relations as it had seemingly answered.

"A Cross Section of All Kinds of People in a Community"

Throughout the 1940s, YW women debated the role they could and should play in the larger society. In 1944, Bell and Wilkins had stressed that the YWCA was ahead of many, if not most, other groups and prompted others to move on the issue.[87] That year, a national YW staff member observed that race was the most discussed issue among the women and girls of the YWCA.[88] It was also the year that the preeminent study of race relations in America, Gunner Myrdal's *An American Dilemma,* was published. Myrdal worried that, while Americans often discussed race, it was not yet a dominant issue in America.[89] An examination of polling data reveals that white Americans had begun to identify "racial problems" as among the most "vital" issues for Americans in the mid-1940s, but not until 1963 did they identify race as "the most important problem facing the United States."[90] As in earlier years, the

YWCA exposed some white Americans to race questions before they were of concern to most white Americans.

By 1949, however, the YWCA offered a more subdued appraisal of its record. Heralding its "forward-looking" approach, authors of a study that year argued that the YWCA's commitment to being a "cross section of all kinds of people in a community" meant that "it can seldom, if ever, be called a spearhead." Other organizations, often smaller and not as well known, were further along.[91] The study also found significant differences in how the white and black women viewed the association: "Negro and white women frequently come to a new interracial experience with different expectations. It was found that white women had usually participated in 'a long educational process' before an interracial policy was adopted. Frequently they had a sense of achievement when a committee had become interracial or when a policy had been passed. The Negro women who became members of the committee had probably not shared the educational process and came to the committee with a sense of beginning rather than of accomplishment."[92] What for many white women was the culmination of years of struggle was, for black women, only an initial step.

Despite (or because of) the YWCA's presentation of itself as a cross section of the larger society, the YWCA faced criticisms from those who saw it as a force for social harm. Gladys Gilkey Calkins, president of the convention that debated the Interracial Charter, wrote in retrospect of "the real risk that liberal opinions on the subject of race would be at once labeled 'radical' and 'communistic.'"[93] In the late 1940s, the YWCA faced a resurgence of attacks both from within and without. In 1948, Joseph Kamp published *Behind the Lace Curtains of the YWCA,* whose cover featured a gauze curtain over the blue triangle logo of the YWCA with a notable modification of the YWCA's initials: a hammer and sickle replaced the "C." Kamp warned his readers about both the YW's influence on individual women (especially younger ones) and the size of the organization. Let others focus on the fate of those behind the "iron curtain"; Kamp identified the danger to America as coming from literally domestic quarters, evil deeds protected from public sight by lace curtains. The YWCA was "30 to 50 times the size of the Communist Party," he wrote.[94] He was not alone in his concerns and, as with previous waves of red-baiting, the critics cited each others' claims to substantiate their own. Eventually, the U.S. House Committee on Un-American Activities included concerns about the YWCA in its publications.[95]

The YWCA's interest in civil rights was of particular concern. Women were acting to overthrow the natural order of both sexual and racial hierarchies, which the critics considered to be the basis of an American and Christian life. They warned of those "frustrated females [who] have gone through bitter struggles to attain their positions" and who espoused a "political dogma based on hatred."[96] Two conservative women, Lucille Crain and Anne Hamilton, argued that the membership had no idea what they were supporting when they followed through on suggestions from the National Public Affairs Committee. Countering the YWCA's self-perception of its women as educated, independent thinkers, Crain and Hamilton argued that the women were accepting "packaged thinking" on issues such as civil rights.[97] Women were not really capable of informed citizenship, and to conservatives, male and female alike, YW women's political activity was only a further sign that reds had been busy.

Assessing the consequences of these efforts is a difficult task. On one hand, the attacks against the YWCA pale in comparison to those against those groups and individuals who were virtually destroyed in the 1940s and 1950s.[98] But local associations were vulnerable to pressure. Funding sources in the community wielded great power; local members expressed concern as to how Community Chests and businesses regarded the YWCA's efforts for social change.[99] Associations around the country reported problems in their communities after Kamp published *Behind the Lace Curtains of the YWCA*. In some cases, funders cut their support for associations, while in others, local membership dropped off.[100] In cities such as Queens, New York, individual women withdrew from the organization, sending their complaints to the House Committee on Un-American Activities and to the press.[101] In other places, the entire local left. In 1949, the YWCA of Atlantic City announced its decision to sever all connections with the national association because of "left-wing 'infiltration'" of the national body.[102]

The national association was somewhat protected from attacks because it received money from a range of sources. Even when it could ride out the attacks, however, they consumed time and money, and its institutional records include voluminous memos and letters revealing its attempts to respond to the attacks.[103] In some cases national leaders advised staying silent, while in others they suggested that locals talk to community leaders and explain the actions of the association. When a funder criticized the San Jose YWCA for engaging in political activities (notably support for a permanent Fair Employment Practices Committee, the FEPC), Grace Loucks Elliott, then executive secretary of the YWCA, cabled back for the secretary to answer "by stating that we are a Christian organization and compelled to be interested in the problems of society as well as of individuals." Elliott's 1 ½-page, single-spaced follow-up letter expanded on the themes of the "international Christian fellowship of women" and the need to educate women for "responsible citizenship," and it also explained how the organization functioned democratically.[104] Like other liberals, YW women defended themselves by appealing to civil liberties and democracy, but first and foremost, the YW's defense against charges of atheistic communism was that they were Christian. The defense did not persuade the professional critics like Joseph Kamp, but it may have provided local associations some assistance when answering questions raised by their communities. YW women's efforts to present their efforts for racial reform in the languages both of democracy and Christianity earned some allies, but also opponents.

❖ ❖ ❖

Over the course of the first half of the twentieth century, white and black YWCA women remained committed to a vision of Christian sisterhood. They referred to connections among women as well as the importance of religion. They continued to link womanhood and religion with race. Testifying for a permanent FEPC in 1944, Emily Hickman, the white lobbyist for the YWCA, explained the YW's involvement: "[W]omen . . . realize that they have been part of a minority group and they know something about what the political and economic discrimination against them meant, and in some cases still means; so that we have a great sympathy for other minority groups."[105] In 1933, Frances Williams had replied to a correspondent who was wary of local religious women's involvement with "foreign work" done in a town. She wrote, "I wager to say also that the best thought on the Negro life of Fairhaven also came from a women's group." Never one to mince words, Williams concluded her letter by asserting, "This in no wise means that women are superior to men, but being a group that has been dominated and oppressed by the honorable males of this world they are inclined to see more quickly the problems of other oppressed groups."[106] The continuity in the language of shared womanhood masks changes in the vision as well as the impact of the larger society. White women adjusted their notion of sisterhood in the face of challenges from black women, in and out of the organization. Other institutional rationales, including both remaining distinct from the YM and the YW's internationalism, provided black women with leverage points.

In many ways the position of religion at the 1946 national convention appeared similar to its status at the 1920 convention, when the YWCA first embraced a political agenda. Each convention included religious services, prayers during the sessions, addresses from religious leaders of the day, and speeches with phrases like "the Kingdom of God." In explaining local YWCAs' progress on race relations, the authors of a subsequent YWCA study relied on motivating factors such as the organization's "Christian ideals," "Christian purpose," and "Christian fellowship." Not only did YWCA women make this connection, they pointed out, but so did the larger public: "It is interesting to note how often civic leaders, not necessarily in sympathy with the organization's interracial aims, commented favorably on the YWCA's forward steps and in almost the same words, 'We expect leadership from the YWCA because of its Christian purpose.'"[107]

There were hints, however, of changes to come. In 1946, delegates were every bit as likely to refer to American democracy as a motivation for social action as they were to appeal to God. In the original constitution (1906/1909), the women declared their purpose as seeking "to bring young women to such a knowledge of Jesus Christ as Saviour and Lord as shall mean for the individual young woman fullness of life and development of character, and shall make the organization as a whole an effective agency in the bringing in of the Kingdom of God among young women." In 1949, members substantially revised the constitution, revising the purpose for the first time. They now defined it as, "To build a fellowship of women and girls devoted to the task of realizing in our common life those ideals of personal and social living to which we are committed by our faith as Christians. In the endeavor we seek to understand Jesus, to share his love for all people, and to grow in the knowledge and love of God."[108] Religion had provided an important motivation, if not sanctification, for their social actions in the early twentieth century. And, in turn, that social action became a way for white and black women to express their religiosity in the late 1920s and 1930s, when conventional formats broke down or lost their appeal. It also provided them an alternate discourse to that of anticommunism. They still testified about the virtues of American democracy, Christian sisterhood, and racial liberalism, but, increasingly, they left behind the evangelical touchstones of Christ as the "Saviour and Lord" or even the "Kingdom of God." The shift reflected their commitment to inclusivity, even on religious grounds, as well as a tempering, in the light of two world wars, a great economic depression, and the social chaos of the mid-twentieth century, of the eschatological idea of the Kingdom of God.[109]

Even so, focusing on their increasing adoption of a democratic language may mask their continuing religious orientation. Democracy remained infused (in their minds) with the traditions of Christianity and, if push came to shove, they meant Protestantism. They were neither simply Christian nor citizens, but rather "Christian citizens."[110] Even in their most "secular" articulation, their vision remained a religious one. As they saw it, democracy, with its Protestant respect for the individual, necessitated both self-governance and respect for minority rights. To achieve rights for minorities through majority rule, black and white women in the association sought to educate people into changes. Legislation, whether through the Interracial Charter or an antilynching law, was necessary, but not sufficient, to change peoples' hearts and minds.[111] The local secretary in Elizabeth, who at the opening of this chapter presented her efforts to get girls to decide for themselves to do the right thing, *and* the unnamed women she advised were representative of a larger process as women of both races sought to educate Americans—white and black—to change themselves and bring in a new world.

EPILOGUE

IN 1896, THE SUPREME COURT delivered its opinion in the landmark case *Plessy v. Ferguson,* ensuring that segregation would be the legal principle guiding daily life in the United States. When the members of the Young Women's Christian Association endorsed its Interracial Charter in March 1946, they acted only a few weeks short of the fiftieth anniversary of *Plessy.* By calling for "the inclusion of Negro women and girls into the main stream of Association life," white women acknowledged that "separate but equal" were hollow words and finally acceded to black women's argument that segregation was not compatible with Christianity, democracy, sisterhood, or fellowship. The involvement of white liberals, such as the women of the YWCA, in the civil rights struggle meant that the white challenge to segregation would no longer be the sole province of radicals.

Black branches, some long established, others newly created, in cities ranging from New York to Los Angeles, from Pittsburgh to Galveston, were (or became) vibrant centers of community activities, including social activism.[1] The Greensboro YWCA was one of the few organizations in North Carolina that offered black women a base from which to lobby for racial change. White liberals were able to use YWCAs as organizational spaces when they chose to get involved in the civil rights struggle.[2] YWCAs were some of the only physical spaces in southern cities for interracial meetings. In the winter of 1960, it was the YWCA whose public cafeteria became the first in Atlanta to serve black demonstrators "without incident."[3]

As black YWCA members realized, however, questions remained: in particular, was a call for integration a major accomplishment or only the first step in a continuing struggle for the eradication of racial discrimination? The years since the Interracial Charter have witnessed intense debates in the association over segregation, race relations, and racism as white members' reactions ranged from eager support for inclusion to full-scale resistance. YWCA leaders had deliberately crafted its language to permit the widest range of associations to sign on. The stress on direction, rather than speed, permitted many associations to claim to be supporting the charter even when others might doubt they were actually acting on it.

While some white women urged changes in the racial order, others were less supportive. In 1948, the white association in Mobile wrote the National Board and all other local associations denouncing the proposed public affairs program because of its actions dealing with "expansion of centralized government controls, collective bargaining, . . . [and] segregation and its accompanying issues." These efforts were a "distortion of [the] YWCA purpose." In particular, the "recommended approach to the Negro problem, evidently is originated by persons who do not understand the people of the South, their approach, their relationships with the Negro race, their understanding, appreciation, affection or interest in the race."[4] In those cities where black members outnumbered their white counterparts, some white women expressed concern that they would be outvoted if their YWCA conducted elections on a citywide basis.[5] When they finally "desegregated" their YWCA in the 1960s, white women in Charlotte, North Carolina, chose to build their new facility in the white suburbs rather than in the downtown, which had become predominantly black.[6] Even in cities where white women were more sympathetic and/or black women had more power, efforts at desegregation had complicated consequences, as some black women left local associations. This may have represented a growing choice of other groups to join, but often it reflected dissatisfaction with the continuing white control over "integrated" associations. William Chafe has observed that with desegregation of the Greensboro YWCA, black women lost an important power base.[7] In cities ranging from Oakland, California, to Germantown, Pennsylvania, to Washington, D.C., black women and girls left the YWCA as they experienced a decreased sense that the institution was still theirs.[8]

Where local white associations actually repudiated the charter, the national YWCA had no enforcement mechanism with which to respond. The YWCA's structure of autonomous locals meant that neither the National Board, nor even the national convention, could penalize those associations. Black women and their white allies attempted to put some teeth into the Interracial Charter in the following years. At the 1955 convention, they succeeded in getting the membership to pass a resolution requiring that local associations review their implementation of the Interracial Charter in preparation for the next convention.[9] It was not until the 1967 convention, some twenty years after the Interracial Charter first passed, that the associations adopted an amendment to disaffiliate local associations that were not "fully integrated in policy and practice." At the same convention, delegates elected Helen Wilkins Claytor (of the Bell and Wilkins study) as the national body's first African American president.[10]

Members increasingly recognized that segregation was not the only racial problem to be addressed. At the YWCA's next national convention, in 1970, presided over by Claytor and held in Houston—the first time the association had held a convention in the South since 1922—black women succeeded in getting the association to make the elimination of racism its "One Imperative." Led by Dorothy Height, who had been active with the YWCA since the 1930s and was also the president of the National Council of Negro Women, the five hundred black delegates threatened a walkout. Ultimately, the membership voted that the "Association will thrust its collective power toward the elimination of racism wherever it exists and by any means necessary." Covering the convention for the *New York Times,* one reporter described the action as a "subordination" of the issue of "women's liberation," a longstanding formulation that presumed white women's issues were somehow universal, while black women's were race specific. Even white supporters saw it as a matter of "setting aside some of our own priorities—women's liberation for example." In contrast, the black women in Houston, like black women of the first decades of the twentieth century, were more likely to see the action on behalf of the race as a means to secure the empowerment of all women. For her part, Height also identified the class issues she saw the organization facing. Drawing upon decades-old language, she told the convention that the YWCA "must get middle-class blacks and white liberals into the ghettos working not for, but with minority groups: listening, not telling, supporting, but with a shift away from the old charity."[11] Times and strategies had changed and the idea that one could move the race forward by focusing on the talented tenth increasingly faced major criticism.

The YWCA's continuing existence as an autonomous women's organization offers clues to links between the woman movement of the late nineteenth and early twentieth centuries and the women's liberation movement beginning in the 1960s. It was the YWCA, rather than the more explicitly political bodies such as the League of Women Voters or the National Woman's Party, that provided continuity between the different "waves" of women's activism.[12] As a growing number of autobiographical and scholarly accounts indicate, the YWCA, particularly through its student groups, played a role in the civil rights movement of the 1950s and 60s. White women such as Rosalie Oakes and black women such as Ella Baker influenced college women's participation in the civil rights struggle. Representatives from the YWCA were observers at the October 1960 meeting that established the Student Nonviolent Coordinating Committee (SNCC). Women such as Casey Hayden and Mary King brought the knowledge and skills they had gained in YWCA activities to other groups, most notably SNCC.[13]

Drawn into the civil rights struggle, many of the white women became active in the subsequent struggle for women's rights. While in SNCC, Hayden and King wrote manifestos analyzing the position of women in society. Other women, including Charlotte Bunch, left the civil rights movement or the New Left in order to form women's groups. The historian Sara Evans, previously active herself in the campus YW at Duke, observed that every "white women from the south I have interviewed or learned about joined the civil rights movement through Church-related activities."[14] Religion, and specifically Protestantism, provided a common experience for white and black women and was an important part of white women's activism. There were, of course, also religiously motivated conservative and reactionary women's groups. Additional work needs to be done to determine how and why women's religion affected political and social orientation.

In delineating changes in the YWCA, white women in the organization presented its becoming "interracial" as "the natural development of something inherent in [the YWCA's] nature from the beginning."[15] An examination of the confrontations between black and white women reveals that the changes were by no means automatic. The efforts of African American women and some sympathetic white women were instrumental in influencing the larger membership to shift policies and practices. In so doing, they affected assumptions about the significance of race relations in the United States. White women of the YWCA reiterated the importance of Christian sisterhood even as their understanding of its implications for race issues changed over time. Black women in the YWCA shared these commitments to varying degrees. They also recognized the leverage they had in linking their concerns to the other priorities of white women in their efforts to make race a national priority and to shape white women's response to it. We are left not with a history of inevitable progress but a history of continuing tension and negotiation.

As white and black women struggled over race, race relations, racism, and racial justice, they produced complicated stories. These accounts suggest that we should think of political culture as common debates, rather than as shared assumptions or conclusions about the way things should be.[16] The stories of race in the YWCA, as in the United States, are ones of ongoing conflict rather than resolution. Examining the history of the YWCA's racial policies and practices serves to highlight continuities over the twentieth century and into the twenty-first in how white people think about race and race relations.

One of the most frequent refrains was (and is) that the association (or America) had solved its race problem, and so it was time to go on to other problems. Throughout the twentieth century, white people kept hoping that they no longer had to address the issue. Leila Frissell, a white woman on the National Board, reported in 1914 that many northern whites "were getting tired of the Southern race problem, thinking 'I have done enough there. There is no need for further work for me.'"[17] Thirty years later, the African American staff warned that some white women read the Interracial Charter as meaning that work "on the Negro question" was no longer needed, and it was time to "choose some other emphasis."[18] And today we find some using Martin Luther King Jr.'s call for a color-blind society as a justification for not addressing racial problems, arguing that attention to race prevents, rather than aids in, a solution.[19]

An analysis of the YWCA's story also lays out the ways in which discussions among white and black women about race often turned into discussions about class or morality or sin. A focus on the behavior of the "better classes" and manners made it difficult to see ways in which racism was systemic and institutional as well as maintained by individuals. If in the early years, this preoccupation led to white women's criticizing black women for lacking manners in the latter's public rebukes of the YWCA, in the latter years, white women often appeared to be preoccupied with whether they were guilty of the "sin" of racism. Speaking of her experiences at the YW, Dorothy Height was concerned in retrospect that at times white women looked at their interracial experiences as a means "to test themselves, rather than to be sensitive to the needs of others."[20] Standing against sin could be a compelling motive for white women, but working toward justice required a social vision as well.

Finally, the examination of the YWCA raises questions about the efficacy of Christian sisterhood as a strategy for solving the problems of race (or class) or bridging differences between women. For more than a quarter century, scholars in women's studies have analyzed the meaning of sisterhood, asking whether "sisterhood" can best be understood as "dubious," "universal," "peculiar," "denied," "all-inclusive," "separate," "advancing," "splintered," "unlikely," or "questioned."[21] The problems associated with using sisterhood as a controlling metaphor stem from assuming that the category means (or should have meant) egalitarian and harmonious relationships, rather than hierarchical and conflicting ones.[22] It seems particularly ironic that feminists, who have ably critiqued the power imbalances in the family and personal relations, would assume that any familial relationship could be a source of natural equality. Families are as easily the site for conflict and struggle as they are for love and harmony. A shared language of sisterhood has not always meant agreement. As Nancy Hewitt has argued, we have allowed "the rhetoric of community" to overshadow "the reality of conflict."[23]

To return to the formulation proposed almost ninety years ago by Lily Hardy Hammond, womanhood, motherhood, and sisterhood were never deeper than race because they could not be separated from race. Racism shapes not only race relations, but the relations of gender and class. Many of the "shared" traits were illusory or problematic. Not all sisters are the same. Not all women are mothers. Not all mothers do the same work. In this society, it was not—and is not—possible simply to *find* a sisterhood of commonality and equality.[24] Saying that womanhood was not deeper than race is disheartening, however, only if we imagine that unity and justice must be built on commonality and sameness. It is important to bear in mind the persistent faith and activism of black and white women like Addie Waites Hunton, Elizabeth Ross Haynes, Eva Del Vakia Bowles, Juliette Aline Derricotte, Frances Harriet Williams, Dorothy Irene Height, Helen Wilkins Claytor, Grace Hoadley Dodge, Leila S. Frissell, Lily Hardy Hammond, Katharine Du Pre Lumpkin, Winnifred Wygal, Sallie L. Hanna, and Mary Shotwell Ingraham, as well as those women whose names have not survived in historical records. The struggles in the YWCA—and in the United States—offer hope that people can strive toward justice, while disagreeing, politely or not.

NOTES

Introduction

1. A. Hunton, "A Deeper Reverence for Home Ties," 59.
2. L. H. Hammond, "Interracial Cooperation," 12.
3. L. H. Hammond, *Southern Women and Racial Adjustment,* 18.
4. Hortense Ridley to Emily Smith, 22 January 1926 (YWCA/RFC 190.5).
5. Zald, *Organizational Change,* xiii. This assessment is of the Young Men's Christian Association, but holds true for the YWCA.
6. In developing this project, I learned much from Joan Jacobs Brumberg's analysis of white Protestant American women and the ways in which their discussion of women in other countries can be used to understand the white American women themselves; see her "Zenanas and Girlless Villages." I also benefitted from studies on "whiteness," and particularly useful works can be found in Robertson, "Kindness or Justice: Women's Associations and the Politics of Race and History."
7. I have relied on an understanding of evangelicalism as referring to the belief in the Bible as the sole word of God, the Trinitarian nature of God, and the role of Jesus as one's personal Saviour. The emphasis on the Bible excluded those who were Roman Catholic, Mormon, or Christian Scientist (as they also relied on other literature or authorities). The emphasis upon the Trinity (Father, Son, and Holy Ghost) ruled out Unitarians and Quakers, among others. See Handy, *Christian America,* chap. 2; Howe, "The Evangelical Movement and Political Culture in the North"; Kett, *Rites of Passage,* 75–79; and McPherson, *The Abolitionist Legacy,* esp. 152–53 and chap. 10.
8. See Curry et al., *Deep in Our Hearts;* Evans, *Journeys That Opened Up the World;* Height, *Open Wide the Freedom Gates;* and Ransby, *Ella Baker.*
9. Martin, in Evans, *Journeys That Opened Up the World,* 246. Martin spelled Barnes's first name as Lillas; I corrected it here.
10. Dorothy Height, "Eliminating Racism by Any Means Necessary" (September 1973), 1 (YWCA/NB), and Height, *Open Wide the Freedom Gates,* 128–30.

11. Young Women's Christian Associations of the U.S.A. (hereafter YWCA of the USA), *Proceedings of the Seventeenth National Convention, 1946,* 29, 70.

12. The classic statement dating the decline of women's organizations to the 1920s is Freedman, "Separatism as Strategy." Jacquelyn Dowd Hall has called for a reperiodization of the civil rights movement that looks for its origins in the 1930s, well before *Brown v. Board of Education;* see her "The Long Civil Rights Movement." For a sophisticated analysis of the Protestant underpinnings of supposedly secular welfare programs and public policy efforts of twentieth-century female reformers, see Fitzgerald, "Losing Their Religion."

13. Sims, *The YWCA—An Unfolding Purpose* and *The Purpose Widens, 1947–1967.*

14. Height, *Open Wide the Freedom Gates,* 119–20.

15. This study refers to the former interchangeably as urban, city, or community YWCAs while using campus, student, or college YWCAs to discuss the latter.

16. *Interracial Charter and Related Policy,* 6, 10.

17. Ibid., 5 (1948 statement quoted).

18. Sabiston and Hiller, *Toward Better Race Relations,* 103–4.

Chapter 1: Building a National Organization

1. Grace Hoadley Dodge (1856–1914), a Presbyterian, was born in New York City to a family that was involved in philanthropy as well as business. She attended Miss Porter's School in Connecticut before returning home to take care of family obligations and to engage in social reform. She was instrumental in founding the working girls' club movement, Teachers College (affiliated with Columbia University), and the Travelers Aid Society. See Graham, *Grace H. Dodge;* Robert D. Cross, "Grace Hoadley Dodge," in James et al., *Notable American Women,* 1:489–92; Katz, "Grace Hoadley Dodge"; Robinson, *Eight Women of the YWCA,* esp. chap. 2; and Lagemann, *Generation of Women,* chap. 1.

2. On generations, see Lagemann, *Generation of Women,* esp. the introduction; Katz, "Grace Hoadley Dodge," 45–47, 268–71; Cross, "Grace Hoadley Dodge," 681. On Schuyler (1837–1926), see Robert D. Cross, "Louisa Lee Schuyler," in James et al., *Notable American Women,* 3:244–46.

3. Dodge, "Introduction," xi.

4. E. Wilson, *Fifty Years of Association Work,* 211.

5. "Miss Grace Dodge, Girls' Friend, Dead," *New York Tribune,* 28 December 1914, 19.

6. For examples of concern for Native American women, heathen women, and the foreign born, see E. Wilson, *Fifty Years of Association Work,* 188, 272–73, 300–302. For "oriental women," see YWCA of the USA, *Proceedings of the Second Biennial Convention, 1909,* 128. For fallen women, see Morton, "Seduced and Abandoned in an American City."

7. There is no recent monograph on the general history of the YWCA in the United States. Three older house histories by Mary S. Sims provide useful information: *Natural History of a Social Institution* (1936); *The YWCA—An Unfolding Purpose* (1950); and *The Purpose Widens, 1947–1967* (1969). Recent work has focused on specific topics (for example, overseas work, programs for the foreign-born, or race) or on

local associations. A. Scott, *Natural Allies,* and Lasch-Quinn, *Black Neighbors,* have discussed the YWCA as part of broader projects.

8. LCA, *Third Annual Report (1860),* 3. This account is drawn from Garrette, *Her New York Story,* 24–31, and Bittar, "The Y.W.C.A. of the City of New York," 14–19. The group began as the Ladies' Christian Association (LCA) but changed its name in 1864 to the Ladies' Christian Union. For the term "layman's revival," see J. D. Hunter, *American Evangelicalism,* 24.

9. Bittar, "The Y.W.C.A. of the City of New York," 15.

10. LCA, *Third Annual Report (1860),* 3, 7.

11. LCU, *Eighth Annual Report for 1866,* 11. The pattern of prayer circles expanding into reform groups was not uncommon; for earlier examples, see Cott, *Bonds of Womanhood,* 134, 142–43.

12. Precise information about women's labor force participation is difficult to come by, although historians agree about the trends. Nancy Woloch gives the percentage of women in the labor force as 9.7 percent in 1860, increasing to 21.2 percent by 1900; see her *Women and the American Experience,* 607. That female labor force was overwhelmingly single; see Weiner, *From Working Girl to Working Mother,* esp. 3–5. For a discussion of contemporary concern about the "working-girl problem," see Murolo, *The Common Ground of Womanhood,* chap. 1.

13. YWCA of NYC, *Thirty-fifth Annual Report, 1906,* 13; LCA, *Third Annual Report (1860),* 7.

14. The LCU constitution, revised in 1863, was reprinted in LCU, *Sixth Annual Report for 1863,* 10–11.

15. LCU, *Twelfth Annual Report for 1870,* 18–19; LCU, *Thirteenth Annual Report for 1871,* 17–18; Young Ladies' Christian Association of the City of New York (hereafter YLCA of NYC), *First Report, 1871,* 3–4; and Bittar, "The Y.W.C.A. of the City of New York," 21–30. Initially the group was known as the Young Ladies' Christian Association of the City of New York, but members revised the name in 1876 to the Young Women's Christian Association of the City of New York; for consistency, I have referred to the group as the New York YWCA.

16. The "Constitution," revised in 1873, reprinted in YLCA of NYC, *Third Report, 1873,* 30.

17. Sims, *Natural History of a Social Institution,* chaps. 1–2. The Boston group was the first in the United States to use the name "Young Women's Christian Association."

18. "Sex not Sects," *Brooklyn Daily Eagle,* 25 February 1888, 2. In 1888, "New York City" did not include Brooklyn and even after consolidation of the cities in 1898, the New York and Brooklyn associations remained separate.

19. E. Wilson, *Fifty Years of Association Work,* 29–49, and Sims, *Natural History of a Social Institution,* 5–6, 82–83.

20. Sims, *Natural History of a Social Institution,* 20–21, 240–43.

21. LCU, *Tenth Annual Report for 1868,* 14. For the concern about working women's leisure, see Peiss, *Cheap Amusements,* esp. chap. 7.

22. Some local YWCAs did remain involved with the issues of reformation; see Morton, "Seduced and Abandoned in an American City." On the Crittenton Homes, see Kunzel, *Fallen Women, Problem Girls.*

23. Quoted in Cochrane, "Compelled to Speak," 48. The New York YWCA restricted

assistance from its employment bureau to Protestant women until the early 1890s; see YWCA of NYC, *Twenty-second Annual Report, 1893,* 40. In some cases, Catholics and Jews avoided the YWCA because of its heavily Protestant culture. In other cases, Catholic and Jewish leaders sought to keep their young people from going to Ys for fear that they would be converted. One impetus for both the Catholic Youth Organization and Young Men's and Young Women's Hebrew Associations was to offer alternatives to Protestant organizations like the YWCA and the YMCA; see Kaufman, *Shul with a Pool,* 52–56.

24. YLCA of NYC, *First Report, 1871,* 4.

25. For examples of the image of motherhood favored by other female reformers, see Meyerowitz, *Women Adrift,* 52–53, 79–80; Boris, "The Power of Motherhood"; and Lasch-Quinn, *Black Neighbors,* chap. 4.

26. LCU, *Twelfth Annual Report for 1870,* 14–15. For the particularly Protestant nature of this approach, see Fitzgerald, "Losing Their Religion," 282–84.

27. YWCA of NYC, *Twenty-third Annual Report, 1894,* 17 (quote), and "Sex not Sects," 2.

28. Mrs. Warren S. [Jean Logan] Buxton, "The Advantages of Consolidation as Viewed by the International Board of Women's and Young Women's Christian Associations," in American Committee of Young Women's Christian Associations, *Proceedings of the Special Convention, 1906,* 7.

29. YLCA of NYC, *Second Report, 1872,* 9.

30. Quoted in Sims, *Natural History of a Social Institution,* 29.

31. Meyerowitz, *Women Adrift,* 83–86.

32. YWCA of NYC, *Fifth Annual Report, 1875,* 9.

33. For the exclusion of factory or domestic workers, see Weiner, *From Working Girl to Working Mother,* 55. Even when policies did not preclude working-class women, the fee structure (intended to make residences self-supporting) could; see Meyerowitz, *Women Adrift,* 84. For white-collar working women who found the YWCA's culture familiar, see Anderson, "Home and Community for a Generation of Women," 36–37, and Rothman, *Woman's Proper Place,* 90.

34. Dodge, "Introduction," xi. Dodge does not identify herself in the text, but see Graham, *Grace H. Dodge,* 99–100.

35. E. Wilson, *Fifty Years of Association Work,* 41.

36. YLCA of NYC, *Fourth Annual Report, 1874,* 10.

37. YWCA of NYC, *Fifth Annual Report, 1875,* 17, and Rothman, *Woman's Proper Place,* 75–76. The association did continue to place women in some domestic positions, including as housekeepers, nurses, and governesses; see YWCA of NYC, *Eighth Annual Report, 1879,* 10.

38. YWCA of NYC, *Eleventh Annual Report, 1882,* 11–13, and E. Wilson, *Fifty Years of Association Work,* 91–92.

39. E. Wilson, *Fifty Years of Association Work,* 78–107, and Sims, *Natural History of a Social Institution,* chaps. 1–2.

40. For a description of this process, for a slightly later period, see Heath, "Negotiating White Womanhood."

41. Woloch, *Women and the American Experience,* 607.

42. Quote appears in Robinson, *Eight Women of the YWCA,* 7. On the origins of the American Committee, see Sims, *Natural History of a Social Institution,* 21–26. For the YMCA's support, see C. Hopkins, *History of the Y.M.C.A.,* 292–94.

43. Joint Committee, YWCA, "To the Friends and Co-Workers," 4.

44. Sims, *Natural History of a Social Institution,* 25, 47–49.

45. YWCA of NYC, *Fifth Annual Report, 1875,* 7. Other differences also divided the two organizations. The associations in the International Board relied primarily on volunteers and stressed the autonomy of local associations; its headquarters were in the president's city, which changed each time a new woman took office. In contrast, the American Committee had centralized operations based in Chicago and hired a professional staff. Regional identity complicated relations as well: the International Board was strongest in the Northeast, while the American Committee was based in the Midwest. Finally, the International Board was critical of the American Committee's close relationship with the YMCA. Student YWs looked to the YM for guidance about policy and structure, while members of the International Board emphasized their place in the independent woman movement.

46. Bittar, "The Y.W.C.A. of the City of New York," 50–52.

47. Joint Committee, YWCA, "To the Friends and Co-Workers," 5–6.

48. Graham, *Grace H. Dodge,* chap. 11, and Sims, *Natural History of a Social Institution,* 47.

49. Sims, *Natural History of a Social Institution,* 24–25, 47–49. For a discussion of Dodge's role see Katz, "Grace Hoadley Dodge," chap. 5; Graham, *Grace H. Dodge,* chap. 11, "Arbitration Seasoned with Hospitality"; and Robinson, *Eight Women of the YWCA,* esp. chap. 2. Active members meant those who were entitled to vote or hold offices as opposed to those who simply participated in programs.

50. See Sims, *The YWCA—An Unfolding Purpose,* 27.

51. YWCA of the USA, *Report of the First Biennial Convention, 1906,* 13.

52. Ibid., 51–52. Ida T. (Mrs. Frank T.) Thurston of Washington, D.C., was a carryover from the International Board (the community YWCAs) who was active in the negotiating efforts between the two bodies.

53. YWCA of the USA, *Proceedings of the Second Biennial Convention, 1909,* 107–8. The YWCA became closely linked to the FCC. The YWCA leaders were on the administrative committee of the council; see G. Wilson, *Religious and Educational Philosophy,* 20.

54. The literature on the social gospel is extensive. For a recent synthesis, see G. Smith, *Search for Social Salvation.* My account draws on C. Hopkins, *Rise of the Social Gospel;* Carter, *The Decline and Revival of the Social Gospel;* Miller, *American Protestantism and Social Issues;* Ahlstrom, *Religious History of the American People,* 2:250–73; Fishburn, *The Fatherhood of God;* Handy, *Christian America;* and Gorrell, *The Age of Social Responsibility.* On the social gospel and gender (or women), see S. Curtis, *Consuming Faith;* Edwards and Gifford, *Gender and the Social Gospel;* and Fishburn, *The Fatherhood of God,* as well as n. 60 below.

55. Mrs. Trawick, "The Social Message of the Church," 64.

56. Ahlstrom, *Religious History of the American People,* 2:272.

57. YWCA of the USA, *Proceedings of the Second Biennial Convention, 1909,* 111.

58. For the religious (Protestant) underpinnings of progressivism, see Crunden, *Ministers of Reform,* and Fitzgerald, "Losing Their Religion."

59. G. Wilson, *Religious and Educational Philosophy,* 41. See also Fishburn, *The Fatherhood of God.*

60. See Fishburn, *The Fatherhood of God,* 13, 20, 32, 169–70; Bederman, "'The Women Have Had Charge of the Church Work Long Enough'"; S. Curtis, "The Son of Man and God the Father"; and Putney, *Muscular Christianity,* 39–44, 73–74, 89–98.

61. Walter Rauschenbusch, "Jesus and the Social Problems of Our Age," in YWCA of the USA, *Proceedings of the Second Biennial Convention, 1909,* 66–68.

62. For one example, see C. Hopkins's classic study, *Rise of the Social Gospel.*

63. A. Scott, *Natural Allies,* 85, and McDowell, *Social Gospel in the South,* 30–31.

64. Quoted in Roberts, *Florence Simms,* 281. One longtime national staff member, Rhoda McCulloch, later explained that "the first piece of social action passed by a convention (1911) came about as a result of the fire at the Triangle factory in New York." See file for "Marion Robinson—Rockefeller Project 1, *Eight Women of the YWCA* and misc. correspondence" (YWCA/NB).

65. YWCA of the USA, *Report of the First Biennial Convention, 1906,* 51–52.

66. Rauschenbusch et al. did discuss other issues, such as race relations; see Rauschenbusch, "The Problem of the Black Man" and "Belated Races and the Social Problems." In 1965, Rayford Logan criticized "the astigmatism" of (white) social gospelers in regards to race; see Logan, *The Betrayal of the Negro,* 171. Both Ronald White and Ralph Luker have challenged this interpretation of the social gospel, arguing for greater involvement by white leaders in the issue of race than has traditionally been presented; see R. White, *Liberty and Justice for All,* and Luker, *The Social Gospel in Black and White.* Also of relevance is the literature on black social gospelers like Reverdy Ransom; see Luker as well as Weisenfeld, "'The More Abundant Life,'" esp. 32–38, and G. Smith, *Search for Social Salvation,* esp. chap. 6. Nonetheless, for most white social gospelers, race was not the primary focus in the first three decades of the twentieth century.

67. On Philadelphia, see [Hunton], *Beginnings among Colored Women,* 7, and Jones, "Struggle among Saints," 162–63.

68. On the race riot, see Osofsky, *Harlem: The Making of a Ghetto,* 46–52.

69. A. Davis, *Spearheads for Reform,* 94–95; Osofsky, "Progressivism and the Negro," 167–68; Lasch-Quinn, *Black Neighbors;* and Crocker, *Social Work and Social Order,* esp. 26, 35, and chaps. 3 and 7.

70. On Brooklyn, see Connolly, *A Ghetto Grows in Brooklyn,* 80–83. For New York, see YWCA of NYC, *Thirty-fifth Annual Report, 1906,* 27–28; Bittar, "The Y.W.C.A. of the City of New York," 54, 145–48; and Weisenfeld, *African American Women and Christian Activism,* chap. 2.

71. Mrs. Hunton, "Women's Clubs," 121–22. For more on Washington, see Radcliffe, *A Simple Matter of Justice,* chap. 1.

72. It is unclear whether the American Committee was actually more open to black participation (than was the International Board) or whether the greater number of black student associations simply reflected that black colleges were permitted to establish separate associations.

73. YWCA National Board, minutes, 5 June 1907, 9; YWCA National Board, minutes, 2 October 1907, 10; and "Brief History of Colored Work" [May 1918], 1 (all YWCA/NB). Although Grace Dodge had largely focused upon the needs of young white working women, her interest in related reforms such as industrial education led her not only to assist in the founding of Teachers College, but also to support the efforts of Booker T. Washington and Victoria Earle Matthews (most notably the latter's White Rose Industrial Association for black women and girls). Her commitment to the "American Negro" was sufficiently broad to win her the appreciation of those in the National Association for the Advancement of Colored People as well; see Graham, *Grace H. Dodge,* 213–15 and chaps. 8–9; E. Davis, *Lifting as They Climb,* 232–33; Jean Blackwell Hutson, "Victoria Earle Matthews," in James et al., *Notable American Women,* 2:510–11; [W. E. B. Du Bois], "A Lost Friend," *Crisis* 9 (February 1915): 183–84.

74. "Brief History of Colored Work," 1.

75. "The First 6 Months [in the Home Department]," *Association Monthly* 1 (August 1907): 328–29.

76. National Board, minutes, 2 October 1907, 10.

77. Robert Wiebe's *Search for Order* is the classic statement of this effort to consolidate, especially in the realms of business and government. In the area of religion, see Ahlstrom, *Religious History of the American People,* 2:265–66. Sophonisba Breckinridge delineates the consolidation of (white) women's groups, while Stephanie Shaw analyzes that of black women's organizations; see Breckinridge, *Women in the Twentieth Century,* 26, and Shaw, "Black Club Women and the Creation of the National Association of Colored Women."

78. McPherson, *Abolitionist Legacy,* 333.

79. Subcommittee on Colored Work, minutes, 23 March 1915 quoted in Jane Olcott Walters, comp., "History of Colored Work: Chronological Excerpts from Reports of Secretaries & Workers and from Minutes Showing Development of the Work among Colored Women, 1907–1920," typescript, 1 (YWCA/NB). Mabel Cratty (1868–1928), a Methodist, was born and raised in Ohio. She graduated with a B.L. from Ohio Wesleyan University in 1890. Cratty then taught or served as a school principal before going to work for the American Committee in 1904. After the 1906 merger, she served as the general secretary of the YWCA until her death in 1928. See William B. Whiteside, "Mabel Cratty," in James et al., *Notable American Women,* 1:403–5; Robinson, *Eight Women of the YWCA,* esp. chap. 3; and Burton, *Mabel Cratty.*

80. For the development of white women's groups in the South, see A. Scott, *The Southern Lady,* and Grantham, "The Contours of Southern Progressivism," 1051–52.

81. "Minutes of a Meeting held in Richmond, Virginia, under the auspices of the South Atlantic Field Committee," transcript, 3 July 1920, 5–6 (YWCA/NB). Helen Alling Davis (1871–1950) was an Episcopalian. She was born in New York and graduated from the Boston Normal School of Gymnastics (later absorbed by Wellesley) in 1896. She worked for local YWCAs in New York State and, after the 1906 merger, for the Northeast Field (New England, New York, and New Jersey). During World War I, she served as general secretary of the YWCA's War Work Council. In 1921, she was an assistant to Mabel Cratty and in 1928, became the associate general secretary.

She retired from the YWCA in 1934. Her sister was Dr. Katherine Bement Davis. See YWCA Biographical Files (YWCA/NB) and "Alumnae Biographical File" and "Alumnae Association: Hygiene and Physical Education Section, Class of 1896, Biographical Data" (WCA).

82. The YWCA changed its regional divisions over time. In the early period, it assigned community YWCAs to eleven or twelve fields; by the 1940s, there were four regions (Eastern, Southern, Central, and Western). The South Atlantic, South Central, and Southwestern *Fields* roughly corresponded to the Southern *Region;* the major exception was the placement of Missouri in the South Central Field, but in the Central Region, and Washington, D.C., as part of the East Central Field, but the Southern Region. I have generally used "the South" to refer to the three southern fields, which consisted of Alabama, Arkansas, Florida, Georgia, Kentucky, Louisiana, Mississippi, Missouri, North Carolina, Oklahoma, South Carolina, Tennessee, Texas, and Virginia. Statistics to compare the number of local YWCAs to the total population were drawn from the YWCA of the USA, *Directory and Statistical Report of the YWCA, 1909,* and Campbell Gibson and Kay Jung, *Historical Census Statistics on Population Totals by Race, 1790 to 1990, and by Hispanic Origins, 1970–1990, for the United States, Regions, Divisions, and States,* Population Division Working Paper 56 (Washington, D.C.: U.S. Census Bureau, 2002), 33–83. The regional divisions for student and city YWCAs differed slightly. The differences have not been explored in this study.

83. For a comparable decision within the white Protestant churches, see Reimers, *White Protestantism and the Negro,* especially chap. 3.

84. The 1890 Mohonk Conference on the Negro Question drew from both white northerners and southerners, but excluded African Americans. Likewise, the Capon Springs Conference for Christian Education in the South (a precursor to the Southern Education Board), held in 1898, had no black attendees. See R. White, *Liberty and Justice for All,* 3–9, 78–82, and McPherson, *Abolitionist Legacy,* 137–38, 179.

85. Subcommittee on Colored Work, minutes, 23 March 1915, 1.

86. See, for instance, Calkins, "The Negro in the Young Women's Christian Association," 39.

87. As late as 1910, only 10.4 percent of African Americans lived in the North and West; see Myrdal, *An American Dilemma,* 183.

88. "Minutes of a Meeting held in Richmond, Virginia," transcript, 3 July 1920, 3.

89. A view of Reconstruction shared by northern and southern whites; see McPherson, *Abolitionist Legacy,* chap. 18.

90. See Osofsky, "Progressivism and the Negro," 153, regarding general hostility toward African Americans.

Chapter 2: Creating the Race Policy

1. Student Committee Report in YWCA National Board, minutes, 2 October 1907, 5 (YWCA/NB).

2. Addie Waites [sometimes spelled Waite or Waits] Hunton (1867?-1943), was born in Norfolk, Virginia, and was raised by an aunt in Boston after the death of her

mother. An Episcopalian, she graduated from the Spencerian College of Commerce in Philadelphia in 1889. She taught in the South, and in 1893 she married William Alphaeus Hunton, a professional worker for the Young *Men's* Christian Association's African American programs. They settled in Atlanta but left following the 1906 race riot and moved to Brooklyn, New York. Addie Hunton was also active with the Brooklyn Equal Suffrage League, the National Association of Colored Women, the National Association for the Advancement of Colored People, the Women's International League for Peace and Freedom, and the International Council of Women of the Darker Races. See Lutz, "'The Dizzy Steep to Heaven,'" esp. chaps. 2–5, and Jean Blackwell Hutson, "Addie Waites Hunton," in James et al., *Notable American Women,* 2:240–41.

3. William Alphaeus Hunton (1863–1916) initially worked for the Norfolk black YMCA as the first paid black local secretary; he later joined the national staff of the YMCA, where he helped develop work for African Americans across the country until his death in 1916; see Mjagkij, *Light in the Darkness,* as well as Addie Hunton's biography of her husband, *William Alphaeus Hunton.*

4. [Hunton], *Beginnings among Colored Women,* 7.

5. "The First Year," *Association Monthly* 1 (January 1908): 561.

6. Mrs. Hunton, "The Work of the National Board of Young Women's Christian Associations," 217.

7. A. Hunton, "Negro Womanhood Defended," 280.

8. Student Committee Report in YWCA National Board, minutes, 2 October 1907, 5. The scholarly literature on the YWCA at the turn of the century is growing; helpful accounts can be found in Jones, "Struggle among Saints"; Neverdon-Morton, *Afro-American Women of the South;* Salem, *To Better Our World;* and Weisenfeld, *African American Women and Christian Activism.*

9. Mrs. Hunton, "Women's Clubs," 122, and Walters, "History of Colored Work," 3.

10. [Hunton], *Beginnings among Colored Women,* 7.

11. Mrs. Hunton, "Women's Clubs," 121, and YWCA National Board, minutes, 1 April 1908, 11 (YWCA/NB). Elizabeth A. Ross Haynes (1883–1953) was a Baptist, later possibly a Congregationalist. Born and raised in Alabama, she earned a B.A. from Fisk University in 1903 and then worked as a teacher in the South. She resigned from the YWCA in 1910 to marry George Edmund Haynes (1880–1960), a one-time YM secretary and social welfare activist who helped found the Urban League. Ross Haynes completed a masters degree in 1923 at Columbia with a thesis entitled "Negroes in Domestic Service in the United States," the first such study. See Ruth Bogin, "Elizabeth Ross Haynes," in Sicherman and Green, *Notable American Women,* 324–25. For consistency, I have referred to her as Ross Haynes even prior to her marriage.

12. Cecelia Holloway Cabaniss Saunders (1883–1966), a Methodist, was born and raised in Charleston, South Carolina. She attended Fisk University and she received her B.A. in 1909. She taught in South Carolina before moving to New York to work for the national YWCA. She left the position when she married Dr. James E. Cabaniss, who died shortly thereafter. In early 1914, she became the general secretary of the black YWCA in New York City, a job she continued even after her marriage to

John D. Saunders (a real estate agent) until her resignation in 1947; see Weisenfeld, "Cecelia Cabaniss Saunders," in Hine et al., *Black Women in America,* 1010.

13. Josephine Virginia Pinyon Holmes (1888–1943), denomination unknown. She grew up in New Jersey and attended Cornell University (1906–10); she subsequently undertook graduate work at Columbia University and the University of Chicago. She worked for the National Board until 1916, when she left to teach high school in Kansas City, Kansas. She resumed work for the National Board during World War I. She married Van S. Holmes of Bennett College in 1921 and moved to Brooklyn, where she worked for the Ashland Place branch and continued to advise the national association as a volunteer. See Olcott, *Work of Colored Women,* 8; additional information provided by Elaine Engst, University Archivist, Cornell University, personal communications to author, 4–5 June 2003.

14. Mrs. Hunton, "Women's Clubs," 121–22.

15. [Hunton], *Beginnings among Colored Women,* 5.

16. Ibid., 3.

17. A. Hunton, "A Deeper Reverence for Home Ties," 59.

18. Logan, *The Betrayal of the Negro,* 11. For more on segregation, see Woodward, *The Strange Career of Jim Crow,* and on cultural images, see Thurber, "The Development of the Mammy Image and Mythology." For the argument that (sexual) violence against women was as critical to the position of the race as lynching, see Hine, "Rape and the Inner Lives of Black Women."

19. A. Hunton, "A Deeper Reverence for Home Ties," 59.

20. A. Hunton, "Negro Womanhood Defended," 280.

21. A discussion of African Americans and class presents all the difficulties inherent in the discussion of white women and class in these years, with an added complication. Due to African Americans' relatively limited financial situation, black men and women who would have been seen as only working class if they had been white actually occupied a class-privileged place in the African American community more comparable to the middle class in the white community; see Lerner, *Majority Finds Its Past,* 73; see also Walker, "City of Brotherly Hate," and D. White, *Too Heavy a Load,* 70.

22. Higginbotham, *Righteous Discontent,* chap. 7; see also Guy-Sheftall, *Daughters of Sorrow,* 70–76; Gilmore, *Gender and Jim Crow,* 138–42; D. White, *Too Heavy a Load,* chap. 2; and Gaines, *Uplifting the Race,* 78–80, 135–36.

23. "Talented tenth" was popularized by W. E. B. Du Bois, but African Americans associated with a wide spectrum of political beliefs used the idea in discussions on how to advance the race. There is a heated debate among scholars as to the strengths and limitations of it as a strategy. Gilmore, *Gender and Jim Crow;* Higginbotham, *Righteous Discontent;* and Weisenfeld, *African American Women and Christian Activism* offer relatively positive assessments of a class-stratified strategy for racial advancement; for a more critical stance, see Gaines, *Uplifting the Race,* esp. the preface.

24. The classic discussion of progressive era notions of uplift is Haber, *Efficiency and Uplift;* on the implications of the idea for African Americans, see Gaines, *Uplifting the Race,* Gilmore, *Gender and Jim Crow,* and D. White, *Too Heavy a Load.*

25. YWCA of NYC, *Thirty-fifth Annual Report, 1906,* 27.

26. A. Hunton, "Negro Womanhood Defended," 282. These views were shared

by other black women. The National Association of Colored Women, with which Hunton was also active in these years, selected "Lifting as We Climb" as its motto; see E. Davis, *Lifting as They Climb,* 21.

27. [Hunton], *Beginnings among Colored Women,* 5–6.

28. Ibid., 16.

29. On evangelical Protestants' equation of American civilization with Christianity (meaning Protestantism), see Handy, *Christian America,* esp. chaps. 2 and 5; for the connections between Americanism, Protestantism, and democracy, see Mead, "American Denominationalism since the Civil War," 1, 6.

30. Walters, "History of Colored Work," 5.

31. Ross [Haynes], report, 3 December 1908, in Walters, "History of Colored Work," 3.

32. The only official standard in these years was adherence to the requirement for membership in a Protestant evangelical church. Women at the national headquarters sought to establish some uniformity in programs—preventive, not relief—and the targeted audience (e.g., young women), but, in practice, local associations, white as well as black, sponsored a wide range of programs.

33. Walters, "History of Colored Work," 7.

34. Ross [Haynes], report, 3 December 1908, in Walters, "History of Colored Work," 4.

35. "Minutes of a Meeting Held in Richmond, Virginia, under the Auspices of the South Atlantic Field Committee," transcript, 3 July 1920, 4 (YWCA/NB).

36. City Committee Report, 5 October 1910, in YWCA National Board, minutes, 7 December 1910, 4 (YWCA/NB).

37. In cities like New York there might be as many as twenty associations scattered around the city in order to make the YWCA accessible to all residents. National leaders urged that multiple associations in a community federate so that there would be a single organization for each city. The agreement was phrased in racially neutral language. Neither it nor the branch policy spelled out the racial composition of central associations. In practice, however, there were no white branches linked to a black central association. African American women, for instance, had been the first to organize an association in Washington, D.C., but the subsequent white association also affiliated directly with the national, rather than as a branch; see Mary S. Sims, "Policy—One Association in a Community," 26 May 1948 (YWCA/NB), and Isobel C. Lawson, "Review of Policies Affecting Organization of Y.W.C.A. Work among Negro Women," 1 (YWCA/RFC 158.3).

38. Ross [Haynes], report, June–December 1910, in Walters, "History of Colored Work," 8.

39. City Committee Report, 5 October 1910, in YWCA National Board, minutes, 7 December 1910, 5. Generally, the recommended minimum African American population was fifteen thousand; see *The Young Women's Christian Association among Colored Women in Cities* (New York: National Board of the Young Womens Christian Associations of the United States of America, 1915), 3 (NU/AUC).

40. J. Curtis, "A Girls' Clubhouse," 295.

41. Work, *Negro Yearbook, 1912,* 95.

42. Walters, "History of Colored Work," 11.

43. "City Notes," *Association Monthly* 4 (January 1911): 496.

44. Ovington, *Walls Came Tumbling Down*, 59.

45. The white woman lasted about six months and left reporting that "a white secretary is not acceptable to the colored women"; quoted in Weisenfeld, *African American Women and Christian Activism*, 58, 61.

46. Walters, "History of Colored Work," 11.

47. Ibid., 11–12.

48. Mrs. Hunton, "Women's Clubs," 121.

49. Walters, "History of Colored Work," 12, and Mrs. Hunton, "Women's Clubs," 121–22. Black women, however, stayed in private living accommodations rather than in the YWCA's dormitory.

50. City Committee Report in YWCA National Board, minutes, 29 May 1912, 15 (YWCA/NB); "History, First Conference of Volunteer and Employed Workers in Colored Young Women's Christian Associations in Cities, New York City, 1912" (YWCA/RFC 108.3); [Addie Waites Hunton], "Conference for Workers in Colored City Associations," *Association Monthly* 6 (August 1912): 262–63.

51. Salem, *To Better Our World*, 142–43.

52. Hunton, report, April–May 1911, in Walters, "History of Colored Work," 11–12.

53. Weisenfeld, *African American Women and Christian Activism*, 102, and more generally chap. 4.

54. Mrs. Hunton, "The Work of the National Board of Young Women's Christian Associations," 216; [Hunton], *Beginnings among Colored Women*, 9–10; and J. Curtis, "A Girls' Clubhouse," 295.

55. Walters, "History of Colored Work," 5, 8, 13–14, 17, 24.

56. City Committee Report in YWCA National Board, minutes, 7 February 1912, 15.

57. Sims, *Natural History of a Social Institution*, 60. Eva Del Vakia Bowles (1875–1943), an Episcopalian, was born in Ohio. She attended Ohio State University and taught in schools in the South. She served as the secretary for the African American branch in New York City starting in 1906 as the first black secretary for a local YW. After attending the New York School of Philanthropy, she served as a caseworker for the Associated Charities of Columbus, Ohio, as one of the first black professional social workers. Joining the YWCA's national staff in 1913, she remained with it until her resignation in 1932. Prior to her death in 1943, she worked for the National Colored Merchants Association and Cincinnati's West End Branch. Over the years, she was also active with the NAACP and the New York Urban League; see Jean Blackwell Hutson, "Eva del Vakia Bowles," in James et al., *Notable American Women*, 1:214–15, and C. Davis, "Eva D[el Vakia] Bowles."

58. Bowles, report, 10 December 1913, in Walters, "History of Colored Work," 26.

59. Walters, "History of Colored Work," 26.

60. Calkins, "The Negro in the Young Women's Christian Association," 40.

61. Mrs. C. A. Winn, "Speech to the National Board," 25 May 1938, 2 (YWCA/NB).

62. Leila S. Frissell, "Conferences," 14–18 May 1914, 2 (YWCA/RFC 108.3). Leila Stiles Frissell (ca. 1856–1932) was a Presbyterian and was raised in New York State

and City. Her major public activities appear to have been for the YWCA. In 1921, she resigned from the National Board for ill health but remained on it as an "honorary member" until her death. Her father, Rev. Amasa Cogswell Frissell, had been an abolitionist minister. One brother, Hollis Burke Frissell, was principal of Hampton Institute (Va.) and on the Tuskegee board of trustees; another, Algernon Sydney Frissell, was a banker who supported both the YMCA and the National Urban League. As such, her generation fits into the pattern described in McPherson's *The Abolitionist Legacy*—that the descendants of evangelical abolitionists often continued an involvement in racial reform, especially through educational efforts. See "The Rev. Amasa C. Frissell," *New York Times,* 8 April 1894, 5; "Frissell," *New York Times,* 10 October 1932, 36; "Algernon Frissell, Banker, Dies at 87," *New York Times,* 10 December 1932, 19; McPherson, *The Abolitionist Legacy,* 149–50; and R. White, *Liberty and Justice for All,* esp. 151, 153, 172–75.

63. Frissell, "Conferences, 1914," 2.

64. John Raleigh Mott (1865–1955), a Methodist, was a lay leader of the Student Christian Movement, in particular the Student Volunteer Movement for Foreign Missions and the YMCA (he became general secretary of the latter in 1915). His book *The Evangelization of the World in This Generation* (1900) set forth the agenda for more than one generation of student missionaries. See R. White, *Liberty and Justice for All,* 189–90, 200–206; C. Hopkins, *History of the Y.M.C.A.;* and Shedd, *Two Centuries of Student Christian Movements,* 289–302.

65. Frissell, "Conferences, 1914."

66. E. Wilson, *Fifty Years of Association Work,* 272.

67. Beach, "The Atlanta Negro Christian Student Convention," 111.

68. Mrs. Trawick, "The Social Message of the Church," 62–65. Mary Maude Wilder Trawick (1875–1963) was a Southern Methodist. She had been a teacher at a settlement in Nashville, prior to her 1909 marriage to Arcadius (Arch) McSwain Trawick (1869–1958), a minister, professor, and YM student secretary. Maude Trawick was president of the board of directors of the Nashville (white) YWCA; in addition to her YW work, she was also a trustee of Fisk University. See R. White, *Liberty and Justice for All,* 201–6.

69. Mrs. Hunton, "The Work of the National Board of Young Women's Christian Associations," 215–16.

70. Ibid., 217.

71. Mrs. J. D. Hammond, "The Building of Homes," 73.

72. For Ronald White's assessment, see *Liberty and Justice for All,* 202–4.

73. Pinyon, Annual Report, 1914 in Walters, "History of Colored Work," 36. The YWCA did send a few secretaries to Africa but mostly concentrated on Asia and South America. The total (forty-nine) sent to Africa over the years was fewer than that to Brazil alone (sixty-seven); see Boyd, *Emissaries: The Overseas Work of the American YWCA,* 321. More needs to be done on African Americans' involvement with missions, but see Jacobs, "Afro-American Women Missionaries Confront the African Way of Life."

74. Pinyon, Annual Report, 1914, in Walters, "History of Colored Work," 36, 38.

75. Holmquist, Report, September 1914, in Walters, "History of Colored Work," 32, and as quoted by Pinyon, Annual Report, 1914, in Walters, "History of Colored

Work," 36. The Department of Method was the umbrella division overseeing both city and student work.

76. YWCA of the USA, *Report of the National Board to the Fifth National Convention, 1915,* 18.

77. Holmes, "Youth Cannot Wait," 128–31. Holmes was Pinyon's married name.

78. The National Board did have a "non-resident" member category, but such members did not consistently attend meetings.

79. Olcott, *Work of Colored Women,* 7.

80. On difficulties for the national staff, see Walters, "History of Colored Work," 41, 47.

81. "Meeting of Sub-committee on Colored Work," 23 March 1915 (YWCA/NB), and Pinyon, Annual Report, 1914, in Walters, "History of Colored Work," 37.

82. YWCA National Board, minutes, 3 February 1915, 1 (YWCA/NB); Bowles, report, 20 October 1915, in Walters, "History of Colored Work," 42 (both quotes); "The Louisville Conference," *Southern Workman* (November 1915) (TIA/MF 5:1025); "Growth of Southern Work," 2 (YWCA/NB); "Brief History of Colored Work" [May 1918], 1 (YWCA/NB); and Bell and Wilkins, *Interracial Practices in Community Y.W.C.A.'s,* 3–4.

Representing the national were staff members Mabel Cratty, Helen Davis, Louise Holmquist, Bertha Condé, Josephine Pinyon, and Eva Bowles, and National Board members Effie Price Gladding and Annie M. Reynolds. The latter two had been at the Asheville conference and on were on the Sub-Committee on Colored Work. The field committees were intermediary bodies between the National Board and local associations and oversaw the work in specific regions. They were officially part of the National Board, but regional women selected the committee members; those who attended included Katharine H. Hawes of the South Atlantic Field and Elizabeth MacFarland of the South Central.

Nominated by the African American staff, the black southerners included Charlotte Hawkins Brown and Lugenia Burns Hope. Most—or all of them—were active with the NACW. The white men were Arcadius Trawick, Thomas Jesse Jones, and John Little, all of whom had attended the 1914 Atlanta conference. The white southern women (from outside the YWCA) included Lily Hardy Hammond and Sara Estelle Haskin [sometimes Haskins], active in a wide range of efforts dealing with race in the South, especially through the Southern Methodist Church.

83. *YWCA among Colored Women in Cities,* 2.

84. "Suggestions from the Committee on Findings at the Conference on Colored Work, Louisville, Ky.," 14–15 October 1915 (YWCA/NB).

85. In the ensuing years, this committee would operate under a variety of names, including the Interlocking Committee, the Committee Between, and eventually, the Colored Work Committee; see "Report of Proceedings of the Conference held by the Young Women's Christian Association, Louisville, Kentucky," 16–17 February 1921, pt. 2:100 (YWCA/NB), and *YWCA among Colored Women in Cities,* 4.

86. For range of practices, see "Report of Proceedings of the Louisville Conference," 1921, pt. 2:89–91, 94–95, 100 ff.

87. "Minutes of a Meeting Held in Richmond, Virginia," transcript, 3 July 1920, 8–9; Winn, "Speech to the National Board, 1938," 2; and Calkins, "The Negro in the

Young Women's Christian Association," 40–45. See also Hall, *Revolt against Chivalry,* 83, 287 n. 70, and Rouse, *Lugenia Burns Hope,* 93–94.

88. "Suggestions from the Conference on Colored Work, Louisville," 1915.

89. "Meeting of Sub-committee on Colored Work," 23 March 1915; see also Frissell, "Conferences, 1914," 2.

90. Bowles, Annual Report, 1915 in Walters, "History of Colored Work," 47–48.

91. "Suggestions from the Conference on Colored Work, Louisville," 1915.

92. Josephine Pinyon, Report to Sub-Committee on Colored Work, 23 November 1915, 1 (YWCA/NB), and her report, 27 October 1915, in Walters, "History of Colored Work," 48.

93. Elizabeth Preston Allen, Katharine Heath Hawes, Lugenia Burns Hope, and Eva Bowles attended the first meeting; see Bowles, report, 18 January 1916, in Walters, "History of Colored Work," 57.

94. "Report of Proceedings of the Louisville Conference," 1921, pt. 2:1–2.

95. The existing evidence suggests that the YWCA drew African Americans from denominations similar to those for whites: particularly Methodist, Baptist, Episcopalian, and Presbyterian. Presbyterians and Methodists dominated among white women, while Methodists and Baptists were the strongest among black women. There were additional differences since black Methodists drew from the African Methodist Episcopal Church (AME), the African Methodist Episcopal Zion Church, and the Colored Methodist Episcopal Church (CME) as well as the Methodist Episcopal Church, while white Methodists were generally from either the Methodist Episcopal Church or the Methodist Episcopal Church, South; there would have been parallel splits for Baptists. For one example of divisions among white women, see the breakdown of delegates at the 1913 national convention; YWCA of the USA, *Proceedings of the Fourth Biennial Convention, 1913,* 60. Of the 927 delegates, there were 265 Presbyterians, 131 Methodists, 101 Baptists, 95 Episcopalians, and 81 Congregationalists, and then several smaller groups. For black women, see (albeit for a later date) "Wilberforce Branch Conference," 19–25 June 1935, 3 (YWCA/NB). Of the 118 registrants, 23 were AME; 21, Methodist; 1, CME; 17, Baptist; 14, Episcopal; 7, Presbyterian; some unknown or only a couple.

96. [Hunton], *Beginnings among Colored Women,* 12.

97. For other examples of African American women who promoted interracial efforts to advance the race, see Higginbotham, *Righteous Discontent,* chap. 4, and Gilmore, *Gender and Jim Crow,* chap. 7. For more on black social gospelers, see G. Smith, *Search for Social Salvation,* esp. chap. 6.

98. [Hunton], *Beginnings among Colored Women,* 11–12.

99. "Minutes of a Meeting held in Richmond, Virginia," transcript, 3 July 1920, 10.

100. See "Suggestions from the Conference on Colored Work, Louisville," 1915; Walters, "History of Colored Work," 58–59; and Pinyon, Report to Sub-Committee on Colored Work, 23 November 1915, 2–3.

101. There is a rapidly expanding literature on the networks of black women. The NACW, as well as the YWCA, facilitated connections; see, for instance, Hunton's columns on the work in the *Crisis, Voice of the Negro,* and *Colored American,* as well as E. Davis, *Lifting as They Climb.* In addition to those listed in n. 8 above, useful scholarly

accounts include D. White, *Too Heavy a Load,* and Shaw, "Black Club Women and the Creation of the National Association of Colored Women."

102. D. White, "The Cost of Club Work," 252–53.

103. "Negro Women to Unite," *Philadelphia Record,* 1916 (TIA/MF 5:1027). For more on clubwomen's pointed critique of black men (and the latter's response), see D. White, *Too Heavy a Load,* esp. chaps. 1–2.

104. Walters, "History of Colored Work," 7. See also Calkins, "The Negro in the Young Women's Christian Association," 46; Salem, *To Better Our World,* 143–44; and Weisenfeld, *African American Women and Christian Activism,* 35.

105. Jane Olcott Walters, the compiler of "History of Colored Work," initially included the comment, but someone crossed it off with instructions to "omit" in the final version; see Walters, "History of Colored Work," 7. See Myrdal, *An American Dilemma,* 794–97, for an analysis of the discussions (or lack thereof) of the "advantages of disadvantages."

106. Walters, "History of Colored Work," 12. Efforts to found a black YWCA resumed in 1915, although advocates did not succeed until 1923.

107. See Ovington, *Walls Came Tumbling Down,* 21–24, on Boston and the YMCA. For debate over a black YWCA in the Boston area, see "So. Colored Woman Starting Jim Crow in Cambridge" *Guardian,* 1922 (TIA/MF 17:62). For Cleveland, see "Colored Girls in Cleveland," *Crisis* 36 (December 1929): 411–12; Jones, *Jane Edna Hunter;* and Kusmer, *A Ghetto Takes Shape,* 124, 149, 249, 265–66.

108. Rabinowitz, *Race Relations in the Urban South,* esp. epilogue.

109. *Afro-American Ledger,* 12 June 1914 (TIA/MF 3:615, 3:620).

110. "Report of Proceedings of the Louisville Conference," 1921, pt. 2:134.

Chapter 3: Working for Democracy

1. L. H. Hammond, *Southern Women and Racial Adjustment,* 27.

2. Lily Hardy Hammond (1859–1925), a Southern Methodist, was born in New Jersey to southerners and was educated in private schools. As a young woman, she spent some time with urban missions in the North before her 1879 marriage to John D. Hammond, a minister. The couple moved to the South, where she was active with the Southern Methodist women's home mission efforts. John Patrick McDowell describes her as its "most prolific writer"; see his *Social Gospel in the South,* 14. For more on Hammond's ideas and activities, see McDowell, *Social Gospel in the South,* esp. chaps. 1, 2, 4, and R. White, *Liberty and Justice for All,* 220–24; for additional biographical information, see Bowden, *Dictionary of American Religious Biography,* 189–90, and her obituary, "Mrs. Lydia [*sic*] Hardy Hammond," *New York Times,* 25 January 1925, sec. 2, p. 7.

3. L. H. Hammond, *Southern Women and Racial Adjustment,* 15.

4. Ibid., 28–29, 27.

5. Sosna, *In Search of the Silent South,* 14. While at Paine, the Hammonds quietly supported the founding of the NAACP; once they left, they were more vocal, joining, for instance, a 1919 call for a national conference on lynching; see "Anti-Lynching Conference, May 5–6," *Crisis* 18 (May 1914): 23–24.

6. L. H. Hammond, *Southern Women and Racial Adjustment,* 18.

7. Ibid., 29.

8. [Hunton], *Beginnings among Colored Women,* 5–6.

9. For a recommendation of Hammond's 1914 *In Black and White: An Interpretation of Southern Life,* see Pinyon, Annual Report, 1914, in Walters, "History of Colored Work," 38. The YWCA published her essay "Interracial Cooperation." Comments on her contributions to the 1915 Louisville conference can be found in "The Louisville Conference," *Southern Workman* (November 1915) (TIA/MF 5:1025).

10. L. H. Hammond, *Southern Women and Racial Adjustment,* 18, 27, 29.

11. L. H. Hammond, "Interracial Cooperation," 13.

12. "Editorial," *Association Monthly* 11 (January 1918): 6.

13. For a discussion of the churches' comparable view, see Ahlstrom, "Preaching the Great Crusade," in *Religious History of the American People,* 2:365–73, and Handy, *Christian America,* 130–33, 146–47.

14. On Baker, see Bristow, *Making Men Moral,* esp. 4–5.

15. "To Subscribers to the United War Work Campaign," 2–5, and Sims, *Natural History of a Social Institution,* 181–82. For a fuller account of the CTCA, see Bristow, *Making Men Moral.*

16. YWCA of the USA, *Report of the National Board to the Sixth National Convention, 1920,* 106.

17. "To Subscribers to the United War Work Campaign," 4, and Putney, *Muscular Christianity,* 188. The YM got about 59 percent, or $119 million.

18. Lane, "Girls They Leave behind Them," 37; Cushman, "The War Work of the YWCA," 191; and YWCA, *Report of Hostess House Committee,* 3.

19. Hannah Mitchell, "Colored Women Represent Their Race in State and Nation," *New York Tribune,* 23 March 1919, sec. 7, p. 9.

20. Davison, "Y.W.C.A.'s War Burden," 498.

21. YWCA, "Report of the National War Work Council," 38–39, 41, and Zeiger, *In Uncle Sam's Service,* 52–53.

22. YWCA, "Report of the National War Work Council," 37.

23. "Hostess Houses and the Home Touch in Camp," 395, and W. Clarke, "The Promotion of Social Hygiene in War Time," 184–85; also see Bristow, *Making Men Moral,* chap. 2, esp. 33–34.

24. Vera Scott Cushman to the Rockefeller Foundation, memorandum, 5 June 1917, 1 (RFA/RAC).

25. Williamson, "Second Line of Defense," 763.

26. See YWCA, *Report of Hostess House Committee,* 5; YWCA, "Report of the National War Work Council," 11–15; W. Clarke, "The Promotion of Social Hygiene in War Time," 184; and Davison, "*Little Sister* of the Red Cross."

27. "What the Women Are Doing for Our Army and Navy"; M. Hopkins, "Hostess Houses"; and Cushman to Rockefeller Foundation, memorandum, 5 June 1917, 2. Nancy Bristow discusses reformers' use of motherhood and home for moral uplift in *Making Men Moral,* 49–50.

28. The YWCA declared that its policy was that dancing was not permitted; YWCA, *Report of Hostess House Committee,* 5–6. Reports of actual practices suggest a more

lenient stance: Olcott, *Work of Colored Women,* 42; W. Clarke, "The Promotion of Social Hygiene in War Time," 184; and YWCA, *Report of Hostess House Committee,* 21, 26.

29. Eva D. Bowles, "Work among Colored Women and Girls under the War Work Council," memorandum, 1 (YWCA/NB).

30. See M. Hopkins, "Hostess Houses," and E. Ward, "Bringing Home to the Army Camps."

31. YWCA, "Report of the National War Work Council," 7, 11.

32. Fosdick, "The War and Navy Departments Commissions on Training Camp Activities," 137, and "To Subscribers to the United War Work Campaign," 8.

33. "What the Women Are Doing for Our Army and Navy"; Cushman to Rockefeller Foundation, memorandum, 5 June 1917; YWCA, "Report of the National War Work Council," 8–9; YWCA, *Report of Hostess House Committee,* 7–8.

34. Paddock, "War Work of YWCA," 208. The phrase "second line of defense" sometimes referred to women's upholding the moral standards; see Williamson, "Second Line of Defense."

35. YWCA, "Report of the National War Work Council," 16, 17.

36. Wyckoff, "Girls behind the Men behind the Guns." See also the YWCA's proposed budget in "To Subscribers to the United War Work Campaign," 8.

37. On training programs for leaders, see Wyckoff, "Girls behind the Men behind the Guns," and Paddock, "War Work of YWCA."

38. The literature on women and World War I (and the prospects of a "new era" for women) is voluminous. For early studies, see Green, *The Role of Women as Production Workers in War Plants,* 3, and I. Clarke, *American Women and the World War.* For a more recent scholarly account, see Greenwald, *Women, War, and Work.*

39. Chafe, *The American Woman,* 52–54.

40. YWCA of the USA, *Report of the National Board to the Sixth National Convention, 1920,* 15, 92–93; the total membership for 1915 was given as 360,865 (on 101). As impressive as the figure of 300,000 workers is, it represented only a small portion of women in industry, estimated as a million and a half by August 1918; YWCA of the USA, *Proceedings of the Sixth National Convention, 1920,* 27.

41. YWCA of the USA, *Report of the National Board to the Sixth National Convention, 1920,* 14–15.

42. Ibid., 11, 14.

43. On the International Institutes, see Mohl, "Cultural Pluralism in Immigrant Education," and DeRoche, "How Wide the Circle of We."

44. YWCA of the USA, *Report of the National Board to the Sixth National Convention, 1920,* 21–28.

45. Ibid., 17–18.

46. African Americans debated both whether they should support the war and whether, in fact, the war would improve their position; see Scheiber and Scheiber, "The Wilson Administration and the Wartime Mobilization of Black Americans"; Jordan, "'The Damnable Dilemma'"; M. Ellis, "'Closing Ranks' and 'Seeking Honors'"; and N. Brown, "'Your Patriotism Is of the Purest Quality.'"

47. Bowles, "Negro Women and the War," 426. For contemporary accounts of black

women's war efforts, see Alice Dunbar-Nelson, "Negro Women in War Work," in E. Scott, *Scott's Official History*, 374–97, and Olcott, *Work of Colored Women*. Scholarly accounts situate the war work in the context of larger efforts for social reform; see Breen, "Black Women and the Great War"; N. Brown, "'Your Patriotism Is of the Purest Quality'"; Salem, *To Better Our World*, chap. 7; and Weisenfeld, *African American Women and Christian Activism*, chap. 5.

48. Paddock, "War Work of YWCA," 211; Paddock was the YWCA's publicity director for war relief efforts.

49. Eva D. Bowles, Report on 1915–1920, to the Convention, 1 (YWCA/NB).

50. The Sub-committee on Colored Work had become a full committee of the Department of Method in early 1917. The War Work Council reported on the work for African American women and girls in its reports, but Bowles opted for the work to be administered through the Committee on Colored Work (which was also known as the Colored Work Committee) so that it would not be overshadowed by the other war work; see Weisenfeld, "'The More Abundant Life,'" 116. See also Walters, "History of Colored Work," 63–64, and Department of Method Report, 4, in YWCA National Board, minutes, 5 February 1919 (YWCA/NB).

51. Paddock, "War Work of YWCA," 211.

52. Josephine Pinyon had left, in part, over the YWCA's failure to live up to a promised pay raise; the YWCA was unable to replace her, apparently, because it was not prepared to pay enough; see Executive Committee, report, 4, in YWCA National Board, minutes, 31 May 1916; Student Committee, report, in YWCA National Board, minutes, 4 October 1916; and Office Department, report, 10, in YWCA National Board, minutes, 6 December 1916 (YWCA/NB).

53. Executive Committee Report, 9, in YWCA National Board, minutes, 2 October 1918, and Department of Method, report, 1, in YWCA National Board, minutes, 2 October 1918 (YWCA/NB), and Olcott, *Work of Colored Women*, 16–17, 21; see also Mjagkij, "Morals and Morale."

Catharine Deaver Lealtad (1886–1989) was an Episcopalian. Raised in Minnesota, Lealtad attended Macalaster College and graduated in 1915 as the first African American to do so. She taught in Ohio before joining the staff of the national YWCA in 1918 as a traveling secretary for student programs. After leaving the YWCA in 1920, she worked for the New York Urban League and then the NAACP as assistant director for its branches. She subsequently became a medical doctor, training at Cornell and in Europe; she worked in international relief efforts after World War II and then joined the staff of Sydenham Hospital in New York City; see Borchett, "Catharine Lealtad."

Crystal Dreda Bird Fauset (1893–1965), a Methodist, was born in Maryland. Fauset was raised in Boston, where she attended the Boston Normal School, graduating in 1914. After teaching for three years, she joined the staff of the national YWCA in 1918, where her primary responsibility was for the Girl Reserve program (the YWCA's youth group). She stayed with the YWCA until the late 1920s, when she joined the Interracial Section of the American Friends Service Committee. In 1931, she completed a B.S. at Teachers College and married Arthur Huff Fauset, a school principal in Philadelphia; the couple moved to Pennsylvania. In 1938, she ran as a Democrat for the Pennsylvania state legislature and became the first black woman in the country to hold such an office; see Ruth Bogin, "Crystal Dreda Bird Fauset," in Sicherman and Green, *Notable American Women,* 224–25.

54. Bowles, Report on 1915–1920, 3.

55. "Broadening Opportunities for Colored Girls," *War Work Bulletin* 30 (May 1918): 2. Out of the postwar budget of $15,000,000, Bowles was awarded $400,000 (or less than 3 percent); see "$400,000 to Be Spent for Work among Colored Girls," *New York Age* (28 September 1918): 1.

56. Hunton and Johnson, *Two Colored Women with the American Expeditionary Forces,* and Zeiger, *In Uncle Sam's Service.*

57. "What the Women Are Doing for Our Army and Navy," 149.

58. YWCA—National Board—War Work Council—Committee on Work among Colored Girls and Women, *Colored American Women in War Work;* and Bowles, "War Work among Colored Girls and Women," 6.

59. Bowles, "Negro Women and the War," 425.

60. In its own account of black women in the war, the YWCA featured hostess house work; see Olcott, *Work of Colored Women.* Recent scholars have also covered the efforts; for more details, see Mjagkij, "Morals and Morale"; Salem, *To Better Our World,* 204, 208–12, 215–19; and Bristow, *Making Men Moral,* chap. 5, among others.

61. Olcott, *Work of Colored Women,* 13; E. Scott, *Scott's Official History,* 32; and Barbeau and Henri, *Unknown Soldiers,* 33–39, 79–82, esp. 36.

62. Eva D. Bowles to Mrs. John Hope, 30 July 1931, 1 (NU/AUC).

63. Olcott, *Work of Colored Women,* 15–16.

64. "$400,000 to Be Spent for Work among Colored Girls" and YWCA, "Report of the National War Work Council," 21.

65. Olcott, *Work of Colored Women,* 13–45, and YWCA, *Report of Hostess House,* 37–41, for a list of all hostess houses.

66. On Morgan's work, see Davison, "*Little Sister* of the Red Cross," 26. Even the YWCA qualified its claim of equality, acknowledging the houses for African Americans differed in size; see YWCA, *Report of Hostess House Committee,* 5. For community resistance, see Olcott, *Work of Colored Women,* 5–6, 14.

67. Olcott, *Work of Colored Women,* 20–21.

68. Lugenia Burns Hope (1871–1947), a Presbyterian, later became a Baptist. Born in St. Louis, she and her family moved to Chicago when she was young. There she worked in settlement houses, including Hull-House, prior to her 1897 marriage to John Hope. In 1898, the Hopes moved to Atlanta, where they remained until John Hope's death in 1936 (by which time he was president of Atlanta University). For her part, Lugenia Hope was active in community groups, helping to found the Neighborhood Union, a settlement that served Atlanta's black communities. She was active with the NAACP and the NACW as well as various interracial efforts, including the Commission on Interracial Cooperation. See Lerner, *Majority Finds Its Past,* 91–93, 109; Hall, *Revolt against Chivalry,* chap. 3; and Rouse, *Lugenia Burns Hope.*

69. Eva D. Bowles to Mrs. John Hope, 29 November 1916 (NU/AUC).

70. Olcott, *Work of Colored Women,* 20.

71. Ibid., 23–24, 28; see also 21, 76–77.

72. For more on Hope, see Rouse, *Lugenia Burns Hope;* on clubwomen's efforts, see YWCA, "Report of the National War Work Council," 19.

73. Lugenia Burns Hope, "Mission of the Hostess House," *New York Age,* 6 July 1918, 6.

74. Olcott, *Work of Colored Women,* 38; see also Florida Ruffin Ridley, "Hostess House as a War Development," *New York Age,* 4 May 1918, 5.

75. Bowles, Report on 1915–1920, 1.

76. Swartz et al., *A New Day for the Colored Woman Worker,* 30. On women's occupations, see Greenwald, *Women, War, and Work,* 20, 22–27.

77. Weiss, "From Black Separatism to Interracial Cooperation," 55–56 (migration figures).

78. Scheiber and Scheiber, "The Wilson Administration and the Wartime Mobilization of Black Americans," 448–49.

79. Mitchell, "Colored Women Represent Their Race."

80. Olcott, *Work of Colored Women,* 8–9. Mary Elizabeth Jackson (1867–1923) was active with the Rhode Island State Federation of Colored Women's Clubs, serving as its president for eight years, and was also involved with the NACW. She was a Free Baptist. Committed to woman suffrage, she served as the vice president of the Alpha Suffrage Club (founded in the face of black women's exclusion from the National American Woman Suffrage Association). While in Rhode Island, she worked for the Bureau of Industrial Statistics of the state's Labor Department. In the 1920s, she was the National Organizer for the Anti-Lynching Crusaders. See her piece "The Self-Supporting Woman and the Ballot," as well as "The Ninth [Anti-Lynching] Crusade," *Crisis* 25 (March 1923): 217. See also Olcott, *Work of Colored Women,* esp. 2, 8–10; E. Davis, *Lifting as They Climb,* 301; Hine et al., *Black Women in America,* 25, 558, 1288–89; and YWCA Biographical Files (YWCA/NB).

81. City Committee Report, 1, in YWCA National Board, minutes, 3 April 1918 (YWCA/NB), and Jackson, "The Colored Woman in Industry," 12–17.

82. Jackson, "The Colored Woman in Industry."

83. Jackson reported her findings in articles for the YWCA and the NAACP; Jackson, "The Colored Woman in Industry," and "Colored Girls in the Second Line of Defense." See also Olcott, *Work of Colored Women,* 124. The YWCA cooperated with groups like the Consumers' League, the Urban League, the Russell Sage Foundation, and the Women's Trade Union League to study the position of black working women; see Swartz et al., *A New Day for the Colored Woman Worker,* as well as Consumers' League of Eastern Pennsylvania, *Colored Women as Industrial Workers in Philadelphia.* See also Bowles, "Work among Colored Women and Girls under the War Work Council," which she submitted in May 1919 to the War Work Council describing both work for working women and publicity efforts.

84. Jackson, "The Colored Woman in Industry," 12, 17.

85. "Minutes of a Meeting held in Richmond, Virginia, under the auspices of the South Atlantic Field Committee," transcript, 3 July 1920, 20–22 (YWCA/NB), and Olcott, *Work of Colored Women,* 46ff. The Blue Triangle was the YWCA's logo.

86. Olcott, *Work of Colored Women,* 66–69, and "Minutes of a Meeting held in Richmond, Virginia," transcript, 3 July 1920, 18.

87. Olcott, *Work of Colored Women,* 46–121.

88. YWCA, "Report of the National War Work Council," 20, and Olcott, *Work of Colored Women,* 51, 86.

89. Department of Method Report, 2, in YWCA National Board, minutes, 3 April 1918 (YWCA/NB).

90. Jackson, "The Colored Woman in Industry," 16.

91. Jackson, "Colored Girls in the Second Line of Defense," 363. Maurine Weiner Greenwald offers a sophisticated analysis of women's (black and white) work options and choices during the war, arguing in part that black women's "bad" work habits (absenteeism, for instance) reflected their efforts to maximize "their earnings during the war by alternating between jobs as domestics and factory hands"; see her *Women, War, and Work,* 23. For her part, Jackson placed her emphasis on the need to educate black women as to the expectations of industrial work, which reflected her understanding that the sector represented the best hope for good jobs.

92. Bowles, Report on 1915–1920, 1.

93. Eva D. Bowles, "The Colored Girl in Our Midst," *Association Monthly* 11 (December 1917): 492.

94. Jackson, "The Colored Woman in Industry," 12–14.

95. Davison, "Y.W.C.A.'s War Burden," 501.

96. Compare Grace L. Coyle, "Colored Girls in Industry," 14 November 1918 (YWCA/NB), and her "Noblesse Oblige: Social Responsibility and an Industrial Club Council," *Association Monthly* 12 (December 1918): 468–69. The East Central Field consisted of Pennsylvania, Maryland, Delaware, and the District of Columbia. Grace Longwell Coyle (1892–1962), a Congregationalist, was born and raised in Massachusetts. Coyle graduated from Wellesley College in 1914 and received a certificate from the New York School of Philanthropy in 1915. She worked for YWCAs in Pennsylvania, joining the national staff in 1918, and worked primarily in programs for industrial women and girls until 1926. After additional education (a master's in 1928 and a Ph.D. in 1931 from Columbia University), Coyle returned to the YW in 1930, staying until 1934 as the executive of the Laboratory Division (which promoted research and programs). She spent the rest of her life developing the field of social work—teaching on the faculty of Western Reserve University, leading professional associations, and writing, especially on the concept of "group work" and social change; see Bremner, "Grace Longwell Coyle."

97. Olcott, *Work of Colored Women,* 127, and the Department of Conventions and Conferences Committee, report, 2, in the YWCA National Board, minutes, 2 October 1918 (YWCA/NB). Adela (sometimes Adelle, Adella, or Adele) F. Ruffin (fl. 1915–38) was a Presbyterian. She studied at Norfolk Mission College (a black high school established by northern Presbyterians) in Virginia and taught at black normal schools and colleges in the South. Ruffin was one of the first black women to be trained at the YWCA's NTS, attending in the summer of 1915 and then becoming the secretary for the newly established black branch in Richmond. In 1917, she joined the national staff as the field supervisor for colored work in the South Atlantic states. After World War I, she was the Colored City Secretary for the South Atlantic Field. In the budget crisis of the mid-1920s, she left the national for positions in local YWCA associations, ending up as the general secretary for the Phyllis Wheatley branch in Asheville, North Carolina. (The YWCA used the spelling "Phyllis" in the branch names honor-

ing Phillis Wheatley.) She held that position until 1938 when she resigned following a reorganization of the branch. See Walters, "History of Colored Work," 41–42; "Men of Richmond," *Crisis* 13 (January 1917), 132; and Olcott, *Work of Colored Women,* 48, 50–59, 127–28. She appears to have been unmarried, although there are occasional references to her as Mrs. Ruffin.

98. Davison, "Y.W.C.A.'s War Burden," 498.

99. Information drawn from the YWCA of the USA, *Year Book Containing Directory and Statistical Material, 1918–1919.*

100. Sims, *Natural History of a Social Institution,* 63, 191.

101. YWCA of the USA, *Report of the National Board to the Sixth National Convention, 1920,* 101, 110.

102. See Mitchell, "Colored Women Represent Their Race."

103. Roosevelt quoted in E. Scott, *Scott's Official History,* 412.

104. Olcott, *Work of Colored Women, 76–77.*

105. Student Friendship War Fund Report, 2–3, in YWCA National Board, minutes, 5 December 1917, and Student Committee Annual Report, 3, in YWCA National Board, minutes, 6 February 1918, 3 (YWCA/NB).

106. "'Colored Women Capable of Leadership'—Miss Bowles," *New York Age,* 25 October 1919, 2.

107. Jackson, "Colored Girls in the Second Line of Defense," 363.

108. Jackson, "The Colored Woman in Industry," 16.

109. "Colored Women Capable of Leadership."

110. *Interracial Cooperation,* 2.

111. Eva D. Bowles, "The Young Womens Christian Association—A Means of Meeting the Colored Girls Need for Self Expression," 1 (YWCA/NB).

112. Scheiber and Scheiber, "The Wilson Administration and the Wartime Mobilization of Black Americans," 457–58.

113. Department of Method Report, 3, in YWCA National Board, minutes, 2 April 1919 (YWCA/NB). The number of paid staff workers with black hostess houses had gone from five in 1917 to thirty-four by early 1919; see War Work Council Report, 1, in YWCA National Board, minutes, 5 February 1919 (YWCA/NB).

114. The expected final funds had dropped from an estimated budget of $2,128,424 to a revised budget of $1,766,210, presumably as people failed to make good on pledges to the War Work Campaign. The reduction was not applied evenly. The revised budget awarded overseas programs $615,000 (35 percent), while their estimated allocation had been $375,000 (or 29 percent of that budget); see Continuation Committee Recommendations, 4, in YWCA National Board, minutes, 4 February 1920 (YWCA/NB).

115. Tindall, *The Emergence of the New South,* 152–55.

116. L. H. Hammond, "Interracial Cooperation," 7.

117. The number of lynchings had gone down between the turn of the century and the start of the World War, but it rose during the war, and victims, more and more, were African Americans murdered in an increasingly brutal manner; see Tindall, *The Emergence of the New South,* 171–72, and Weiss, "From Black Separatism to Interracial Cooperation," 56. In 1919, the number doubled to seventy-two from thirty-six in 1917. The Ku Klux Klan had been revitalized in 1915 in the wake of the premiere

of *Birth of a Nation,* and by 1923 its membership had risen to more than three million; Tindall, *The Emergence of the New South,* 186–95.

118. Dykeman and Stokely, *Seeds of Southern Change,* 66. Will W. Alexander (1884–1956), a Methodist, was born and raised in Missouri. He was ordained as a minister when he was still in his teens. Alexander worked with the YMCA during World War I and was instrumental in helping to found the Commission on Interracial Cooperation; *Seeds of Southern Change* is a biography of Alexander.

119. Founded in 1919, the CIC grew out of the YMCA's War Work Council; see Dykeman and Stokely, *Seeds of Southern Change;* Myrdal, *An American Dilemma,* 842–50; A. Ellis, "Commission on Interracial Cooperation"; Burrows, "Commission on Interracial Cooperation"; and Pilkington, "The Trials of Brotherhood."

120. On the struggles that women faced inside the CIC, see A. Ellis, "Commission on Interracial Cooperation," and Hall, *Revolt against Chivalry,* 65, 123–25, 257.

121. Glenda Gilmore has persuasively demonstrated the importance of the world war in giving (some) southern white women an experience of working interracially as well as an appreciation for the importance of interracial efforts to the greater social good. Many of these women had or would develop YWCA ties; see her *Gender and Jim Crow,* esp. chap. 7.

122. "Interracial Cooperation: An Open Letter to the College Men of the South from the University Commission," in *Interracial Cooperation,* 5–7.

123. *Interracial Cooperation,* 2.

124. L. H. Hammond, "Interracial Cooperation," 8.

125. Ibid., 12–13; for the "bond of a common womanhood," see L. H. Hammond, *Southern Women and Racial Adjustment,* 18.

126. L. H. Hammond, "White Man's Debt to the Negro," 69.

127. Eva Bowles, Report, 18 January 1917, in Walters, "History of Colored Work," 57.

128. Pilkington, "The Trials of Brotherhood," 70–71. For one interracialist's equation of the whites of the Ku Klux Klan with blacks of the NAACP (and contrasting both to a more desirable involvement with the CIC), see A. Taylor, "Black versus White," 15.

129. Helen P. Wallace, "Foreword," in Olcott, *Work of Colored Women,* 3. Helen Peters Wallace (1875–1943), a Baptist, was born in Buffalo. She received her A.B. from Vassar in 1897. In 1899, she married Dr. Charlton Wallace (but was divorced in 1919). Helen Wallace was elected to the National Board in 1913 but resigned in 1919 (presumably because she left New York City). While on the board, she served as chairman of the Department of Method (which oversaw student and community YWs). During World War I, she also served as chairman of the Committee on Colored Work for the YW's War Work Council. From 1922 to 1932, she was a nonresident member of the National Board and was also active with the Cincinnati YWCA as president from 1923 to 1931; see YWCA Biographical Files (YWCA/NB).

130. Colored Work Committee, minutes, 25 April 1919, 2 (YWCA/NB) (for description of poster); Walters, "History of Colored Work," 71 (for designation as "first" poster); and Eva Bowles, report, included in the City Committee, minutes, 28 February 1921, 8 (YWCA/RFC 225.5) (for comment about having to "brown up posters"). The poster was used in an exhibit on YWCA programs for a secretarial conference

in 1919. It is unclear if there was further distribution of the poster (correspondence with Maida Goodwin, archivist, Sophia Smith Collection).

131. Olcott, *Work of Colored Women*, 11, 58. Katharine Heath Hawes (1876–1956) was a Presbyterian. Based in Richmond, Hawes served as the chairman of the South Atlantic Field Committee during the 1910s and early 1920s. She was one of the first faculty members and female trustees for the Presbyterian General Assembly's Training School for Layworkers, founded in 1914 in Richmond (information provided by April Swofford, Presbyterian School of Christian Education, personal communication to author, 12 September 2005).

132. Bureau of Colored Work, minutes, 25 February 1921, 3–5 (YWCA/NB). As with Elizabeth Preston Allen, the change had come because Hawes had finally met educated black women.

133. Frederickson, "'Each One Is Dependent on the Other.'"

134. Darlene Clark Hine's analysis of "the culture of dissemblance" as a key strategy for encounters between whites and blacks was useful to me in thinking through these interactions; see Hine, "Rape and the Inner Lives of Black Women."

135. L. H. Hammond, *Southern Women and Racial Adjustment*, 29. For discussions of white southern liberals' defense of segregation, see Kneebone, *Southern Liberal Journalists;* Sosna, *In Search of the Silent South;* Tindall, *The Emergence of the New South*, 181–82; and A. Ellis, "Commission on Interracial Cooperation."

136. L. H. Hammond, "Interracial Cooperation," 8.

137. Emma Bailey Speer to Mrs. Murrell Gray Ross (3 December 1925), 3, in Executive Committee of the YWCA National Board, minutes, 25 November 1925 (YWCA/NB).

138. For a discussion of this issue, see Painter, "'Social Equality.'"

139. L. H. Hammond, "White Man's Debt to the Negro," 67.

140. Adelle [*sic*] Ruffin, "Down New Streets," *Association Monthly* 12 (August 1918): 274.

141. Mrs. Charlton Wallace, "The Colored Work Committee of the National Board of The Young Women's Christian Association," draft for her foreword to Olcott, *Work of Colored Women*, 1, 3 (YWCA/NB).

142. Bowles, Report on 1915–1920, 7.

143. Bowles, "Work among Colored Women and Girls under the War Work Council," 2–3.

144. Colored Work Committee, minutes, 4 April 1919, 1, and Colored Work Committee, minutes, 29 May 1919, 5 (YWCA/NB).

145. Bowles, Report on 1915–1920, 6–7.

146. Catharine D. Lealtad to Mrs. John Hope, 5 March 1920, 1 (NU/AUC), and Salem, *To Better Our World*, 328 n. 52.

147. Helen A. Davis to Mrs. John Hope, 17 January 1920, 1 (NU/AUC).

148. "Colored Women Capable of Leadership."

149. Mary E. Jackson, Report, City Committee, minutes, 26 May 1919, 2 (YWCA/RFC 225.7), and Olcott, *Work of Colored Women*, 69–72. See also Mjagkij, "Morals and Morale."

150. "Causes of Race Friction," in *Interracial Cooperation*, 6.

151. Quoted in Myrdal, *An American Dilemma*, 845.

152. Salem, *To Better Our World,* 242, 328 n. 52, and Lutz, "'The Dizzy Steep to Heaven,'" 248–49.

153. Lealtad, "The National Y.W.C.A. and the Negro."

154. Lealtad to Hope, 5 March 1920; see also [Catharine Lealtad] to Mary B. Talbert, 12 January 1921 (NAACP/LC), where she described Bowles as "spineless."

155. Bowles, Report on 1915–1920, 7.

156. Colored Work Committee, minutes, 15 November 1918, 2 (YWCA/NB).

157. YWCA of the USA, *Report of the National Board to the Sixth National Convention, 1920,* 86; see also 55, 59, and 89.

158. L. H. Hammond, *Southern Women and Racial Adjustment,* 29.

159. Eva D. Bowles, Report to the Department of Research and Method, 1920, 3 (YWCA/NB).

160. My thanks to Mollie Keller, who first suggested the metaphor of the "big sister."

Chapter 4: Developing Christian Citizenship

1. "Report of Proceedings of the Conference held by the Young Women's Christian Association, Louisville, Kentucky," 16–17 February 1921, pt. 1:5 (YWCA/NB).

2. Mary Morris Burnett Talbert (1866–1923), a Congregationalist, then Baptist, was born in Ohio. She received an S.P.B. from Oberlin College in 1886 (in 1896, it was made a B.A.). She taught in Arkansas before her 1891 marriage to William H. Talbert, a realtor from New York. The couple lived in Buffalo and Mary Talbert took additional courses at the University of Buffalo. She was active with both black clubwomen's efforts, serving as the president of the NACW from 1916 to 1920 and was on the board of the NAACP; see Lillian S. Williams, "Mary Morris Burnett Talbert," in Hine et al., *Black Women in America,* 1137–39.

3. The ICW was the world equivalent of the National Council of Women (NCW)—an umbrella organization for women's groups. It held quinquennial conventions, to which the NCW would send a delegation to represent the United States. See Cott, *Grounding of Modern Feminism,* 255–57, and Rupp, "Constructing Internationalism."

4. Mary White Ovington to Mrs. J. C. Merriman, 27 October 1920; Myra Kingman Merriman to Mary W. Ovington, 20 November 1920; [Mary White Ovington] to Mrs. Josiah C. Merriman, 1 December 1920; Myra Kingman Merriman to Miss Ovington, 13 December 1920; Mary B. Talbert to Miss [Catherine] Lealtad, 3 January [1921] (all NAACP/LC). I appreciate Nancy F. Cott's bringing the YWCA materials in this collection to my attention because the materials were located in NAACP files pertaining to the National Woman's Party. See also [Edna] Sandlin to [Sara] Lyon, 29 October 1920, typed copy (YWCA/NB), as well as the press coverage in the next note.

5. Coverage included "Even in Norway—Thou Art There, Oh Colorphobia," *Cleveland Advocate,* 9 October 1920, 8; "The International Council of Women," *Crisis* 21 (December 1920): 57–58; "A Question of Facts," *Crisis* 21 (February 1921): 151; "National Board, Y.W.C.A., Hostess to 19 Colored Women," *New York Age,* 18 December 1920, 1; "Women Getting Together," *New York Age,* 25 December 1920, 4; "Discrimi-

nation in Y.W.C.A. Hotel in Paris is Disclosed," *New York Age,* 29 January 1921, 1; and "Women at Conference Entertained," *Savannah Tribune,* 10 October 1920 (TIA/MF 12:729).

6. [Mary White Ovington] to Mrs. Paul G. Darrot, 27 April 1921 (NAACP/LC).

7. [Mary White Ovington] to Mrs. Paul Gaston Darrot, 9 May 1921 (NAACP/LC).

8. Sandlin to Lyon, 29 October 1920. The letter was circulated among YWCA personnel and an edited version sent to the black press; see "National Board, YWCA, Hostess to 19 Colored Women," 7, and "Discrimination in YWCA Hotel in Paris is Disclosed," 2.

9. W. E. B. Du Bois to Mrs. Paul Gaston Darrot, 27 January 1921 (NAACP/LC), published as "A Letter," *Crisis* 21 (April 1921): 246–47.

10. Statement from the National Board of the YWCA, 19 January 1921 (NAACP/LC).

11. Bureau of Colored Work, minutes, 20 January 1921, 2 (YWCA/NB), and Ellen Sullivan Darrot to Mary W. Ovington, 4 May 1921 (NAACP/LC); Ethel Sullivan Darrot [chair of the YWCA's publicity committee] to Fred R. Moore (editor), printed in "Discrimination in YWCA Hotel in Paris Is Disclosed," 5.

12. Du Bois to Darrot, 27 January 1921, 1–2. See City Committee Report, 15, in YWCA National Board, minutes, 29 May 1912 (YWCA/NB).

13. YWCA National Board, minutes, 21 February 1921, 20 (YWCA/NB), and Bureau of Colored Work, minutes, 20 January 1921, 2.

14. In thinking through "racial etiquette," I was helped by Susan Kerr Chandler's analysis of "prescribed behaviors" in "African American Social Workers in the World War I Era," esp. 3, as well as Myrdal, *An American Dilemma,* 36.

15. Merriman to Ovington, 13 December 1920, 2, publicized in, for example, "Discrimination in YWCA Hotel in Paris is Disclosed," 4; see also [Catharine Lealtad] to Mary B. Talbert, 12 January 1921, 1 (NAACP/LC). For an analysis of the relation between economic means and manners, see D. White, "The Cost of Club Work," 259. Although some black women had more financial resources, the women emphasized proper comportment as possible for all women and important to advancing the race.

16. "Report of Proceedings of the Louisville Conference," 1921, pt. 1:12.

17. Chafe, *The American Woman,* 3, 20.

18. For the membership statistics, see YWCA of the USA, *Proceedings of the Sixth National Convention, 1920,* 282; Breckinridge, *Women in the Twentieth Century,* 11–14; and Ryan, *Womanhood in America,* 204. Women in the YWCA were holding their first convention since 1915 because wartime restrictions had led to cancellation of earlier conventions.

19. YWCA of the USA, *Report of the National Board to the Sixth National Convention, 1920,* 27. Like others at the time, YWCA members referred to organized women's activities as the "woman movement," rather than "woman's" or "women's."

20. Ibid., 15, 18, 46–47, 25, 26.

21. Ibid., 54.

22. Ibid., 14–15. On self-governing groups, see Wyckoff, "The Girls behind the Men behind the Guns."

23. By 1922, there would be an Industrial Assembly for working women that would meet during national conventions; YWCA of the USA, *Proceedings of the Seventh National Convention, 1922,* 267–302. Business and professional "girls" (essentially white- and pink-collar workers) followed suit in 1924 with the Business and Professional Women's Assembly; see YWCA of the USA, *Proceedings of the Eighth National Convention, 1924,* 334–44.

24. YWCA of the USA, *Proceedings of the Sixth National Convention, 1920,* 41, 43.

25. Ibid., 74.

26. Ibid., 44, 45, 71. Helen Miller Gould Shepard (1868–1938), a member of the Dutch Reformed church, was born in New York City, a daughter of Jay Gould. Noted as a philanthropist with a special interest in religious work (including the YM's programs for railroad workers and the YW's foreign efforts), she had been on the American Committee and was an original member of the National Board. She was instrumental in financing the construction of the YW's national headquarters. In 1913, she married Finley J. Shepard, a railroad executive. Beginning in the 1920s, she financed conservative women's groups, including the Daughters of the American Revolution; see Delegard, "Women Patriots," 477–87; Bannan, "Management by Women," 208–9, 228–29; and "Mrs. F. J. Shepard Dies of a Stroke," *New York Times,* 21 December 1938, 1.

27. YWCA of the USA, *Proceedings of the Sixth National Convention, 1920,* 45. The fact that students, who were historically associated with the more conservative American Committee, were the first to push for liberalizing the religious requirement has prompted speculation as to why. Mary Sims, a longtime staffer, argued that the student YWs of the late nineteenth century had been strongest in colleges in the Midwest, "a section more conservative in its religious expression than the east"; see her *Natural History of a Social Institution,* 110. By the 1920s, however, YWs were well represented on campuses across the country; see YWCA of the USA, *Year Book Containing Directory and Statistical Material, 1918–1919,* 56–76.

Anne Firor Scott has suggested that the students of the 1910s and 1920s could have been the children of community YW women and expanded upon their mothers' progressivism; see *Natural Allies,* 108–9. Paula Fass's work on youth culture in the 1920s observes that, by the 1920s, the Ys (both YM and YW) were fairly self-selective groups. Whereas previously, Ys had drawn from a large part of the student population, they became (essentially) fraternities for the socially conscious as other student groups became the locus for more popular students; see Fass, *The Damned and the Beautiful,* 140–41, 335, 346. Perhaps, also, the consequences of self-governance were at play as students were able to decide for themselves what they wanted. The women of the American Committee (the governing body of student associations prior to the 1906 merger) who fought to ensure the YW's connection to Protestant churches were no longer students; they were the older volunteer and paid staff members who worked for the national group.

28. YWCA of the USA, *Proceedings of the Sixth National Convention, 1920,* 97.

29. Ibid., 53; the vote carried by a 6 to 1 margin (see page 76).

30. Ibid., 102–3, for the list of the ideals. For an account of the struggle, see Frederickson, "Citizens for Democracy," 81–83. The points had already been endorsed

by the FCC and various denominations; see Gorrell, *The Age of Social Responsibility,* 299–301. The YMCA endorsed a weaker version.

31. YWCA of the USA, *Proceedings of the Sixth National Convention, 1920,* 97–98 (emphasis added).

32. Ibid., 106, 109.

33. Ibid., 109–15. For the businessmen's threat, see Mary Van Kleeck, "Relation of the Young Women's Christian Association to the Problems of Labor," ibid., 250.

34. Ibid., 98–99.

35. Ibid., 110–12.

36. Ibid., 111–12, 117–18. For a sampling of coverage of the event, see "Mrs. Shepard Quits Board of the Y.W.C.A.: Disapproves of Progressive Platform of the National Convention at Cleveland," *New York Times,* 18 April 1920, 9; H. Stewart, "Where the 'Y' Stands *Now,*" 107; "The Y.W.C.A. under Fire," *Survey* 44 (16 August 1920): 603; and "Suffering for Righteousness Sake," *Christian Work* (12 February 1921): 188.

37. YWCA of the USA, *Proceedings of the Sixth National Convention, 1920,* 112.

38. H. Stewart, "Where the 'Y' Stands *Now,*" 104.

39. Frederickson, "Citizens for Democracy," 82–83.

40. Robinson, *Eight Women of the YWCA,* 97.

41. Coyle quoted by Bremner, "Grace Longwell Coyle," 170. Many YWCA staffers studied at Columbia University—especially Teachers College—where John Dewey taught; see, G. Wilson, *Religious and Educational Philosophy,* 38, 115.

42. Abby A. Rockefeller, "The Young Women's Christian Association and Legislation," *Association Monthly* 14 (March 1920): 121. Abby Greene Aldrich Rockefeller (1874–1948), a Baptist was born in Rhode Island and attended a private school. She was active with the Providence YW. In 1901 she married John D. Rockefeller Jr. and moved to New York City. Noted as a philanthropist, she served on the YWCA's National Board, where she was active with housing for women and interracial issues; Neil Harris, "Abby Greene Aldrich Rockefeller," in James et al., *Notable American Women,* 3: 185–87.

43. YWCA of the USA, *Report of the National Board to the Seventh National Convention, 1922,* 161–68.

44. Ibid., 164, and YWCA of the USA, *Proceedings of the Ninth National Convention, 1926,* 118–19.

45. The phrase "Women's Lobby on Capitol Hill" was Sophonisba Breckinridge's term; see *Women in the Twentieth Century,* 260. See also Alice Standish Buell, "What Is the Women's Joint Congressional Committee?" *Association Monthly* 15 (September 1921): 368; Muncy, *Creating a Female Dominion in American Reform,* 104; Johnson, "Organized Women as Lobbyists in the 1920's"; and Cott, *Grounding of Modern Feminism.*

46. YWCA of the USA, *Report of the National Board to the Eighth National Convention, 1924,* 145–48; Margaret Jefferys Hobart, "Woman Suffrage and the Kingdom of God," *Association Monthly* 13 (November 1919): 429–30; Young Women's Christian Associations—National Board, *Politics Needs Christian Citizenship: Women and Legislation* (New York City, [1923]); Young Women's Christian Associations—National Board, *Politics Needs Christian Citizenship: Citizenship in the County* (New York City,

[1923]); and Young Women's Christian Associations—National Board, *Politics Needs Christian Citizenship: Our Children* (New York City, [1923]) (all YWCA/NB).

47. Clemens, "Organizational Repertoires and Institutional Change," 769.

48. "Blacklisting the Y.W.C.A.," and Krehbiel, "The Attack on the Los Angeles Y.W.C.A."

49. Krehbiel, "The Attack on the Los Angeles Y.W.C.A.," 612; see also Layton, "The Better America Federation," 142–43.

50. "Christianity under Fire," *Social Service Bulletin* 11 (May 1921): 1.

51. "Blacklisting the Y.W.C.A.," 668; see Executive Committee, minutes, 26 January 1921, in YWCA National Board, minutes, 2 February 1921, 17–18 (YWCA/NB). See also Spratt, "The Pittsburgh YWCA and Industrial Democracy in the 1920s," 6–11.

52. Miller, *American Protestantism and Social Issues,* 31–33.

53. Krehbiel, "The Attack on the Los Angeles Y.W.C.A.," 613.

54. "Blacklisting the Y.W.C.A.," and Spratt, "The Pittsburgh YWCA and Industrial Democracy in the 1920s."

55. An American Citizen, "Why Don't Women Investigate Propaganda?" *Dearborn Independent,* 22 March 1924, 10–13 (see 11 for one version of the "spider web" chart including the YWCA [compiled 1922–23]); Leonard Cline, "The War on the Peace Seekers," pt. 1, *New Republic* 39 (2 July 1924): 149–50, and "The War on the Peace Seekers," pt. 2 (9 July 1924): 184–85; and Hapgood, *Professional Patriots,* esp. 103–6, 172–73. For secondary literature on the spider web and women's reform efforts in the 1920s, see A. Davis, *American Heroine,* 263–65; Lemons, *The Woman Citizen,* chap. 8, esp. 210, 214–16; Jensen, "All Pink Sisters"; Cott, *Grounding of Modern Feminism,* esp. 242, 249–50, 259, 356–57 n. 11; Nielsen, *Un-American Womanhood;* and Morgan, "'Home and Country.'"

56. YWCA of the USA, *Report of the National Board to the Seventh National Convention, 1922,* 9.

57. "Voice of the Churches," *Survey* 45 (March 26, 1921): 912–13.

58. YWCA of the USA, *Proceedings of the Sixth National Convention, 1920,* 73.

59. Ibid., 102; see Reimers, *White Protestantism and the Negro,* 54–55.

60. Mary Catherine Jackson McCrorey (1869–1944) was born in Georgia and graduated from (what would become) Atlanta University. A Presbyterian, she taught in schools in the South, and, in 1916, she married Henry Lawrence McCrorey, president of Biddle University (later Johnson C. Smith University). She helped to found the Phyllis Wheatley branch of the Charlotte YWCA and was active with the CIC in North Carolina and the National Council of Negro Women; see Glenda Elizabeth Gilmore, "Mary Jackson McCrorey," in Hine et al., *Black Women in America,* 767–68. She was not the Mary Jackson who worked for the YWCA during World War I.

61. YWCA of the USA, *Proceedings of the Sixth National Convention, 1920,* 122.

62. Ibid., 121.

63. YWCA of the USA, *Report of the National Board to the Sixth National Convention, 1920,* 16; see also Weisenfeld, *African American Women and Christian Activism,* 100–14.

64. YWCA of the USA, *Proceedings of the Sixth National Convention, 1920,* 323. By 1920, African American women served on three local boards of directors: Detroit, New York, and Philadelphia; see Bureau of Colored Work, minutes, 23 November

1920, 1 (YWCA/NB). In the winter of 1919–20, the Committee on Colored Work had reorganized as the Bureau of Colored Work.

65. The excluded delegates were offered a meal in the dining room of the local (white) YWCA. On the banquet, see "The Latest Farce from the YWCA," *Cleveland Advocate,* 24 April 1920, 1 (quote), and "A Question," *Crisis* 20 (July 1920): 119.

66. YWCA of the USA, *Proceedings of the Sixth National Convention, 1920,* 323.

67. Bowles provided black women with information about the structure and requirements for branches so they could convert wartime centers into permanent branches; Eva D. Bowles, Report to the Department of Research and Method, 1920, 1 (YWCA/NB). See also "Minutes of a Meeting held in Richmond, Virginia, under the auspices of the South Atlantic Field Committee," transcript, 3 July 1920, 6 (YWCA/NB).

68. "Suggestions from the Committee on Findings at the Conference on Colored Work, Louisville, Ky.," 14–15 October 1915 (YWCA/NB).

69. "Minutes of a Meeting held in Richmond, Virginia," transcript, 3 July 1920, 2.

70. [Lugenia Burns Hope] to unknown, draft of letter, 29 May 1920, 1. Hope may have been distinguishing between paid workers and volunteers like herself because she believed the former were not as critical of the white women in the organization—either because these black women actually agreed with white women or because they were dependent on white women for jobs and therefore hesitant to criticize white women.

71. Conference of Representative Negro Women, minutes, 6 April 1920, and "Requests" to the National Board of the Young Women's Christian Association (both YWCA/NB).

Charlotte Eugenia Hawkins Brown (1883–1961), a Congregationalist and later a Baptist, was born in North Carolina but moved with her family to Cambridge, Massachusetts, as a child. She attended Salem State Normal School for two years before going to Sedalia, North Carolina, to teach in an American Missionary Association (AMA) school. When the AMA pulled out, she became head and chief fundraiser for the school, which was renamed Palmer Memorial Institute and eventually expanded to offering junior college courses. Married to Edward Brown in 1911, she and her husband separated shortly after. Charlotte Brown was active with the North Carolina Federation of Colored Women's Clubs; see Ruth Ann Stewart, "Charlotte Hawkins Brown," in Sicherman and Green, *Notable American Women,* 111–13. See also Glenda Gilmore's deconstruction of the myths of Brown's life in her *Gender and Jim Crow,* chap. 7.

Mary Jane McLeod Bethune (1875–1955) was a Presbyterian and later a Methodist. Born in South Carolina, she was educated at the Scotia Seminary in North Carolina and the Moody Institute in Chicago. In 1898, she married Albertus Bethune, although the couple separated relatively quickly. She taught before she founded what would become Bethune-Cookman College, in Daytona, Florida. Active with the NACW, she served as its president in the 1920s. In the 1935, she helped start the National Council of Negro Women (NCNW); its founding meeting was in the black YWCA in Harlem. Bethune served as the NCNW's first president. In the 1930s, she worked for the federal National Youth Administration and organized the Federal Council on

Negro Affairs (the "black cabinet"); see Elaine M. Smith, "Mary McLeod Bethune" in Hine et al., *Black Women in America*, 113–27.

72. For more on the networks, see Rouse, *Lugenia Burns Hope*, 5, 55, 100, and Hall, *Revolt against Chivalry*, 286 n. 66.

73. Lucy Craft Laney (1854–1933) was born free in Georgia. She was a Presbyterian. Laney graduated in the first class of Atlanta University, in 1873. She founded and directed the Haines Normal and Industrial Institute in Augusta, Georgia. There she mentored women like McCrorey and Bethune who worked at Haines; Sadie Daniel St. Clair, "Lucy Craft Laney," in James et al., *Notable American Women*, 2:365–67.

74. "Requests" to the National Board of the YWCA.

75. Lumpkin, *The Making of a Southerner*, 212.

76. Eva D. Bowles to [Lugenia Burns Hope], 10 April 1920 (NU/AUC).

77. Eva D. Bowles to Mrs. John Hope, 17 February 1930 (NU/AUC).

78. D. White, *Too Heavy a Load*, 103–9.

79. Katharine Hawes, in "Minutes of a Meeting held in Richmond, Virginia," transcript, 3 July 1920, 42, and "Report of Proceedings of the Louisville Conference," 1921, pt. 2:9.

80. "Too Much Paternalism in the 'Ys'" *Cleveland Advocate*, 1 May 1920, 8.

81. Besides Eva Bowles, the women from New York were white: Helen A. Davis, the executive for the Field Work Department; Mabel Head, the associate executive for the Department of Method; and Katharine Scott, the associate executive for the Department of Field Work. The women from the South Atlantic Field held the following posts: Katharine Heath Hawes (white) was the overall chairman for the field; Martha (Mrs. Walter S.) McNeill (white) was chairman of the field's Committee on Colored Work; Leona Macgeorge (white) was the city secretary; and Ruffin was the colored city secretary.

82. "Meeting held in offices of the South Atlantic Field Committee," circulated minutes, 3 July 1920 (NU/AUC). While the wording is the same as that in the national YW's copy (YWCA/NB), the pagination is not.

83. "Report of Proceedings of the Louisville Conference," 1921, pt. 2:8.

84. Mary J. McCrorey to Mrs. Hope, 27 January 1921, 1 (NU/AUC).

85. "Meeting held in South Atlantic Field Committee," circulated minutes, 3 July 1920, 2; compare to "Minutes of a Meeting held in Richmond, Virginia," transcript, 3 July 1920, 3, 6, 7.

86. Unknown, "Who are the 'people' of the 'community'?" no date, 1 (NU/AUC).

87. "Meeting held in South Atlantic Field Committee," circulated minutes, 3 July 1920, 4.

88. "Minutes of a Meeting held in Richmond, Virginia," transcript, 3 July 1920, 18.

89. Ibid., 24. No figures were provided for the white turnover other than to assert that it was also high.

90. Unknown, "Who are the 'people' of the 'community'?" 2, and "Minutes of a Meeting held in Richmond, Virginia," transcript, 3 July 1920, 24.

91. "Minutes of a Meeting held in Richmond, Virginia," transcript, 3 July 1920, 8–10.

92. Ibid., 38, and "Report of Proceedings of the Louisville Conference," 1921, pt. 2:8.

93. "Requests" to the National Board of the YWCA, 1.

94. "Minutes of a Meeting held in Richmond, Virginia," transcript, 3 July 1920, 37–38.

95. Ibid., 38–39. In claiming to represent "300,000 negro women of the south," the women were referring to the membership of the southern black clubwomen's movement, which they led.

96. Ibid., 40–41.

97. Unknown, "Who are the 'people' of the 'community'?" 1.

98. National Association of Colored Women, Eleventh Biennial Convention, 1920, executive board, minutes, 16 July 1920, 18–19 (NACW/MF 1).

99. Bureau of Colored Work, minutes, 24 September 1920, 3 (YWCA/NB).

100. Ibid., 4.

101. Eva Bowles to [Lugenia Burns Hope], 25 January 1920, reprinted in Lerner, *Black Women in White America,* 479–80; see also Eva D. Bowles to Mrs. Hope, 30 November 1920 (NU/AUC).

102. "National Board Y.W.C.A., Tells of Work with Colored Girls," *New York Age,* 14 May 1921, 2.

103. The "Outstanding Colored Women" included Addie Waites Hunton and Charlotte Hawkins Brown, but also other non-YW prestigious black women such as Mary McLeod Bethune and Nannie Burroughs; see "Summaries of Conferences: Conference of Outstanding Colored Women," excerpts of minutes, news release, statement, attendance list (YWCA/NB). For coverage in the black press, see "National Board, Y.W.C.A., Hostess to 19 Colored Women"; "Colored and White Women in Conference in New York City at Y.W.C.A.," *Philadelphia Tribune,* 11 December 1920, 1; and "Colored and White women Confer at Y.W.C.A.," *Atlanta Independent,* 16 December 1920 (TIA/MF 12:734).

104. "Report of Proceedings of the Louisville Conference," 1921, attendance lists; Bureau of Colored Work, minutes, 25 February 1921, 3–4 (YWCA/NB); and Eva D. Bowles to Mrs. Hope, 8 March 1921 (NU/AUC). Bowles reported thirty-three "colored" women and thirty-one white present. Also see Neverdon-Morton, *Afro-American Women of the South,* 217–18; Rouse, *Lugenia Burns Hope,* 105; and Hall, *Revolt against Chivalry,* 86.

105. "Report of Proceedings of the Louisville Conference," 1921, pt. 1:6.

106. Ibid., pt. 2:66, 67.

107. Ibid., pt. 2:7.

108. Ibid., pt. 2:84–85.

109. Ibid., pt. 2:183.

110. Whites from a wide range of ideological backgrounds enjoyed hearing African Americans sing spirituals—Alexander Hamilton Stephens, the one-time vice-president of the Confederacy did, but so did Henry Ward Beecher; see A. Ward, *Dark Midnight When I Rise,* 148–50, 383–84. At some point during almost any interracial meeting in the 1920s and 1930s, black attendees would sing such songs. Increasingly as the years went on, African Americans worked to see that the songs would be sung

by both blacks and whites; see Frances Williams, memo to the subcommittee on race of the [YWCA] National Student Council, 30 November 1936, 2 (GTH/AHC).

111. "Report of Proceedings of the Louisville Conference," 1921, pt. 2:190–91.

112. Ibid., pt. 2:191.

113. Lumpkin, *The Making of a Southerner,* 212.

114. "The Educational Work of the Young Women's Christian Association," 19 February 1923, 24 (YWCA/RFC 157.1).

115. "Conference of the Young Women's Christian Association on Colored Work, Louisville, Ky., 15–17 February 1921," Findings. Delegates also endorsed the findings of the Women's Inter-Racial Conference in Memphis.

116. Mrs. H. L. McCrorey to Mrs. Hope, 6 July 1931 (NU/AUC). On Hope's subsequent activities, see Rouse, *Lugenia Burns Hope,* 107 ff.

117. YWCA of the USA, *Report of the National Board to the Sixth National Convention, 1920,* 16.

118. For a description from a YW leader from the 1930s and 1940s of facilities around the country, see Calkins, "The Negro in the Young Women's Christian Association," 61–62; for more on Calkins, see chap. 7 below.

119. Hedgeman, *Trumpet Sounds,* 30–33. Anna Arnold Hedgeman (1899–1990), a Methodist was born in Iowa and raised in Minnesota. She attended Hamline University, graduating in 1922. She taught at Rust College for two years and over the next twelve years found positions in local YWs in Ohio, New Jersey, New York, and Pennsylvania. In 1933, she married Merritt Hedgeman, a concert artist. She held a variety of positions in local and federal government in the ensuing years. In 1963, she helped organize the March on Washington; see her autobiography, *Trumpet Sounds,* and Nancy Marie Robertson, "Anna Arnold Hedgeman," in Ware, *Notable American Women,* 285–86.

120. "City Question Box," 892–93, and Mrs. C. A. Winn, "Speech to the National Board," 25 May 1938, 3 (YWCA/NB).

121. Bureau of Colored Work, minutes, 31 May 1921, 4; Bureau of Colored Work, minutes, 28 October 1921, 2; and "Suggested By-Laws of the Branch for Colored Women" (all YWCA/NB).

122. YWCA of the USA, *Proceedings of the Eighth National Convention, 1924,* 39.

123. "City Question Box"; discussion in the "Report of Proceedings of the Louisville Conference," 1921, pt. 2:94–95, 89, 96, 100; and Bureau of Colored Work, minutes, 31 May 1921, 4–5. Bowles stressed its role as advisory. For information on the affiliating committee, see "Minutes of a Meeting held in Richmond, Virginia," transcript, 3 July 1920, 21; and YWCA of the USA, *Report of the National Board to the Eighth National Convention, 1924,* 32.

124. Work, *Negro Yearbook, 1925–1926,* 281–82.

125. See Bureau of Colored Work, minutes, 31 May 1921, 1, for the announcement of Brown's appointment. Brown described her appointment as being to the National Board, but she was appointed only to the South Atlantic Field Committee in Richmond, which was affiliated with, but distinct from, the National Board in New York City. See also Antoinette D. (Mrs. Lewis H.) Lapham to Charlotte Hawkins Brown, 21 June 1921, and Martha (Mrs. Walter S.) McNeill to Mrs. John Hope, 16 March 1921 (both NU/AUC).

126. Eva D. Bowles to Mrs. John Hope, 14 February 1922, and Mrs. John Hope to Eva D. Bowles, 15 March 1922, drafts (both NU/AUC). Bowles presented it as a victory specifically for African Americans, but other YWCA records do not support that interpretation. Instead the elimination of the field structure was done to save money; see Bannan, "Management by Women," 162–70. When the field offices were eliminated, the surviving staff members, such as Ruffin, were initially reassigned to the national headquarters in New York.

127. Young Women's Christian Associations of the U.S.A., Eighth National Convention, 1924: Credential Blanks: Durham (YWCA/RFC 28.3–28.4), and Young Women's Christian Associations of the U.S.A., Ninth National Convention, 1926: Credential Blanks: Asheville (YWCA/RFC 28.9). Cordella Arthur Winn (1878–1965), an Episcopalian, was raised in Ohio. She was a graduate of the Columbus Normal School, with additional coursework at Ohio State University. At some point, she married Malcolm Winn, a medical worker, but it is unclear when he died. Cordella Winn had been a social worker in Columbus, Ohio, when she was brought into the YWCA in 1918 for war work programs. She remained with the YWCA until 1938, when she left to join the faculty of Florida A&M at Tallahassee. Winn was the sister of Eva Bowles; see Olcott, *Work of Colored Women,* 90–91, and YWCA/NB.

128. Calkins, "The Negro in the Young Women's Christian Association," 64; Winn, "Speech to the National Board, 1938," 2; Cordella A. Winn, report, July 1938, 11 (YWCA/NB); and Work, *Negro Yearbook, 1925–1926,* 280–81. The Council on Colored Work replaced the existing Bureau of Colored Work, which was primarily a staff body. Key staff members attended council meetings.

129. For a description of the agreement, see Winn, "Speech to the National Board, 1938," 3.

130. "Report of Proceedings of the Louisville Conference," 1921, pt. 1:15.

131. "The Y.W.C.A. Convention," *Southern Workman* 53 (June 1924): 244.

132. Elizabeth Ross Haynes to Mrs. Washington, 2 December 1924 (MCT/MSRC).

133. James Grossman and Stephanie Shaw discuss the role of YWCAs in northern cities (Chicago and Detroit, respectively), while Glenda Gilmore looks at its role in a southern city (Charlotte). See Grossman, *Land of Hope,* 116, 133, 143, 186; Shaw, *What a Woman Ought to Be and to Do,* 189–90; and Gilmore, *Gender and Jim Crow,* 192–95.

134. Eva D. Bowles, Annual Report to the City Department, 1922, 3 (YWCA/NB).

135. Eva D. Bowles, Annual Report to the City Department, 1927, 3 (YWCA/NB).

136. YWCA of the USA, *Report of the National Board to the Seventh National Convention, 1922,* 167, and YWCA of the USA, *Proceedings of the Eighth National Convention, 1924,* 354–55. They, for instance, joined with the National Committee on the Cause and Cure of War (NCCCW). Led by Carrie Chapman Catt, the NCCCW essentially focused on foreign policy, while the WJCC tackled domestic issues; see Johnson, "Organized Women as Lobbyists in the 1920's," 43.

137. YWCA of the USA, *Report of the National Board to the Seventh National Convention, 1922,* 9, 279. For the general support of isolationism, especially among progressives, see Goldman, *Rendezvous with Destiny,* 291.

138. Its efforts were similar to those of the women's boards of missions for various

Protestant churches. For more on the YWCA's overseas work, see Boyd, *Emissaries: The Overseas Work of the American YWCA.*

139. YWCA of the USA, *Proceedings of the Sixth National Convention, 1920,* 124; this decision was repeatedly reaffirmed by attendees at subsequent conventions despite the advice of the National Board, which regarded it as unduly restrictive during hard times.

140. YWCA of the USA, *Proceedings of the Eighth National Convention, 1924,* 117.

141. Eva D. Bowles, "The Young Womens Christian Association—A Means of Meeting the Colored Girls Need for Self Expression," 2 (YWCA/NB).

142. YWCA of the USA, *Proceedings of the Eighth National Convention, 1924,* 117.

143. Marguerite Hersey, "Words of Life: Fresh Fields for Youth to Conquer," *Association Monthly* 15 (February 1921): 46.

144. Executive Committee, minutes, 11 October 1922 in YWCA National Board, minutes, 1 November 1922, 40 (YWCA/NB). There was no comment on the fact that the request came from Mary Talbert (of the Paris incident). For more on the Anti-Lynching Crusaders, see "The Ninth Crusade," *Crisis* 25 (March 1923): 213–17, and Terborg-Penn, "African-American Women's Networks in the Anti-Lynching Crusade," 157–59.

145. Council on Colored Work, minutes, 9–10 May 1923, 2, and Council on Colored Work, minutes, 8–9 November 1923, 2 (YWCA/NB).

146. Council on Colored Work, minutes, 7–8 February 1924, 3 (YWCA/NB). For coverage see "Mrs. J. D. Rockefeller Jr. in Anti-Lynching Move," *New York Tribune,* 19 May 1924, and "Negroes Now Members of Committees—Council on Colored Work Active," *New York Sun,* 18 May 1924 (both TIA/MF 22:192).

147. Lucy R. Somerville, "Of the People, By the People, For the People," *Association Monthly* 15 (December 1921): 472.

148. "Report of Proceedings of the Louisville Conference," 1921, pt. 2:63–64.

149. Council on Colored Work, minutes, 8–9 November 1923, 5.

150. Lumpkin, *The Making of a Southerner,* 191. Katharine Du Pre Lumpkin (1897–1988) was an Episcopalian. Born in Georgia and raised there and in South Carolina, she graduated from Brenau College in 1915. She worked as a student YWCA secretary on the campus before moving to New York City where she earned an M.A. from Columbia University (1919). She joined the national staff as a traveling student secretary in 1920 and remained until 1925. She received a Ph.D. from the University of Wisconsin (1928). See her autobiography, *The Making of a Southerner,* and Hall, "Katharine Du Pre Lumpkin," in Ware, *Notable American Women,* 400–402.

Frances Sanders Taylor's study of southern student YWCAs from 1920 to 1944 has been invaluable to my understanding of their efforts, although I have focused more on how they did (or did not) affect the larger organization; see her "'On the Edge of Tomorrow.'"

151. YWCA of the USA, *Report of the National Board to the Eighth National Convention, 1924,* 84; Holmes, "Youth Cannot Wait," 129 (quote). Holmes, who had been the sole African American at the 1915 convention, was by this time executive secretary of the Brooklyn black YWCA and an advisor to the national student group.

152. "Report of Proceedings of the Louisville Conference," 1921, pt. 2:55.

153. Hedgeman, *Trumpet Sounds,* 32, also 87–88.

154. For discussions of the conversionary nature of such meetings, see McDowell, *Social Gospel in the South.* Jacquelyn Dowd Hall has critiqued the limitations to the cathartic nature of interracial meetings for white women; see Hall, *Revolt against Chivalry,* 94, 105–6, 190 n. 100. See also Frederickson, "'Each One Is Dependent on the Other,'" 315–17.

155. "Claims That at Y.W.C.A. Camp at Blue Ridge, N.C., Intermarriage of Whites and Negroes Was Advocated," *Manufacturers Record,* 13 August 1925, 66.

156. Emma Bailey Speer to Mrs. Murrell Gray Ross (3 December 1925), 2, in Executive Committee of the YWCA National Board, minutes, 25 November 1925 (YWCA/NB). Emma Bailey Speer (1872–1961) a Presbyterian, was born in Pennsylvania. She attended Bryn Mawr College for two years before marrying Robert Elliott Speer (a missionary and, later, a lay leader of the Presbyterian General Assembly) in 1893. She was a charter member of the National Board of the YWCA; with the death of Grace Dodge, Speer became president of the National Board, serving during 1915–32. Following her retirement, she remained as honorary president until 1947, when her husband died; see "Mrs. R. E. Speer, 88, Leader in Y.W.C.A.," *New York Times,* 26 April 1961, 39, and Robinson, *Eight Women of the YWCA,* esp. chap. 4.

157. [Katharine Du Pre Lumpkin], Report of a Recent Situation in Columbia, S.C., 14 November 1924 (KDL/UNC).

158. Council on Colored Work, 9–10 May 1923, 2. Sallie Little Hanna (ca. 1870–1957), a Presbyterian, was born in Michigan. She attended Lindenwood College in Missouri before leaving in 1888 to marry John M. Hanna, a businessman. In 1902 they moved to Dallas, where she was active with the local YWCA. She joined the National Board in 1914, usually serving as a nonresident member. She was president of the national convention from 1926 to 1930. Hanna was also active with churchwomen's associations and was chairman of the Texas Association of Southern Women for the Prevention of Lynching; see Hall, *Revolt against Chivalry,* 178, and YWCA Biographical Files (YWCA/NB).

159. Executive Committee, minutes, 11 May 1921, 3, in YWCA National Board, minutes, 1 June 1921 (YWCA/NB).

160. YWCA of the USA, *Proceedings of the Eighth National Convention, 1924,* 114.

161. YWCA of the USA, *Proceedings of the Seventh National Convention, 1922,* 225, and YWCA of the USA, *Report of the National Board to the Seventh National Convention, 1922,* 120.

Chapter 5: Defending a Women's Organization

1. Quoted in Herbert N. Shenton, director, "Reconnaissance Study: YMCA-YWCA Relations in the Field in the United States of America," typescript, 1930, 330–31 (YWCA/NB; also at YMCA/MN). The respondent was identified only as a member of the YWCA's National Board, but I assume it was a white member.

2. YWCA of the USA, *Proceedings of the Tenth National Convention, 1928,* 59.

3. Council on Colored Work, minutes, 13 December 1929, 3 (YWCA/NB). Lucy Diggs Slowe (1885–1937) was a Presbyterian. Born in Virginia, she moved to Baltimore in 1898. In 1908, Slowe graduated from Howard University, where she was a founder of Alpha Kappa Alpha. She earned a master's from Columbia University in

1915. After a career in secondary education, she became dean of women at Howard. She helped to found the NCNW in 1935; Marion Thompson Wright, "Lucy Diggs Slowe," in James et al., *Notable American Women,* 3: 299–300.

4. Israel, "The Man's Viewpoint," 539; "Synopsis of Case Histories of Y.M.C.A. and Y.W.C.A. Relationships," 15 March 1926, 22 (YMCA/MN); and Bannan, "Management by Women," 62–63.

5. For examples of the language, see "Women and Girls Question," 2.

6. Men and women discussed many options in these years: doing sex-segregated work for members of the opposite sex, starting coeducational programs, developing joint activities, merging one into the other, or creating a new group. Generally, I have not distinguished between the choices since they raised similar issues.

7. YWCA of the USA, *Proceedings of the Eighth National Convention, 1924,* 40–41, 161. Henrietta Roelofs (1878–1942) was born in Michigan and graduated from Lake Erie College in 1906. She was a Congregationalist. Roelofs joined the national YW staff in 1906. She held a variety of posts, but her last major position with the organization was as executive secretary of the Public Affairs Committee in the 1930s. One of her priorities was peace; she helped organize the Conference on the Cause and Cure of War and was one of the officers of the NCCCW. When she retired from the YW in 1939, she continued work with the National Peace Conference. Her life partner, Rhoda McCulloch (1884–1978), was also on the national staff, primarily as editor of the YWCA's monthly periodical; see "Miss Roelofs Dies; Peace Group Head," *New York Times,* 28 January 1942, 19; and YWCA/NB.

8. Edith M. Gates, "YMCA and YWCA Cooperate in Physical Education," *Journal of Physical Education,* 27 (January 1930): 84–86.

9. For a similar observation about Southern Methodist men and women, see Hall, *Revolt against Chivalry,* 283 n. 36.

10. Shenton, "Reconnaissance Study: YMCA-YWCA Relations," 297.

11. C. Hopkins, *History of the Y.M.C.A.,* and Macleod, *Building Character in the American Boy.*

12. "Extract from a letter from Dwight C. Drew," [1914] (YMCA/MN); "Questionnaire sent out by E. G. Gay" [1914] (YMCA/MN); and C. Hopkins, *History of the Y.M.C.A.,* 39, 240–42.

13. C. Hopkins, *History of the Y.M.C.A.,* 194, 518. See also Karlin, "Disciples of Mercury," 184, 207.

14. See Putney, *Muscular Christianity,* esp. chap. 2.

15. C. Hopkins, *History of the Y.M.C.A.,* 401, 456–58; see also Lupkin, "Manhood Factories." Robyn Muncy has speculated that the male focus on buildings was based on the historical importance of owning property to male definitions of citizenship (Muncy, comment, American Historical Association annual meeting, 7 January 1995).

16. C. Hopkins, *History of the Y.M.C.A.,* 456–58, 503.

17. The general shift is described in Zald, *Organizational Change,* chaps. 2 and 3.

18. One of the 1888 "McBurney principles," listed in Doggett, *Life of Robert R. McBurney,* 146; for the debate club incident, see C. Hopkins, *History of the Y.M.C.A.,* 395.

19. *Atlanta Constitution* editorial, quoted in C. Hopkins, *History of the Y.M.C.A.*, 389; see also 227, 390–91, 393, 476, 478, 234–35, for more on the ties between employer and employee. Jane Karlin has observed that by the late nineteenth century, not only had businessmen replaced ministers as the pivotal leaders of the YMCA, but the structure of the YMCA itself resembled that of a business; see her "Disciples of Mercury," 71–72, 79–80, 152–53.

20. For the struggle over control of the Philadelphia YMCA, see Fones-Wolf, *Trade Union Gospel*, 130–39, 157.

21. Winter, *Making Men, Making Class*, 43–45.

22. C. Hopkins, *History of the Y.M.C.A.*, 220.

23. W. E. B. Du Bois, "The Y.M.C.A.," *Crisis* 31 (November 1925): 11.

24. Nina Mjagkij has observed that at the time of the YM's founding in the 1850s, there was little interest in black men because they were largely seen as property, rather then as men who could own property; see her *Light in the Darkness*, 2. For an elaboration on black men's strategy to advance the race, see her "True Manhood: The YMCA and Racial Advancement." Christine Lutz offers a slightly different take on how black YM men, especially Hunton, saw manhood; see her dissertation, "'The Dizzy Steep to Heaven,'" 121–23, 127–28.

25. Shenton, "Reconnaissance Study: YMCA-YWCA Relations," 344, 356; see Fisher, *Public Affairs and the Y.M.C.A.*, for information on progressive local YMs in New York and Cleveland; and C. Hopkins, *History of the Y.M.C.A.*, 384.

26. Men also had more choices of organizations to join and progressive men may well have opted to join other groups.

27. On schools, Shenton, "Reconnaissance Study: YMCA-YWCA Relations," 311. The YWCA's NTS was strongly influenced by the social gospel while the political and theological views of the YM's schools varied. On the NTS, see Bannan, "Management by Women." On the YM's schools, see C. Hopkins, *History of the Y.M.C.A.*, 610–14.

28. The following account is drawn from Mittelman, "'A Spirit That Touches the Problems of Today,'" 47–53.

29. Pence, *The Y.M.C.A. and Social Need*, 151. In 1929, the national YM eliminated its industrial department altogether; see Winter, *Making Men, Making Class*, 147.

30. Marshall Tribby to D. C. Drew, 1 March 1926, 2 (YMCA/MN). Many local YMs held onto restrictive rules, such as those against dancing and playing cards.

31. Lyman, *The World Almanac and Book of Facts for 1927*, 260, gives the YWCA's membership as 605,912, the General Federation of Women's Clubs' as 3,000,000, and the YM's as 988,522.

32. Mildred Corbett, "The Y.M.C.A. National Council Meeting: The Men's Organization Considers its Relation to Work with Women and Girls," *Womans Press* 19 (December 1925): 865.

33. Mary Sims, a longtime YW secretary, conveys the women's annoyance with being treated as a subset of the YMCA and their belief that this caused people to support the YM better than they supported the YW; see Sims, *Natural History of a Social Institution*, 14–15, 73.

34. [Richard C. Morse], "A Memorandum" [1917] (YMCA/MN).

35. YWCA of the USA, *Proceedings of the Ninth National Convention, 1926*, 130.

36. On programs that did not take equipment, see "Y.W.C.A.—Y.M.C.A. Relationships: From the Point of View of the Town Department," 14 November 1927, 3 (YMCA/MN).

37. YWCA of the USA, *Proceedings of the Ninth National Convention, 1926,* 133–34.

38. C. Hopkins, *History of the Y.M.C.A.*, 493, 502–3.

39. Regina Bannan discusses pressure from funders like the Gambles in Cincinnati and the Rockefellers on the national YWCA; see Bannan, "Management by Women," 55–63 and chap. 4.

40. "Facing the Merger Problem," *Association Forum* 10 (October 1929): 12.

41. Estelle Freedman's classic work on women's institutions lays out the reasons that they were significant to women's power and discusses the society-wide pressures on women's organizations in the 1920s; see Freedman, "Separatism as Strategy."

42. Crocker, *Social Work and Social Order,* esp. 39–40, 216–17.

43. Yohn, *Contest of Faiths,* esp. chap. 6.

44. See discussions in Hill, *The World Their Household;* J. Hunter, *The Gospel of Gentility;* and MacHaffie, *Herstory.*

45. *Relative Place of Women in the Church in the United States,* 4, 21. See also YWCA of the USA, *Report of the National Board to the Ninth National Convention, 1926,* 76–82, and YWCA of the USA, *Report of the National Board to the Tenth National Convention, 1928,* 88.

46. "A Survey of Y.M.C.A.—Y.W.C.A. Relations," *Womans Press* 23 (October 1929): 672, and YWCA of the USA, *Proceedings of the Eighth National Convention, 1924,* 364.

47. Mabel Cratty and S. Wirt Wiley to John D. Rockefeller Jr., 21 January 1928, typed copy, and Thomas B. Appelget to S. Wirt Wiley, 28 November 1928, typed copy (both YMCA/MN).

48. Meeting of Y.M.C.A. and Y.W.C.A. Secretaries Representing the Northwest and Pacific Coasts, minutes, 30 April 1928, 2 (YMCA/MN).

49. Shenton, "Reconnaissance Study: YMCA-YWCA Relations," 276.

50. Harris, "Christian Associations and the Community," 779.

51. Israel, "The Man's Viewpoint," 540.

52. First Joint Meeting of the Commissions on Cooperation, report, 17 December 1925, 4 (YWCA/RFC 158.5); Second Joint Meeting of the YMCA and YWCA Commissions, minutes, 16 March 1926, 6, 9 (YMCA/MN). Walter Mabie Wood (1871–1941), a Presbyterian, was born in Ohio. He received an A.B. from Indiana University in 1893. His employment was primarily with the YMCA. He retired from the Philadelphia association in 1935.

53. "Women and Girls Question," 2–3, 25.

54. Robert E. Lewis, "The Point of View: Women in the Y, II," in *Cleveland Red Triangle* (March 1926): 3 (YMCA/MN).

55. First Joint Meeting of the Commissions on Cooperation, report, 17 December 1925, 4.

56. YWCA of the USA, *Proceedings of the Tenth National Convention, 1928,* 37.

57. Judge Ben Lindsey first coined the term "companionate marriage" in Lindsey and Evans, *Revolt of Modern Youth.* Along with issues of social hygiene and sex

education, it was a popular topic for discussion groups, especially for younger men and women. The list of topics for the African American girls club in Elizabeth, N.J., in 1928–29 included the History of Negro Literature, the Bryn Mawr Summer School for Women Workers, and Companionate Marriage; see Elizabeth, New Jersey YWCA, "Timeline of Events in the History of the Y.W.C.A. of Eastern Union County" (YWCA/NJ). The classic piece on companionate marriage is Simmons, "Companionate Marriage and the Lesbian Threat." Jodi Vandenberg-Daves's article "The Manly Pursuit of a Partnership between the Sexes: The Debate over YMCA Programs for Women and Girls, 1914–1933" is a sophisticated analysis of the conflict between the YM and YW from the men's point of view. Her focus is on explaining the internal struggles within the YM (which I have elided). The differences in our analyses recapitulate those between the YM and the YW in the 1920s.

58. "Women and Girls Question," 2, 25, 26.

59. Gustav-Wrathall, *Take the Young Stranger by the Hand,* chap. 3, esp. pp. 71, 78–79, 88, and Chauncey, "Christian Brotherhood or Sexual Perversion?"

60. Historically, men in the YM had defined their group as part of a "men's movement." As late as 1929, one of the most prolific writers for the YM, Paul Super, embraced the term as he argued against admitting women to the YM. Nonetheless, those voices were becoming quieter in the association; see his *Formative Ideas in the YMCA,* 175.

61. YWCA of the USA, *Report of the National Board to the Tenth National Convention, 1928,* 85.

62. For possible topics, Gregg, "What Women Are Thinking," 300. On the commission, see YWCA of the USA, *Report of the National Board to the Ninth National Convention, 1926,* 47–50, and YWCA of the USA, *Proceedings of the Ninth National Convention, 1926,* 165–71. For the legislative and educational priorities, ibid., 45, 122–24.

63. Gregg, "What Women Are Thinking," 300–303.

64. For the idea of "twinness," see the Commission on Cooperation with the YMCA, report of meeting, 17 March 1925, 9 (YWCA/NB).

65. Elizabeth B. Herring to W. H. Baxley, 22 March 1926, 1–2 (YMCA/MN).

66. Emma Bailey Speer, "'What Does the Woman Want?' Men Wonder, But Women Know," *Womans Press* 22 (July 1928): 456–57; it was reprinted from *Association Men* (the YM's periodical).

67. Reported in YWCA National Board, minutes, 18 November 1925, 4 (YWCA/NB).

68. Young Women's Christian Associations of the U.S.A., "Proceedings of the Ninth Biennial Convention, 1926," stenotype, 129 (YWCA/RFC 29.1). Examples of the YMCA's comparatively conservative stand on social issues can be found in Shenton, "Reconnaissance Study: YMCA-YWCA Relations," 325.

69. "Voice of the Churches," *Survey* 45 (26 March 1921): 913.

70. Spratt, "The Pittsburgh YWCA and Industrial Democracy in the 1920s," 11.

71. "The Industrial Policy of the Young Men's Christian Association," *Industry* 3 (1 August 1921): 1.

72. "Y.M.C.A.—Y.W.C.A. National Secretaries Conference: Boys' and Girls' Work," [21 February 1927], 1–2 (YMCA/MN).

73. Shenton, "Reconnaissance Study: YMCA-YWCA Relations," 273.

74. Ames, *Cooperation between the YW and YMCA,* 41–44.

75. Ibid., 59.

76. For a southern example (Laurel, Mississippi), see Eleanor Copenhaver, "Chronological Statement of Attack on Southern Industrial Conference," 21 February 1929 (YWCA/NB).

77. See "Doubtful Speakers: Men" and "Doubtful Speakers: Women," reprinted in Nielsen, *Un-American Womanhood,* 143–49. YW staff members listed included Leslie Blanchard (erroneously on the men's list, identified as "pacifist"), executive of the student department, and Lucy P. Carner ("radical"), executive in the industrial department. Board members included Mary E. Woolsey [*sic,* Woolley] ("pacifist, radical"). See also "Organizations Interlocking with Radical Groups, either thro [*sic*] their Directorates of Legislative Programs," in ibid., 153. Francesca Morgan brought these lists to my attention.

Coverage of the DAR's attack mentioning the YWCA included "The Blue Menace of the Black Lists," *Christian Century* 45 (29 March 1928): 400; "D.A.R. Head Defends Order's Blacklist," *New York Times,* 3 April 1928, 31; "Sees Klan's Hand in D.A.R. Blacklist," *New York Times,* 6 April 1928, 20; and Villard, "What the Blue Menace Means."

For more on the DAR's shift from being moderate to conservative and its ensuing campaign against progressive women's groups, see Morgan, "'Home and Country,'" and Delegard, "Women Patriots."

78. For the term "professional patriots," see Hapgood, *Professional Patriots.*

79. "History of Attacks," 9 June 1927, 1, included with H. Roelofs, "Memorandum on 'Attacks' on the Y.W.C.A.," 25 June 1927 (YWCA/NB); see also Henrietta Roelofs, "'I'll Tell the World': Does the Public Really Know the Y.W.C.A.?" *Womans Press* 21 (September 1927): 613–15. The wording is similar to that of the WJCC's Special Committee on Attacks; see Nielsen, *Un-American Womanhood,* 130–31.

80. Before her resignation, Ida Jones (one of the staff members) shared her experiences with the YW membership; YWCA of the USA, *Proceedings of the Ninth National Convention, 1926,* 116–17. See also her correspondence about the spider web chart with the Military Intelligence Division: Ida L. Jones to Col. James H. Reeves, 26 April 1927 and 12 May 1927; James H. Reeves to Ida L. Jones, 30 April 1927; and Col. Stanley H. Ford to Ida L. Jones, 20 May 1927 (all MID/NA). Francesca Morgan shared this correspondence with me. See also editorial comment in *New Republic* 51 (13 July 1927): 187, and Margaret M. Hatch, "What Can We Learn from Fort Wayne?" *Womans Press* 21 (September 1927): 612.

81. Elsie D. Harper, Visitation Report: Fort Wayne, Indiana, 20 January 1947, 2 (YWCA/NB).

82. For the impact of Community Chests on settlement houses, see Carson, *Settlement Folk,* 183–84, and Trolander, *Professionalism and Social Change,* 23, 51, 89. For the impact on the YW, see Sims, *Natural History of a Social Institution,* 229–30. The National Board reports and proceedings for the national conventions evinced concern over the impact of Community Chests throughout the decade; see, for instance, YWCA of the USA, *Report of the National Board to the Eighth National Convention, 1924,* 31, 192.

83. "Findings for the Branch Leadership Conference, Institute, West Virginia," 24 June–2 July 1931, 6 (YWCA/NB).

84. C. Hopkins, *History of the Y.M.C.A.*, 564–66.

85. "Proposals Making Possible Identical Status of the Sexes as Affecting Recognition, Rights, and Responsibility in Association Affairs," 3 (YMCA/MN).

86. For the YWCA's commitments, see Mary Sims, "YMCA—YWCA Field Relations Studied," *Association Men* (December 1930): 172.

87. For "race solidarity," see YWCA of the USA, *Report of the National Board to the Ninth National Convention, 1926,* 86; for Corbett's wording, see YWCA of the USA, *Report of the National Board to the Tenth National Convention, 1928,* 79, and YWCA of the USA, *Proceedings of the Tenth National Convention, 1928,* 61. See also YWCA of the USA, *Report of the National Board to the Eleventh National Convention, 1930,* 116.

88. Hill, *The World Their Household,* 6, and Frederickson, "'Each One Is Dependent on the Other,'" 317, 324 n. 53.

89. Council on Colored Work, minutes, 12 March 1926, 3 (YWCA/NB). While black men had more representation at the national level on boards of directors than did women in the YWCA, they usually were not on boards at the local level.

90. Council on Colored Work, minutes, 9 November 1928, 1 (YWCA/NB), and Tobias, "The Work of the YM and YWCA with Negro Youth," 283. For a fuller analysis of black men's strategy in the YM, see Mjagkij, *Light in the Darkness.* Channing Heggie Tobias (1882–1961), CME, was born in Georgia. He received a B.A. from Paine College in 1902 and a B.D. from Drew Seminary in 1905. In 1911, he became a student secretary for the YMCA; in 1923 he was the senior secretary for the colored men's department, a position he held until he left in 1946. He then worked for the Phelps-Stokes Fund until he retired in 1953. That year, he was chosen as chairman of the board of the NAACP; see "Channing Tobias of N.A.A.C.P. Dead," *New York Times,* 6 November 1961, 37.

91. Baker, *Negro-White Adjustment,* 141. See also the Council on Colored Work, minutes, 9 January 1931, 3 (YWCA/NB).

92. Eva D. Bowles, Annual Report to the City Department for 1929, 2 (YWCA/NB), and letter quoted in Shenton, "Reconnaissance Study: YMCA-YWCA Relations," 431.

93. Council on Colored Work, minutes, 13 December 1929, 3.

94. The Phyllis Wheatley Branch of the YWCA to the Hunton Branch of the YMCA [Lynchburg, Va.], 17 June 1929 (YWCA/RFC 158.5 and 218.2).

95. Bowles, Annual Report for 1929, 2.

96. Shenton, "Reconnaissance Study: YMCA-YWCA Relations," 262.

97. Eva D. Bowles, Annual Report to the City Department for 1927, 3 (YWCA/NB). Bowles's assessment was shared with the larger membership in preparation for the 1928 convention; see YWCA of the USA, *Report of the National Board to the Tenth National Convention, 1928,* 12.

98. Council on Colored Work, minutes, 13 December 1929, 4.

99. Quoted in Shenton, "Reconnaissance Study: YMCA-YWCA Relations," 429. The wording also appeared in the YWCA's draft of the discussions; see "Statement Frames [*sic*] by Y.M.C.A. and Y.W.C.A. Commissions," draft, in YWCA National Board, minutes, 7 April 1926, addendum III, 34 (YWCA/NB).

100. For the YM's comments on the draft, see attachments for Mildred Corbett

to Mabel Cratty and Wirt Wiley, 17 March 1926 (YMCA/MN); compare to the version agreed upon and published: "Tentative Conclusions of the Joint Meeting of the Commissions on the Relation between the Y.M.C.A. and the Y.W.C.A.," in YWCA National Board, minutes, 7 April 1926, addendum V, 40–41.

101. Shenton, "Reconnaissance Study: YMCA-YWCA Relations" summarized in C. Hopkins, *History of the Y.M.C.A.*, 565.

102. Edith Abbott and S. P. Breckinridge to George B. McKibbon, Committee on Policy, Young Men's Christian Association [of Chicago], 21 May 1931, 2 (YWCA/NB).

103. J. W. Ogg to Neil MacMillan Jr., 19 June 1928 (YMCA/MN).

104. "Work for Women and Girls and Cooperation with the Young Women's Christian Association," 1 May 1933, 3 (YMCA/MN). Charles Hopkins gives the date as 1933, although the first survey registering female members did not come out until 1934; see his *History of the Y.M.C.A.*, 565.

105. By 1942, although 43 percent of the men's associations permitted women as members, only 23 percent would let them vote. As late as 1947, the YM's National Council (its national governing body) still did not include women; C. Hopkins, *History of the Y.M.C.A.*, 565–66, 721.

106. Vandenberg-Daves, "The Manly Pursuit of a Partnership," 1334.

107. YWCA of the USA, *Report of the National Board to the Tenth National Convention, 1928*, 12.

108. The city had neither a black YM nor a black YW; see Elizabeth, New Jersey, YWCA, Board of Directors, minutes, 1922–1928, and Department of Girls' Work, records, 1922–1928 (all YWCA/NJ).

109. There were limits to when African Americans could use the pool, but the new policy marked a departure from almost total exclusion; see "Chronological History of the Interracial Practices, Boston Y.W.C.A., 1918–1944," 9 (YWCA/MA). For their part, by the 1920s, African American women in Boston seemed to have decided to wait to be admitted to the main association, rather than accept a segregated branch; see Cochrane, "'And the Pressure Never Let Up.'"

110. Florence R. Ridley, "Elect Colored Woman on Y.W.C.A. Board," *Indianapolis Recorder*, 26 October 1929 (TIA/MF 45:852).

111. Bell and Wilkins, *Interracial Practices in Community Y.W.C.A.'s*, 6, 8–9. For the progression of interracial issues and activities in another group, that of Southern Methodist churchwomen (many of whom were in the YWCA), see Frederickson, "'Each One Is Dependent on the Other,'" esp. 315–17.

112. "Committee on Colored Work," Memorandum, May 1929 (YWCA/NB).

113. [Cordella Winn and Frances Williams], "Outgrowths of the Interracial Structure of the Y.W.C.A.—Current Administrative Practices," [1934], 10 (YWCA/NB).

114. Frances Harriet Williams (1898–1992), a Presbyterian was born in Kentucky and raised in St. Louis. She graduated from Mount Holyoke in 1919 and went on to postgraduate work at the New York School for Social Work. From 1921 to 1928, she worked as a student secretary for the national YWCA. She left to earn a master's degree from the University of Chicago, which she did in 1931. In 1932, Williams returned to the YW and worked for the Laboratory Division, leaving in 1940 to become a race relations advisor in the federal Office of Price Administration. In the

late 1940s, she was on the staff of President Truman's Committee on Civil Rights. See F. Taylor, "'On the Edge of Tomorrow,'" and Hill and Miller, *Black Women Oral History Project,* 10: 275–308. Frances Williams's mother, Fannie B. Miller (Mrs. Frank L.) Williams, served on the first Council on Colored Work.

115. Jenness, *Twelve Negro Americans,* 166–68; the white student secretary is not identified. Juliette Aline Derricotte (1897–1931) may have been a Presbyterian. Born in Georgia, she graduated from Talladega College in 1918 and then attended the NTS in the summer. From 1918 to 1929, she served as a student secretary for the YWCA. She received her master's degree from Columbia University in 1927; in 1929 she left the YW to become dean of women at Fisk University in Nashville. See Jean Cazort, "Juliette Derricotte," in Hine et al., *Black Women in America,* 332–33.

116. Frances Williams, memo to the subcommittee on race of the [YWCA] National Student Council, 30 November 1936, 4 (GTH/AHC).

117. Frances [Williams] to Jule [Juliette Derricotte] and Jane [Juanita Saddler], no date [ca. 1926] (YWCA/RFC 134.6).

118. Katharine Du Pre Lumpkin to Leslie [Blanchard], 3 December 1923, 1–2 (KDL/UNC).

119. Council on Colored Work, minutes, 15–16 January 1925, 2 (YWCA/NB).

120. Eva D. Bowles, Annual Report to City Department for 1926 (YWCA/NB), 5.

121. Eva Bowles, "The Y.W.C.A. and Racial Understanding," *Womans Press* 23 (September 1929): 624.

122. L. H. Hammond, *Southern Women and Racial Adjustment,* 29.

123. "Statement Sent to Northern Cities Who Are Approaching Colored Work for the First Time," 24 September 1925 (YWCA/NB).

124. "Summary of Discussion on Industrial Work among Girls" and Eleanor Copenhaver, "Supplementary Notes Covering the Discussion of the Industrial Staff and Those Concerned with Work in Colored Branches," 5 October 1928 (both YWCA/NB).

125. Dorothy Guinn, Annual Report for 1932–1933, 1–3 (YWCA/NB); Guinn joined the national staff in 1932. The lack of concern from locals for industrial women was a problem for white associations as well, but given fewer economic resources in black communities, there were racial consequences.

126. Craney quoted in Annette M. Dieckmann, "Towards Unity in Industry: How Various Organizations Are Studying the Problem of the Colored Worker in Industry," *Womans Press* 21 (April 1927): 259, and YWCA of the USA, *Proceedings of the Ninth National Convention, 1926,* 205–6.

127. "25 Colored Women Attend Regional Y.W. Conference: First Inter-Racial Y.W.C.A. Meeting in South is Held at Richmond, Va.," *New York Age,* 12 February 1927 (TIA/MF 30:552), and Council on Colored Work, minutes, 14 January 1927, 3 (YWCA/NB).

128. Council on Colored Work, minutes, 8 January 1926, 4 (YWCA/NB).

129. See, for instance, the preconvention files for the Ninth National Convention [1926, Milwaukee] (YWCA/RFC 29.3) for the efforts that went into securing interracial accommodations. For a discussion of the policy's implementation, see Council on Colored Work, minutes, 6 March 1931 (YWCA/NB). The YW's efforts garnered

public attention, as in 1927 when the hotels of Portland, Oregon, refused to admit African American delegates so the YW held the convention in Sacramento instead; "Portland's Negro Ban Hits Y.W.C.A. Session," *New York Times,* 29 May 1927, E6.

130. Council on Colored Work, minutes, 10 February 1928 (YWCA/NB).

131. I am grateful to Priscilla Murolo for this observation.

132. Eva Bowles to Mildred Corbett, 6 October 1925 (YWCA/RFC 158.5).

133. Freedman, "Separatism as Strategy"; Freedman has revised this analysis in her "Separatism Revisited." See also Sarah Deutsch's discussion of women's groups that also continued to exist as such, in "Learning to Talk More Like a Man."

134. YWCA of the USA, *Report of the National Board to the Twelfth National Convention, 1932,* 24, 117; Eva D. Bowles, Annual Report to the City Department for 1930, 3–4; and "A Meeting to consider the Interracial Situation and the Public Affairs Program," minutes, 26 April 1933, 1 (both YWCA/NB).

135. Council on Colored Work, minutes, 8 October 1926, 3–4 (YWCA/NB).

136. Alice Dunbar-Nelson, "As in a Looking Glass," 28 September 1928, in *Works of Alice Dunbar-Nelson,* 3:232–33, and *Give Us Each Day,* 264.

Chapter 6: Changing Strategies

1. This account is drawn from [Arthur Raper], *Report of the Commission on Interracial Cooperation Regarding the Automobile Accident in Dalton, Georgia, November 6, 1931* (Atlanta: Commission on Interracial Cooperation, 1931), reprinted in *Interracial News Bulletin* [March 1932]: 7–11 (YWCA/NB); correspondence of the National Board and staff; and the press coverage (see n. 4 below).

2. Platt, *E. Franklin Frazier Reconsidered,* 100; Langston Hughes, "Cowards from the Colleges," *Crisis* 41 (August 1934): 226–28; Franklin, foreword to Love, *One Blood,* xvii–xviii; and *Norfolk Journal and Guide,* 14 November 1931, 1; see also Love, *One Blood,* 49.

3. "Juliette Derricotte Dies," *New York Times,* 8 November 1931, sec. 2, p. 7, and W. E. B. Du Bois, "Dalton, Georgia," *Crisis* 39 (March 1932): 85–87.

4. A sample of the coverage includes "Juliette Derricotte, Dean of Women at Fisk University, Former Student Y.W. Secretary, Killed in Accident," *New York Age,* 14 November 1931, 1; "Denies That White Doctors Refused Medical Treatment to Victims of Automobile Accident in Dalton, Ga.," *New York Age,* 21 November 1931, 1; "Dead Fisk Women Suffered Because Ga. Hospitals Were for Whites Only," *Afro-American,* 21 November 1931, 18; Walter White, "The Color Line," *New York Herald Tribune,* 12 December 1931, 14; "Editorial," *Nation* 33 (30 December 1931): 711; J. B. Matthews, "Tragic Result of Jim Crow Discrimination," *World Tomorrow* 15 (January 1932): 28; and "Does Your Hospital Aid Them?" *Women and Missions* 9 (April 1932): 18.

5. Ethel Bedient Gilbert to Leslie Blanchard, 10 November 1931, 9.

6. YWCA of the USA, *Report of the National Board to the Eleventh National Convention, 1930,* 125; Walton, "Y.W.C.A. Has Achieved Great Work for Negro" and Sims, "The Y.W.C.A. at Detroit."

7. Sims, "The Y.W.C.A. at Detroit," 356, and Council on Colored Work, minutes, 9 May 1930, 1–2 (YWCA/NB).

8. YWCA of the USA, *Proceedings of the Eleventh National Convention, 1930,* 246, and Council on Colored Work, minutes, 9 May 1930, 2.

9. Council on Colored Work, minutes, 9 May 1930, 3. Winnifred Crane Wygal (1884–1972), a member of Riverside Church in New York City, was born in Missouri. She received her B.A. from Drury College (in Missouri) in 1906, with additional study at Teachers College and Union Theological Seminary in New York City. She taught high school before serving as a student secretary at University of Nevada from 1912 to 1917. She joined the national YW in 1919, working in the student division and then as secretary for religious resources; she retired in 1944. Wygal worked to develop religious services and a lay theology, writing, among other works, *We Plan Our Own Worship Services* (1940); see Memorial Service Program, 1972 (WW/SL), and YWCA Biographical Files (YWCA/NB).

10. Council on Colored Work, minutes, 9 May 1930, 2.

11. Walton, "Y.W.C.A. Has Achieved Great Work for Negro," and Sims, "The Y.W.C.A. at Detroit," 335.

12. Sims, "The Y.W.C.A. at Detroit," 356.

13. Eva D. Bowles, Annual Report to the City Department for 1930, 3 (YWCA/NB), and Walton, "Y.W.C.A. Has Achieved Great Work for Negro."

14. Sims, "The Y.W.C.A. at Detroit," 356.

15. "Findings of All-Day Meeting of Young Women's Christian Associations of Eastern Pennsylvania, New Jersey and Delaware for Consideration of Interracial Relationships," 1 December 1936, 4 (YWCA/NB).

Campus Ys (both associations and participants) declined beginning in the 1920s; see Solomon, *In the Company of Educated Women,* 165–66. The number of student associations went from 767 in 1922 to 447 by 1940. By the late 1930s, students represented only 4 percent of the total YW membership; see YWCA National Board, *The Students Standards Study,* 3, 7.

The number of industrial women, a smaller percentage to begin with, had also been declining from a peak in 1929 of 51,206 to a membership of 39,026 in 1936. The 1931 national reorganization that ended the Colored Work Department also eliminated the Industrial Department; see A. Stewart, *Industrial Work of the Y.W.C.A.,* 11, 19. For more on the declining involvement of working women in the YWCA, see Mittelman, "'A Spirit That Touches the Problems of Today,'" esp. chap. 5. Dorothea Browder of the University of Wisconsin is working on a dissertation on industrial women in the YWCA.

16. "Relief Work Done in 137th Street Y.W.C.A." *New York Age,* 17 December 1931, 5.

17. The YM's 1933 decision to permit locals to allow women as members made many of the women's efforts to negotiate with the YM moot. Correspondence between the national YW and its locals continued to reveal problems in the 1930s; see "Relationship with YMCA: Local Relations Summaries" (YWCA/RFC 158.6).

18. YWCA of the USA, *Report of the National Board to the Eleventh National Convention, 1930,* 64, 102–3.

19. For the revisions through 1934, see Sims, *Natural History of a Social Institution,* 233–37. In the case of community YWs, the changes reflected an effort to involve the

non-evangelical women, including those from Roman Catholic and the Orthodox churches, active in the International Institutes (the YWCA's programs for first and second generation Americans) or the industrial programs; see "Editorial," *Womans Press* 18 (May 1924): 311. Women in the YWCA were not alone in struggles over the meaning of religion in these years. For arguments that the social gospel in particular led to a "religion without theology" (to use R. A. R. Edwards's phrase) and then to secularization, see R. Edwards, "Jane Addams, Walter Rauschenbusch, and Dorothy Day," esp. 152; S. Curtis, *Consuming Faith;* and Fox, "The Culture of Liberal Protestant Progressivism, 1875–1925." While they are persuasive about the difficulties that religious liberals had retaining their religion, it seems significant that it was members of the Young Women's *Christian* Association who took on racial issues at a time when explicitly secular women's groups did not. YW women's continued activism, couched in religious terms, suggests limitations to a portrayal of secularization as an inevitable juggernaut.

20. Local and student associations *could* hold onto the older requirement of membership in an evangelical Protestant church or adopt the new personal statements. Increasingly, the latter prevailed over the former. The national YW was more likely to invite ministers and proponents of the liberal or modern wing of Protestantism (rather than fundamentalist) to speak or teach. No doubt there was more variation at the local level, but those voices were increasingly silent in the national venues.

21. YWCA of the USA, *Report of the National Board to the Eleventh National Convention, 1930,* 60, 139, and YWCA of the USA, *Proceedings of the Eleventh National Convention, 1930,* 126–27.

22. YWCA of the USA, *Report of the National Board to the Eleventh National Convention, 1930,* 139.

23. Anna Rice in her speech to the convention, see YWCA of the USA, *Proceedings of the Eleventh National Convention, 1930,* 145.

24. YWCA of the USA, *Report of the National Board to the Eleventh National Convention, 1930,* 122.

25. YWCA of the USA, *Proceedings of the Eleventh National Convention, 1930,* 52.

26. Bowles, Annual Report for 1930, 5.

27. Walton, "Y.W.C.A. Has Achieved Great Work for Negro."

28. For accounts of the impact that Derricotte had on white college students, see Rossman, "Conversation with Fern Babcock Grant" and R. Smith, *White Man's Burden,* esp. chap. 3 and 166, 182–89, 213–14.

29. Baker, *Negro-White Adjustment,* 242–43. In 1922, the YWCA changed the title of its magazine from the *Association Monthly* to the *Womans Press.*

30. Council on Colored Work, minutes, 9 May 1930, 5.

31. L. H. Hammond, *Southern Women and Racial Adjustment,* 31–32.

32. Lily Hammond, *In the Vanguard of a Race,* 175.

33. Quoted in Eva D. Bowles to Cordella Winn, 3 March 1932, 2 (YWCA/NB).

34. Winnifred Wygal, "The Death of Miss Derricotte," *Christian Century* 49 (13 January 1932): 58.

35. Winnifred Wygal, diary, 7 November 1931 (WW/SL).

36. Winnifred Wygal to Leslie Blanchard, 14 November 1931, 5 (YWCA/NB).

37. *Interracial News Bulletin* [March 1932], 5.

38. See F. Taylor, "'On the Edge of Tomorrow,'" for a more sustained analysis of the student efforts.

39. National Student Council, minutes, 9 December 1931, 7 (YWCA/NB).

40. [Leslie Blanchard] to [Winnifred Wygal], 12 November 1931, 1 (YWCA/NB).

41. YWCA of the USA, *Proceedings of the Twelfth National Convention, 1932,* 35.

42. On the reorganization, see Bannan, "Management by Women," esp. 290–95 and chap. 6, as well as A. Stewart, *Industrial Work of the Y.W.C.A.,* 11, 14–20.

43. Grace L. Coyle to Otto Mayer, 17 February 1933, 1 (YWCA/NB). Marion Vera Cuthbert (1896–1989), a Baptist, was born in Minnesota. She attended the University of Minnesota but completed her B.A. at Boston University in 1920. She worked in a private school for African Americans in Alabama before joining Talladega College as dean of women from 1927 to 1930 (while Juliette Derricotte served as its first female trustee). Cuthbert earned an M.A. in 1931 from Columbia. She joined the YWCA's national staff in 1932, but she left in 1940 to complete her Ph.D. in 1942 from Teachers College; see Linda M. Perkins, "Marion Vera Cuthbert," in Ware, *Notable American Women,* 146–47.

44. Eva Bowles to May Belcher et al. [the Branch General Secretaries], 20 October 1931 (YWCA/NB).

45. Mrs. C. A. Winn, "Speech to the National Board," 25 May 1938, 2 (YWCA/NB).

46. Margaret Hiller to Lucy Carner, 22 March 1932, 1 (YWCA/NB). By the 1930s, the Public Affairs Committee, a joint effort of the National Board and national staff, had absorbed the work of the Legislative Committee and Legislative Service Division.

47. Henrietta Roelofs, "Cooperation with Other Organizations: Commission on Interracial Cooperation," 17 March 1932 (YWCA/NB).

48. Baker, *Negro-White Adjustment,* 32.

49. See, for example, Eva D. Bowles to Cordella Winn, 3 March 1932.

50. Carter G. Woodson, "And So Miss Bowles Goes the Way of Moorland," *New York Age,* 4 June 1932, 4.

51. Marion Robinson's interview with Margaret Mead [not the anthropologist], notes on "race" in "Marion Robinson—Rockefeller Project 1, *Eight Women of the YWCA* and misc. correspondence, 1960–1966" (YWCA/NB). Regina Bannan brought these notes to my attention.

52. C. Davis, "Eva D[el Vakia] Bowles," 55.

53. YWCA of the USA, *Proceedings of the Twelfth National Convention, 1932,* 244–45.

54. For information on both lynchings and financial cutbacks, see Bowles's report to the Council on Colored Work, minutes, 7 November 1930, 1–2 (YWCA/NB); for the national figures, see Sitkoff, *New Deal for Blacks,* 269.

55. YWCA of the USA, *Proceedings of the Twelfth National Convention, 1932,* 177, 230, 237–38, 249–52; for more on Hanna, see chap. 4 above.

56. Ibid., 251.

57. Frances Williams, "Analysis of Significant Work Done by Public Affairs Committee on Lynching, April 1933 to November 1934," 2 (YWCA/NB). For an analysis of the impact of lynchings beyond the immediate victims, see Hall, *Revolt against Chivalry,* 136, 301 n. 17.

58. YWCA of the USA, *Proceedings of the Twelfth National Convention, 1932,* 250. The wording is from a resolution passed at the first annual meeting of the ASWPL, see "Mob Violence Described as 'Menace to Public Safety' at First Annual Meeting of Anti-Lynching Association," *Atlanta Constitution,* 22 November 1931, 2 (NU/AUC).

59. YWCA of the USA, *Proceedings of the Twelfth National Convention, 1932,* 250.

60. Bunce, "First Meeting: A Letter from Gertrude Ware Bunce," 3.

61. Williams, "Analysis of Significant Work Done by the PAC," 2.

62. Hall, *Revolt against Chivalry,* 177–78.

63. Frederickson, "'Each One Is Dependent on the Other,'" 324.

64. In his study of the CIC, Edward Burrows pointed out that education programs were cheaper than programs that would have delivered social services to African Americans; see his "Commission on Interracial Cooperation," 173.

65. [Richard W. Edmonds], "Every Lynching as a Greater Crime than that of the Criminal Lynched," *Manufacturers Record* (9 August 1920): 88. Edmonds's opposition to lynching was unrelated to support for the YWCA; throughout the 1920s, his paper attacked the YWCA for advocating social equality and socialist teachings (see chap. 4 above).

66. Winn, "Speech to the National Board, 1938," 4.

67. Henrietta Roelofs, Memorandum on Meeting of Interracial Group, 9 May 1933, 1 (YWCA/NB).

68. [Henrietta Roelofs and Marion Cuthbert], "The Objectives of the Y.W.C.A. Considered in Relation to Its Interracial Work," 26 May 1933 (YWCA/NB).

69. Meeting on Race Relations, minutes, 6 June 1933, 3 (YWCA/NB).

70. Ibid., 5.

71. Ibid., 6. Lillian Anderson Alexander (1876–1957) was a Baptist. Born in Ohio, she graduated from the University of Minnesota. She moved to New York in 1917 to work for the Urban League during World War I. In 1918, she married Dr. Ernest R. Alexander, a dermatologist. She was active with both the black branch in Harlem and the National Board, especially the latter's public affairs division. Beginning in 1924, she served on the board of directors of the NAACP; see "Mrs. Lillian A. Alexander," *Crisis* 64 (October 1957): 483–84.

72. See issues of the *Womans Press* from September 1933 to February 1934. Articles included Bruno Lasker, "Race Relations as a World Problem," *Womans Press* 27 (September 1933): 388–89, 413; Frances Williams and Lucy P. Carner, "Varieties of Racial Experience," *Womans Press* 27 (November 1933): 491; and Louise Young, Jessie Daniel Ames, Margaret K. Smith, and Carrie E. Meares, "Symposium on Race," *Womans Press* 28 (February 1934): 84–86.

73. Louise Young, "Toward a Christian Philosophy of Race," *Womans Press* 28 (February 1934): 84. For more on Young, see Hall, *Revolt against Chivalry,* 313 n. 39, and McDowell, *Social Gospel in the South,* chap. 4.

74. Rose H. Quinn to Henrietta Roelofs, typed copy, 12 January 1934, and Katharine F. Deitz, "Confidential Report of Meeting to Discuss Objectives of the Y.W.C.A. considered in relation to its inter-racial work," 11 September 1933 (YWCA/NB).

75. YWCA of the USA, *Proceedings of the Fourteenth National Convention, 1936,* 31.

76. YWCA of the USA, *Actions of the Thirteenth National Convention, 1934,* 30, 58.

For an analysis of the pivotal role that the YWCA played in the efforts for antilynching legislation, see M. Brown, *Eradicating This Evil*, esp. chaps. 6–7.

77. Hall, *Revolt against Chivalry*, 292–93 n. 138. For examples of actions by local associations, see Philadelphia in Mittelman, "'A Spirit That Touches the Problems of Today,'" 210, or Elizabeth, New Jersey, YWCA, Board of Directors, minutes, January 1935 (YWCA/NJ).

78. Frances Williams to Henrietta Roelofs, 27 February 1934 (YWCA/NB).

79. On the ASWPL, see Hall, *Revolt against Chivalry*.

80. YWCA of the USA, *Actions of the Thirteenth National Convention, 1934*, 29.

81. Williams, "Analysis of Significant Work Done by the PAC" and "Public Affairs News Service: Minority Groups—The Negro," [ca. 1938] (YWCA/NB).

82. YWCA of the USA, *Actions of the Thirteenth National Convention, 1934*, 29.

83. YWCA National Board, *The Standards Study, 1938–1940*, 46–48.

84. Public Affairs Committee, Sub-committee on Race, "A Meeting to Consider the Interracial Situation and Public Affairs Program," 26 April 1933, 2, and "A Few Interracial Practices in the Y.W.C.A.," 22 April 1932 (both YWCA/NB).

85. "Y.W.C.A. Speakers Discuss Communism, Segregation, Southern Attitudes at Meeting," *Afro-American*, 12 May 1934 (TIA/MF 48:778).

86. Cordella A. Winn, "Why a Branch among Negroes?" *Womans Press* 30 (March 1936): 133.

87. F. Taylor, "'On the Edge of Tomorrow,'" and Philpott, "History of the Student YMCA, 1900–1941," recount efforts to desegregate the student meetings.

88. Baker, *Negro-White Adjustment*, 146–48, 185–88.

89. Strong opposition to the Costigan-Wagner bill from white southern senators ensured its defeat; see Sitkoff, *New Deal for Blacks*, esp. chap. 11.

90. Williams, "Analysis of Significant Work Done by the PAC," 1.

91. The areas where the ASWPL was active witnessed a decrease in lynchings; see Hall, *Revolt against Chivalry*, 236.

92. Frances Williams, "I. The Negro," 9 September 1935 (YWCA/NB).

93. YWCA of the USA, *Proceedings of the Fifteenth National Convention, 1938*, 148, 201–2.

94. YWCA of the USA, *Proceedings of the Twelfth National Convention, 1932*, 205, 229.

95. The National Board also referred to a number of women who had served as state senators; YWCA of the USA, *Report of the National Board to the Sixteenth National Convention, 1940*, 133.

96. Hurlin, *Salaries and Qualifications of YWCA Professional Workers*, 14.

97. Quoted by Karen Mittelman in "'A Spirit That Touches the Problems of Today,'" 96.

98. This understanding of women's role in creating the American welfare state draws upon Gordon, "Black and White Visions of Welfare"; Koven and Michel, "Womanly Duties"; Sklar, "Historical Foundations of Women's Power in the Creation of the American Welfare State"; and Muncy, *Creating a Female Dominion in American Reform*. For a more extensive list and an elaboration of the argument, see Robertson, "Kindness or Justice: Women's Associations and the Politics of Race and History."

99. Henriette Roelofs to Mary E. Dreier, 9 June 1933, and Henrietta Roelofs to Elizabeth Eastman, 14 June 1933 (both YWCA/NB).

100. Susan Hartmann has observed, however, that it was the YWCA, along with the National Council of Jewish Women, the National Council of Catholic Women, and Church Women United, who were most likely to engage in interracial activities and support civil rights legislation at a time when other middle-class, white-dominated women's organizations, such as the General Federation of Women's Clubs, the American Association of University Women, and the National Woman's Party, ignored or downplayed the concerns of African American women; see Hartmann, *The Other Feminists,* esp. chap. 6.

101. Gordon, "Black and White Visions of Welfare," 573.

102. Durr, *Outside the Magic Circle,* chap. 6, "Initiation into Politics," 101–2, 114–15 (quote); see also Robin Muncy's observation of the consequences of women's ties to Roosevelt and the declining power of their "dominion," in *Creating a Female Dominion in American Reform,* 155. Sarah Deutsch has observed similar constraints on Boston female reformers who compromised in their efforts to win support from (male) politicians; see Deutsch, "Learning to Talk More Like a Man."

103. YWCA of the USA, *Proceedings of the Fifteenth National Convention, 1938,* 51.

104. Out of Linda Gordon's network of white women active with the New Deal, only two of the almost eighty white women had noticeable YWCA connections (Grace Coyle and Lucy Randolph Mason). Of her comparable list of almost seventy black women, at least 20 percent of them had YW connections. The number could be even higher if women's connections with local associations were known. Alice Dunbar-Nelson, for instance, was an advisor to a local Girl Reserves club in Washington; see Gordon, "Black and White Visions of Welfare," 589–90.

105. Winn, "Speech to the National Board, 1938," 4.

106. Dorothy Irene Height (1912–) was a Baptist, and later a Methodist. Born in Richmond, and raised in Pennsylvania, she received a B.A. in 1932 and an M.A. in 1933 from New York University. She was a social worker in New York City and then joined the staff of the Harlem YWCA in the 1937 and then the Phyllis Wheatley YWCA (Washington, D.C.) in 1939. She joined the staff of the National Board in 1944, working in a variety of positions until her retirement in 1977. Mentored by Mary McLeod Bethune, Height became president of the NCNW. See Eleanor Hinton Hoytt, "Dorothy Irene Height," in Hine et al., *Black Women in America,* 1:552–55; Height, *Open Wide the Freedom Gates;* and "Dorothy I. Height," in Hill and Miller, *Black Women Oral History Project,* 5:33–295.

107. Cordella A. Winn, report, July 1938, 12 (YWCA/NB).

108. Juanita J. Saddler, "Statement Made to the Student Staff Regarding Interracial Education," May 1933 (YWCA/RFC 134.6). Juanita Jane Saddler (ca. 1892–1970) was a member of Riverside Church in New York City. Raised in Oklahoma, she graduated from Fisk University in 1915. After teaching, she joined the staff of the national YWCA in 1920 and worked with the student division until 1933. In 1935, she earned an M.A. from Teachers College. In the 1950s she worked with community groups in Boston to promote integration. "Juanita Saddler of Y.W.C.A. Dies," *New York Times,* 13 January 1970, 45, and YWCA Biographical Files (YWCA/NB).

109. YWCA of the USA, *Report of the National Board to the Fourteenth National Convention, 1936,* 12.

110. YWCA of the USA, *Proceedings of the Fourteenth National Convention, 1936,* 8–9, 122.

111. Ibid., 122, 125, 129, 131.

112. Ibid., 123–24; see also Mamie Davis, ibid., 128.

113. "Public Affairs News Service: Minority Groups—The Negro," 5–6, and Hurlin, *Salaries and Qualifications of YWCA Professional Workers,* esp. 11, 16.

114. National Services Division, staff meeting, minutes, 14 November 1935, 2 (YWCA/NB).

115. Special Meeting Called by the Chairman of the Executive Committee to Consider Race Relations, 27 November 1937, minutes, 3 (YWCA/NB); *Branch Study* quoted in Winn, report, July 1938, 1.

116. L. C. Haworth, "Are We Agents of Communism?" *Association Forum* 11 (October 1930): 13.

117. Dilling, *Roosevelt Red Record,* 221, 290, and Dilling, *Red Network,* 338; for information on Dilling, see Delegard, "Women Patriots," 497–99, and Jeansonne, *Women of the Far Right.*

118. Dilling, *Should Christians Support the Y's?* 1–3.

119. Florence Dennison to Belle Ingels, 16 October 1936, 1 (YWCA/RFC 158.5).

120. Mrs. Frederic M. Paist to "Madam President" [sent to presidents of local associations], 27 December 1934, 1 (YWCA/NB).

121. Love, *One Blood,* esp. 49, 69, 248, 252.

122. Frances Williams, memo to the subcommittee on race of the [YWCA] National Student Council, 30 November 1936, 3–4 (GTH/AHC).

123. Frances Williams to Mrs. Ernest [Lillian] Alexander, 22 October 1937 (YWCA/NB). Williams had left the Student Department in the late 1920s, but she rejoined the staff of the research division after Bowles's resignation in 1932. Derricotte and Williams were contemporaries; Derricotte was born only one year earlier. The difference may be attributable simply to the fact that Derricotte remained rooted in the South, while Williams was educated and lived in the North. But their differing stances remind us that there were differences among black women as well as between white and black women.

Chapter 7: Struggling over Segregation

1. Elizabeth, New Jersey, YWCA, Business and Professional Department, report, September 1941, 1 (YWCA/NJ). MacCracken was white, as was the entire local board of directors.

2. Elizabeth, New Jersey, YWCA, Business and Professional Department, report, October 1941 (YWCA/NJ).

3. Bell and Wilkins, *Interracial Practices in Community Y.W.C.A.'s,* 67.

4. See Elizabeth, New Jersey, YWCA, Publicity Scrapbook: "Girls' Minstrel Show at Battin" [*Elizabeth Daily Journal,* ca. 12 May 1921] and "Girl Minstrels Score Triumph" [*Elizabeth Daily Journal,* 13 May 1921] (YWCA/NJ). While I have found no official policy banning minstrel shows, national YWCA publications had attempted

to discourage them for years. See Burner, *Potters and Pipers,* 56, and Height, *Step by Step with Interracial Groups,* 17. Amateur minstrel shows were a popular activity for white Americans well into the twentieth century; see Wittke, *Tambo and Bones.*

5. YWCA of the USA, *Proceedings of the Sixteenth National Convention, 1940,* 84–85.

6. Ibid., 16.

7. YWCA of the USA, *Report of the National Board to the Sixteenth National Convention, 1940,* 13.

8. YWCA of the USA, *Future Emphases and Some Questions of Policy, 1940,* 3.

9. Ibid., 2, and YWCA of the USA, *Proceedings of the Sixteenth National Convention, 1940,* 157–99, 247–51.

10. YWCA of the USA, *Proceedings of the Sixteenth National Convention, 1940,* 168.

11. Ibid., 163.

12. Ibid., 76–82.

13. Ibid., 201–2.

14. Ibid., 81.

15. Ibid., 116–17. Birmingham did not have a black woman on its board.

16. Ibid., 140. At both the 1936 and 1938 national conventions, the Student Assembly sought to have the YWCA rethink its acceptance of segregation. Despite the students' success in getting the conventions to pass resolutions to address the issue, the National Board failed to act, citing other commitments; Bell and Wilkins, *Interracial Practices in Community Y.W.C.A.'s,* 1–2.

17. YWCA of the USA, *Proceedings of the Sixteenth National Convention, 1940,* 257–58.

18. In analyzing the YM's approach to cooperating with women and the YW, Charles Hopkins observed that studies "became a device for postponing commitment to a definite policy"; see his *History of the Y.M.C.A.,* 565.

19. YWCA of the USA, *Proceedings of the Sixteenth National Convention, 1940,* 265. Beginning in 1940, the YWCA planned its national conventions to meet every three years (hence "triennium").

20. YWCA of the USA, *Proceedings of the Seventeenth National Convention, 1946,* 21.

21. Calkins, "The Negro in the Young Women's Christian Association," 73–74.

22. For the YWCA's own account of these efforts, see Creedy, *Women behind the Lines;* see also Knapp, "Experimental Social Policymaking during World War II." The United Service Organizations (USO) included the YWCA, the YMCA, the Jewish Welfare Board, the Knights of Columbus, the Salvation Army, the National Catholic Community Services, and the National Travelers Aid Association, while the American War-Community Services was composed of the YWCA, the Family Welfare Association of America, the Child Welfare League, the National Organization of Public Health Nursing, the National Urban League, and the American Federation of International Institutes.

23. YWCA of the USA, *Proceedings of the Seventeenth National Convention, 1946,* 13.

24. Mrs. Sherwood [Eleanor Copenhaver] Anderson, Testimony to the Senate

Committee on Judiciary, *Poll Taxes, Pt. 1: Hearings on S. 1280,* 77th Cong., 2nd sess., 1941, 82–84.

25. L. Smith, "There Are Things To Do," 10. For discussions of the racial angle in the war, see Myrdal, *An American Dilemma,* 517, 814–15, 1004–7, 1016.

26. See comments on the talk by Roy Wilkins and Vivian C. Mason in "Résumé of [Negro] Leadership Conference, Institute, West Virginia, 23–30 June 1942," 6 (YWCA/NB). See also Calkins, "The Negro in the Young Women's Christian Association," 76–77, and Myrdal, *An American Dilemma,* 850, 1005–6.

27. Atwood, *The Racial Factor in Y.M.C.A.'s,* 131.

28. Emily Hickman, Testimony to the Senate Committee on Education and Labor, *Fair Employment Practices Act, Hearings on S739–2,* 78th Cong., 2nd sess., 1944, 54–55, and her Testimony to the House Committee on Labor, *To Prohibit Discrimination in Employment, vol. 1: Hearings on H.R. 3986, H.R. 4004, H.R. 4005,* 78th Cong., 2nd sess., 1944, 211. Legislation on behalf of a permanent FEPC failed, but some states and cities passed related laws; see Calkins, "The Negro in the Young Women's Christian Association," 78.

29. Bell and Wilkins, *Interracial Practices in Community Y.W.C.A.'s,* 7; see also Height, *Open Wide the Freedom Door,* 110–11.

30. For Williams's efforts, see Frances Williams to Walter White, 1 November 1937 (YWCA/NB); on Barnett's suit, see [Yolanda Barnett] to Eleanor [French], 29 March 1944 (YWCA/NB); Jay A. Ulrice to Ralph W. Harbison, 25 September 1946, plus enclosures [excerpts from YWCA records] (YMCA/MN); and "Dining Car Suit Settled," *New York Times,* 22 November 1945, 27.

31. Fern [Babcock] to Eleanor [French], 3 April 1944, and Lillian Norwood to Mrs. Henry A. Ingraham, typed copy, 17 March 1944 (both YWCA/NB).

32. Helen Natalie Jackson Wilkins Claytor (1907–2005), an Episcopalian, was born in Minneapolis. She graduated from the University of Minnesota in 1928. She worked in YW branches in Trenton, New Jersey, and Kansas City, Missouri, until the death of her first husband, Earl Wilkins (a journalist) in 1941. She then joined the national staff to develop interracial education programs. She moved to Grand Rapids, Michigan, following her marriage in 1943 to Robert W. Claytor (a physician). In 1946, she joined the National Board, and in 1967 was elected president of the YWCA (the first African American woman to hold the position), serving until 1973. Roy Wilkins, of the NAACP, was her brother-in-law, and Claytor was active with both the NAACP and the Urban League. See "Helen Wilkins Claytor, 98, Ex-President of Y.W.C.A.," *New York Times,* 11 May 2005, 10 (B), and YWCA Biographical Files (YWCA/NB).

33. Bell and Wilkins, *Interracial Practices in Community Y.W.C.A.'s,* 58, 25.

34. Ibid., 60.

35. By the late 1940s, against the desires of industrial women, their assembly was merged with that of the Business and Professional Girls; it was subsequently redefined as Young Adult Work, focusing on recreational activities for young unmarried members rather than their occupational identity. For more on the diminishing involvement of students and industrial workers, see chap. 6, n. 15, above.

36. Bell and Wilkins, *Interracial Practices in Community Y.W.C.A.'s,* 118.

37. YWCA—National Board, *Issues for the Young Women's Christian Association,* 52–53, 58–59; Laura Smith Ebaugh to Mrs. Henry A. Ingraham, ca. April 1944; and

[Laura Smith Ebaugh], "Analysis of the Report of Interracial Practices in Community Y.W.C.A.'s," 2 (both YWCA/NB).

38. [Compilation of Responses Regarding the Interracial Study, December 1944], for Mobile, Ala., ca. December 1944 (YWCA/NB).

39. YWCA of the USA, *Proceedings of the Seventeenth National Convention, 1946*, 11. Mary Shotwell Ingraham (1887–1981) was a Quaker. Born in Brooklyn, she received an A.B. from Vassar in 1908. That year, she married Henry Andrews Ingraham, a lawyer, and the couple lived in Brooklyn. Active with the local association, she joined the National Board in 1930. As president of the National Board of the YWCA from 1940 to 1946, she was involved with both the YW's war work and the interracial efforts. She helped to found the USO. In 1946, Harry Truman awarded her the presidential Medal for Merit for that work, with a citation that noted she had led in efforts to address interracial problems; Ingraham was the first woman to receive the award. See "Mary S. Ingraham Is Dead at 94; Helped Guide City Creation of City U.," *New York Times*, 20 April 1981, 10(D), and YWCA Biographical Files (YWCA/NB).

40. Cuthbert, "The Role of the YWCA," 175.

41. YWCA of the USA, *Proceedings of the Seventeenth National Convention, 1946*, 29.

42. Height, *Open Wide the Freedom Door*, 115, and YWCA of the USA, *Proceedings of the Seventeenth National Convention, 1946*, 62.

43. *Interracial Charter and Related Policy*, 6.

44. YWCA of the USA, *Proceedings of the Seventeenth National Convention, 1946*, 74.

45. Ibid., 75–76.

46. Ibid., 87.

47. Ibid., 63–64.

48. Ibid., 92–93 (on the charter) and 65–92 (on the recommendations).

49. "Women Way Ahead," *New York Age*, 16 March 1946, 6; "Women's Parley Votes for Full Integration," *Chicago Defender* (AUVF: YWCA); "Racial Equality in Y.W.C.A. Urged," *New York Times*, 6 March 1946, 22; "Y.W.C.A. Delegates Push Interracial Cooperation," *Christian Science Monitor*, 6 March 1946, 12; and "Y.W.C.A. Votes to Integrate Negro Women into Activities," *Los Angeles Times*, 6 March 1946, 2.

50. Lynn, *Progressive Women in Conservative Times*, 49.

51. George Edmund Haynes, "Along the Interracial Front," *New York Age*, 6 April 1946, 6. On the FCC's action, see Reimers, *White Protestantism and the Negro*, 112–13.

52. Susan Hartmann points to the general isolation of white women in the 1940s from African American women; see her "Women's Organizations during World War II." For an account of the efforts of the American Association of University Women to desegregate after the YW, see Leone, "Integrating the American Association of University Women, 1946–1949."

53. YWCA of the USA, *Proceedings of the Seventeenth National Convention, 1946*, "Appendix," xii.

54. Constance W. (Mrs. Arthur Forrest) Anderson to the Senate Committee on Judiciary, 5 February 1948, re: *Punishment for the Crime of Lynching: Hearings on S. 42, S. 1352, S. 1465*, 80th Cong., 1948, 198.

55. *To Secure These Rights,* 148. For information on the report, see Sosna, *In Search of the Silent South,* 150–52. Frances Williams, a longtime YW staffer, was the assistant to the executive secretary on the staff of the committee.

56. Sosna, *In Search of the Silent South,* 164.

57. Calkins, "The Negro in the Young Women's Christian Association," 95.

58. *Interracial Charter and Related Policy,* 20.

59. Genevieve Lowry to Mrs. J. Ross Tuttle, 24 May 1946, 2 (YWCA/NB).

60. Ibid., 3.

61. Sabiston and Hiller, *Toward Better Race Relations,* 80.

62. Fannie Pitt Byrd, "Satisfaction in One's Job," *New York Age,* 13 April 1946, 6. See also Lynn, *Progressive Women in Conservative Times,* 54.

63. Unidentified source quoted by Sabiston and Hiller, *Toward Better Race Relations,* 174.

64. "Résumé of [Negro] Leadership Conference, 23–30 June 1942," 8.

65. Lowry to Tuttle, 24 May 1946, 1.

66. Sabiston and Hiller, *Toward Better Race Relations,* 63.

67. Ibid., 175.

68. Byrd, "Satisfaction in One's Job."

69. Hurlin, *Salaries and Qualifications of YWCA Professional Workers,* 11, 16. On lower pay, see also YWCA of the USA, *Proceedings of the Seventeenth National Convention, 1946,* 51, 113.

70. Bell and Wilkins, *Interracial Practices in Community Y.W.C.A.'s,* 85; also Sabiston and Hiller, *Toward Better Race Relations,* 57–58.

71. YWCA of the USA, *Proceedings of the Seventeenth National Convention, 1946,* 86, 92.

72. [Myra Smith], draft of speech to the 1949 national convention, 7 (YWCA/NB). The comment was not included in the published version of her speech, so it is unclear whether she publicly revealed the problem; see YWCA of the USA, *Proceedings of the Eighteenth National Convention, 1949,* 104.

73. Studies included Wilkerson, *Interracial Programs of Student YWCA's,* and Sabiston and Hiller, *Toward Better Race Relations.*

74. Height and Lee, *The Christian Citizen and Civil Rights.*

75. Height, *Step by Step with Interracial Groups,* 36.

76. Lowry to Tuttle, 24 May 1946, 1–2, and YWCA of the USA, *Report of the National Board to the Sixteenth National Convention, 1940,* 66.

77. Lowry to Tuttle, 24 May 1946, 2.

78. Sabiston and Hiller, *Toward Better Race Relations,* 173–74.

79. Bell and Wilkins, *Interracial Practices in Community Y.W.C.A.'s,* 51; also Sabiston and Hiller, *Toward Better Race Relations,* 168, and YWCA of the USA, *Proceedings of the Sixteenth National Convention, 1940,* 79.

80. YWCA of the USA, *Proceedings of the Seventeenth National Convention, 1946,* 84, 86.

81. Sabiston and Hiller, *Toward Better Race Relations,* 85, also 42, 174.

82. Statistics drawn from Young Women's Christian Associations—National Board, "Community Young Women's Christian Associations of the U.S.A.," August 1942 (YWCA/NB), and YWCA of the USA, *Figures Talk Back, 1948.*

83. Sabiston and Hiller, *Toward Better Race Relations,* 21, 116; YWCA of the USA, *Proceedings of the Seventeenth National Convention, 1946,* 87.

84. Bell and Wilkins, *Interracial Practices in Community Y.W.C.A.'s,* 53, and Sabiston and Hiller, *Toward Better Race Relations,* 56.

85. Sabiston and Hiller, *Toward Better Race Relations,* 19, 85, 91, 165, 168–69.

86. Ibid., 57–58.

87. Bell and Wilkins, *Interracial Practices in Community Y.W.C.A.'s,* 109–10, 112–13; also YWCA of the USA, *Proceedings of the Seventeenth National Convention, 1946,* 74.

88. Myra Smith, "Integration of Minority Groups into the Total Life of the Country," 6 October 1944, 1 (YWCA/NB). Calkins contends that, by the time of the 1946 national convention, most YW women were aware of the issue; see "The Negro in the Young Women's Christian Association," 87.

89. Myrdal, *An American Dilemma,* 26–27.

90. Sheatsley, "White Attitudes toward the Negro," 217–18, 237 n. 2.

91. Sabiston and Hiller, *Toward Better Race Relations,* 103–4.

92. Ibid., 86–87.

93. Calkins, "The Negro in the Young Women's Christian Association," 92. Gladys Gilkey Calkins (1897–1988), a Presbyterian, was born in Massachusetts. She received a B.A. from Cornell in 1919. In 1920, she married James Birdsall Calkins (a civil engineer). Active with the YWCA of Rochester, Calkins joined the National Board in 1936. She served as president of the YWCA of the USA, presiding over the national convention in 1946 and 1949. In 1960, Calkins completed an M.A. at George Washington University; her thesis was entitled "The Negro in the Young Women's Christian Association: A Study of the Development of YWCA Interracial Policies and Practices in Their Historical Setting." See "Gladys G. Calkins, 90, Y.W.C.A.'s President," *New York Times,* 18 February 1988, B10, and YWCA Biographical Files (YWCA/NB).

The president of the YWCA of the USA was a distinct position from that of the president of the National Board; the latter was the head of the executive body of the national association. The 1949 YWCA convention eliminated the former position.

Calkins was well aware of red-baiting, as Elizabeth Dilling had listed two of her brothers (Rev. Charles W. Gilkey and Rev. James Gordon Gilkey), along with a number of YWCA officials, in the "Who Is Who in Radicalism" section of her book; see Dilling, *Red Network,* 284. In fact, one of the red "credentials" listed for Charles Gilkey was that his wife was a YWCA leader.

94. Kamp, *Behind the Lace Curtains of the YWCA,* 9. With the lace curtain image, Kamp may have, in fact, intended a comparison to the iron curtain. The YWCA had ratified the Interracial Charter the same day (5 March 1946) that Winston Churchill gave his now famous "iron curtain" speech.

95. Crain and Hamilton, *Packaged Thinking for Women;* "The Red Streak in the Y.W.C.A." in *Sunday School Times* (5 March 1949): 193–94, 199, 216; and U.S. House of Representatives, Committee on Un-American Activities, *100 Things You Should Know about Communism;* see esp. 49. David Caute has estimated that over one million copies were distributed, *The Great Fear,* 101.

96. U.S. House of Representatives, Committee on Un-American Activities, *100 Things You Should Know about Communism,* 61.

97. Crain and Hamilton, *Packaged Thinking for Women,* 14, 23, 29–30.

98. For the destructiveness of anticommunist attacks, see Durr, *Outside the Magic Circle,* chaps. 15 and 18, and Caute, *The Great Fear.*

99. Bell and Wilkins, *Interracial Practices in Community Y.W.C.A.'s,* 26, 37, and YWCA of the USA, *Proceedings of the Seventeenth National Convention, 1946,* 137.

100. The National Board records include incidents in the following cities (among others): Elmira, N.Y.; Ridgewood, N.J.; Omaha, Neb.; and Winston-Salem, N.C.; see YWCA Local Associations Records (YWCA/RFC 194.4, 191.6, 264.2, and 200.2).

101. When members of the Queens, New York, YWCA's board of directors quit in 1947, charging communist influence, they pointed to similarities between the YWCA songbook and one used by the Communist Party; examples included "John Brown's Body" and a song condemning "Jim Crow" segregation; see "3 Queens YW Chiefs Quit to 'Expose Reds,'" *Brooklyn Daily Eagle,* 15 October 1947 (*BE*/BPL); "3 Officers Quit Y.W.C.A. in Queens," *New York Times,* 16 October 1947, 29; and YWCA Local Associations Records—Jamaica, New York (YWCA/RFC 195.1 and 267.1).

Although initial coverage of the Queens attack was covered only in the metropolitan papers, the women subsequently publicized their charges nationally, sending information to cities ranging from Madison, Wisconsin, to Bogalusa, Louisiana, and from Spokane, Washington, to Boston; see "Communism Files, 1945–1952" (YWCA/NB), and "Former Queens Y.W. Leader Again Charges Communism in Group," *Brooklyn Daily Eagle,* 3 February 1948, and "Open National Drive to Rout YWCA Reds," *Brooklyn Daily Eagle,* 16 March 1948 (both *BE*/BPL).

102. "Atlantic City YWCA Quits National Body," *New York Times,* 4 March 1949, 5, and "Status of Branch Seen Y.W.C.A. Topic," *New York Times,* 7 March 1949, 34. For additional information, see YWCA Local Associations Records—Atlantic City (YWCA/RFC 189.4 and 264.7).

103. For an assessment of the impact of anticommunism on other women's organizations in these years, see Rupp and Taylor, *Survival in the Doldrums,* 139–41 (on the National Woman's Party), and Hartmann, *The Home Front and Beyond,* 156–57.

104. H. E. Gray to Mrs. C. F. Nedderson, 13 November 1946, typed copy; Edna Pearce to Grace Loucks Elliott, 16 November 1946, typed copy; Grace Loucks Elliott to Edna Pearce, 19 November 1946, day letter; and Mrs. Harrison S. Elliott to Edna Pearce, 19 November 1946 (all YWCA/NB).

105. Hickman, Testimony to the House Committee on Labor, *To Prohibit Discrimination in Employment,* 216.

106. Frances Williams to Clarence King, 20 May 1933, 2 (YWCA/NB).

107. Sabiston and Hiller, *Toward Better Race Relations,* 172.

108. YWCA of the USA, *Proceedings of the Eighteenth National Convention, 1949,* Appendix, xiii.

109. Among those having influence on the YWCA in these years was Reinhold Niebuhr, who spoke at YWCA events; Calkins, "The Negro in the Young Women's Christian Association," 70. Niebuhr was critical of the unlimited optimism of the social gospel and proposed a more realistic theology that nonetheless addressed social issues. During these years, YWCA women held onto an optimism that must have irritated Niebuhr—their language and ideas resonated more with Rauschenbusch's or Dewey's rather than his.

110. Sabiston and Hiller, *Toward Better Race Relations,* vii and Height and Lee, *The Christian Citizen and Civil Rights.*

111. Constance W. Anderson to Mrs. A. A. Richards, typed copy, 29 November 1948, 2 (YWCA/NB).

Epilogue

1. For statistics on participants in branches, see YWCA of the USA, *Figures Talk Back, 1948,* 10–13, 16–17, 26–27. For an account of New York, see Weisenfeld, *African American Women and Christian Activism;* for Pittsburgh, see Spratt, "To Be Separate or One."

2. Chafe, *Civilities and Civil Rights,* 30–34.

3. "5 Negroes Served in Atlanta Y.W.C.A.," *New York Times,* 1 December 1960, 27.

4. Mrs. A. A. Richards to Public Affairs Committee, National Board of the Y.W.C.A. [copy retyped by the national association], 11 October 1948 (YWCA/NB).

5. "Findings of the Workshop on Interracial Practices," Vassar Alumnae House, Poughkeepsie, New York, 30 November-4 December 1948, 8 (YWCA/NB).

6. Busby, "'The Price of Integration.'"

7. Chafe, *Civilities and Civil Rights,* 243.

8. For the Linden Street Branch in Oakland, see Lynn, *Progressive Women in Conservative Times,* 54–55; on the Colored Branch in Germantown, see Felix, "Committed to Their Own," chaps. 4 and 5; on the Phyllis Wheatley YWCA of Washington, D.C., see Radcliffe, *A Simple Matter of Justice,* chaps. 1 and 2.

9. YWCA of the USA, *Proceedings of the Twentieth National Convention, 1955,* 278.

10. "Y.W.C.A. Elects First Negro Head," *New York Times,* 30 April 1967, 84; "Helen Wilkins Claytor, 98, Ex-President of Y.W.C.A.," *New York Times,* 11 May 2005, B 10; and Height, *Open Wide the Freedom Gates,* 127.

11. "Parley of Y.W.C.A. Asks End to Racism," *New York Times,* 19 April 1970, 30, and Height, *Open Wide the Freedom Gates,* 127–29. See also Lynn, *Progressive Women in Conservative Times,* 146–48.

12. For a more developed analysis of the role of the YWCA from the late 1940s to the 1960s, see Lynn, *Progressive Women in Conservative Times,* esp. 3, and chaps. 2 and 5–6, and her "Gender and Progressive Politics: A Bridge to Social Activism of the 1960s."

13. Useful personal accounts include those of Charlotte Bunch, in Braude, *Transforming the Faith of Our Fathers;* Dorothy Dawson Burlage and Casey Hayden, in Curry et al., *Deep in Our Hearts;* Sara Evans, Charlotte Bunch, Nancy D. Richardson, Valerie Russell, Renetia Martin, and Frances E. Kendall, in Evans, *Journeys That Opened Up the World;* Height, *Open Wide the Freedom Gates;* and King, *Freedom Song,* chap. 1. Biographies and scholarly accounts include: Evans, *Personal Politics;* F. Taylor, "'On the Edge of Tomorrow,'" 216–18; Ransby, *Ella Baker;* and Rossinow, "'The Break-through to New Life.'"

14. Evans, *Personal Politics,* 35. On King and Hayden, see King, *Freedom Song,* chap. 12.

15. Calkins, "The Negro in the Young Women's Christian Association," 1.

16. Sklar, "Historical Foundations of Women's Power in the Creation of the American Welfare State," 43–93, esp. 79–80 n. 4.

17. Leila S. Frissell, "Conferences," 14–18 May 1914, 2 (YWCA/RFC 108.3).

18. Genevieve Lowry to Mrs. J. Ross Tuttle, memo, 24 May 1946, 2 (YWCA/NB).

19. For a critique of the conservative misuse of King's vision, see Hall, "The Long Civil Rights Movement," 1236–38.

20. Quoted in Lynn, *Progressive Women in Conservative Times,* 50–51.

21. See Burkett, "In Dubious Sisterhood: Class and Sex in Spanish Colonial South America" (1977); Sherrick, "Toward Universal Sisterhood" (1982); Gwin, *Black and White Women of the Old South: The Peculiar Sisterhood in American Literature* (1985); Janiewski, *Sisterhood Denied: Race, Gender, and Class in a New South Community* (1985); Dill, "Race, Class, and Gender: Prospects for an All-Inclusive Sisterhood" (1983); Reynolds, *A Separate Sisterhood: Women Who Shaped Southern Education in the Progressive Era* (2002); Monteith, *Advancing Sisterhood? Interracial Friendships in Contemporary Southern Fiction* (2000); Marshall, *Splintered Sisterhood: Gender and Class in the Campaign against Woman Suffrage* (1997); Higginbotham, "Unlikely Sisterhood," chap. 4 in her *Righteous Discontent* (1993); and Bolt, *Sisterhood Questioned: Race, Class, and Internationalism in the American and British Women's Movements, c. 1880s-1970s* (2004).

22. This assumption is suggested in the title of Nancy Schrom Dye's work, *As Equals and as Sisters.*

23. Hewitt, "Beyond the Search for Sisterhood," 315; see also Mittelman, "'A Spirit That Touches the Problems of Today,'" 262–63.

24. Liu, "Teaching the Differences among Women from a Historical Perspective," 268–69, and Rupp, "Constructing Internationalism," 1598–1600.

BIBLIOGRAPHY

Archival Collections

AUVF	Atlanta University—Vertical Files. Robert W. Woodruff Library of the Atlanta University Center, Archives and Special Collections Department (Atlanta, Ga.).
BE/BPL	*Brooklyn Eagle* article morgue. Brooklyn Public Library (Brooklyn, N.Y.).
GTH/AHC	Grace Towns Hamilton Collection. Atlanta History Center (Atlanta, Ga.).
KDL/UNC	Katharine Du Pre Lumpkin Papers. Southern Historical Collection. Manuscripts Department, Wilson Library, University of North Carolina (Chapel Hill, N.C.).
MCT/MSRC	Mary Church Terrell Collection: file for the International Council of Women of the Darker Races. Moorland-Spingarn Research Center, Manuscript Division, Howard University (Washington, D.C.).
MID/NA	Military Intelligence Division, Correspondence, 1917–1941 (War Department): RG 165, National Archives and Records Administration (Washington, D.C.).
NAACP/LC	National Association for the Advancement of Colored People Papers: file for the National Woman's Party. Library of Congress (Washington, D.C.).
NACW/MF	National Association of Colored Women's Clubs, Records, 1895–1992, Part 1: Minutes of National Conferences, Publications, and President's Office Correspondence—microfilm.
NU/AUC	Neighborhood Union Collection. Robert W. Woodruff Library of the Atlanta University Center, Archives and Special Collections Department (Atlanta, Ga.).
RFA/RAC	Rockefeller Foundation Archives. Rockefeller Archives Center (Sleepy Hollow, N.Y.).

TIA/MF	Tuskegee Institute Archives: News Clippings File, microfilm (Tuskegee, Ala.).
WCA	Wellesley College Archives (Wellesley, Mass.).
WW/SL	Winnifred Wygal papers. Schlesinger Library, Radcliffe Institute, Harvard University (Cambridge, Mass.).
YMCA/MN	Kautz Family YMCA Archives. University of Minnesota Libraries (Minneapolis, Minn.).
YWCA/MA	Boston, Massachusetts, Young Women's Christian Association Records. Schlesinger Library, Radcliffe Institute, Harvard University (Cambridge, Mass.).
YWCA/NB	Young Women's Christian Association, National Board Records. Sophia Smith Collection, Smith College (Northampton, Mass.).
YWCA/NJ	Young Women's Christian Association of Elizabeth, New Jersey Records. YWCA of Eastern Union County, New Jersey (Elizabeth, N.J.).
YWCA/RFC	Young Women's Christian Association, Records File Collection, microfilm. Sophia Smith Collection, Smith College (Northampton, Mass.).

Published Annual Reports and Convention Materials

AMERICAN COMMITTEE OF YOUNG WOMEN'S CHRISTIAN ASSOCIATIONS

American Committee of Young Women's Christian Associations. *Proceedings of the Special Convention, 3–4 January 1906.* Chicago: American Committee of Young Women's Christian Associations, 1906.

LADIES' CHRISTIAN ASSOCIATION OF THE CITY OF NEW YORK

Ladies' Christian Association of the City of New York. *Third Annual Report (1860).* New York, 1860.

LADIES' CHRISTIAN UNION OF THE CITY OF NEW YORK

Ladies' Christian Union of the City of New York. *Sixth Annual Report for 1863.* New York, 1864.

Ladies' Christian Union of the City of New York. *Eighth Annual Report for 1866.* New York, 1866.

Ladies' Christian Union of the City of New York. *Tenth Annual Report for 1868.* New York, 1868.

Ladies' Christian Union of the City of New York. *Twelfth Annual Report for 1870.* New York, 1870.

Ladies' Christian Union of the City of New York. *Thirteenth Annual Report for 1871.* New York, 1871.

YOUNG LADIES' CHRISTIAN ASSOCIATION OF THE CITY OF NEW YORK

Young Ladies' Christian Association of the City of New York. *First Report, 1871.* New York, 1871.

Young Ladies' Christian Association of the City of New York. *Second Report, presented 1872.* New York, 1873.
Young Ladies' Christian Association of the City of New York. *Third Report, presented 1873.* New York, 1874.
Young Ladies' Christian Association of the City of New York. *Fourth Annual Report, presented 1874.* New York, 1875.

YOUNG WOMEN'S CHRISTIAN ASSOCIATION OF THE CITY OF NEW YORK

Young Women's Christian Association of the City of New York. *Fifth Annual Report, presented 1875.* New York, 1876.
Young Women's Christian Association of the City of New York. *Eighth Annual Report, 1879.* New York, 1879.
Young Women's Christian Association of the City of New York. *Eleventh Annual Report, 1882.* New York, 1882.
Young Women's Christian Association of the City of New York. *Twenty-Second Annual Report, 1893.* New York, 1893.
Young Women's Christian Association of the City of New York. *Twenty-Third Annual Report, 1894.* New York, 1894.
Young Women's Christian Association of the City of New York. *Thirty-Fifth Annual Report, 1906.* New York, 1906.

YOUNG WOMEN'S CHRISTIAN ASSOCIATIONS—NATIONAL BOARD

Young Women's Christian Associations—National Board. *Issues for the Young Women's Christian Associations: A Nation-Wide Discussion.* New York: National Board, 1945.

YOUNG WOMEN'S CHRISTIAN ASSOCIATIONS OF THE U.S.A.

Young Women's Christian Associations of the U.S.A. *Actions of the Thirteenth National Convention, 2–8 May 1934.* New York: National Board of the YWCA, 1934.
Young Women's Christian Associations of the U.S.A. *Future Emphases and Some Questions of Policy Confronting the Y.W.C.A.* New York: National Board of the YWCA, 1940.
Young Women's Christian Associations of the U.S.A. *Proceedings of the Fourth Biennial Convention, 9–15 April 1913.* New York: National Board of the YWCA, 1913.
Young Women's Christian Associations of the U.S.A. *Proceedings of the Sixth National Convention, 13–20 April 1920.* New York: National Board of the YWCA, 1920.
Young Women's Christian Associations of the U.S.A. *Proceedings of the Seventh National Convention, 20–27 April 1922.* New York: National Board of the YWCA, 1922.
Young Women's Christian Associations of the U.S.A. *Proceedings of the Eighth National Convention, 30 April–6 May 1924.* New York: National Board of the YWCA, 1924.
Young Women's Christian Associations of the U.S.A. *Proceedings of the Ninth National Convention, 21–27 April 1926.* New York: National Board of the YWCA, 1926.
Young Women's Christian Associations of the U.S.A. *Proceedings of the Tenth National Convention, 14–20 April 1928.* New York: National Board of the YWCA, 1928.

Young Women's Christian Associations of the U.S.A. *Proceedings of the Eleventh National Convention, 24 April–1 May 1930.* New York: National Board of the YWCA, 1930.

Young Women's Christian Associations of the U.S.A. *Proceedings of the Twelfth National Convention, 5–11 May 1932.* New York: National Board of the YWCA, 1932.

Young Women's Christian Associations of the U.S.A. *Proceedings of the Business Sessions of the Fourteenth National Convention, 29 April–5 May 1936.* New York: National Board of the YWCA, 1936.

Young Women's Christian Associations of the U.S.A. *Proceedings of the Fifteenth National Convention, 22–28 April 1938; section 1: Business of the Convention.* New York: National Board of the YWCA, 1938.

Young Women's Christian Associations of the U.S.A. *Proceedings of the Seventeenth National Convention, 2–8 March 1946.* New York: National Board of the YWCA, 1946.

Young Women's Christian Association of the U.S.A. *Proceedings of the Eighteenth National Convention, 7–14 March 1949.* New York: National Board of the YWCA, 1949.

Young Women's Christian Association of the U.S.A. *Proceedings of the Twentieth National Convention, 21–27 April 1955.* New York: National Board of the YWCA, 1955.

Young Women's Christian Associations of the U.S.A. *Report of the National Board to the Fifth National Convention, 5–11 May 1915.* New York: National Board of the YWCA, 1915.

Young Women's Christian Associations of the U.S.A. *Report of the National Board to the Sixth National Convention, 13–20 April 1920.* New York: National Board of the YWCA, 1920.

Young Women's Christian Associations of the U.S.A. *Report of the National Board to the Seventh National Convention, 20–27 April 1922.* New York: National Board of the YWCA, 1922.

Young Women's Christian Associations of the U.S.A. *Report of the National Board to the Eighth National Convention, 30 April–6 May 1924.* New York: National Board of the YWCA, 1924.

Young Women's Christian Associations of the U.S.A. *Report of the National Board to the Ninth National Convention, 21–28 April 1926.* New York: National Board of the YWCA, 1926.

Young Women's Christian Associations of the U.S.A. *Report of the National Board to the Tenth National Convention, 14–21 April 1928.* New York: National Board of the YWCA, 1928.

Young Women's Christian Associations of the U.S.A. *Report of the National Board to the Eleventh National Convention, 25 April–1 May 1930.* New York: National Board of the YWCA, 1930.

Young Women's Christian Associations of the U.S.A. *Report of the National Board to the Twelfth National Convention, 5–11 May 1932.* New York: National Board of the YWCA, 1932.

Young Women's Christian Associations of the U.S.A. *Report of the National Board*

to the Fourteenth National Convention, on the Biennium, 1934–1936. New York: National Board of the YWCA, 1936.
Young Women's Christian Associations of the U.S.A. *Report of the National Board to the Sixteenth National Convention, on the Biennium, 1938–1940.* New York: National Board of the YWCA, 1940.
Young Women's Christian Associations of the U.S.A. *Report of the First Biennial Convention, 5–6 December 1906.* New York: National Board of the YWCA, 1906.
Young Women's Christian Associations of the U.S.A. *Report of the Proceedings of the Second Biennial Convention, 11–26 April 1909.* New York: National Board of the YWCA, 1909.

Articles, Books, Theses, and Dissertations

Ahlstrom, Sydney E. *A Religious History of the American People.* 2 vols. New Haven: Yale University Press, 1972; Garden City, N.Y.: Image Books, 1975.
Ames, J. Quincy. *Cooperation between the Young Women's and the Young Men's Christian Associations.* Chicago: Young Men's Christian Association, 1929.
Anderson, M. Christine. "Home and Community for a Generation of Women: A Case Study of the Cincinnati Y.W.C.A. Residence, 1920–1940." *Queen City Heritage* 43 (Winter 1985): 34–41.
Atwood, J. Howell. *The Racial Factor in Y.M.C.A.'s: A Report on Negro-White Relationships in Twenty-four Cities.* New York: Association Press, 1946.
Baker, Paul E. *Negro-White Adjustment: An Investigation and Analysis of Methods in the Interracial Movement in the United States.* New York: Association Press, 1934.
Bannan, Regina. "Management by Women: The First Twenty-Five Years of the YWCA National Board, 1906–1931." Ph.D. diss., University of Pennsylvania, 1994.
Barbeau, Arthur E., and Florette Henri. *The Unknown Soldiers: Black American Troops in World War I.* Philadelphia: Temple University Press, 1974.
Beach, Harlan P. "The Atlanta Negro Christian Student Convention." *Student World* 7 (July 1914): 109–14.
Bederman, Gail. "'The Women Have Had Charge of the Church Work Long Enough': The Men and Religion Forward Movement of 1911–1912 and the Masculinization of Middle-Class Protestantism." *American Quarterly* 41 (September 1989): 432–65.
Bell, Juliet O., and Helen J. Wilkins. *Interracial Practices in Community Y.W.C.A.'s: A Study under the Auspices of the Commission to Gather Interracial Experience as Requested by the Sixteenth National Convention of the Y.W.C.A.'s of the U.S.A.* New York: Womans Press, 1944.
Bittar, Helen. "The Y.W.C.A. of the City of New York, 1870–1920." Ph.D. diss., New York University, 1979.
"Blacklisting the Y.W.C.A." *Survey* 45 (5 February 1921): 668.
Bolt, Christine. *Sisterhood Questioned: Race, Class, and Internationalism in the American and British Women's Movements, c. 1880s–1970s.* New York: Routledge, 2004.
Borchett, Susan. "Catharine Lealtad." In *African-American Women: a Biographical Dictionary,* edited by Dorothy C. Salem, 324–25. New York: Garland, 1993.

Boris, Eileen. "The Power of Motherhood: Black and White Activist Women Redefine the 'Political.'" *Yale Journal of Law and Feminism* 2 (Fall 1989): 25–49.

Bowden, Henry Warner, ed. *Dictionary of American Religious Biography.* Westport, Conn.: Greenwood, 1977.

Bowles, Eva D. "Negro Women and the War." *Southern Workman* 47 (September 1918): 425–26.

———. "War Work among Colored Girls and Women." *A.M.E. Review* 35 (July 1918): 3–7.

Boyd, Nancy. *Emissaries: The Overseas Work of the American YWCA, 1895–1970.* New York: Woman's Press, 1986.

Braude, Ann, ed. *Transforming the Faith of Our Fathers: Women Who Changed American Religion.* New York: Palgrave Macmillan, 2004.

Breckinridge, Sophonisba P. *Women in the Twentieth Century: A Study of Their Political, Social, and Economic Activities.* New York: McGraw-Hill, 1933.

Breen, William J. "Black Women and the Great War: Mobilization and Reform in the South." *Journal of Southern History* 44 (August 1978): 421–40.

Bremner, Robert H. "Grace Longwell Coyle." In *Notable American Women: The Modern Period—A Biographical Dictionary,* edited by Barbara Sicherman and Carol Hurd Green, 169–71. Cambridge, Mass.: Harvard University Press, 1980.

Bristow, Nancy K. *Making Men Moral: Social Engineering during the Great War.* New York: New York University Press, 1996.

Brown, Mary Jane. *Eradicating This Evil: Women in the American Anti-Lynching Movement, 1892–1940.* New York: Garland, 2000.

Brown, Nikki L. M. "'Your Patriotism Is of the Purest Quality': African American Women and World War I." Ph.D. diss., Yale University, 2002.

Brumberg, Joan Jacobs. "Zenanas and Girlless Villages: The Ethnology of American Evangelical Women, 1870–1910." *Journal of American History* 69 (September 1982): 347–71.

Bunce, Gertrude. "First Meeting: A Letter from Gertrude Ware Bunce." In *Three Meetings on Interracial Interests,* edited by Gertrude Ware Bunce and Frances Williams, 2–4. New York: Womans Press, 1934.

Burkett, Elinor C. "In Dubious Sisterhood: Class and Sex in Spanish Colonial South America." *Latin American Perspectives* 4 (Winter/Spring 1977): 18–26.

Burner, Oolooah. *Potters and Pipers.* New York: Womans Press, 1924.

Burrows, Edward F. "The Commission on Interracial Cooperation, 1919–1944: A Case Study on the History of the Interracial Movement in the South." Ph.D. diss., University of Wisconsin, Madison, 1954.

Burton, Margaret E. *Mabel Cratty: Leader in the Art of Leadership.* New York: Womans Press, 1929.

Busby, Michelle. "'The Price of Integration': The Story of the Charlotte YWCA in the 1960s." In Mjagkij and Spratt, *Men and Women Adrift,* 206–30.

Calkins, Gladys Gilkey. "The Negro in the Young Women's Christian Association: A Study of the Development of YWCA Interracial Policies and Practices in Their Historical Setting." Master's thesis, George Washington University, 1960.

Carson, Mina. *Settlement Folk: Social Thought and the American Settlement Movement, 1885–1930.* Chicago: University of Chicago Press, 1990.

Carter, Paul A. *The Decline and Revival of the Social Gospel: Social and Political Lib-*

eralism in American Protestant Churches, 1920–1940. Ithaca: Cornell University Press, 1954.

Caute, David. *The Great Fear: The Anti-Communist Purge under Truman and Eisenhower.* New York: Simon and Schuster, 1978.

Chafe, William H. *The American Woman: Her Changing Social, Economic, and Political Roles, 1920–1970*. New York: Oxford University Press, 1972.

———. *Civilities and Civil Rights: Greensboro, North Carolina, and the Black Struggle for Freedom*. New York: Oxford University Press, 1981.

Chandler, Susan Kerr. "African American Social Workers in the World War I Era." Ph.D. diss., University of California, Berkeley, 1993.

Chauncey, Jr., George. "Christian Brotherhood or Sexual Perversion? Homosexual Identities and the Construction of Sexual Boundaries in the World War I Era." *Journal of Social History* 19 (1985): 189–212.

"City Question Box." *Womans Press* 18 (January 1924): 892–93.

Clarke, Ida Clyde. *American Women and the World War.* New York: Appleton, 1918.

Clarke, Walter. "The Promotion of Social Hygiene in War Time." *Annals of the American Academy of Political and Social Science* 79 (September 1918): 178–88.

Clemens, Elisabeth S. "Organizational Repertoires and Institutional Change: Women's Groups and the Transformation of U.S. Politics, 1890–1920." *American Journal of Sociology* 98 (January 1993): 755–98.

Cochrane, Sharlene Voogd. "'And the Pressure Never Let Up': Black Women, White Women, and the Boston YWCA, 1918–1949." In *Women in the Civil Rights Movement: Trailblazers and Torchbearers, 1941–1965*, edited by Vicki L. Crawford, Jacqueline Anne Rouse, and Barbara Woods, 259–69. Brooklyn: Carlson Publishing, 1990.

———. "Compelled to Speak: Women Confronting Institutional Racism, 1910–1950." *New England Journal of Public Policy* 7 (Fall/Winter 1991): 47–59.

Connolly, Harold X. *A Ghetto Grows in Brooklyn*. New York: New York University Press, 1977.

Consumers' League of Eastern Pennsylvania. *Colored Women as Industrial Workers in Philadelphia*. Philadelphia: Consumers' League, 1920.

Cott, Nancy F. *The Bonds of Womanhood: "Women's Sphere" in New England, 1790–1835*. New Haven: Yale University Press, 1977.

———. *The Grounding of Modern Feminism*. New Haven: Yale University Press, 1987.

Crain, Lucille Cardin, and Anne Burrows Hamilton. *Packaged Thinking for Women*, supplement to *American Affairs* 10 (October 1948).

Creedy, Brooks Spivey. *Women behind the Lines: YWCA Program with War Production Workers, 1940–1947*. New York: Woman's Press, 1949.

Crocker, Ruth Hutchinson. *Social Work and Social Order: The Settlement Movement in Two Industrial Cities, 1889–1930*. Urbana: University of Illinois Press, 1992.

Crunden, Robert M. *Ministers of Reform: The Progressives' Achievement in American Civilization, 1889–1920*. New York: Basic Books, 1982.

Curry, Constance, Joan C. Browning, Dorothy Dawson Murlage, Penny Patch, Theresa Del Pozzo, Sue Thrasher, Elaine DeLott Baker, Emmie Schrader Adams, and Casey Hayden. *Deep in Our Hearts: Nine White Women in the Freedom Movement.* Athens: University of Georgia Press, 2000.

Curtis, Julia Childs. "A Girls' Clubhouse." *Crisis* 6 (October 1916): 294–96.

Curtis, Susan. *A Consuming Faith: The Social Gospel and Modern American Culture.* Baltimore: Johns Hopkins University Press, 1991.

———. "The Son of Man and God the Father: The Social Gospel and Victorian Masculinity." In *Meanings for Manhood: Constructions of Masculinity in Victorian America,* edited by Mark C. Carnes and Clyde Griffen, 67–78. Chicago: University of Chicago Press, 1990.

Cushman, Vera Scott. "The War Work of the Young Women's Christian Association." *American Review of Reviews* 57 (February 1918): 191–92.

Cuthbert, Marion. "The Role of the Young Women's Christian Association." In *The Christian Way in Race Relations,* edited by William Stuart Nelson, 162–82. New York: Harper, 1948.

Davis, Allen F. *American Heroine: The Life and Legend of Jane Addams.* New York: Oxford University Press, 1973.

———. *Spearheads for Reform: The Social Settlements and the Progressive Movement, 1890–1914.* New York: Oxford University Press, 1967.

Davis, Clarice Winn [Mrs. Arthur P.]. "Eva D[el Vakia] Bowles." In *Dictionary of American Negro Biography,* edited by Rayford W. Logan and Michael R. Winston, 54–55. New York: Norton, 1982.

Davis, Elizabeth Lindsay, comp. *Lifting as They Climb: The National Association of Colored Women.* [Washington, D.C.: National Association of Colored Women, 1933].

Davison, Mrs. Henry P. "The *Little Sister* of the Red Cross." *Good Housekeeping* 66 (March 1918): 25–26, 126–30.

———. "The Y.W.C.A.'s War Burden." *Public* 21 (20 April 1918): 498–501.

Delegard, Kirsten Marie. "Women Patriots: Female Activism and the Politics of American Anti-Radicalism, 1919–1925." Ph.D. diss., Duke University, 1999.

DeRoche, Celeste. "How Wide the Circle of We: Cultural Pluralism and American Identity, 1910–1954." Ph.D. diss., University of Maine, 2000.

Deutsch, Sarah. "Learning to Talk More Like a Man: Boston Women's Class-Bridging Organizations, 1870–1940." *American Historical Review* 97 (April 1992): 379–404.

Dill, Bonnie Thornton. "Race, Class, and Gender: Prospects for an All-Inclusive Sisterhood." *Feminist Studies* 9 (Spring 1983): 131–50.

Dilling, Elizabeth Kirkpatrick. *The Red Network: A Who's Who and Handbook of Radicalism for Patriots.* Kenilworth, Ill.: by the author, c. 1934–35, 5th printing, 1936.

———. *The Roosevelt Red Record and Its Background.* Kenilworth, Ill.: by the author, 1936.

———. *Should Christians Support the Y's?* Chicago: Patriotic Research Bureau, 1939.

Dodge, Grace H. "Introduction." In *Wage-Earning Women,* by Annie Marion MacLean. New York: Macmillan, 1910.

Doggett, L. L. *Life of Robert R. McBurney.* Cleveland: F. M. Barton, 1902.

Dunbar-Nelson, Alice. *Give Us Each Day: The Diary of Alice Dunbar-Nelson.* Edited by Gloria T. Hull. New York: Norton, 1984.

———. *The Works of Alice Dunbar-Nelson.* Edited by Gloria T. Hull. Vol. 3. New York: Oxford University Press, 1988.

Durr, Virginia Foster. *Outside the Magic Circle: The Autobiography of Virginia Foster Durr.* New York: Simon and Schuster, 1985.

Dye, Nancy Schrom. *As Equals and As Sisters: Feminism, the Labor Movement, and the Women's Trade Union League of New York.* Columbia: University of Missouri Press, 1980.

Dykeman, Wilma, and James Stokely. *Seeds of Southern Change: The Life of Will Alexander.* New York: Norton, 1962.

Edwards, R. A. R. "Jane Addams, Walter Rauschenbusch, and Dorothy Day: A Comparative Study of Settlement Theology." In Edwards and Gifford, *Gender and the Social Gospel,* 150–66.

Edwards, Wendy J. Deichmann, and Carolyn De Swarte Gifford, eds. *Gender and the Social Gospel.* Urbana: University of Illinois Press, 2003.

Ellis, Ann Wells. "The Commission on Interracial Cooperation, 1919–1944: Its Activities and Results." Ph.D. diss., Georgia State University, 1975.

Ellis, Mark. "'Closing Ranks' and 'Seeking Honors': W. E. B. Du Bois in World War I." *Journal of American History* 79 (June 1992): 96–124.

Evans, Sara. *Personal Politics: The Roots of Women's Liberation in the Civil Rights Movement and the New Left.* New York: Random House, 1979, Vintage, 1980.

Evans, Sara M., ed. *Journeys That Opened up the World: Women, Student Christian Movements, and Social Justice, 1955–1975.* New Brunswick, N.J.: Rutgers University Press, 2003.

Fass, Paula S. *The Damned and the Beautiful: American Youth in the 1920s.* New York: Oxford University Press, 1977.

Felix, Stephanie Yvette. "Committed to Their Own: African American Women Leaders in the YWCA—The YWCA of Germantown, Philadelphia, Pennsylvania, 1870–1970." Ph.D. diss., Temple University, 1999.

Fishburn, Janet Forsythe. *The Fatherhood of God and the Victorian Family: The Social Gospel in America.* Philadelphia: Fortress Press, 1981.

Fisher, Galen M. *Public Affairs and the Y.M.C.A., 1844–1944: With Special Reference to the United States.* New York: Association Press, 1948.

Fitzgerald, Maureen. "Losing Their Religion: Women, the State, and the Ascension of Secular Discourse, 1890–1930." In *Women Twentieth-Century Protestantism,* ed. Margaret Lamberts Bendroth and Virginia Lieson Brereton, 280–303. Urbana: University of Illinois Press, 2002.

Fones-Wolf, Ken. *Trade Union Gospel: Christianity and Labor in Industrial Philadelphia, 1865–1915.* Philadelphia: Temple University Press, 1989.

Fosdick, Raymond B. "The War and Navy Departments Commissions on Training Camp Activities." *Annals of the American Academy of Political and Social Science* 79 (September 1918): 130–42.

Fox, Richard Wightman. "The Culture of Liberal Protestant Progressivism, 1875–1925." *Journal of Interdisciplinary History* 23 (Winter 1993): 639–60.

Frederickson, Mary E. "Citizens for Democracy: The Industrial Programs of the YWCA." In *Sisterhood and Solidarity: Workers' Education for Women, 1914–1984,* edited by Joyce L. Kornbluh and Mary Frederickson, 75–106. Philadelphia: Temple University Press, 1984.

———. "'Each One Is Dependent on the Other': Southern Churchwomen, Racial Reform, and the Process of Transformation, 1880–1940." In Hewitt and Lebsock, *Visible Women,* 296–324.

Freedman, Estelle. "Separatism as Strategy: Female Institution Building and American Feminism, 1870–1930." *Feminist Studies* 5 (Fall 1979): 512–29.

———. "Separatism Revisited: Women's Institutions, Social Reform, and the Career of Miriam Van Waters." In *U.S. History as Women's History: New Feminist Essays,* edited by Linda K. Kerber, Alice Kessler-Harris, and Kathryn Kish Sklar, 170–88. Chapel Hill: University of North Carolina Press, 1995.

Gaines, Kevin K. *Uplifting the Race: Black Leadership, Politics, and Culture in the Twentieth Century.* Chapel Hill: University of North Carolina Press, 1996.

Garrette, Eve. *Her New York Story: The Ladies' Christian Union, New York, 1858–1958.* New York: privately printed, 1958.

Gilmore, Glenda Elizabeth. *Gender and Jim Crow: Women and the Politics of White Supremacy in North Carolina, 1896–1920.* Chapel Hill: University of North Carolina Press, 1996.

Goldman, Eric F. *Rendezvous with Destiny: A History of Modern American Reform.* Rev. ed. New York: Vintage Books, 1956.

Gordon, Linda. "Black and White Visions of Welfare: Women's Welfare Activism, 1890–1945." *Journal of American History* 78 (September 1991): 559–90.

Gorrell, Donald K. *The Age of Social Responsibility: The Social Gospel in the Progressive Era, 1900–1920.* Macon, Ga.: Mercer University Press, 1988.

Graham, Abbie. *Grace H. Dodge: Merchant of Dreams.* New York: Womans Press, 1926.

Grantham, Dewey W. "Review Essay: The Contours of Southern Progressivism." *American Historical Review* 86 (December 1981): 1035–59.

Green, Constance McL. *The Role of Women as Production Workers in War Plants in the Connecticut Valley.* Northampton, Mass: Smith College, 1946.

Greenwald, Maurine Weiner. *Women, War, and Work: The Impact of World War I on Women Workers in the United States.* Westport, Conn: Greenwood, 1980.

Gregg, Mrs. Abel J. "What Women Are Thinking: The Y.W.C.A. Talks It Over." *Survey* (1 December 1926): 300–03.

Grossman, James R. *Land of Hope: Chicago, Black Southerners, and the Great Migration.* Chicago: University of Chicago Press, 1989.

Gustav-Wrathall, John Donald. *Take the Young Stranger by the Hand: Same-Sex Relations and the YMCA.* Chicago: University of Chicago Press, 1998.

Guy-Sheftall, Beverly. *Daughters of Sorrow: Attitudes toward Black Women, 1880–1920.* Brooklyn: Carlson Publishing, 1990.

Gwin, Minrose. *Black and White Women of the Old South: the Peculiar Sisterhood in American Literature.* Knoxville: University of Tennessee Press, 1985.

Haber, Samuel. *Efficiency and Uplift: Scientific Management in the Progressive Era, 1890–1920.* Chicago: University of Chicago Press, 1964.

Hall, Jacquelyn Dowd. "The Long Civil Rights Movement and the Political Uses of the Past." *Journal of American History* 91 (March 2005): 1233–63.

———. *Revolt against Chivalry: Jessie Daniel Ames and the Women's Campaign Against Lynching.* New York: Columbia University Press, 1979.
Hammond, L. H. "Interracial Cooperation." In *Interracial Cooperation: Helpful Suggestions Concerning Relations of White and Colored Citizens,* 7–14. New York: National Board of the YWCA [ca. 1920].
———. *Southern Women and Racial Adjustment,* John F. Slater Fund, Paper #19. [Lynchburg, Va.: J. P. Bell], 1917.
———. "The White Man's Debt to the Negro." *Annals of the American Academy of Political and Social Science* 49 (September 1913): 67–73.
Hammond, Lily Hardy. *In the Vanguard of a Race.* New York: Council of Women for Home Missions and Missionary Education Movement of the United States and Canada, 1922; reprinted in [Lily Hardy] Hammond *Race and the South: Two Studies, 1914–1922.* New York: Arno Press, 1972; page citation is to reprint edition.
Hammond, Mrs. J. D. "The Building of Homes." In A. M. Trawick, *The New Voice in Race Adjustments,* 69–74.
Handy, Robert T. *A Christian America: Protestant Hopes and Historical Realities.* 2d ed. New York: Oxford University Press, 1984.
Hapgood, Norman, ed. *Professional Patriots.* New York: Albert and Charles Boni, 1927.
Harris, Frederick. "The Christian Associations and the Community." *Social Forces* 4 (June 1926): 776–80.
Hartmann, Susan M. *The Other Feminists: Activists in the Liberal Establishment.* New Haven: Yale University Press, 1998.
———. "Women's Organizations during World War II: The Interaction of Class, Race, and Feminism." In *Woman's Being, Woman's Place: Female Identity and Vocation in American History,* edited by Mary Kelley, 313–28. Boston: G. K. Hall, 1979.
Heath, Sarah. "Negotiating White Womanhood: The Cincinnati YWCA and White Wage-Earning Women, 1918–1929." In Mjagkij and Spratt, *Men and Women Adrift,* 86–110.
Hedgeman, Anna Arnold. *The Trumpet Sounds: A Memoir of Negro Leadership.* New York: Holt, Rinehart, and Winston, 1964.
Height, Dorothy I. *Open Wide the Freedom Gates: a Memoir.* New York: Perseus Books, 2003.
———. *Step by Step with Interracial Groups.* New York: Womans Press, 1946.
Height, Dorothy I., and J. Oscar Lee. *The Christian Citizen and Civil Rights: a Guide to Study and Action.* New York: Federal Council of Churches, 1949.
Hewitt, Nancy A. "Beyond the Search for Sisterhood: American Women's History in the 1980s." *Social History* 10 (October 1985): 299–321.
Hewitt, Nancy A., and Suzanne Lebsock, eds. *Visible Women: New Essays in American Activism.* Urbana: University of Illinois Press, 1993.
Higginbotham, Evelyn Brooks. *Righteous Discontent: The Women's Movement in the Black Baptist Church, 1880–1920.* Cambridge, Mass.: Harvard University Press, 1993.
Hill, Patricia R. *The World Their Household: The American Woman's Foreign Mission Movement and Cultural Transformation, 1870–1920.* Ann Arbor: University of Michigan Press, 1985.

Hill, Ruth Edmonds, and Patricia King Miller, eds. *The Black Women Oral History Project.* 10 vols. Westport, Conn: Meckler Publishing, 1991.

Hine, Darline Clark. "Rape and the Inner Lives of Black Women in the Middle West: Preliminary Thoughts on the Culture of Dissemblance." *Signs* 14 (Summer 1989): 912–20.

Hine, Darline Clark, Elsa Barkley Brown, and Rosalyn Terborg-Penn, eds. *Black Women in America: An Historical Encyclopedia.* Brooklyn: Carlson Publishing, 1993.

Holmes, Josephine Pinyon. "Youth Cannot Wait." *Crisis* 28 (July 1924): 128–31.

Hopkins, C. Howard. *History of the Y.M.C.A. in North America.* New York: Association Press, 1951.

Hopkins, Charles Howard. *The Rise of the Social Gospel in American Protestantism, 1865–1915.* New Haven: Yale University Press, 1940.

Hopkins, Mary Alden. "The Hostess Houses: Oases in the Desert of Army Discipline." *Independent* (16 March 1918): 453.

"Hostess Houses and the Home Touch in Camp." *House Beautiful* 44 (December 1918): 374–75, 395.

Howe, Daniel Walker. "The Evangelical Movement and Political Culture in the North during the Second Party System." *Journal of American History* 77 (March 1991): 1216–39.

Hunter, James Davison. *American Evangelicalism: Conservative Religion and the Quandary of Modernity.* New Brunswick, N.J.: Rutgers University Press, 1983.

Hunter, Jane. *The Gospel of Gentility: American Women Missionaries in Turn-of-the-Century China.* New Haven: Yale University Press, 1984.

Hunton, Addie W. "A Deeper Reverence for Home Ties." *Colored American Magazine* 12 (June 1907): 58–59.

———. "Negro Womanhood Defended." *Voice of the Negro* 1 (July 1904): 280–82.

———. *William Alphaeus Hunton: A Pioneer Prophet of Young Men.* New York: Association Press, 1938.

[Hunton, Addie W.] *Beginnings among Colored Women.* New York: National Board of the YWCA, 1913.

Hunton, Mrs. W. A. "Women's Clubs: Caring for Young Women." *Crisis* 2 (July 1911): 121–22.

———. "The Work of the National Board of Young Women's Christian Associations." In A. M. Trawick, *The New Voice in Race Adjustments,* 215–19.

Hunton, Addie W., and Kathryn M. Johnson. *Two Colored Women with the American Expeditionary Forces.* Brooklyn: Brooklyn Eagle Press, 1920.

Hurlin, Ralph G. *Salaries and Qualifications of YWCA Professional Workers.* New York: Russell Sage Foundation, 1943.

The Interracial Charter and Related Policy. New York: National Board of the YWCA, 1955.

Interracial Cooperation: Helpful Suggestions Concerning Relations of White and Colored Citizens. New York: National Board of the YWCA, [ca. 1920].

Israel, Henry. "The Man's Viewpoint: Sidelights on the Present Situation Regarding the Y.M.C.A.'s Work With Women." *Womans Press* 22 (August 1928): 538–41.

Jackson, Mary E. "Colored Girls in the Second Line of Defense." *Association Monthly* 12 (October 1918): 363–64.

———. "The Colored Woman in Industry." *Crisis* 17 (November 1918): 12–17.

———. "The Self-Supporting Woman and the Ballot." *Crisis* 10 (August 1915): 187–88.

Jacobs, Sylvia M. "Afro-American Women Missionaries Confront the African Way of Life." In *Women in Africa and the African Diaspora,* edited by Rosalyn Terborg-Penn, Sharon Harley, and Andrea Benton Rushing, 121–32. Washington, D.C.: Howard University Press, 1987.

James, Edward T., Janet Wilson James, and Paul S. Boyer, eds. *Notable American Women: 1607–1950, A Biographical Dictionary.* 3 vols. Cambridge, Mass.: Belknap Press, 1971.

Janiewski, Dolores E. *Sisterhood Denied: Race, Gender, and Class in a New South Community.* Philadelphia: Temple University Press, 1985.

Jeansonne, Glenn. *Women of the Far Right: The Mothers' Movement and World War II.* Chicago: University of Chicago Press, 1996.

Jenness, Mary. *Twelve Negro Americans.* New York: Friendship Press, 1936.

Jensen, Joan M. "All Pink Sisters: The War Department and the Feminist Movement in the 1920s." In *Decades of Discontent: The Women's Movement, 1920–1940,* edited by Lois Scharf and Joan M. Jensen, 199–222. Boston: Northeastern University Press, 1987.

Johnson, Dorothy E. "Organized Women as Lobbyists in the 1920's." *Capitol Studies* 1 (Spring 1972): 41–58.

Joint Committee, Young Women's Christian Associations. "To the Friends and Co-Workers in the International Board of the Women's and Young Women's Christian Associations and of the American Committee" [published letter], 1 October 1905.

Jones, Adrienne Lash. *Jane Edna Hunter: A Case Study of Black Leadership, 1910–1950.* Brooklyn: Carlson Publishing, 1990.

———. "Struggle among Saints: African American Women and the YWCA, 1870–1920." In Mjagkij and Spratt, *Men and Women Adrift,* 160–87.

Jordan, William. "'The Damnable Dilemma': African-American Accommodation and Protest during World War I." *Journal of American History* 81 (March 1995): 1562–83.

Kamp, Joseph P. *Behind the Lace Curtains of the YWCA: A Report on the Extent and Nature of Infiltration by Communist, Socialist and Other Left Wing Elements, and the Resultant Red Complexion of Propaganda Disseminated In, By, and Through the Young Woman's Christian Association.* New York: Constitutional Educational League, 1948.

Karlin, Jane Feinberg. "Disciples of Mercury: the Commercial Education Program of the Young Men's Christian Association, 1851–1916." Ph.D. diss., New York University, 1993.

Katz, Esther. "Grace Hoadley Dodge: Women and the Emerging Metropolis, 1856–1914." Ph.D. diss., New York University, 1980.

Kaufman, David. *Shul with a Pool: The "Synagogue-Center" in American Jewish History.* Hanover, N.H.: Brandeis University Press, 1999.

Kett, Joseph F. *Rites of Passage: Adolescence in America, 1790 to the Present.* New York: Basic Books, 1977.

King, Mary. *Freedom Song: A Personal Story of the 1960s Civil Rights Movement.* New York: Quill, 1987.

Knapp, Gretchen. "Experimental Social Policymaking during World War II: The United Service Organizations (USO) and the American War-Community Services (AWCS)." *Journal of Policy History* 12 (2000): 321–37.

Kneebone, John T. *Southern Liberal Journalists and the Issue of Race, 1920–1944.* Chapel Hill: University of North Carolina Press, 1985.

Koven, Seth and Sonya Michel. "Womanly Duties: Maternalist Politics and the Origins of Welfare States in France, Germany, Great Britain, and the United States, 1880–1920." *American Historical Review* 95 (October 1990): 1076–1108.

Krehbiel, Edward. "The Attack on the Los Angeles Y.W.C.A." *Survey* 44 (16 August 1920): 611–13.

Kunzel, Regina G. *Fallen Women, Problem Girls: Unmarried Mothers and the Professionalization of Social Work, 1890–1945.* New Haven: Yale University Press, 1993.

Kusmer, Kenneth L. *A Ghetto Takes Shape: Black Cleveland, 1870–1930.* Urbana: University of Illinois Press, 1976.

Lagemann, Ellen Condliffe. *A Generation of Women: Education in the Lives of Progressive Reformers.* Cambridge, Mass.: Harvard University Press, 1979.

Lane, Rose Wilder. "The Girls They Leave behind Them." *Sunset* 41 (November 1918): 36–38.

Lasch-Quinn, Elisabeth. *Black Neighbors: Race and the Limits of Reform in the American Settlement House Movement, 1890–1945.* Chapel Hill: University of North Carolina Press, 1993.

Layton, Edwin. "The Better America Federation: A Case Study of Superpatriotism." *Pacific Historical Review* 30 (1961): 137–44.

Lealtad, Catharine D. "The National Y.W.C.A. and the Negro." *Crisis* 19 (April 1920): 317–18.

Lemons, J. Stanley. *The Woman Citizen: Social Feminism in the 1920s.* Urbana: University of Illinois Press, 1973; reprint, Charlottesville: University Press of Virginia, 1990; page citation is to the reprint edition.

Leone, Janice. "Integrating the American Association of University Women, 1946–1949." *Historian* 51 (May 1989): 423–45.

Lerner, Gerda, ed. *Black Women in White America: A Documentary History.* New York: Random House, 1972; Vintage, 1973.

———. *The Majority Finds Its Past: Placing Women in History.* New York: Oxford University Press, 1979.

Lindsey, Ben B., and Wainwright Evans, *Revolt of Modern Youth.* New York: Boni and Liveright, 1925.

Liu, Tessie. "Teaching the Differences among Women from a Historical Perspective: Rethinking Race and Gender as Social Categories." *Women's Studies International Forum* 14 (1991): 265–76.

Logan, Rayford W. *The Betrayal of the Negro: from Rutherford B. Hayes to Woodrow Wilson.* New York: Collier Books, 1965.

Love, Spencie. *One Blood: The Death and Resurrection of Charles R. Drew.* With a foreword by John Hope Franklin. Chapel Hill: University of North Carolina Press, 1996.

Luker, Ralph E. *The Social Gospel in Black and White: American Racial Reform, 1885–1912.* Chapel Hill: University of North Carolina Press, 1991.

Lumpkin, Katharine Du Pre. *The Making of a Southerner.* New York: Knopf, 1946.

Lupkin, Paula. "Manhood Factories: Architecture, Business, and the Evolving Urban Role of the YMCA, 1865–1925." In Mjagkij and Spratt, *Men and Women Adrift,* 40–64.

Lutz, Christine Anne. "'The Dizzy Steep to Heaven': The Hunton Family, 1850–1970." Ph.D. diss., Georgia State University, 2001.

Lyman, Robert Hunt. *The World Almanac and Book of Facts for 1927.* New York: New York World, 1927.

Lynn, Susan. "Gender and Progressive Politics: A Bridge to Social Activism of the 1960s." In *Not June Cleaver: Women and Gender in Postwar America, 1945–1960,* edited by Joanne Meyerowitz, 103–27. Philadelphia: Temple University Press, 1994.

———. *Progressive Women in Conservative Times: Racial Justice, Peace, and Feminism, 1945 to the 1960s.* New Brunswick, N.J.: Rutgers University Press, 1992.

MacHaffie, Barbara J. *Herstory: Women in Christian Tradition.* Philadelphia: Fortress Press, 1986.

Macleod, David I. *Building Character in the American Boy: The Boy Scouts, YMCA, and Their Forerunners, 1870–1920.* Madison: University of Wisconsin Press, 1983.

Marshall, Susan E. *Splintered Sisterhood: Gender and Class in the Campaign Against Woman Suffrage.* Madison: University of Wisconsin Press, 1997.

McDowell, John Patrick. *The Social Gospel in the South: The Woman's Home Mission Movement in the Methodist Episcopal Church, South, 1886–1939.* Baton Rouge: Louisiana State University Press, 1982.

McPherson, James M. *The Abolitionist Legacy from Reconstruction to the NAACP.* Princeton: Princeton University Press, 1975.

Mead, Sidney. "American Denominationalism since the Civil War: I. From Denominationialism to Americanism." *Journal of Religion* 36 (January 1956): 1–16.

Meyerowitz, Joanne J. *Women Adrift: Independent Wage Earners in Chicago, 1880–1930.* Chicago: University of Chicago Press, 1988.

Miller, Robert Moats. *American Protestantism and Social Issues, 1919–1939.* Chapel Hill: University of North Carolina Press, 1958.

Mittelman, Karen Sue. "'A Spirit That Touches the Problems of Today': Women and Social Reform in the Philadelphia Young Women's Christian Association, 1920–1945." Ph.D. diss., University of Pennsylvania, 1987.

Mjagkij, Nina. *Light in the Darkness: African Americans and the YMCA, 1852–1946.* Lexington: University of Kentucky Press, 1994.

———. "Morals and Morale: The YWCA with Black Troops in World War I." Paper presented at the Southern Conference on Women's History, Spartanburg, SC, June 1988.

———. "True Manhood: The YMCA and Racial Advancement, 1890–1930." In Mjagkij and Spratt, *Men and Women Adrift,* 138–59.

Mjagkij, Nina, and Margaret Spratt, eds. *Men and Women Adrift: The YMCA and the YWCA in the City.* New York: New York University Press, 1997.

Mohl, Raymond A. "Cultural Pluralism in Immigrant Education: The YWCA's International Institutes, 1910–1940." In Mjagkij and Spratt, *Men and Women Adrift*, 111–37.

Monteith, Sharon. *Advancing Sisterhood? Interracial Friendships in Contemporary Southern Fiction*. Athens: University of Georgia Press, 2000.

Morgan, Francesca Constance. "'Home and Country': Women, Nation, and the Daughters of the American Revolution, 1890–1930." Ph.D. diss., Columbia University, 1998.

Morton, Marian J. "Seduced and Abandoned in an American City: Cleveland and Its Fallen Women, 1869–1936." *Journal of Urban History* 11 (August 1985): 443–69.

Muncy, Robyn. *Creating a Female Dominion in American Reform, 1890–1935*. New York: Oxford University Press, 1991.

Murolo, Priscilla. *The Common Ground of Womanhood: Class, Gender, and Working Girls' Clubs, 1884–1928*. Urbana: University of Illinois Press, 1997.

Myrdal, Gunnar with the assistance of Richard Sterner and Arnold Rose. *An American Dilemma: The Negro Problem and Modern Democracy*. New York: Harper, 1944.

Neverdon-Morton, Cynthia. *Afro-American Women of the South and the Advancement of the Race, 1895–1925*. Knoxville: University of Tennessee Press, 1989.

Nielsen, Kim E. *Un-American Womanhood: Antiradicalism, Antifeminism, and the First Red Scare*. Columbus, Ohio State University Press, 2001.

Olcott, Jane, comp. *The Work of Colored Women*. New York: Colored Work Committee, War Work Council, National Board of the YWCA, [1919].

Osofsky, Gilbert. *Harlem: The Making of a Ghetto—Negro New York, 1890–1930*. 2d ed. New York: Harper, 1971.

———. "Progressivism and the Negro: New York, 1900–1915." *American Quarterly* 16 (Summer 1964): 153–68.

Ovington, Mary White. *The Walls Came Tumbling Down*. New York: Harcourt, Brace, 1947.

Paddock, A. Estelle. "War Work of Young Women's Christian Association." *Annals of the American Academy of Political and Social Science* 79 (September 1918): 208–12.

Painter, Nell Irvin. "'Social Equality,' Miscegenation, Labor, and Power." In *The Evolution of Southern Culture*, edited by Numan V. Bartley, 47–67. Athens: University of Georgia Press, 1988.

Peiss, Kathy. *Cheap Amusements: Working Women and Leisure in Turn-of-the-Century New York*. Philadelphia: Temple University Press, 1986.

Pence, Owen. *The Y.M.C.A. and Social Need: a Study of Institutional Adaptation*. New York: Association Press, 1939.

Philpott, Harry M. "A History of the Student Young Men's Christian Association, 1900–1941." Ph.D. diss., Yale University, 1947.

Pilkington, Charles Kirk. "The Trials of Brotherhood: The Founding of the Commission on Interracial Cooperation." *Georgia Historical Quarterly* 69 (Spring 1985): 55–80.

Platt, Anthony M. *E. Franklin Frazier Reconsidered*. New Brunswick, N.J.: Rutgers University Press, 1991.

Putney, Clifford. *Muscular Christianity: Manhood and Sports in Protestant America, 1880–1920*. Cambridge, Mass.: Harvard University Press, 2001.

Rabinowitz, Howard N. *Race Relations in the Urban South, 1865–1890.* Urbana: University of Illinois Press, 1980.

Radcliffe, Florence J. *A Simple Matter of Justice: The Phyllis Wheatley YWCA Story.* Pompano Beach, Fla.: Exposition Press of Florida, 1985.

Ransby, Barbara. *Ella Baker and the Black Freedom Movement: A Radical Democratic Vision.* Chapel Hill: University of North Carolina Press, 2003.

Rauschenbusch, Walter. "Belated Races and the Social Problems." *The Methodist Review Quarterly* 63 (April 1914): 252–59.

———. "The Problem of the Black Man." *The American Missionary* n.s., 5 (March 1914): 732–33.

Reimers, David M. *White Protestantism and the Negro.* New York: Oxford University Press, 1965.

The Relative Place of Women in the Church in the United States: Tentative Report of the Joint Committee appointed by the Council of Women for Home Missions, the Federation of Woman's Boards of Foreign Missions of North America, and the Federal Council of Churches of Christ in America, to Study the Place of Women's Organized Work in the Church. New York, 1927.

Reynolds, Katherine Chaddock. *A Separate Sisterhood: Women Who Shaped Southern Education in the Progressive Era.* New York: Peter Lang, 2002.

Roberts, Richard. *Florence Simms: A Biography.* New York: Womans Press, 1926.

Robertson, Nancy Marie. "Kindness or Justice: Women's Associations and the Politics of Race and History." In *Private Action and the Public Good,* edited by Walter W. Powell and Elisabeth S. Clemens, 193–205. New Haven: Yale University Press, 1998.

Robinson, Marion O. *Eight Women of the YWCA.* New York: National Board of the Young Women's Christian Association of the USA, 1966.

Rossinow, Doug. "'The Break-through to New Life': Christianity and the Emergence of the New Left in Austin, Texas, 1956–1964." *American Quarterly* 46 (September 1994): 309–40.

Rossman, Parker. "Seeking a Dynamic Student Christian Movement: A Conversation with Fern Babcock Grant." *Christian Century* 100 (20 April 1983): 373–75.

Rothman, Sheila M. *Woman's Proper Place: A History of the Changing Ideals and Practices, 1870 to the Present.* New York: Basic Books, 1978.

Rouse, Jacqueline Anne. *Lugenia Burns Hope: Black Southern Reformer.* Athens: University of Georgia Press, 1989.

Rupp, Leila J. "Constructing Internationalism: The Case of Transnational Women's Organizations, 1888–1945." *American Historical Review* 99 (December 1994): 1571–1600.

Rupp, Leila J., and Verta Taylor. *Survival in the Doldrums: The American Women's Rights Movement, 1945 to the 1960s.* Columbus, OH: Ohio State University Press, 1990.

Ryan, Mary P. *Womanhood in America: From Colonial Times to the Present.* 3rd ed. New York: Franklin Watt, 1983.

Sabiston, Dothory, and Margaret Hiller. *Toward Better Race Relations.* New York: Woman's Press, 1949.

Salem, Dorothy. *To Better Our World: Black Women in Organized Reform, 1890–1920.* Brooklyn: Carlson Publishing, 1990.

Scheiber, Jane Lang, and Harry N. Scheiber. "The Wilson Administration and the Wartime Mobilization of Black Americans, 1917–1918." *Labor History* 10 (Summer 1969): 433–58.

Scott, Anne Firor. *Natural Allies: Women's Associations in American History.* Urbana: University of Illinois Press, 1991.

———. *The Southern Lady from Pedestal to Politics, 1830–1930.* Chicago: University of Chicago Press, 1970.

Scott, Emmett J., ed. *Scott's Official History of The American Negro in the World War.* [Chicago: Homewood Press, 1919].

Shaw, Stephanie J. "Black Club Women and the Creation of the National Association of Colored Women." *Journal of Women's History* 3 (Fall 1991): 10–25.

———. *What a Woman Ought to Be and to Do: Black Professional Women Workers during the Jim Crow Era.* Chicago: University of Chicago Press, 1996.

Sheatsley, Paul B. "White Attitudes toward the Negro." *Daedalus* 95 (Winter 1966): 217–38.

Shedd, Clarence P. *Two Centuries of Student Christian Movements: Their Origin and Intercollegiate Life.* New York: Association Press, 1934.

Sherrick, Rebecca L. "Toward Universal Sisterhood." *Women's Studies International Forum* 5 (1982): 655–61.

Sicherman, Barbara, and Carol Hurd Green, eds. *Notable American Women: The Modern Period—A Biographical Dictionary.* Cambridge, Mass.: Harvard University Press, 1980.

Simmons, Christina. "Companionate Marriage and the Lesbian Threat." *Frontiers* 4 (Fall 1979): 54–59.

Sims, Mary S. *The Natural History of a Social Institution—The Young Women's Christian Association.* New York: Womans Press, 1936.

———. *The Purpose Widens, 1947–1967.* New York: National Board of the Young Women's Christian Association of the U.S.A., 1969.

———. *The YWCA—An Unfolding Purpose.* New York: Woman's Press, 1950.

———. "The Y.W.C.A. at Detroit." *Crisis.* 37 (October 1930): 335, 356.

Sitkoff, Harvard. *A New Deal for Blacks: The Emergence of Civil Rights as a National Issue: The Depression Decade.* New York: Oxford University Press, 1978.

Sklar, Kathryn Kish. "The Historical Foundations of Women's Power in the Creation of the American Welfare State, 1830–1930." In *Mothers of a New World: Maternalist Politics and the Origins of Welfare States,* edited by Seth Koven and Sonya Michel, 43–93. New York: Routledge, 1993.

Smith, Gary Scott. *The Search for Social Salvation: Social Christianity and America, 1880–1925.* Lanham, MD: Lexington Books, 2000.

Smith, Lillian. "There Are Things To Do." *South Today* (Winter 1942–1943); reprinted as a pamphlet [with some revisions], page citations for that version.

Smith, Ruth. *White Man's Burden: a Personal Testament.* New York: Vanguard Press, 1946.

Solomon, Barbara Miller. *In the Company of Educated Women: A History of Women and Higher Education in America.* New Haven: Yale University Press, 1985.

Sosna, Morton. *In Search of the Silent South: Southern Liberals and the Race Issue.* New York: Columbia University Press, 1977.

Spratt, Margaret A. "The Pittsburgh YWCA and Industrial Democracy in the 1920s." *Pennsylvania History* 59 (January 1992): 5–20.

———. "To Be Separate or One: The Issue of Race in the History of the Pittsburgh and Cleveland YWCAs, 1920–1946." In Mjagkij and Spratt, *Men and Women Adrift,* 188–205.

Stewart, Annabel M. *The Industrial Work of the Y.W.C.A.: Report of a Study Made for the Laboratory Division of the National Board of the Young Women's Christian Associations.* New York: Womans Press, 1937.

Stewart, Harry A. "Where the 'Y' Stands *Now.*" *Good Housekeeping* 70 (June 1920): 49, 104, 107–08, 110.

Super, Paul. *Formative Ideas in the YMCA.* New York: Association Press, 1929.

Swartz, Nelle, Mary E. Jackson, Eva Bowles, Rose Schneiderman, Elizabeth Walton, James H. Hubert, Henriette R. Walter, and Mrs. Percival Knauth. *A New Day for the Colored Woman Worker: A Study of Colored Women in Industry in New York City.* New York: [C. P. Young], 1919.

Taylor, Alva W. "Black versus White." *The Christian Century* (14 July 1921): 14–15.

Taylor, Frances Sanders. "'On the Edge of Tomorrow': Southern Women, the Student YWCA, and Race, 1920–1944." Ph.D. diss., Stanford University, 1984.

Terborg-Penn, Rosalyn. "African-American Women's Networks in the Anti-Lynching Crusade." In *Gender, Class, Race, and Reform in the Progressive Era,* edited by Noralee Frankel and Nancy S. Dye, 148–61. Lexington: University Press of Kentucky, 1991.

Thurber, Cheryl. "The Development of the Mammy Image and Mythology." In *Southern Women: Histories and Identities,* edited by Virginia Bernhard, Betty Brandon, Elizabeth Fox Genovese, and Theda Purdue, 87–108. Columbia: University of Missouri Press, 1992.

Tindall, George B. *The Emergence of the New South, 1913–1945.* Baton Rouge: Louisiana State University Press, 1967.

To Secure These Rights: The Report of the President's Committee on Civil Rights. Washington, D.C.: G.P.O., 1947.

"To Subscribers to the United War Work Campaign Conducted at the Request of President Wilson in November, 1918." n.p., [1919].

Tobias, C. H. "The Work of the Young Men's and Young Women's Christian Associations with Negro Youth." *Annals of the American Academy of Political and Social Science* 140 (November 1928): 283–86.

Trawick, A. M., ed. *The New Voice in Race Adjustments: Addresses and Reports Presented at the Negro Christian Student Conference, Atlanta, Georgia, 14–18 May 1914.* New York: Student Volunteer Movement, 1914.

Trawick, Mrs. Arch. "The Social Message of the Church." In A. M. Trawick, *The New Voice in Race Adjustments,* 62–65.

Trolander, Judith Ann. *Professionalism and Social Change: from the Settlement House Movement to Neighborhood Centers, 1886 to the Present.* New York: Columbia University Press, 1987.

U.S. House of Representatives, Committee on Un-American Activities. *100 Things You Should Know About Communism.* Washington, D.C.: G.P.O., December 1948.

Vandenberg-Daves, Jodi. "The Manly Pursuit of a Partnership between the Sexes:

The Debate over YMCA Programs for Women and Girls, 1914–1933." *Journal of American History* 78 (March 1992): 1324–46.
Villard, Oswald Garrison. "What the Blue Menace Means." *Harpers Magazine* 157 (October 1928): 529–40.
Walker, Clarence E. "City of Brotherly Hate." *Reviews in American History* 21 (March 1993): 75–79.
Walton, Lester A. "Y.W.C.A. Has Achieved Great Work For Negro." *New York World* (8 June 1930): 8.
Ward, Andrew. *Dark Midnight When I Rise: The Story of the Jubilee Singers Who Introduced the World to the Music of Black America.* New York: Farrar, Straus, and Giroux, 2000.
Ward, Estelle Frances. "Bringing Home to the Army Camps." *House Beautiful* 45 (February 1919): 76–77, 100.
Ware, Susan, and Stacy Braukman, eds. *Notable American Women: A Biographical Dictionary—Completing the Twentieth Century.* Cambridge, Mass.: Harvard University Press, 2004.
Weiner, Lynn Y. *From Working Girl to Working Mother: The Female Labor Force in the United States, 1820–1980.* Chapel Hill: University of North Carolina Press, 1985.
Weisenfeld, Judith. *African American Women and Christian Activism: New York's Black YWCA, 1905–1945.* Cambridge, Mass.: Harvard University Press, 1997.
———. "'The More Abundant Life': The Harlem Branch of the New York City Young Women's Christian Association, 1905–1945." Ph.D. diss., Princeton University, 1992.
Weiss, Nancy J. "From Black Separatism to Interracial Cooperation: The Origins of Organized Efforts for Racial Advancement, 1890–1920." In *Twentieth-Century America: Recent Interpretations,* 2nd ed., edited by Barton J. Bernstein and Allen J. Matusow, 52–85. New York: Harcourt Brace Jovanovich, 1972.
"What the Women Are Doing for Our Army and Navy." *Outlook* (23 January 1918): 149–51.
White, Deborah Gray. "The Cost of Club Work, the Price of Black Feminism." In Hewitt and Lebsock, *Visible Women,* 247–69.
———. *Too Heavy a Load: Black Women in Defense of Themselves.* New York: W. W. Norton, 1999.
White, Ronald C., Jr. *Liberty and Justice for All: Racial Reform and the Social Gospel (1877–1925).* New York: Harper and Row, 1990.
Wiebe, Robert H. *The Search for Order, 1877–1920.* New York: Hill and Wang, 1967.
Wilkerson, Yolanda B. *Interracial Programs of Student YWCA's: An Inquiry under the Auspices of the National Student Young Women's Christian Association.* New York: Woman's Press, 1948.
Williamson, Louise G. "The Second Line of Defense: The War Work of the Young Women's Christian Association." *Missionary Review of the World* 40 (October 1917): 763–68.
Wilson, Elizabeth. *Fifty Years of Association Work among Young Women, 1866–1916: A History of Young Women's Christian Associations in the United States of America.* New York: National Board of the YWCAs of the U.S.A., 1916.
Wilson, Grace H. *The Religious and Educational Philosophy of the Young Women's Christian Association: A Historical Study of the Changing Religious and Social*

Emphasis of the Association as They Relate to Changes in its Educational Philosophy and to Observable Trends in Current Religious Thought, Educational Philosophy, and Social Situations. New York: Teachers College, Columbia University Press, 1933.

Winter, Thomas. *Making Men, Making Class: The YMCA and Workingmen, 1877–1920.* Chicago: University of Chicago Press, 2002.

Wittke, Carl. *Tambo and Bones: A History of the American Minstrel Show.* Durham, N.C.: Duke University Press, 1930.

Woloch, Nancy. *Women and the American Experience.* 3rd ed. Boston: McGraw-Hill, 2000.

"The Women and Girls Question: A Variety of Opinions on the Significance of This Problem to the Y.M.C.A." *Association Forum* 11 (January 1931): 1–4, 25–26.

Woodward, C. Vann. *The Strange Career of Jim Crow.* 3rd ed. New York: Oxford University Press, 1974.

Work, Monroe N. *Negro Yearbook and Annual Encyclopedia of the Negro for 1912.* Tuskegee, Ala.: Tuskegee Institute, 1912.

———. *Negro Yearbook: An Annual Encyclopedia of the Negro, 1925–1926.* Tuskegee, Ala.: Negro Year Book Publishing, 1925.

Wyckoff, Elizabeth Porter. "The Girls behind the Men behind the Guns: What the YWCA Is Doing for Them." *Ladies Home Journal* 35 (October 1918): 3.

Yohn, Susan M. *A Contest of Faiths: Missionary Women and Pluralism in the American Southwest.* Ithaca: Cornell University Press, 1995.

Young Women's Christian Associations of the United States of America—National Board. *Directory and Statistical Report of the Young Women's Christian Associations of the United States of America, June 1909.* New York: National Board of the YWCA of the USA, 1909.

———. *Year Book Containing Directory and Statistical Material of the Young Women's Christian Associations, 1918–1919.* New York: National Board of the YWCA of the USA, 1919.

Young Women's Christian Associations of the United States of America—National Board—Department of Data and Trends. *Figures Talk Back: From the Annual Statistical Reports of Community Y.W.C.A.'s for the Year 1948.* New York: National Board of the YWCA of the USA, 1948.

Young Women's Christian Associations of the United States of America—National Board—Laboratory Division. *The Standards Study, 1938–1940: A Study of National Structure and National-Local Relations.* New York: National Board of the YWCA of the USA, 1940.

———. *The Student Standards Study: Structure and Relationships of Student Y.W.C.A.s.* New York: National Board of the YWCA of the USA, 1940.

Young Women's Christian Associations of the United States of America—National Board—War Work Council. *Report of Hostess House Committee.* New York City: National Board of the YWCA of the USA, [1919].

———. "Report of the National War Work Council of the Young Women's Christian Associations of the United States of America," October 1919, included in: Young Women's Christian Associations of the U.S.A., *Report of the National Board to the Sixth National Convention, 13–20 April 1920.* New York: National Board of the YWCA of the USA, 1920.

Young Women's Christian Associations of the United States of America—National Board—War Work Council—Committee on Work among Colored Girls and Women. *Colored American Women in War Work.* New York: National Board of the YWCA of the USA, July 1918.

Zald, Mayer N. *Organizational Change: The Political Economy of the YMCA.* Chicago: University of Chicago Press, 1970.

Zeiger, Susan. *In Uncle Sam's Service: Women Workers with the American Expeditionary Forces, 1917–1919.* Ithaca: Cornell University Press, 1999.

INDEX

NANCY MARIE ROBERTSON is associate professor of history in the School of Liberal Arts of Indiana University–Purdue University Indianapolis, where she directs the women's studies program. She also holds positions in the philanthropic studies and American studies programs. She previously worked on a number of public history projects, including the Margaret Sanger Papers, and for several nonprofit and corporate archives.

Women in American History

Women Doctors in Gilded-Age Washington: Race, Gender, and Professionalization *Gloria Moldow*

Friends and Sisters: Letters between Lucy Stone and Antoinette Brown Blackwell, 1846–93 *Edited by Carol Lasser and Marlene Deahl Merrill*

Reform, Labor, and Feminism: Margaret Dreier Robins and the Women's Trade Union League *Elizabeth Anne Payne*

Private Matters: American Attitudes toward Childbearing and Infant Nurture in the Urban North, 1800–1860 *Sylvia D. Hoffert*

Civil Wars: Women and the Crisis of Southern Nationalism *George C. Rable*

I Came a Stranger: The Story of a Hull-House Girl *Hilda Satt Polacheck; edited by Dena J. Polacheck Epstein*

Labor's Flaming Youth: Telephone Operators and Worker Militancy, 1878–1923 *Stephen H. Norwood*

Winter Friends: Women Growing Old in the New Republic, 1785–1835 *Terri L. Premo*

Better Than Second Best: Love and Work in the Life of Helen Magill *Glenn C. Altschuler*

Dishing It Out: Waitresses and Their Unions in the Twentieth Century *Dorothy Sue Cobble*

Natural Allies: Women's Associations in American History *Anne Firor Scott*

Beyond the Typewriter: Gender, Class, and the Origins of Modern American Office Work, 1900–1930 *Sharon Hartman Strom*

The Challenge of Feminist Biography: Writing the Lives of Modern American Women *Edited by Sara Alpern, Joyce Antler, Elisabeth Israels Perry, and Ingrid Winther Scobie*

Working Women of Collar City: Gender, Class, and Community in Troy, New York, 1864–86 *Carole Turbin*

Radicals of the Worst Sort: Laboring Women in Lawrence, Massachusetts, 1860–1912 *Ardis Cameron*

Visible Women: New Essays on American Activism *Edited by Nancy A. Hewitt and Suzanne Lebsock*

Mother-Work: Women, Child Welfare, and the State, 1890–1930 *Molly Ladd-Taylor*

Babe: The Life and Legend of Babe Didrikson Zaharias *Susan E. Cayleff*

Writing Out My Heart: Selections from the Journal of Frances E. Willard, 1855–96 *Edited by Carolyn De Swarte Gifford*

U.S. Women in Struggle: A *Feminist Studies* Anthology *Edited by Claire Goldberg Moses and Heidi Hartmann*

In a Generous Spirit: A First-Person Biography of Myra Page *Christina Looper Baker*

Mining Cultures: Men, Women, and Leisure in Butte, 1914–41 *Mary Murphy*

Gendered Strife and Confusion: The Political Culture of Reconstruction *Laura F. Edwards*

The Female Economy: The Millinery and Dressmaking Trades, 1860–1930 *Wendy Gamber*

Mistresses and Slaves: Plantation Women in South Carolina, 1830–80 *Marli F. Weiner*
A Hard Fight for We: Women's Transition from Slavery to Freedom in South Carolina *Leslie A. Schwalm*
The Common Ground of Womanhood: Class, Gender, and Working Girls' Clubs, 1884–1928 *Priscilla Murolo*
Purifying America: Women, Cultural Reform, and Pro-Censorship Activism, 1873–1933 *Alison M. Parker*
Marching Together: Women of the Brotherhood of Sleeping Car Porters *Melinda Chateauvert*
Creating the New Woman: The Rise of Southern Women's Progressive Culture in Texas, 1893–1918 *Judith N. McArthur*
The Business of Charity: The Woman's Exchange Movement, 1832–1900 *Kathleen Waters Sander*
The Power and Passion of M. Carey Thomas *Helen Lefkowitz Horowitz*
For Freedom's Sake: The Life of Fannie Lou Hamer *Chana Kai Lee*
Becoming Citizens: The Emergence and Development of the California Women's Movement, 1880–1911 *Gayle Gullett*
Selected Letters of Lucretia Coffin Mott *Edited by Beverly Wilson Palmer with the assistance of Holly Byers Ochoa and Carol Faulkner*
Women and the Republican Party, 1854–1924 *Melanie Susan Gustafson*
Southern Discomfort: Women's Activism in Tampa, Florida, 1880s–1920s *Nancy A. Hewitt*
The Making of "Mammy Pleasant": A Black Entrepreneur in Nineteenth-Century San Francisco *Lynn M. Hudson*
Sex Radicals and the Quest for Women's Equality *Joanne E. Passet*
"We, Too, Are Americans": African American Women in Detroit and Richmond, 1940–54 *Megan Taylor Shockley*
The Road to Seneca Falls: Elizabeth Cady Stanton and the First Woman's Rights Convention *Judith Wellman*
Reinventing Marriage: The Love and Work of Alice Freeman Palmer and George Herbert Palmer *Lori Kenschaft*
Southern Single Blessedness: Unmarried Women in the Urban South, 1800–1865 *Christine Jacobson Carter*
Widows and Orphans First: The Family Economy and Social Welfare Policy, 1865–1939 *S. J. Kleinberg*
Habits of Compassion: Irish Catholic Nuns and the Origins of the Welfare System, 1830–1920 *Maureen Fitzgerald*
The Women's Joint Congressional Committee and the Politics of Maternalism, 1920–1930 *Jan Doolittle Wilson*
"Swing the Sickle for the Harvest Is Ripe": Gender and Slavery in Antebellum Georgia *Daina Ramey Berry*
Christian Sisterhood, Race Relations, and the YWCA, 1906–46 *Nancy Marie Robertson*

The University of Illinois Press
is a founding member of the
Association of American University Presses.

University of Illinois Press
1325 South Oak Street
Champaign, IL 61820-6903
www.press.uillinois.edu